SOUTHERN BIOGRAPHY SERIES
*William J. Cooper, Jr., Editor*

John Brown Gordon

# John Brown Gordon

SOLDIER · SOUTHERNER · AMERICAN

## Ralph Lowell Eckert

LOUISIANA STATE UNIVERSITY PRESS

*Baton Rouge and London*

Copyright © 1989 by Louisiana State University Press
Manufactured in the United States of America
First printing
98  97  96  95  94  93  92  91  90  89    5  4  3  2  1

Designer: Laura Roubique Gleason
Typeface: Trump Mediaeval
Typesetter: The Composing Room of Michigan, Inc.
Printer: Thomson-Shore, Inc.
Binder: John H. Dekker & Sons, Inc.

Library of Congress Cataloging-in-Publication Data
Eckert, Ralph Lowell, 1949–
    John Brown Gordon : soldier, southerner, American / Ralph Lowell
    Eckert.
        p.    cm. — (Southern biography series)
    Bibliography: p.
    Includes index.
    ISBN 0-8071-1455-3 (alk. paper)
    1. Gordon, John Brown, 1832–1904.  2. Legislators—United States—
Biography.  3. United States. Congress. Senate—Biography.
4. Generals—Southern States—Biography.  5. Confederate States of
America. Army—Biography.  6. Georgia—Politics and
government—1865–1950.  7. United States—History—Civil War,
1861–1865—Campaigns.  I. Title.  II. Series.
E664.G66E25  1989
973.6'092'4—dc19
[B]                                                          88-30339
                                                                CIP

Frontispiece: John Brown Gordon in the uniform of a major general, Confederate
States of America. *Courtesy of the Library of Congress*

*For my parents,*
Ralph G. and Sue M. Eckert

# Contents

# Illustrations

# Maps

# Acknowledgments

Thanking the many individuals and institutions who aided my work is truly a pleasurable task. The staffs of the libraries and archives listed in the bibliography provided invaluable assistance as they guided me through their collections. Warren W. Hassler and the late T. Harry Williams were instrumental in directing my research during its early stages; however, I owe my greatest debt to William J. Cooper, Jr. His careful reading of every page, his willingness to discuss Gordon at length, and his intelligent, probing criticism constantly challenged me to revise and clarify my arguments. Similarly, Ken Startup, Gaines Foster, Chet Wolford, and Stan Hilton read all or parts of the manuscript and offered important suggestions and thoughtful criticisms that greatly improved the style and substance of this biography.

Special thanks must go to the late Hugh H. Gordon III, who labored to reassemble the letters, mementos, and personal papers of his great-grandfather that had long ago been divided among various family members. His success in persuading relatives to donate their holdings to the University of Georgia ensured the preservation of a personal record of the general. In addition, Mr. Gordon and his wife, Mimi, graciously invited me into their home and gave me access to all family papers prior to donation. I owe a debt of gratitude to several other persons who opened their homes to me and provided a "home away from home" that researchers too long on the road genuinely appreciate. To Bob Schell, Bob and Janet Hersh, Michael Trull, Sue Ellen Eckert, Jerry McAndrews, the late Jim "Moose" Mostoller, Harry Smyser, Roy Lisko, Jim and Joy Oriole, Bob and Debbie Hunter, Rich Lawson, Jesse and Annie Mae Dier, Ron Mohney, Jim and Cindy

Rogers, and John and Carole Wallin, thanks for your hospitality and most of all for your friendship. I also wish to thank Norma Hartner, whose dedication and typing ability were indispensable; Elaine Smyth, whose editorial skills have improved this book; and Gary Lee Hall, whose excellent maps clarify battlefield movements. Lastly, I am deeply grateful to my wife, Jeanne, not only for her typing efforts but for her steadfast support and patience through the years of bringing this book to publication.

# Abbreviations

| | |
|---|---|
| ADAH | Alabama Department of Archives and History, Montgomery |
| AHS | Atlanta Historical Society |
| Duke | Manuscript Department, Duke University Library, Durham, North Carolina |
| Emory | Special Collections, Woodruff Library, Emory University, Atlanta, Georgia |
| GDAH | Georgia Department of Archives and History, Atlanta |
| GHS | Georgia Historical Society, Savannah |
| UGA | University of Georgia Libraries, Athens |
| HL | The Huntington Library, San Marino, California |
| LC | Manuscript Divison, Library of Congress, Washington, D.C. |
| LSU | Louisiana and Lower Mississippi Valley Collections, LSU Libraries, Louisiana State University Library, Baton Rouge |
| NA | National Archives, Washington, D.C. |
| NCDAH | North Carolina Division of Archives and History, Raleigh |
| Princeton | Princeton University, Princeton, New Jersey |
| SCL | South Caroliniana Library, University of South Carolina, Columbia |
| SHC | Southern Historical Collection, Library of the University of North Carolina at Chapel Hill |
| TSLA | Tennessee State Library and Archives, Nashville |

John Brown Gordon

# Introduction

"The General is dead." The news traveled rapidly from city to countryside as word swept across Georgia, then the South, and finally the nation. It seemed impossible that death had finally claimed the Gallant Gordon. Despite his advanced age and the seriousness of his sudden illness, most Georgians were stunned. For decades, Gordon had seemed an Olympian figure; there was something indestructible in the bearing of the scarred veteran who had suffered so severely during the Civil War. Gravely wounded five times at Sharpsburg, he had survived and, remarkably, returned to duty in less than seven months. In the postwar decades, he had often been beset by illness and injury only to recover rapidly and resume his indefatigable course. Gordon had faced death many times before and always emerged victorious. And yet, early on the morning of January 10, 1904, Georgia and the nation learned that Gordon was dead.

The death of John Brown Gordon released a deluge of grief and sorrow unparalleled in Georgia history. The deep sense of loss was not, however, confined either to Georgia or to the South; eulogies and memorials poured in from every section of the country. A saddened President Theodore Roosevelt expressed his pride in counting Gordon among his friends, for a "more gallant, generous, and fearless gentleman and soldier has not been seen by our country"—high praise indeed for a man who less than a half-century before had fought to dissolve the Union that Roosevelt governed. The praise accorded Gordon in the days and months following his death was extraordinary even by nineteenth-century standards. Clearly, the depth of sentiment that marked Gordon's passing carried well beyond the usual commemoration of a public figure's demise. His brilliant military record with the Army of Northern Virginia, his efforts both as a politician and as a businessman to defend and promote the interests of his native South, and his contributions to national reconciliation set him apart from most public figures of his time. Gordon was by no means ordinary.[1]

The effusiveness of the tributes paid to the Georgian bears out this assertion. Gordon's military career captured the imagination of northerners and southerners alike. His successor as commander-in-chief of the United Confederate Veterans observed, "His imposing and magnificent soldierly bearing, coupled with his splendid ringing voice, and magnetic oratory gave him a god-given talent, not equalled or possessed by any other officer in either army—that of getting in front of his troops, and in a few ringing appeals, inspiring them almost to madness, and being able to lead them into the very Jaws of death." Others remembered Gordon as the "beau ideal of military leaders," the "idol of the whole army," and "one of the knightliest soldiers in all the tide of time." Only Robert E. Lee had a stronger hold on the admiration and affection of the Confederate veterans. With his native military instinct, Gordon "exemplified in the highest degree the best qualities of the American volunteer soldier."[2]

Although unstinting in their praise of his military performance, most eulogists recognized that Gordon's martial prowess was only one dimension of his character. It was his devotion to the South and his commitment to the reunited nation that they most heartily extolled. One Georgian believed it was generally conceded that Gordon possessed "the unique distinction, not only in the south, but as well in the eyes of all the world, as being, beyond a doubt, the greatest and most conspicuous southerner." "True to his section and the traditions of his native south," Gordon labored tirelessly on its behalf in both public service and private life. He particularly devoted himself to preserving an accurate account "of the honesty and nobility of the motives and contentions" of southerners who had gone to war in 1861.[3]

1. New York *Times*, January 13, 1904; Atlanta *Constitution*, January 13, 1904.

2. Atlanta *Journal*, January 14, 1904; Atlanta *Constitution*, January 15, 13, 8, 1904; Houston *Chronicle*, quoted in Atlanta *Journal*, January 16, 1904; Baltimore *Sun*, quoted in Atlanta *Journal*, January 12, 1904.

3. Atlanta *Constitution*, January 11, 1904; Houston *Post*, quoted in Atlanta *Journal*, January 13, 1904; Nashville *Banner*, quoted in Atlanta *Journal*, January 13, 1904.

"He loved the South and was loyal to its interests and its spirit," another wrote, "but he rose completely above the plane of sectional feeling." Instead of dwelling upon the differences that precipitated the war, Gordon "sought to allay the rancorous feelings engendered by strife without imputing unworthy motives to the union cause." He was "among the first to lead in the great work of reconciliation of the sections" and quickly became "one of the most eloquent and persuasive advocates" of national pacification. Enjoying "to an exceptional extent the respect and admiration of those whom he had opposed in war, and also of his political opponents in congress," he preached a new nationalistic message to which almost all Americans could subscribe. Gordon, in a New Yorker's opinion, "did more by word and pen and deed than any other southern man to assuage the feeling of animosity and restore real harmony and fraternal good will between the north and south." Recognizing Gordon as "the great apostle of reconciliation and obliteration of sectional feeling," a Connecticut editor urged citizens of all sections to "unite in paying due tribute to the memory of one than whom no stauncher patriot and lover of his country and constitution now lives." Gordon "died as he lived—an American, a patriot, a southern gentleman, a Christian." Such eulogies leave no doubt that Gordon's contemporaries thought his passing a profound loss to Georgia, the South, and the nation.[4]

Even so, there were some who did not hold the general in nearly so high regard. Indeed, in the four decades after the Civil War, Gordon made more than his share of enemies, especially in politics. Although most praised his service on behalf of the South during Reconstruction, others roundly condemned almost every aspect of his senatorial record. They called him a "political gymnast" or, worse, a self-serving politician, "venal and corrupt, without principles, without policy." Critics accused him of betraying the Democratic party and selling the South out too cheaply when he entered into the electoral dispute surrounding the election of 1876 and the bargaining that culminated in the Compromise of 1877. Collis P. Huntington's smug references to Senator Gordon as "one of our men" convinced some that he had

4. "Soldier and Gentleman," *Outlook: A Weekly Newspaper*, LXXVI (January, 1904), 152; Nashville *Banner*, quoted in Atlanta *Journal*, January 13, 1904; Atlanta *Constitution*, January 11, 15, 1904; Baltimore *Sun*, quoted in Atlanta *Journal*, January 12, 1904; Horatio C. King of Brooklyn *Eagle*, quoted in Atlanta *Constitution*, January 14, 1904; Atlanta *Journal*, January 14, 10, 1904; Mobile *Register*, quoted in Atlanta *Journal*, January 13, 1904; Bridgeport (Conn.) *Morning Telegram*, quoted in Atlanta *Journal*, January 14, 1904.

become "a servant of the corporation," a paid handmaiden of the railroad magnate. And further evidence that Gordon was willing to use his office for pecuniary gain seemed to come in May, 1880, when he suddenly resigned his Senate post amid a cloud of controversy. Despite denials, it appeared that he had betrayed the public trust once again, by exchanging his office for a more remunerative railroad position.[5]

Opponents of the general found more to criticize than merely what they regarded as his unprincipled political course. His adventuresome, even reckless, business career convinced one contemporary that he was "the living realistic 'Mulberry Sellers' of America," whose "skin games and south sea bubbles" furnished "material enough for a dozen first-class farces." Gordon's long list of business failures prompted charges of fraud and deception, as thousands of unsuspecting investors became hopelessly ensnared in his grand projects. Some critics scored him for his involvement with Georgia's pernicious convict lease system while others condemned his association with the Ku Klux Klan. Others, even a few of his former Confederate comrades-in-arms, assailed him for embellishing his military record and shamelessly using it for personal advantage—as one put it, Gordon "made a brazen trumpet of himself & goes about blowing it." And as the Georgian led the movement for national reconciliation in the late nineteenth century, he came under fire from unreconstructed Rebels for too readily embracing the conquerors of the Confederacy.[6]

Obviously, Gordon was not a one-dimensional character. Few southerners were more beloved than was the man styled the Hero of Appomattox; nevertheless, the passion with which his critics reviled him forces one to reconsider the accolades bestowed upon him. Curiously, historians have paid relatively little attention to the Georgian. A comprehensive, critical study of Gordon's public career, which spanned more than four of America's most turbulent decades, has strangely been lacking. Historical treatment of his life consists of an uncritical biography, scattered accounts of certain aspects of his mili-

5. Mrs. William H. Felton [Plain Talk], *Gen. J. B. Gordon, as a Financier and Statesman* [her letters to the Macon *Telegraph*, May, 1886] (Macon, Ga., 1886), pamphlet located in Rebecca Latimer Felton Collection, UGA; Robert Toombs to A. H. Stephens, March 25, 1879, in Ulrich B. Phillips (ed.), *The Correspondence of Robert Toombs, Alexander H. Stephens, and Howell Cobb* (Washington, D.C., 1913), 740; San Francisco *Chronicle*, December 23, 1883.

6. Augusta *Chronicle*, September 29, 1890; Lafayette McLaws to General Munford, May 9, 1895, in Munford-Ellis Family Papers, Duke.

tary service, and isolated references to his postwar political activities and business involvements. Although a dearth of private papers—primarily the result of an 1899 fire that destroyed not only his home but almost all his personal correspondence—partially explains this lack of scholarly attention, Gordon clearly deserves better.

In my effort to present a thorough and balanced account of the life of General John B. Gordon, I have faced the task of all biographers: to determine both his influence upon the times and the impact of the times upon him. Accordingly, I have developed all areas of Gordon's career, not focusing upon any single portion at the expense of the others. Even though his participation in the Civil War was unquestionably the most dramatic chapter of his life, it is his postwar career that warrants much more extensive investigation and analysis. Barely thirty-three years of age at the end of the war, Gordon remained in the public spotlight for nearly forty years more. He made his most important contributions to American history during the last third of the nineteenth century and, in doing so, left an indelible imprint upon his state, his section, and his nation. It is this imprint that I wish to examine. Equally important, however, is the need to understand the myriad of historical forces—often contradictory and conflicting forces—that operated upon him. Identifying these influences and ascertaining how they affected the Georgian will yield additional insight into the political, social, and economic mentality of both the South and the nation in the difficult years after the war. A citizen-soldier in an army of professionals, a leading spokesman for the South, an active participant in the industrial, commercially oriented New South, and a major promoter of national reconciliation—John Brown Gordon should properly be numbered among the most important figures in southern and American history during the last half of the nineteenth century.

# I · The Early Years

During a political campaign in the 1880s, John Brown Gordon returned to the place of his birth along the Flint River in Upson County, Georgia. As he surveyed the familiar surroundings he found that the "river isn't nearly so wide and the hills are not nearly so high" as he remembered them. Gaining the perspective that comes only with the passage of years, Gordon nonetheless fondly recalled the days of his youth in Georgia. Later, reflecting on a career laced with countless military and political battles, he wistfully observed that whatever martial spirit may have been born in him "was greatly stimulated by the frequent rallies of the farmers and planters to meet reported raids by the Indians." For, indeed, the Upson County of Gordon's youth lay on the fringe of the frontier, with the recently dispossessed Creek Indians only fifty miles west of the Flint River.[1]

Four earlier generations of Gordons had helped push forward the American frontier. The first of Gordon's forebears to reach the North American continent sailed from Aberdeen, Scotland, in 1724. John George Gordon, John Brown's great-great-grandfather, disembarked in Charleston, South Carolina, but soon moved to Maryland and then on to Spotsylvania Court House, Virginia, before finally settling down. Like most Americans of the period, the first four generations of Gordons in the New World demonstrated a remarkable willingness to pick up and move at almost any time. Gordon's ancestors spread out through the South, but most remained in North Carolina and

---

1. Atlanta *Journal*, October 11, 1931; John B. Gordon, *A Boyhood Sketch* (N.p., n.d.), 1; John B. Gordon, "Boyhood in the South," *Youth's Companion: An Illustrated Weekly Paper for Young People and Families*, LXXIV (January, 1900), 15–16.

Georgia. His father, the Reverend Zachariah Herndon Gordon, was born in Wilkes County, North Carolina, and moved to Georgia in the early 1800s. Once situated in Upson County in the mid–1820s, he rapidly established himself as one of the county's most prominent ministers and added to his distinction by acquiring and running a large plantation. It was on this plantation, on February 6, 1832, that John Brown Gordon was born.[2]

John was the fourth of twelve children born to Zachariah and Malinda Cox Gordon. Although successful in Upson County, the reverend moved his family to Walker County in northwestern Georgia around 1840. He settled about ten miles from Lafayette, on property he dubbed Gordon Springs because of the great abundance of mineral water that flowed from twelve main springs in the space of a quarter of an acre. The elder Gordon took advantage of their medicinal value by building a large hotel that served as a summer resort, and in the decade preceding the Civil War, Gordon Springs became one of the "most fashionable watering places in Georgia." Ironically, it was in the peaceful fields and valleys surrounding the Gordon homestead in northwestern Georgia, over which John roamed during his adolescence, that the Battle of Chickamauga—one of the Civil War's bloodiest struggles—would later rage.[3]

While Gordon cultivated respect for the out-of-doors and developed what would become remarkable skill as a horseman, religion also played a formative role in his early life. "Among my earliest recollections," he wrote many years later, "are the great gatherings of

2. Frances Beal Smith Hodges, *The Gordons of Spotsylvania County, Virginia with Notes on Gordons of Scotland* (Wichita Falls, Tex., 1934), 12, 20–21; Paul W. Gregory, *Early Settlers of the Reddies River* (Wilkes County, N.C., 1972), 59–63; Allen P. Tankersley, "Zachariah Herndon Gordon: His Life and His Letters on the Battle of King's Mountain," *Georgia Historical Quarterly*, XXXVI (September, 1952), 233–37; Carolyn Walker Nottingham and Evelyn Hannah, *The Early History of Upson County* (Macon, Ga., 1930), 58; *Atlanta Journal*, April 3, 1932; *History of the Baptist Denomination in Georgia: With Biographical Compendium and Portrait Gallery of Baptist Ministers and Other Georgia Baptists* (2 vols.; Atlanta, 1881), II, 228–29, hereinafter cited as *History of Georgia Baptists*.

3. Sarah Harriet Butts (comp.), *The Mothers of Some Distinguished Georgians* (New York, 1902), 1–2; *History of Georgia Baptists*, II, 228–29; *Atlanta Journal*, April 3, 1932; George White, *Statistics of the State of Georgia: Including an Account of its Natural, Civil and Ecclesiastical History; Together with a Particular Description of Each County, Notices of the Manners and Customs of its Aboriginal Tribes, and a Correct Map of the State* (Savannah, 1849), 584–85; John B. Gordon, *Reminiscences of the Civil War* (New York, 1903), 198–99; U.S. Census, 1840, Walker County, Ga., 84; U.S. Census, 1850, Walker County, Ga., Free Schedule, 342.

the people at the old country church" in his father's charge. Young John, in addition to attending regular church services, often accompanied the reverend as he traveled about Georgia, preaching the gospel. At one church meeting when Gordon was but seven years of age, he came forward and made his profession of faith. Placed upon a rough pine table so that all might hear, Gordon related how he had "decided to put my trust in the Lord" when a team of mules he was driving earlier in the week had gotten away from him on a muddy hill. The congregation, convinced by the earnestness of the youth's account of his religious experience, immediately voted to receive him into their membership. Although reared as a Baptist, Gordon later became a Presbyterian and helped establish several churches on the outskirts of Atlanta. He remained an active Christian all his life, in no small part because of the influence of his father and the religious instruction of his youth.[4]

Gordon's early education differed little from what the sons of most small planters received at the time. He attended rural schools until his father became dissatisfied with the quality of instruction in Walker County. The reverend established a school on his own and assumed responsibility for securing and paying a good teacher. He also provided housing at a nominal cost for neighborhood boys who attended the institution. After finishing his father's school, Gordon ventured to Lafayette, where he entered Pleasant Green Academy, reputedly "one of the best schools in all northwest Georgia." The reputation was evidently well deserved, because when Gordon completed his studies there near the end of 1850, he enrolled at the University of Georgia in Athens as a second semester sophomore. He established himself as an excellent student and soon joined the Demosthenian Literary Society on campus. In a declamation competi-

4. Gordon, Boyhood Sketch, 4–5, 7; Atlanta Journal, February 15, 1932, October 11, 1931; Nottingham and Hannah, Upson County, 346, 844; Caroline Lewis Gordon, "De Gin'ral an' Miss Fanny" (MS in Gordon Family Collection, UGA). After settling in Kirkwood, four miles from Atlanta, in the late 1860s, Gordon helped build Decatur Presbyterian Church in neighboring Decatur. He became one of the ruling elders and remained active until June, 1892, when he and other Kirkwood parishioners left the parent church. Moving as a colony, they established Kirkwood Presbyterian Church, nearer their homes. Caroline McKinney Clarke, The Story of the Decatur Presbyterian Church, 1825–1975 (N.p., 1975), 46, 83–84; Kirkwood Presbyterian Church, in Georgia Historical Records Survey Inventory of Presbyterian Church Records in Georgia, GDAH; Testimony Taken by the Joint Select Committee to Inquire into the Condition of Affairs in the Late Insurrectionary States (13 vols.; Washington, D.C., 1872), Georgia, Vol. I, in House Reports, 42nd Cong., 2nd Sess., No. 22, Pt. 6, p. 340.

tion with sixteen of his fellow sophomores at the end of his first semester, Gordon won first place and was awarded a gold medal.[5]

Gordon remained a superb student during his junior year, at the end of which the faculty again chose him to compete as one of six class orators. Even though no prizes or medals were awarded for this contest, Gordon devoted a great deal of effort to preparing "an elaborate eulogy" honoring a man his father greatly admired, Henry Clay, of Kentucky. He had written his address and committed it to memory when the faculty notified him only days before the commencement exercises that university policy prohibited eulogies of living statesmen. This decision obviously upset him, for as he recalled, "[i]t was Clay, or nothing. Even if a subject could be thought of, the time was too short for suitable presentation." Nevertheless, the faculty refused to make any exceptions. It was with a touch of wry humor that Gordon later confessed, "I am afraid that my grief was not as profound as it should have been over the death of Henry Clay, which occurred a few days before commencement, and just in time to permit the delivery of my eulogy."[6]

Gordon began his senior year at the university in August, 1852. Despite possessing one of the highest grade averages, if not the highest, in his class, he did not graduate from college, because on October 14 he withdrew from school. Why he left the university so precipitately cannot be determined with certainty. The Reverend Z. H. Gordon had sent a letter to the faculty requesting that his son be allowed to leave, so it is likely that young Gordon resigned in order to return home and assist his father in developing his coal mines or in managing the family plantation. However, in a brief biographical sketch written in 1878, Henry Grady, who was then very close to the current senator from Georgia, wrote that Gordon left college "for the purpose of marrying—a frustrated elopement being the history of this event." In either case, Gordon never returned to the University of Georgia and thus never earned a college degree. Still, there could be no question of his ability; while in college, Gordon had amply dem-

5. Gordon, *Boyhood Sketch*, 1–3, 8–13; James Alfred Sartain, *History of Walker County, Georgia* (Dalton, Ga., 1932), 159, 163; Sketches of Alumni of University of Georgia, in UGA; Demosthenian Society Minute Book, 1851–52, in UGA; Athens *Southern Banner*, August 7, 21, 1851; Atlanta *Constitution*, November 24, 1878; C. L. Gordon, "De Gin'ral an' Miss Fanny"; Atlanta *Constitution*, January 15, 1904.

6. Gordon, *Boyhood Sketch*, 13; Minutes of the Faculty, June 18, 1852, in UGA; Athens *Southern Banner*, August 11, 1852; Athens *Herald*, August 5, 1852; Atlanta *Constitution*, November 24, 1878.

onstrated his academic competence. The faculty of the university sent his father a letter stating "that had he [John] remained he would have taken the senior honor." Moreover, he had revealed in his penchant for public speaking an indication of the outstanding oratorical powers that would later prove so valuable.[7]

After leaving the university, Gordon evidently returned to northwestern Georgia, but he did not remain there long. In 1854, he moved to Atlanta, where he pursued a career in law. Under the tutelage of two of Atlanta's most respected attorneys, Basil H. Overby and Logan E. Bleckley, Gordon read law, and took and passed the bar examination. He immediately joined the Overby & Bleckley firm but experienced considerable difficulty in attracting clients. As a result, his career as a lawyer was to be short-lived; nevertheless, his brief association with Overby & Bleckley proved far more valuable than did the legal training he received.[8]

Shortly after joining the law firm, Gordon met Mrs. Overby's younger sister, Fanny Rebecca Haralson. Smitten at first sight, Gordon began courting the daughter of General Hugh Anderson Haralson of La Grange, Georgia. He pursued her with such intensity and sincerity that in less than a month she consented to become his wife. Gordon married Fanny on her seventeenth birthday, September 18, 1854, in a private ceremony in the bedroom of her desperately ill father at Myrtle Hill, the Haralsons' ancestral home near La Grange. General Haralson's death one week later undoubtedly cast a pall over the early days of John and Fanny's marriage, but this union developed into one of the most solid and most stabilizing influences in Gordon's life. A charming, intelligent lady, Fanny was the love of his life and he of hers. Long after their death, the Gordons' daughter Caroline fondly remembered her parents' marriage as "a perfect union—unmarred by

7. Minutes of the Faculty, October 14, 1852; Atlanta *Constitution*, November 24, 1878; C. L. Gordon, "De Gin'ral an' Miss Fanny." A letter from young Gordon to a close friend in Athens in the summer of 1853 seems to indicate that he had compelling reasons for withdrawing from the university the previous fall and that he did not leave under a cloud of controversy. In the letter, written from Gordon Springs, Gordon requested information about commencement for his class and about the trains traveling to Athens. Obviously, he wanted to return to the university to be with his classmates when they were graduated. Gordon to Governor Lumpkin, July 21, 1853, in Keith Morton Read Collection, UGA.

8. Atlanta *Constitution*, November 24, 1878; C. L. Gordon, "De Gin'ral an' Miss Fanny"; Allen D. Candler and Clement A. Evans (eds.), *Georgia: Comprising Sketches of Counties, Towns, Events, Institutions, and Persons, Arranged in Cyclopedia Form* (3 vols.; Atlanta, 1906), II, 138.

discord through all their years together." Throughout nearly fifty years of marriage, Fanny provided "her beloved John" with trusted counsel, unwavering support, and unquestioned devotion.[9]

Gordon and his young bride returned to Atlanta following the death of Fanny's father. But by late 1855, when his law practice had not improved appreciably, Gordon felt compelled to seek other employment elsewhere. He chose journalism and Milledgeville, where as a newspaper reporter he covered the 1855–56 session of the Georgia General Assembly. When the legislature adjourned in March, 1856, Gordon returned to northwestern Georgia and joined his father in a coal-mining enterprise in the mountainous tri-state region of Alabama, Georgia, and Tennessee. In the years preceding the Civil War, the Gordons formed the Castle Rock Coal Company, which profitably developed several mines in the mineral-rich region. The younger Gordon initially settled in Dade County, in the north-western-most corner of Georgia, but later crossed the state line, moving to Jackson County, Alabama. Later commenting on the geographical propinquity of the three states, he wrote, "I lived so near the lines that my mines were in Georgia, my house in Alabama, and my post-office in Tennessee."[10]

The mountainous regions of these states possessed numerous features that set them apart from the southern mainstream. Dominated by the southern extension of the Appalachian Mountains, the northern-most counties of Georgia and Alabama were geographically isolated and in fact more closely tied, economically and socially, to the similarly mountainous area of eastern Tennessee. Steep ridges,

9. C. L. Gordon, "De Gin'ral an' Miss Fanny"; Marriage Records, Court of Ordinary, Troup County, Georgia, Vol. D, p. 66, in GDAH; Mrs. Bryan Wells Collier, *Biographies of Representative Women of the South* (6 vols.; n.p., 1920–38), IV, 229 (copy in AHS). Three of the four Haralson sisters eventually married the partners of the law firm Overby, Bleckley, and Gordon. The fourth, Leonora, or "Nora," married James M. Pace of Covington, Georgia, who served on Gordon's staff during the Civil War. William J. Northen (ed.), *Men of Mark in Georgia: A Complete and Elaborate History of the State from its Settlement to the present time, chiefly told in biographies and autobiographies of the most eminent men of each period of Georgia's progress and development* (7 vols.; Spartanburg, S.C., 1974), II, 34; Collier, *Representative Women*, IV, 229.

10. Atlanta *Constitution*, December 3, 1876, November 24, 1878, June 8, 1880; C. L. Gordon, "De Gin'ral an' Miss Fanny"; Gordon, *Reminiscences*, 3; Ethel M. Armes, *The Story of Coal and Iron in Alabama* (Birmingham, 1910), 183; Gordon to Barlow, January 29, April 7, September 21, 1868, all in Samuel Latham Mitchill Barlow Papers, HL; Detroit *Free Press*, quoted in La Grange *Reporter*, January 24, 1878, cited in Allen P. Tankersley, *John B. Gordon: A Study in Gallantry* (Atlanta, 1955), 75.

narrow valleys, and the poor quality of soil, as well as the cooler climate, prevented the growth of large-scale agriculture but in turn encouraged subsistence farming. In these sparsely populated counties, whites overwhelmingly predominated, yet few thrived. Although the mountains held an abundance of mineral wealth, mining operations were still in an early stage of development. It was a region of few slaves, few slaveholders, small slaveholdings, and small landholdings. Despite the chronic poverty present in the mountains, Gordon evidently prospered with his coal mines. By 1860, he had acquired $3,500 in real estate, $14,900 in personal property, and several slaves and servants.[11] Also, John and Fanny felt financially secure enough to start a family; two sons, Hugh and Frank, were born to the couple in the late 1850s.[12]

As he established himself economically, Gordon also gravitated toward politics. Initially a Whig (perhaps as a consequence of his father's long-time Whiggish affiliation), Gordon left the party as it disintegrated in the mid–1850s, and became a Democrat. His rise to political prominence in northern Alabama was not spectacular, but in the half-decade prior to the outbreak of war, he distinguished himself among the mountain folk "as a brilliant and captivating orator." He actively participated in every campaign in the state and, in the words of Henry Grady, "was accounted one of the best of the campaign orators, always drawing immense crowds." Although few of his antebellum political speeches and writings have survived, it is apparent that as the sectional crisis deepened, Gordon moved increasingly into the secessionists' camp.[13]

In a commencement address delivered before the literary societies

11. Robert P. Brooks, *The Agrarian Revolution in Georgia, 1865–1912* (Madison, Wis., 1914), 69–114; Phillip J. Green, "Secession in Georgia, 1860–1861," *North Dakota Historical Quarterly Journal,* XVII (1927), 255; U.S. Census, 1860, Jackson County, Ala., Free Schedule, 476–77, Slave Schedule, 432. More details concerning the economy and society of north Georgia and north Alabama can be found in the 1860 census, especially in the statistics, population, agriculture, and manufacturing tables. See also Stephen Hahn, *The Roots of Southern Populism: Yeoman Farmers and the Transformation of the Georgia Upcountry, 1850–1890* (New York, 1983), Pt. I, "The Poor Man's Best Government," especially pp. 15–49. Even though Hahn deals with Georgia upcountry whites, most of his observations concerning their social values and political culture are applicable to whites in the more mountainous regions to the north and northwest.

12. The Gordons would eventually have six children: Hugh (b. 1855), Frank (b. 1857), Frances (b. 1863), John, Jr. (b. 1865), Caroline Lewis (b. 1873), and Carolina (b. 1877).

13. Atlanta *Constitution,* November 24, 1878.

of Oglethorpe University on July 18, 1860, Gordon expounded upon the "progress of civil liberty." He openly questioned whether a government "from which you cannot receive, for your person and your property, protection from any and all enemies on the common domain" was worth preserving. He hoped the current political controversy would be peaceably resolved, but he stressed that southerners must be permitted to retain their slaves and to carry them into the territories. African slavery was, for him, "the Mightiest Engine in the universe for the civilization, elevation and refinement of mankind— the surest guarantee of the continuance of liberty among ourselves." If their alternatives were reduced to "dismemberment of this Union" or "fanatical dictation and Abolition rule," Gordon warned his fellow southerners not to hesitate for even a moment. "The spirit of RESISTANCE is the spirit of LIBERTY. . . . [L]et us do our duty, protect our liberties, and leave the consequences with God, who alone can control them." Rather than admit that slavery was an evil or a tyrannical institution, Gordon urged his audience to "take the position everywhere, that it [slavery] is morally, socially, and politically *right*—and that it is, in truth, the hand-maid of civil liberty." In Gordon's mind, southern slavery and southern liberty were inextricably intertwined.[14]

Consequently, Gordon campaigned extensively in the summer and fall of 1860 on behalf of the southern Democratic presidential candidate, John C. Breckinridge. According to one newspaper account, "he was literally everywhere, and was pronounced a marvel of eloquence in address and endurance." At Huntsville, before one of the largest gatherings of the campaign, he spoke on the same platform with Alabama's foremost fire-eater, William Lowndes Yancey. Gordon's interest in the momentous questions of the day steadily intensified in the weeks following the defeat of Breckinridge and the election of Abraham Lincoln. He traveled to Montgomery in early January, 1861, so that he might be present while the secession convention debated the fate of Alabama. On the evening that Alabama seceded, a frenzied crowd outside Montgomery Hall prevailed upon him to deliver a brief address. Gordon then moved on to Milledgeville, where on January 19, 1861, Georgia secessionists also

14. Milledgeville *Federal Union*, July 24, 1860; Milledgeville *Southern Recorder*, July 24, 1860; John B. Gordon, *Progress of Civil Liberty. An Address Delivered Before the Thalian and Phi Delta Societies, of Oglethorpe University, Georgia, at the Last Annual Commencement* (Macon, 1861), 13–16.

voted to leave the Union. As in Montgomery, Gordon spoke at the insistence of an excited throng and fanned the flames of southern independence.[15]

Gordon's passionate championing of secession placed him at odds with many of his hill-country neighbors. Although residents of extreme northeastern Alabama had voted overwhelmingly for Breckinridge, only a minority supported immediate secession. They did not oppose the principle of secession but rather questioned the need for such precipitate action. Exactly why Gordon favored immediate secession cannot be determined owing to a lack of material; nevertheless, historical studies offer possible insights. Northern Alabamians who supported both Breckinridge and secession were generally younger and wealthier than their opponents and usually held more slaves. Only in his late twenties, heavily engaged in mining operations, and already owning slaves, Gordon could certainly fit this description. As he was not the typical yeoman farmer who dominated this mountainous region, he may have had more in common with planters in the Black Belt than he did with his neighbors. Gordon realized that Abraham Lincoln's election threatened the geographical expansion of slavery, but even more important than the threat to the future of slavery was the perceived restriction of southern liberty that came with the Republican victory. Acutely aware of the linkage between slavery and freedom as a result of everyday contact with black slavery, white southerners, especially slaveholders, regarded all forms of restriction or dependence as essentially equivalent to slavery itself. Thus Gordon's advocacy of secession seems most likely to have been rooted in his desire to protect and defend southern rights and southern constitutional interpretations. In any event, he stood ready to do more than merely campaign for disunion.[16]

Once the state of his birth and the state of his residence had seceded, Gordon returned to his home in northeastern Alabama to await the reaction of the Republican administration. Many in his district called upon him to stand for election to the Confederate

15. Atlanta *Constitution*, November 24, 1878.
16. William L. Barney, *The Secessionist Impulse: Alabama and Mississippi in 1860* (Princeton, 1974), 61–76, 180–88, 267–79; J. Mills Thornton III, *Politics and Power in a Slave Society: Alabama, 1800–1860* (Baton Rouge, 1978), xviii–xxi, 343–47, 401–61; Gordon, *Reminiscences*, 14–25. See also Hahn, *Southern Populism*; Michael P. Johnson, *Toward a Patriarchal Republic: The Secession of Georgia* (Baton Rouge, 1977); and William J. Cooper, Jr., *The South and the Politics of Slavery, 1828–1856* (Baton Rouge, 1978), 58–74.

Congress, but how seriously Gordon entertained the suggestion is unknown. It became a moot point when, in the days following the firing on Fort Sumter, President Abraham Lincoln called for 75,000 militiamen. For Gordon, his course of action was clear—he must offer his military services to the newly created Confederate States of America. Even so, as he remembered many years later, "the struggle between devotion to my family on the one hand and duty to my country on the other was most trying to my sensibilities." Fortunately for John, Fanny promptly allayed such misgivings by boldly announcing that she would leave their two young sons with his mother and accompany her husband to the war. So in April, 1861, the twenty-nine-year-old Gordon began preparing for the uncertain ordeal that lay ahead. John B. Gordon was going to war.[17]

17. Atlanta *Constitution*, November 24, 1878; Gordon, *Reminiscences*, 3–4, 150.

# II · Initiation

Shortly after the firing on Fort Sumter, Gordon helped raise a company of volunteers from the tri-state region of Georgia, Tennessee, and Alabama. Well-known among the mountain folk, he was elected captain. The company organized as cavalry but soon discovered that quotas for horsemen had already been filled. Disappointed, yet still imbued with the passion of the times, Gordon and his men reluctantly abandoned their horses and "resolved to go at once to the front as infantry." Without waiting for orders to move, the company began the journey to Milledgeville, then the capital of Georgia, where it would enlist. In Atlanta, however, the would-be soldiers received a telegram from Governor Joseph E. Brown, informing them that the number of volunteers had far exceeded all quotas and advising them to go home until circumstances warranted their recall. Unwilling to disband, the individualistic mountaineers set up camp on the outskirts of town while imploring the governors of other states to accept their services.[1]

Gordon's company received its name as it marched through the streets of Atlanta on the way to its temporary camp. Moving in ragtag fashion with no two men in step, this motley group of volunteers displayed no semblance of uniformity save their fur caps adorned with raccoon tails. When a curious onlooker inquired as to the company's name, Gordon took it upon himself—as a name had yet to be determined—to announce proudly, "'This company is the Mountain Rifles.'" Instantly, however, a member of Gordon's command objected. "In a tone not intended for his captain," the tall mountaineer

1. John B. Gordon, *Reminiscences of the Civil War* (New York, 1903), 3–5, 7–8.

proclaimed, "'Mountain hell! we are no Mountain Rifles; we are the Raccoon Roughs.'" So in a single stroke, the undisciplined mountain-man, and not his captain, named this soon-to-be-famous company.[2]

When word arrived that Alabama governor A. B. Moore had accepted the service of the company, the Raccoon Roughs set out for Montgomery. Gordon and his men reveled in the unbounded optimism that characterized the early days of the Confederacy. He described the trip by train from Atlanta to Montgomery as "one unbroken scene of enthusiasm." The throngs that flocked to the depots along the track frequently prevailed upon Gordon, the only captain aboard, to speak briefly, and in doing so, drew from him promises that were to prove impossible to honor. He later recalled that in his "ardor and inexperience," he pledged that neither he nor his men would ever retreat. With only the vaguest knowledge of military science and barely an inkling of what lay ahead, the young captain had much to learn.[3]

Upon arrival in Montgomery, the Raccoon Roughs were assigned to the 6th Alabama Regiment of Infantry. Although regulations called for ten companies per regiment, Governor Moore authorized the 6th to include two extra companies in order to accommodate those to whom he had promised immediate assignment. The twelve-company, 1,400-man complement made the regiment one of the largest in the Confederate army. When regimental elections took place in early May, Gordon was unanimously elected major. He received his commission as major of the 6th Alabama on May 14, 1861, and formally enlisted as a twelve-month volunteer three days later.[4]

Near the end of May, the 6th Alabama, now uniformed in Confederate gray but still sporting their distinctive "'coonskin' head-dress," moved to Corinth, Mississippi, to undergo military training. Following a "brief and uneventful" encampment there, the regiment received orders on June 4, 1861, to proceed to Richmond as quickly as possible. The long journey from Mississippi to Virginia passed without serious incident; still, the trip left an indelible impression on Gordon. Forced to travel through east Tennessee, a hotbed of Unionist sentiment, Gordon encountered unmistakable signs of the region's divided allegiances. Whenever crowds gathered at the depots

2. *Ibid.*, 8–9.
3. *Ibid.*, 9–12.
4. *Ibid.*, 13, 26; Gordon's Service File, in Military Service Records, NA; Military Records of the Sixth Alabama, and Military Records of John B. Gordon, both in ADAH.

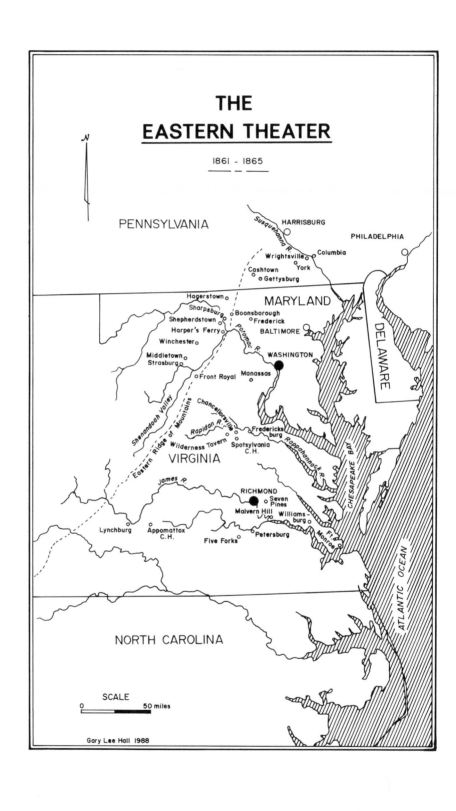

# THE
# EASTERN THEATER

1861 - 1865

N

PENNSYLVANIA

Susquehanna R.

HARRISBURG

PHILADELPHIA

Wrightsville
Columbia
Cashtown
York
Gettysburg

Hagerstown
MARYLAND
Sharpsburg
Boonsborough
Shepherdstown
Frederick
Harper's Ferry
BALTIMORE
Winchester
Potomac R.
DELAWARE
WASHINGTON
Middletown
Strasburg
Front Royal
Manassas

Shenandoah Valley
Eastern Ridge of Mountains
Chancellorsville
Rapidan R.
Fredericksburg
Wilderness Tavern
Spotsylvania C.H.
VIRGINIA
Rappahannock R.
CHESAPEAKE BAY

James R.
RICHMOND
Seven Pines
Malvern Hill
Williamsburg
Lynchburg
Appomattox C.H.
Petersburg
Ft. Monroe
Five Forks

ATLANTIC OCEAN

NORTH CAROLINA

SCALE
0          50 miles

Gary Lee Hall 1988

where the train stopped, both cheers and jeers greeted the Alabamians. In many towns along the way, the flags of both the North and the South flew openly, almost mockingly, often on opposite sides of the street. Aware of the possibility of trouble between his troops and Union sympathizers, Gordon took particular care to restrain his men and avoid any action on their part that might precipitate a conflict. His vigilance was rewarded as the 6th Alabama peacefully passed through the mountainous region of Tennessee.[5]

Gordon and his men arrived in Virginia around June 10 and found the state burning with war fever as it hectically prepared for military action. Soon after reporting to Richmond, the 6th moved northward to Manassas Junction and joined other Confederate regiments rapidly arriving from throughout the South. In the first major organization of troops of the Confederate Army of the Potomac, General P. G. T. Beauregard assigned the Alabama regiment to the 2nd Brigade of the I Corps, under the command of Brigadier General Richard S. Ewell. Gordon and the rest of Ewell's brigade occupied forward positions near Fairfax Station, where they monitored Federal movements until July 17 when the Union army began its advance on Manassas. During the brigade's retirement to the main Confederate line, Gordon commanded a portion of the rearguard element, and when he rejoined the main body, he excitedly told his comrades that "he had seen the enemy."[6]

Even after the Battle of First Manassas four days later, Gordon could boast of little more than a "feel of the enemy." Early on the morning of July 21, Ewell, joyful at the prospect of battle, lustily invited Gordon to join him for a quick breakfast. "'Come and eat a cracker with me,'" offered the eccentric Ewell. "'[W]e will breakfast together here and dine together in hell.'" The young major, "who had never been under fire except at long range, on scouting expeditions, or on the skirmish-line," found the invitation neither appetizing nor inspiring. After breakfast, Ewell ordered Gordon to make a reconnaissance across Bull Run; yet just when Gordon had deployed his skir-

5. Charles T. Jones, Jr., "Five Confederates: The Sons of Bolling Hall in the Civil War," *Alabama Historical Quarterly*, XXIV (1962), 139–41; *The War of the Rebellion: A Compilation of the Official Records of the Union and Confederate Armies* (130 vols.; Washington, D.C., 1880–1901), Ser. I, Vol. LI, Pt. 2, p. 128, hereinafter cited as *OR*, and unless otherwise noted, all references are from Series I; Gordon, *Reminiscences*, 26–28.

6. *OR*, Vol. II, 944, 447, 440; Jones, "Five Confederates," 142–44; Gordon, *Reminiscences*, 32.

mishers and prepared to open fire, his commander suddenly recalled him. The anticipated order for a general advance had not yet been delivered, so the Alabama troops recrossed the stream and awaited further orders. These early morning movements exemplified the extent of Gordon's participation at First Manassas. Although constantly expecting action, he spent the entire day and part of the evening marching and countermarching around Bull Run, but never actually engaged the enemy. When, at last, well after dark, he returned to the same position he had held at daybreak, Gordon must have reflected upon his part in the first major clash of the war. True, he had seen the enemy, but he had still not undergone the trial by fire that would prove his mettle. For that he would have to wait almost a year.[7]

In the months following the Union rout at Manassas, the 6th Alabama remained in the vicinity of Bull Run. Gordon devoted much of his time to training and drilling his men, as well as to preparing himself for the rigors of command. Like all other conscientious citizen-soldiers without professional training in arms, Gordon had to teach himself the techniques of contemporary warfare. No record of what he read or how he educated himself in the science of war has survived, but it is probable that he utilized whatever military manuals he could find. Gordon certainly understood the importance of drill and discipline. A private in the 6th, bemoaning the tedium and discipline of army life, wrote home, "Drilling everyday—very hot and dull times, . . . our employment is the same as ever—a very dull routine it is." Despite its monotony, Gordon realized that ceaseless drilling was the only way to achieve effective control of troops in combat. As there was no further campaigning during 1861, Gordon and the troops posted along Bull Run occupied the remaining months of the summer and fall with drilling, doing picket duty, rebuilding bridges destroyed during the movements of July, and preparing for winter by constructing cabins.[8]

Gordon's command went into winter quarters on the banks of Occoquan Creek near the mouth of Bull Run. As winter settled in, Gordon, like so many other soldiers, suffered the disappointment that came with the inactivity of camp life. In a December letter to the

7. Jones, "Five Confederates," 145; Gordon, *Reminiscences*, 37–39; OR, Vol. II, 536–37.
8. Gordon, *Reminiscences*, 48; Jones, "Five Confederates," 145–48.

War Department he asked for a furlough in order to return home to raise a regiment, but his promotion to lieutenant colonel of the 6th on December 26, 1861, dispelled all thoughts of leaving Virginia. Although undoubtedly pleased with his advancement, Gordon found few other reasons to celebrate as the frigid winds of winter engulfed Virginia.[9]

The severity of the Virginia winter amazed Gordon as he witnessed the hardships it wrought upon the soldiers from the Deep South. In spite of their efforts to gather supplies and prepare for the unaccustomed cold weather, the men suffered terribly. Both food and warm clothing were in short supply; consequently, sickness spread throughout the Confederate camp. Measles became one of the primary killers, but Gordon encountered diseases that "ran through the whole catalogue of complaints to which boyhood and even babyhood are subjected . . . everything almost except teething, nettle rash, and whooping-cough," and he even suspected that some were afflicted with the last of these ailments. Gordon himself suffered intensely from a crippling attack of diarrhea, which confined him to private quarters for six weeks in February and March. He returned to duty on March 28 and continued preparing for the battles that warmer weather would bring.[10]

April not only signaled a return to spring but also brought movement on the part of the Union forces. Major General George B. McClellan initiated the long-expected move on Richmond when his troops began landing at the base of the Virginia peninsula at Fortress Monroe. On April 6, the 6th Alabama, now part of Brigadier General Robert E. Rodes's brigade, left northern Virginia by train for Yorktown on the peninsula. While en route, the troop-laden train on which Gordon and his wife were traveling collided head on with an empty train speeding in the opposite direction. "Nearly every car on the densely packed train," he recalled, "was telescoped and torn into pieces; and men, knapsacks, arms, and shivered seats were hurled to the front and piled in horrid mass against the crushed timbers and ironwork." Although many were killed and scores injured, both Gor-

9. OR, Vol. V, 737; Gordon, Reminiscences, 48; Secretary of War Judah P. Benjamin to Major J. B. Gordon, December 21, 1861, in Gordon Family Collection, UGA; Gordon's Service File; Sixth Alabama Records.

10. Gordon's Service File; Gordon, Reminiscences, 49–50; Jones, "Five Confederates," 146–49.

don and his wife fortunately escaped serious injury. The young Georgian was learning that disease and accident, as in all wars, often exacted a greater toll than did rifle or cannon fire.[11]

Finally arriving in Yorktown, Gordon and the rest of the brigade labored to improve the weak defenses around the town. D. H. Hill, commander of the division to which Rodes's brigade was assigned, kept his command "at work day and night to remedy the defects, strengthen the intrenchments and secure shelter for the men." While engaged in these efforts, the Alabama regiment underwent reorganization, and on April 28, 1862, the men of the 6th unanimously elected Gordon their colonel. The improvements to the Yorktown defenses went for naught, as the entire Confederate line evacuated the town on the night of May 3. Portions of Hill's division engaged at Williamsburg on May 5, but Gordon and the 6th did not become involved. As the Confederates retreated up the peninsula, Gordon saw no action. His command served as the rear guard of the army for a time, but the mud and slush of Virginia's deeply rutted roads proved far more troublesome than was the advancing Union army. The rain-drenched countryside turned into a seemingly bottomless sea of mud in which wagons, horses, and artillery repeatedly bogged down. On at least one occasion, Gordon waded into the mud himself to help his men who were laboring to free some mired artillery pieces. With justifiable pride, he claimed that "not a gun or caisson was lost, and there was never again among those brave men a moment's hesitation about leaping in the mud and water whenever it became necessary on any account." Despite the severe conditions of the march, Gordon's shivering, tired, and hungry troops finally limped into the incomplete breastworks behind the banks of the Chickahominy River east of Richmond. In this wooded swampland, Gordon finally faced his first real trial by fire less than three weeks later.[12]

The Battle of Fair Oaks, or Seven Pines, fought on May 31 and June 1, 1862, developed when General Joseph E. Johnston decided to crush a portion of McClellan's army located south of the Chickahominy. A torrential downpour that lasted throughout the evening of May 30,

11. OR, Vol. V, 935–36, 961; Vol. XI, Pt. 1, pp. 601–602; Gordon, Reminiscences, 52.

12. OR, Vol. XI, Pt. 3, p. 426; Pt. 1, pp. 601–605; Sixth Alabama Records; Gordon's Service File; E. A. Pollard [A Distinguished Southern Journalist], The Early Life, Campaigns and Public Services of Robert E. Lee, with a Record of the Campaigns and Heroic Deeds of his Companions in Arms (New York, 1871), 536, hereinafter cited as Companions in Arms; Gordon, Reminiscences, 52–54.

however, complicated his plans for a rapid convergence of his divisions to overwhelm the somewhat isolated Federals. When D. H. Hill's division plunged forward the following morning, the normally marshy land around Seven Pines was completely flooded, in some places to a depth of three feet.[13]

Gordon and the rest of Rodes's brigade experienced considerable difficulty in moving through the swampland to their point of attack south of the Williamsburg Road. A washed-out bridge forced the men to wade through waist-deep water and delayed their arrival on the field of battle. Only Gordon's and one other regiment were in position at the appointed time of attack. Gordon, sensing in his men the apprehension and dread that haunt most soldiers just prior to their first real battle, and undoubtedly experiencing it himself, addressed his men in the moments before their advance. He reminded them of "Beast" Butler's actions in New Orleans, spoke of the disaster that would befall both them and their cause if they were defeated, and implored them to do their duty. Fortified by Gordon's oratory, the 6th moved forward on signal and deployed as skirmishers covering the brigade's entire front because most of Rodes's men were still struggling to get in position. The thick undergrowth, the ever-present briars, the felled trees, and the spongy soil of this northern end of White Oak Swamp made Gordon's advance both difficult and exhausting; nevertheless, his men drove the enemy's pickets back to their first line of entrenchments.[14]

With the entire brigade now on the field and deployed, Rodes ordered Gordon to concentrate his regiment and move it to the extreme right. Once in position, the 6th pressed forward with the rest of the brigade and, despite heavy fire, forced the Federals to retreat from their first line of defense. At this point, Rodes halted his brigade so that he could reform and reorganize his line before assaulting the next Union position. The order to stop never reached Gordon, and as a result, the 6th continued its advance past the first line of earthworks and into hastily abandoned enemy camps. Gordon, seeing that the troops on his left had halted, quickly stopped his men, ordered them about, and marched them back to the point where Rodes was dressing

13. OR, Vol. XI, Pt. 1, p. 943; Gustavus W. Smith, "Two Days of Battle at Seven Pines (Fair Oaks)," in Robert Underwood Johnson and Clarence Clough Buel (eds.), Battles and Leaders of the Civil War (4 vols.; 1887–88; rpr. New York, 1956), II, 225–27.
14. OR, Vol. XI, Pt. 1, pp. 971–72, 979.

his brigade line. When Rodes called for the advance to resume, Gordon ordered his men forward but to his immense consternation found the entire regiment continuing to march to the rear as previously ordered. The men had not been ordered about.[15]

Immediately realizing that his order had been misunderstood and "impressed with the importance of arresting the movement at once," Gordon galloped to a point equidistant between his line and the Federals, where he called and gestured for his men to turn and move on the enemy. The startled 6th then faced about and delivered its charge at the double-quick. In his official report, Gordon noted that this incident "though insignificant in itself, is worthy of record, as evincing the spirit of the brave men under my command." It might be added that the regiment's orderly retrograde movement, consistent with previous orders, and its rapid about-face reflected extremely favorably upon Gordon and the discipline he had inculcated into his command.[16]

The assault upon the second Federal line sorely tested Gordon's control of his troops. Most of his officers, including his brother, were disabled, and he alone remained on horseback.[17] Although a magnificent target for the numerous Union soldiers who drew a bead on this lone horseman, Gordon escaped unscathed, despite numerous bullets piercing his clothing. As he approached the abatis guarding the front of the Federal line, his horse was killed, forcing him to advance on foot. Gordon led his men into a labyrinth in which felled trees, the dense growth of vines and briars, and two to three feet of water made "an almost impassable barrier." Advancing in the face of intense fire, the Alabamians suffered severely, often finding it necessary to prop up the wounded when they fell lest they drown. In spite of these difficulties, the regiment continued to drive the enemy back steadily.[18]

As the 6th moved through the swampy abatis, Gordon's right sud-

---

15. *Ibid.*, 971–73, 979–80.

16. *Ibid.*, 980.

17. When the 6th Alabama organized in Montgomery in May, 1861, three Gordon brothers—John, Eugene, and Augustus—enlisted. At Seven Pines, Gordon saw his nineteen-year-old brother, Augustus, severely wounded, but he was unable to stop and aid him. Sixth Alabama Records; Gordon, *Reminiscences*, 56–57; Frances Beal Smith Hodges, *The Gordons of Spotsylvania County, Virginia with Notes on Gordons of Scotland* (Wichita Falls, Tex., 1934), 21–22.

18. Pollard, *Companions in Arms*, 536–37; Gordon, *Reminiscences*, 56–57; OR, Vol. XI, Pt. 1, pp. 972–73, 980.

denly came under a withering fire from Union troops who had moved forward when they saw the 6th's flank unsupported. This destructive enfilading fire compelled Gordon to halt his men and refuse his flank in an effort to protect his right and rear. Further advance was impossible until the supporting brigade under Brigadier General Gabriel J. Rains moved up. Despite urgent pleas from Gordon and Rodes and a written order from Hill, Rains's brigade, "although within sight and but a few hundred yards distant," never advanced to protect Gordon's right. As a result, Federal fire virtually annihilated Gordon's right flank company before the order to withdraw was given. Only one officer and twelve of the fifty-six men in the company escaped unharmed. Rodes, seeing that nothing could be accomplished as long as the brigade's right wing was exposed, ordered his entire command to fall back. With the fighting near an end and with sunset approaching, Rodes, nearly exhausted from a painful arm wound sustained earlier in the day, turned his decimated brigade over to the young colonel of the 6th. After assuming command and reporting to D. H. Hill, Gordon moved the brigade to the rear, where it camped for the evening. Even in the darkness, rest did not come immediately, for the brigade spent much of the evening searching out and attending to the wounded who had not yet been removed from the battlefield. The brigade remained in reserve during the next day's fighting.[19]

The grisly aftermath of battle became painfully apparent to Gordon in the days following the conflict at Seven Pines. His inspection of the battlefield revealed a scene he found "sickening and shocking to those whose sensibilities were not yet blunted by almost constant contact with such sights." Gordon found himself almost overwhelmed by the human wreckage spread out before him. The dead bodies of soldiers of both sides littered the fields and swamps in which they had fought on May 31. These images and the emotions stirred by the grim task of burying the dead burned deeply into Gordon's mind. When reminiscing about his Civil War experiences, he called his recollections of the months he spent in the swampland east of Richmond "some of the saddest memories of those four years." Yet, it was in these "miasmatic swamps" of the Chickahominy that the Georgian first learned the lessons of war.[20]

For a young soldier with no previous military training or experi-

19. *OR*, Vol. XI, Pt. 1, pp. 944, 973–74, 976, 977, 980; Gordon *Reminiscences*, 57–58.
20. Gordon, *Reminiscences*, 54, 70.

ence, Gordon had performed quite well. Even if made only to ease his own nervousness, Gordon's speech to his men prior to their advance served to strengthen their resolve to stand fast. He would employ his oratorical powers frequently throughout the war and obviously to good effect. After another battle later in the war, one of his men claimed that he never again wanted to hear his commander speak before going into action, "because he makes me feel like I could storm h——ll." More important, Gordon demonstrated the ability to inspire not only with his words but with his deeds as well. Six feet tall, slight of build, and straight as a ramrod, Gordon looked every inch a soldier. His coal-black hair, high forehead, closely cropped chin beard, and piercing gray eyes marked him as "a man of natural eminence," but it was his martial bearing and commanding presence, especially on horseback in combat, that distinguished him as one of the most picturesque Confederate officers. Once engaged at Seven Pines, he displayed the coolness and courage that allowed him to make full use of the sound military sense that he possessed. One contemporary later noted, "[I]t was here [at Seven Pines] that Gen. Gordon for the first time, displayed those remarkable qualities: serene intrepidity, perfect self-possession, fertility of resource, & rapidity of decision & movement, that in the opinions of the Military . . . [would lend] such distinction to his subsequent career." Even in the heaviest of fire, he remained on horseback as long as possible in order to maintain more effective control of his regiment—a difficult task in any combat, but one complicated by the terrain over which the 6th advanced. Gordon's firm control of the regiment proved that he had mastered his manuals and had been equally successful in imparting his knowledge to his men.[21]

Gordon's Alabamians similarly exhibited remarkable discipline in their first fight under trying conditions. Their casualty lists bore bloody evidence of their dauntlessness in the face of intense fire and difficult terrain. The entire brigade suffered, but the 6th was hammered the worst, losing nearly 60 percent of the men it carried into action. Yet, under their young colonel, they never wavered. If in the

21. Pollard, *Companions in Arms*, 540; John S. Lewis to General Trousdale, June 13, 1865, in William Trousdale Papers, TSLA; Morris Schaff, *The Sunset of the Confederacy* (Boston, 1912), 57; John S. Wise, "Two Great Confederates. General John B. Gordon and General James Longstreet: Characterizations by a Friend of Both," *American Monthly Review of Reviews*, XXIX (February, 1904), 204; Caroline Lewis Gordon, "De Gin'ral an' Miss Fanny" (MS in Gordon Family Collection, UGA).

final analysis, as one historian averred, "the discipline of the regiment depended largely on the personality of the colonel," the men of the 6th were well served. Clearly, Gordon had admirably prepared them for combat. Moreover, he had won their complete confidence by his direction of the regiment and his conduct during the battle. The gallant and cool manner in which Gordon handled his men in combat had persuaded Rodes to turn brigade command over to the Georgian, even though he was the brigade's youngest colonel, both in age and in time in grade.[22]

Just as Gordon had undergone his baptism of fire at Seven Pines, so too had Fanny first faced the emotional strain of a battle in which her husband was engaged. With cannonade rocking the countryside around Richmond and the roar of the raging battle increasing, Fanny's anxiety mounted steadily. Unable to bear the tension any longer, she prevailed upon her elderly uncle, John Sutherland Lewis, to accompany her as she moved closer to the action. There, upon a hill, he remembered, "she listened in silence. Pale and quiet, with clasped hands, she sat statue-like, with her face toward the field of battle." She displayed remarkable self-control, only occasionally revealing her inner turmoil and then merely with a "quick-drawn sigh." But when she learned of John's safety and "the excessive tension was relaxed, . . . the intensity of mental strain to which she had been subjected . . . [left her] well-nigh prostrated." Although almost unnerved by this initial trial, Fanny soon recovered and gradually developed "a sublime fortitude" that enabled her to endure similar harrowing experiences during the next three years.[23]

After the battle at Seven Pines, Gordon continued in command of Rodes's brigade. His temporary advancement over the other regimental commanders was "not only unexpected, but unwelcome and extremely embarrassing." Despite his apprehensions, Gordon warmly recalled many years later that his brother officers "did everything in their power to lessen my embarrassment and uphold my hands." By late June, Rodes, still quite feeble from his unhealed wound sustained on May 31, returned to duty, thus freeing Gordon to resume command of the 6th. He was at the head of the Alabamians

22. Lewis to Trousdale, June 13, 1865, in Trousdale Papers; Pollard, *Companions in Arms*, 537; *OR*, Vol. XI, Pt. 1, pp. 975–76; T. Harry Williams, *Hayes of the Twenty-third: The Civil War Volunteer Officer* (New York, 1965), 24–27.
23. Quoted in Gordon, *Reminiscences*, 58–59.

when the newly organized Army of Northern Virginia marched out from the Richmond entrenchments to meet McClellan's army.[24]

The Seven Days' Battles began on June 25, when General Robert E. Lee, successor to General Johnston, seized the initiative from Mc-Clellan by attacking north of the Chickahominy. Almost continuous fighting and constant movement marked the actions of the two armies during the following week. Although near the battlefields of the first two days, Gordon and his regiment did not see action until the fighting at Gaines' Mill late in the afternoon of June 27. From his position on the extreme left of the Confederate line, D. H. Hill attacked with his five brigades deployed in a solid divisional front. Rodes's brigade, moving in the center of the division, found that its line of advance carried it through an all but impenetrable swamp. Amid the tangled undergrowth, the orderly, organized advance rapidly degenerated into great confusion as brigade lines overlapped and regiments lost contact with one another.[25]

The 6th passed through this "most densely wooded morass" in good order, but when it emerged from the swamp, Gordon found that the regiment had become separated from the rest of the brigade. After reforming his men, Gordon advanced into a long, open field where he encountered heavy fire from both artillery and infantry. He continued to move forward until his total isolation became dangerously apparent, whereupon he halted his men and ordered them to lie down while awaiting support. When reinforcements failed to arrive, Gordon calmly withdrew the 6th "in perfectly good order" to the cover of the swamp. Efforts by Rodes and his regimental commanders to reassemble the brigade and resume the advance failed as nightfall brought an end to the day's fighting. After a sleepless evening on the battlefield attending to the wounded, the brigade marched in pursuit of the retreating Federals on June 28. At day's end, a nearly prostrated Rodes once again relinquished command of the brigade to Gordon.[26]

Gordon and the brigade were not seriously engaged again until July 1. With its change of base from White House on the Pamunkey River to Harrison's Landing on the James all but completed, McClellan's army withdrew behind its fortified lines atop Malvern Hill. The Federals were "strongly posted on a commanding hill, all the ap-

24. Gordon, *Reminiscences*, 58.
25. *OR*, Vol. XI, Pt. 2, pp. 624–25, 631.
26. *Ibid.*, 625–26, 631–32, 633, 637.

proaches to which could be swept by his artillery, and were guarded by swarms of infantry securely sheltered by fences, ditches and ravines." The firepower of the nearby gunboats on the James added to the impregnability of the Union position. Despite his belief that an attack would be exceedingly hazardous, D. H. Hill prepared his division for an assault up the slopes of Malvern Hill.[27]

Shortly before sundown, the division moved forward. Gordon, having been ordered to charge the Union batteries some seven to eight hundred yards in his front, led his brigade uphill across an open field. His men moved on, weathering "a most destructive fire," and climbed to within two hundred yards of the deadly batteries. There grapeshot and canister from the Federal artillery coupled with infantry fire made it "impossible to advance without support," so Gordon ordered his command to "lie down and open fire." While waiting for promised support, Gordon fearlessly walked among his men offering words of encouragement as they exchanged blows with Union infantry. An artillery shell exploded at his feet, filling his eyes with sand and dirt, but the blast blinded him only momentarily. Enemy bullets shattered the handle of his pistol, pierced his canteen, and ripped away part of the front of his coat, but Gordon again escaped uninjured. He held his brigade under the Federal guns on the heights until nightfall, when darkness permitted a withdrawal with less loss of life. Gordon and the other brigade commanders collected their scattered commands in the darkness and bivouacked near the base of Malvern Hill. McClellan's troops retreated during the night, thereby ending the first serious threat to Richmond.[28]

Although disappointed by his inability to capture the Federal batteries, Gordon proudly reported that "the dead of this [Rodes's] brigade marked a line nearer the batteries than any other." But the price in blood had been high: almost one-half of the men he carried into battle on July 1 lay on the field, killed or wounded. Gordon concluded his report of the battle by stating "that nothing so increases an officer's confidence in our strength as to lead such troops into battle." In the same vein, for the men in the ranks, nothing buoyed their spirits more than to be led into battle by a man like Gordon. His splendid conduct in the face of heavy fire led observers to declare that "the capacity of inspiring courage in action, & holding men long

27. *Ibid.*, 627–28.
28. *Ibid.*, 628–29, 634–35, 643; Gordon, *Reminiscences*, 73–75.

under fire is an endowment characteristic, unique, almost peerless in the young officer."[29]

Following the assault on Malvern Hill, Gordon retained command of Rodes's brigade and remained with D. H. Hill's division. Except for some minor skirmishing, Gordon and his men confined their activity to monitoring Union movements around Richmond during July and August. But by the middle of August, most of McClellan's army had slipped away from its base on the James without any significant Confederate interference. Lee, "greatly mortified" that the Federals "got off so easily," nevertheless recalled Hill and his division to the Army of Northern Virginia in late August when it moved northward. Gordon and the rest of Hill's command missed the Battle of Second Manassas on August 30 but finally rejoined the army three days later at Chantilly.[30]

Inaugurating Lee's first invasion of the North, Rodes's brigade, with Gordon at its head, crossed the Potomac into Maryland on September 4. When he had learned the day before that his men were to be given the honor of crossing the river first, Gordon took the opportunity to address the Alabamians under his command. He told them that they richly deserved such an honor, for in all their previous fights they had bestowed only glory upon themselves and the cause for which they fought. The young colonel reminded them to remain true to their colors and uphold their reputation, so that southern independence might be realized and peace and liberty restored to the country.[31]

Once the bulk of his army had safely crossed the Potomac, Lee divided his forces. He sent Jackson and a major portion of the army to capture the Federal garrison at Harper's Ferry while D. H. Hill and Longstreet continued their northward march. Lee recognized the danger of dividing his army, but he believed that the disorganization that plagued the Union army after Second Manassas remained. Such was not the case, however, as McClellan had resumed command and begun to pursue Lee with unexpected speed. West of the mountains, D. H. Hill had been ordered to guard the roads leading north from Harper's Ferry, to gather up escaping Federals, and to protect the

29. OR, Vol. XI, Pt. 2, p. 635; Lewis to Trousdale, June 13, 1865, in Trousdale Papers.

30. OR, Vol. XI, Pt. 3, pp. 673–74, 677; Vol. XII, Pt. 3, pp. 917, 942; Vol. LI, Pt. 2, pp. 1075–76; Vol. XIX, Pt. 1, pp. 144–45, 1018–19.

31. OR, Vol. XIX, Pt. 1, p. 1019; Pollard, *Companions in Arms*, 538; Soldier [pseud.] to Messrs. Editors, November 2, 1862, in Sixth Alabama Records.

passes over South Mountain. He saw no particular danger to the passes until a personal inspection on the morning of September 14 revealed that only a large force could defend them. Even then Hill was reluctant to move his entire division forward until more could be learned about the Union presence. But as noon approached and the main body of the Union army came into view below him, Hill ordered the remainder of his division to South Mountain and hastily called upon Longstreet for reinforcements.[32]

Rodes's twelve hundred Alabamians arrived atop South Mountain shortly after one o'clock. Having recently returned to duty, Rodes moved his brigade to the left of the road running through Turner's Gap and occupied a hill three-quarters of a mile to the north. This "bare hill" held the key to the defense of the Confederate left, for it not only commanded the ridge controlling the gap but also dominated a road leading to the Confederate rear, west of the mountain. To hold this vital hill, Rodes extended his line by ordering his extreme left regiment, Gordon's 6th, to move farther to the left along the crest of the hill. While Rodes continued to stretch his already thin line, the Federals, outflanking him "on either side by at least half a mile," began their advance. In clear view below the Confederates, three divisions of seasoned Union troops, ably led by experienced officers, moved against Rodes's single brigade. The Federal advance up the steep eastern face of the mountain against an enemy well posted among trees and rocks was slow, but steady.[33]

Once atop South Mountain, Gordon exhorted his men "not to allow their courage to falter in the event of his fall, but to acquit themselves nobly, that their names as heroes might live forever." This time, however, words were not enough, for Gordon and the other men of Rodes's brigade spent the rest of the afternoon and evening merely delaying the inevitable. Outflanked, outnumbered, and isolated, Rodes's men found it impossible to hold any position for an extended period. Broken into small groups by the rocky terrain, they were forced to fight until nearly overwhelmed, then fall back and form a new line, and there continue to resist until compelled to retreat again. On the extreme left of Rodes's line, Gordon's regiment faced a grave danger in that the "apparently interminable right" of the advancing Federals greatly overlapped his flank. Despite this consis-

32. *OR*, Vol. XIX, Pt. 1, pp. 145–46, 1019–20, 1034.
33. *Ibid.*, 214–15, 267, 272, 1020, 1034.

tent threat to his rear and the continuous pressure on his front, Gordon kept his regiment "constantly in hand."[34]

Stubborn resistance finally yielded to the weight of Union numbers as Gordon and the rest of the brigade were forced off the hill. Rodes, seeing his left crumbling, established a new line around the peak of another hill by changing fronts and facing his entire brigade to the left. In this manner, though still unable to form a united line owing to the terrain, Rodes's regiments continued their fight as nightfall approached. The brigade suffered severely, with some of the units completely shattered and demoralized. "Fortunately for the whole command," reported Rodes, Gordon's regiment remained intact as the sole organized force opposing the enemy and formed "a Nucleus around which the defeated could rally." Exposed to both enfilading and direct fire, and repeatedly in danger of being surrounded, the 6th retreated slowly, "held together by its able commander." Gordon's men succeeded in making "one more desperate stand" near the top of the highest peak shortly before darkness brought an end to the fighting. During this last action, Gordon audaciously exposed himself upon a huge rock while shouting orders and encouragement to his men. Gordon's regiment and remnants of the brigade retained control of the key points covering Turner's Gap until about 11 P.M., when they were ordered to march to Sharpsburg. As Rodes's brigade moved off the mountain, one-third of its number remained, dead or wounded.[35]

After reaching Sharpsburg early on the morning of September 15, Gordon's men moved to occupy the center of the Confederate line, about one-half mile northeast of the town. Under occasional artillery fire from the arriving Federal batteries across Antietam Creek, they passed that day and the next preparing for battle. The single bloodiest day of battle in the Civil War opened at first light on the morning of September 17. McClellan's army savagely assaulted the Confederate left, defended by Lieutenant General Thomas J. Jackson, and the battle raged there almost continuously until midmorning. Lee, without the luxury of ready reserves except those hurriedly marching from Harper's Ferry, found it necessary to pull troops from the right and

34. *Ibid.*, 1034–35; Soldier [pseud.] to Messrs. Editors, November 2, 1862, in Sixth Alabama Records.

35. Soldier [pseud.] to Messrs. Editors, November 2, 1862, in Sixth Alabama Records; *OR*, Vol. XIX, Pt. 1, pp. 1035–36, 1021; Lewis to Trousdale, June 13, 1865, in Trousdale Papers.

center of his line to relieve the hard-pressed left. When three of D. H. Hill's five brigades were shifted to the left, the remaining two brigades—Rodes's and Brigadier General G. B. Anderson's—side-stepped to the left in an attempt to cover the entire center themselves. Hill posted them along a narrow sunken road that ran east from the Hagerstown Pike for about five hundred yards and then southeast for another five hundred yards. In the hours that followed, the events on this peaceful farm lane caused it to be known ever thereafter as the Bloody Lane.[36]

Occupying that portion of the road immediately adjacent to its bend to the southeast, the 6th Alabama held the most advanced point along this defensive front. The sunken road formed a natural rifle pit that shielded its defenders, who further strengthened their position by dismantling wooden fences and piling rails in front of the lane. The fury on the Confederate left raged unabated until midmorning when action died away, as both sides had seemingly fought themselves to the point of exhaustion. With the carnage on the left drawing to a close, Hill's two brigades awaited the onslaught that appeared certain to descend upon them. General Lee, convinced that the next attack would fall on his center, rode along the narrow lane and offered words of encouragement to his troops. He called upon them to hold their ground at all costs, for a breakthrough on their front would mean disaster for the entire army. Gordon, in an effort to assure General Lee and to make his men even more resolute, loudly proclaimed in a voice for all to hear, "These men are going to stay here, General, till the sun goes down or victory is won." As Lee moved away from the road, the attack began.[37]

Watching the blue-clad troops advance through the undulating fields on his front, Gordon could not help but marvel at the "thrilling spectacle." The Union forces marched forward with parade-ground-like precision in four magnificently aligned columns while their band trailed in the rear, playing martial music. "'What a pity to spoil with bullets such a scene of martial beauty!'" Gordon thought to himself. "But there was nothing else to do. Mars is not an aesthetic god." His enthrallment with this brilliant military pageant gave way to the tactical necessity of resisting the advancing blue columns. Unaccustomed to receiving charges, Gordon considered his alternatives as it became increasingly clear that the enemy planned to carry his

36. *OR*, Vol. XIX, Pt. 1, pp. 149, 1022–23, 1036–37.
37. Gordon, *Reminiscences*, 84; *OR*, Vol. XIX, Pt. 1, p. 1037.

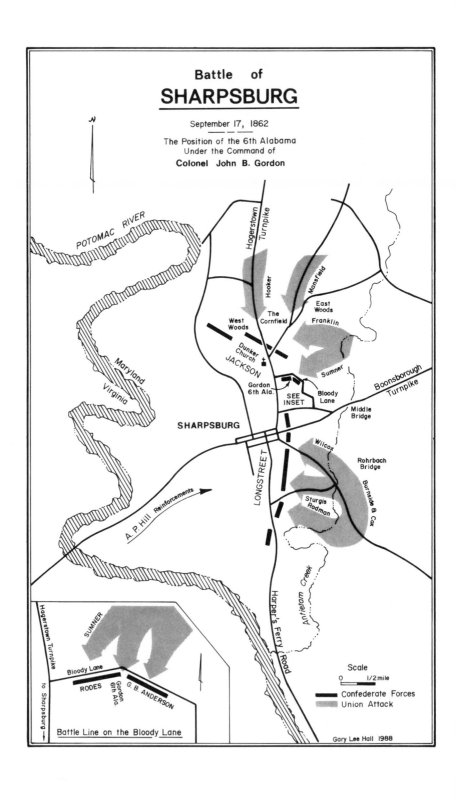

# Battle of
# SHARPSBURG

September 17, 1862

The Position of the 6th Alabama
Under the Command of
**Colonel John B. Gordon**

POTOMAC RIVER

Hagerstown Turnpike

Hooker

Mansfield

East Woods

Franklin

The Cornfield

West Woods

Maryland

Virginia

Dunker Church

JACKSON

Gordon 6th Ala.

SEE INSET

Bloody Lane

Sumner

Boonsborough Turnpike

Middle Bridge

SHARPSBURG

LONGSTREET

Wilcox

Rohrbach Bridge

A. P. Hill Reinforcements

Sturgis Rodman

Burnside & Cox

Harper's Ferry Road

Antietam Creek

Scale

0    1/2 mile

Confederate Forces
Union Attack

Hagerstown Turnpike

SUMNER

Bloody Lane

RODES

Gordon 6th Ala.

G. B. ANDERSON

to Sharpsburg

Battle Line on the Bloody Lane

Gary Lee Hall 1988

position by weight of numbers in a bayonet attack. How could his one line resist four Union lines? Realizing that his men could not possibly disable enough of the enemy to break the assault, Gordon rejected his impulse to open fire as soon as the Federals came within range. Instead, he decided to hold his regiment's fire until the enemy was almost on top of them, "and then turn loose a sheet of flame and lead into their faces." Believing that no troops could withstand such a sudden shock, the young colonel determined that none of his men should fire "until the Federals were so close upon us that every Confederate bullet would take effect." He positioned himself in the center of the regiment and ordered his men to lie down and await his command.[38]

As the Union troops drew near, an oppressive stillness hung over the field; neither artillery nor musketry fire could be heard. On came the Yankees, ever closer. When the eagle insignia on the Yankee buttons were clearly visible, anxious Confederates begged to open fire, but Gordon simply replied, "Not yet. . . . Wait for the order." And the Federals came on. They had moved unhindered to within thirty paces of where Gordon stood when, at last, he shouted, "Fire!"[39]

The rifles of the 6th Alabama simultaneously flamed and, in little more than an instant, virtually the entire Federal front line disappeared, consumed by the blast. Before the stunned Federals could recover, the men of the 6th arose and poured a continuous fire into the blue ranks, compelling their immediate retreat beyond the range of Gordon's deadly rifles. Although the front line had been shattered, the other three remained intact and, once reformed, they charged Gordon's position a second time and were again bloodily repulsed. So it was with the third and fourth attempts. Unable to weather the storm of lead any longer, the Union troops lay down, taking shelter behind the crest of the ridge some eighty yards in front of the road, and opened fire. Both forces tried numerous flanking movements, but in the main, the battle at the Bloody Lane became a small-arms fight between two closely drawn lines of infantry, each seeking to dislodge the other by musketry fire alone.[40]

In the initial Union volley, Gordon suffered his first wound of the

38. Gordon, *Reminiscences*, 84–86.
39. *Ibid.*, 86–87; Soldier [pseud.] to Messrs. Editors, November 2, 1862, in Sixth Alabama Records.
40. Gordon, *Reminiscences*, 87–88.

war when a ball passed through the calf of his right leg. He continued to walk among his men, encouraging them both by word and deed even after a second ball struck him higher up on the same leg. An hour later, a third ball ripped through his left arm, "making a hideous and most painful wound, mangling the tendons and muscles, and severing a small artery." His men caught sight of the blood streaming down his arm and pleaded for him to go to the rear and have his wounds attended to, but Gordon refused to leave. He remembered his earlier promise to Lee. As he looked to the sun and hoped for nightfall, he thought to himself that "it [the sun] moved very slowly; in fact, it seemed to stand still." A short while later, a fourth Union ball pierced his shoulder, leaving a wad of clothing and the ball's base in the wound. Although extremely weak from the loss of blood, he remained alert and upright. Gordon, seeing that his extreme right companies were being torn apart by an enfilading fire, moved unsteadily in that direction to correct the situation. He had staggered only a few yards when a fifth Minié ball struck him squarely in the face and passed through his left cheek and out through the jaw, just missing his jugular vein. Knocked unconscious, the battered colonel fell face forward into his cap and might have drowned in his own blood had not a "thoughtful" Yankee earlier shot a hole in his hat.[41]

Gordon's fall went unnoticed for a time, because when he came to, he found himself alone. Dazed by the shock of his multiple wounds, he experienced many curious thoughts and weird sensations. As he lay there in his own blood, Gordon imagined that half his head had been carried away. Wondering if he was alive or dead, he reasoned that a dead man could not move a limb, so he tried to move one of his legs. His success not only proved to him that he was alive but brought him to his senses, whereupon he crawled approximately one hundred yards to the rear, where a new line was being formed.[42] There he collapsed and was borne away on a litter.[43]

41. *Ibid.*, 89–90; Pollard, *Companions in Arms*, 538–39.

42. It would appear that immediately after Gordon's fall, the lieutenant colonel of the 6th attempted to draw back the right of the regiment in order to eliminate the deadly enfilading fire that Gordon had been moving toward when he received his head wound. After obtaining Rodes's permission to execute such a move, the lieutenant colonel mistakenly ordered all of the 6th to retreat and also told an adjoining regimental commander that the move was intended for the entire line. As all of the brigade fell back from its strong position at the Sunken Road, Rodes made numerous attempts to rally his men and form new lines in the rear of his former position. In all probability, it was one of these new lines that Gordon crawled to after he regained consciousness. *OR*, Vol. XIX, Pt. 1, pp. 1037–38.

43. *OR*, Vol. XIX, Pt. 1, pp. 1037–38; Pollard, *Companions in Arms*, 538–39; Soldier

Gordon and other badly wounded men were placed in a barn where they could safely be treated. When revived by stimulants late that evening, he found his friend Dr. Weatherly attending him. Immediately perceiving the distress etched on the surgeon's face, Gordon asked, "What do you think of my case, Weatherly?" Although the answer was hopeful, Gordon knew better and replied, "You are not honest with me. You think I am going to die but I am going to get well." These were brave words for a man whose blackened face was so swollen that both eyes were almost completely hidden and whose right leg, left arm, and left shoulder were covered in bandages and propped upon pillows. Not long thereafter, Fanny, who had remained close to the front, reached him. Gordon feared his appearance might shock her, so he summoned up his remaining strength and attempted to reassure her by calling, "Here's your handsome (?) husband; been to an Irish wedding!" Fanny's response, as might be expected, was a "suppressed scream."[44]

Gordon's immense loss of blood and his severe wounds left him in critical condition for several months. The necessity of wiring his jaw shut further complicated his weakened condition because it made eating both "difficult and discouraging." He had to be frequently fed "concentrated nourishment"—brandy and beef tea—in order to rebuild his strength and guard against "constant drainage." His young wife faithfully attended to this and much more. She bathed him, dressed his wounds, and sat devotedly by his bedside, ministering to his needs. When Gordon contracted erysipelas in his left arm and the doctors instructed her to paint the arm with iodine three or four times daily, Gordon "complained" that she painted his wounds three or four hundred times a day. Fanny's vigilance and tender nursing strengthened both Gordon's body and his indomitable will to recover and return to the Army of Northern Virginia.[45]

A return to duty would most certainly mean greater command responsibilities for Gordon. In all his battles, he had performed superbly. Rodes thought Gordon deserved special attention for his conduct at South Mountain, where he not only acted with his customary gallantry but handled his regiment "in a manner . . . [Rodes had] never heard or seen equalled during this war." Gordon's firm control

[pseud.] to Messrs. Editors, November 2, 1862, in Sixth Alabama Records; Atlanta Constitution, November 26, 1878.

44. Gordon, Reminiscences, 90–91; Atlanta Constitution, March 25, 1881.

45. Gordon, Reminiscences, 91–92; Pollard, Companions in Arms, 539–40; Atlanta Constitution, March 25, 1881.

of his men under extremely trying conditions played a major role in averting disaster on the Confederate left on September 14. D. H. Hill, seconding Rodes's praise, reported simply that "Gordon, the Christian hero, excelled his former deeds at Seven Pines and in the battles around Richmond." The division commander maintained that in the English language there was no means of expressing any higher compliment to the man he called "the Chevalier Bayard of the army." With such glowing words of praise, promotion seemed inevitable.[46]

On October 27, 1862, General Lee recommended that Gordon be promoted to brigadier general and assigned to command Rains's brigade. Lee's plans, however, were soon to be frustrated. As he learned shortly thereafter, the War Department had already promoted Colonel Alfred H. Colquitt and given him command of this brigade, which he had led at South Mountain and Sharpsburg. With this vacancy closed and Gordon's immediate, or even eventual, return to active duty seriously in doubt, the War Department decided not to confirm Gordon's November 1, 1862, appointment as a brigadier general. If able to endure the rigors of campaigning, Gordon would be reappointed. But prospects for his return to duty did not look good because of his wounds and weakened condition.[47]

Although Gordon spent much of his convalescent period in Virginia at Staunton and Winchester, he did travel south in early 1863. While he was there, residents of Alabama evidently attempted to induce him to stand for election to the Confederate Congress, but Gordon declined the honor. The winter of 1862–63 passed as Gordon painfully convalesced.[48]

46. *OR*, Vol. XIX, Pt. 1, pp. 1038, 1035, 1021, 1027.
47. *Ibid.*, Pt. 2, pp. 684, 697–98; Gordon's Service File; Military Records of Gordon.
48. Pollard, *Companions in Arms*, 539; Soldier [pseud.] to Messrs. Editors, November 2, 1862, in Sixth Alabama Records; Atlanta *Constitution*, June 8, 1880; Gordon to Major G. R. Fairbanks, February 26, 1863, in Fairbanks Collection, Jessie Ball duPont Library, University of the South, Sewanee, Tenn. Fanny was assisted by her servant Sarah, Gordon's body servant Jim, and another body servant that General Wade Hampton sent to aid Mrs. Gordon. This slave, Buddy Hampton, remained with the Gordons until shortly before the colonel resumed active duty, at which time Buddy returned to his master. After the war, Gordon and his wife, wishing to recognize his services, invited Buddy to Atlanta, where they helped him complete his education. He was so grateful and impressed with the Gordons' actions that he made sure his own children had the same educational opportunities. During a visit around 1930, Buddy Hampton proudly told Gordon's grandson that all of his children held college degrees. Hugh H. Gordon, Jr., "General Wade Hampton's Slave" (MS in Gordon Family Collection, UGA).

# III · Brigadier

Despite the severity of the wounds he sustained at the Battle of Sharpsburg, Gordon recovered with remarkable quickness. He returned to active duty after less than seven months of what he called "prolonged and tedious" convalescence. On March 30, 1863, with his facial wound still unhealed, Gordon reported for duty, ready to assume brigade responsibilities, even though he had not been confirmed as a general officer. A new command had to be found for him because there were no openings in his old division for brigadiers with Georgia or Alabama troops. Consequently, on April 11, 1863, Gordon was assigned to command the brigade in Major General Jubal A. Early's division that had previously been led by Brigadier General Alexander R. Lawton. Although distressed by his parting from the men with whom he had gone to war, Gordon nonetheless looked forward to leading his new brigade. Gordon's brigade comprised six Georgia regiments, making it one of the largest Confederate brigades. He had less than three weeks with his new command before carrying it into action, but an inspector immediately commented upon the positive effect of his leadership and discipline. Gordon and his men were ready when the Union army under Major General Joseph Hooker assumed the offensive during the last week of April, 1863.[1]

1. Gordon's Service File, in Military Service Records, NA; *OR*, Vol. XXV, Pt. 2, p. 717; E. A. Pollard [A Distinguished Southern Journalist], *The Early Life, Campaigns and Public Services of Robert E. Lee, with a Record of the Campaigns and Heroic Deeds of his Companions in Arms* (New York, 1871), 540, hereinafter cited as *Companions in Arms*; John B. Gordon, *Reminiscences of the Civl War* (New York, 1903), 92, 95; Jubal Anderson Early, *Autobiographical Sketch and Narrative of the War Between the States* (Philadelphia, 1912), 192, hereinafter cited as *Narrative of the War*.

Although most of the fighting during the Chancellorsville campaign took place in the wooded maze surrounding that crossroads hamlet, Gordon played a prominent role in actions on the other front, near Fredericksburg. His brigade constituted a portion of the force under Early that Lee left at Fredericksburg to defend the town and protect the army's rear against any enemy movement from that direction. When Union troops under Major General John Sedgwick attacked Early's command on the morning of May 3, they brushed the badly outnumbered Confederates aside. Then, rather than pursuing Early, who retreated southward, Sedgwick moved westward via the Plank Road toward Lee's rear at Chancellorsville. Ascertaining the Federals' movement, Early made plans to return to Fredericksburg the following morning. He would first seize the heights that he had been forced to abandon and then attack Sedgwick, in conjunction with Confederate troops moving back on the Plank Road.[2]

Early's battle plan called for Gordon's brigade to lead the assault on the Fredericksburg heights. Shortly after daybreak, Early placed Gordon's brigade in position and then moved to another portion of his line to supervise troop dispositions. With all the preparations nearly completed, Early rode back to accompany Gordon during the assault. When Early returned to where he had left the young brigadier, he could not find the Georgia brigade. Gordon, acting under a "misapprehension" of orders, was at that moment advancing without support. Although shocked that his plans for a carefully coordinated advance had been destroyed, Early quickly grasped the situation. He realized that Gordon might already be engaged, so he immediately ordered the rest of his command forward.[3]

Whether Gordon simply mistook Early's order or whether that order had been vaguely or incorrectly worded made little difference at the time, because Gordon believed he had been instructed to advance at once. In any event, fortune smiled on Gordon's "serious misunderstanding" of his orders, for the Confederates recaptured the Fredericksburg heights with relative ease. By occupying the hills west of Fredericksburg, Gordon enabled Early to cut Sedgwick's connection with the town and thus to isolate the Federal command. Much had been accomplished, despite the prematurity of the move. Perhaps there was more truth than humor in Gordon's contention years later

2. Early, *Narrative of the War*, 193–211, 217–21; *OR*, Vol. XXV, Pt. 1, pp. 796–97, 800–801, 1000–1001.

3. Gordon, *Reminiscences*, 100; Early, *Narrative of the War*, 221–23.

that Early "playfully but earnestly" chided him after the attack that only his success had saved the Georgian from a court-martial for disobeying orders.[4]

Having again secured Fredericksburg, Early turned westward to fall upon Sedgwick. When, late in the afternoon, Early resumed the offensive in conjunction with portions of Lee's forces, Gordon attacked the Federals' left flank. He cleared the enemy from the ridges in his front and advanced a considerable distance before darkness arrested his progress. He had driven the enemy's flank back, but found it impossible to move into the rear of Sedgwick's forces. During the night of May 4, Sedgwick withdrew his entire command across the Rappahannock. Portions of Gordon's brigade quickly moved to the river the next morning and captured a number of Federals. When Hooker began pulling the rest of his army back across the river later in the day, the Chancellorsville-Fredericksburg drama drew to a close.[5]

In the aftermath of the Chancellorsville campaign, Gordon's conduct received a favorable review. On May 11, 1863, Lee reappointed him brigadier general with his rank to date from May 7. The commanding general also sought to return Gordon to the command of Rodes's old brigade, which he had previously served with and had temporarily commanded. But the commissioned officers in the brigade Gordon led into battle for the first time around Fredericksburg were so taken with the fiery young Georgian that they unanimously petitioned Lee to allow him to remain with them. Gordon, as a Georgia native, expressed his willingness to stay and lead this brigade, which he felt was composed of as "superb material [as] ever filled the ranks of any command in any army." In the face of such mutual admiration, Lee decided to retain the new brigadier in his present position.[6]

After Chancellorsville, as Lee planned a second invasion of the North, he reorganized the Army of Northern Virginia; the death of

4. Early, *Narrative of the War*, 223–24; Gordon, *Reminiscences*, 100–101; Jubal A. Early to Messrs. Editors, May 11, May 19, 1863, both in Jubal Anderson Early Papers, LC; Douglas Southall Freeman, *Lee's Lieutenants: A Study in Command* (3 vols.; New York, 1942–44), II, 629; *OR*, Vol. XXV, Pt. 1, p. 1001.

5. *OR*, Vol. XXV, Pt. 1, pp. 801–802, 1001–1002; Early, *Narrative of the War*, 225–33.

6. *OR*, Vol. XXV, Pt. 1, p. 810; Douglas Southall Freeman and Grady McWhiney (eds.), *Lee's Dispatches* (New York, 1957), 94; Gordon's Service File; Gordon, *Reminiscences*, 95.

Stonewall Jackson necessitated a reshuffling of both general officers and troops. Lee increased the number of corps to three and assigned newly promoted Lieutenant General R. S. Ewell to command the restructured II Corps. Gordon's brigade remained with Early's division as a part of the corps. Although Lee appreciated the difficulties of undertaking offensive operations with a new and untried command system, he determined that the benefits outweighed the concomitant dangers. An invasion would not only seize the initiative and disrupt Federal plans for the summer but also perhaps force the recall of Union troops assailing other points in the Confederacy, and it might provide impetus for the peace movement in the North. Moreover, it would move the fighting out of war-ravaged Virginia and allow the army to secure abundant provisions in Pennsylvania. Above all else, Lee realized, "he had to invade the North for provisions."[7]

On June 4, the II Corps, under its new commander, left its camps around Fredericksburg and began moving toward the Shenandoah Valley. Ewell's corps, composed of three divisions under Major General Jubal A. Early, Major General Edward Johnson, and Major General Robert E. Rodes, spearheaded Lee's second great northward thrust. Gordon's brigade reached Culpeper Court House on June 7, after a series of short, leisurely marches, often only eight or ten miles in length. After the first day, Gordon found the marches "much more agreeable and less fatiguing," especially when a light rain settled the dust. In spite of the easy traveling and the improbability of encountering serious action soon, Gordon's thoughts centered upon his wife, who remained behind in Richmond. He missed her terribly but did not think it wise for her to follow too closely, as he had no idea where or how far the army might go. Gordon implored her to write to her "big old ugly" often, for he cherished her letters as "the most beautiful evidences of a wife's devotion" he had ever seen. With her loving letters to comfort him during their separation, he might endure "such a cheerless jaut [sic]."[8]

The II Corps resumed its march on June 10. It passed through Sperryville and Washington before crossing over the Blue Ridge Mountains at Chester Gap. Late on the evening of June 12, after an exhausting six-hour, seventeen-mile march, Ewell's corps reached Front Royal. Early the following morning, Gordon's brigade forded

7. Gordon, Reminiscences, 137–40; Douglas Southall Freeman, R. E. Lee: A Biography (4 vols.; New York, 1934–35), III, 8–19.

8. OR, Vol. XXVII, Pt. 2, pp. 439, 459; Gordon to his wife, June 7, 1863, in Gordon Family Collection, UGA.

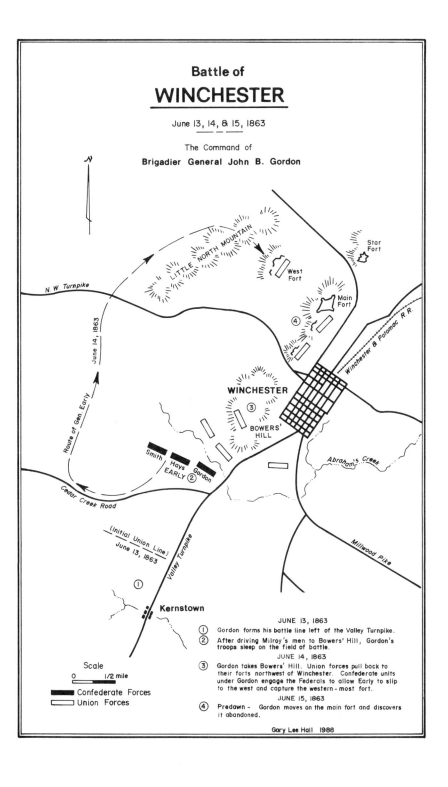

# Battle of
# WINCHESTER

June 13, 14, & 15, 1863

The Command of

**Brigadier General John B. Gordon**

N. W. Turnpike

Star Fort

LITTLE NORTH MOUNTAIN

West Fort

June 14, 1863

Main Fort

④

Route of Gen. Early

Winchester & Potomac R.R.

WINCHESTER

③

BOWERS' HILL

Smith Hays Gordon
EARLY ②

Abraham's Creek

Cedar Creek Road

(Initial Union Line)
June 13, 1863

Valley Turnpike

Millwood Pike

①

Kernstown

Scale

0        1/2 mile

� Confederate Forces
▭ Union Forces

JUNE 13, 1863

① Gordon forms his battle line left of the Valley Turnpike.

② After driving Milroy's men to Bowers' Hill, Gordon's troops sleep on the field of battle.

JUNE 14, 1863

③ Gordon takes Bowers' Hill. Union forces pull back to their forts northwest of Winchester. Confederate units under Gordon engage the Federals to allow Early to slip to the west and capture the western-most fort.

JUNE 15, 1863

④ Predawn – Gordon moves on the main fort and discovers it abandoned.

Gary Lee Hall  1988

the Shenandoah River and moved down the Valley Turnpike toward Winchester and a Federal force of six to eight thousand men under Major General Robert H. Milroy. Approximately three miles south-west of Winchester, near Kernstown, Early ordered Gordon to form his brigade in a line of battle to the left of the turnpike and to clear the Federals from a ridge in his front. Gordon's men advanced smartly and, in conjunction with skirmishers of Brigadier General Harry Hays's brigade, drove the enemy from a strong position behind a stone wall, across the fields beyond, and back to Bowers' Hill and the main fortifications at Winchester. Darkness brought an end to Gordon's pursuit, but both Ewell and Early were pleased with the actions of the Georgian. Early reported that Gordon's late-afternoon affair "reflected equal credit upon himself and his brigade." The corps commander described Gordon's "rapid and skillful advance" as "one of the finest movements" he had witnessed during the war—one that "won for the troops and their gallant commander the highest commendation." The men slept on the field that night, trying to get a well-deserved rest, despite a drenching rain.[9]

Gordon's actions the next day demonstrated the tactical effectiveness of a skillfully employed diversion. At daybreak on June 14, Gordon and Hays advanced skirmishers and easily took possession of Bowers' Hill, as the Federals had withdrawn their artillery and most of the infantry during the night. From atop the hill, Ewell and Early watched the enemy busily strengthening their works to the west and northwest of the town. Early determined that despite these efforts to fortify the Union position, the key fort in the Federal defensive scheme could be attacked from a concealed position on Little North Mountain. While he marched three of his brigades under cover to the point of attack, Early left Gordon in command of a force on Bowers' Hill with orders "to amuse the enemy and hold him in check in front." Gordon's demonstration, using skirmishers and artillery throughout the afternoon, allowed Early to move his men unobserved to the point of attack. His assault, about an hour before sundown, completely surprised the enemy "whose entire attention . . . was engrossed by Gordon." Early occupied the western-most fort, which forced the Federals to fall back to their main fortifications, closer to Winchester, as darkness ended the attack.[10]

9. *OR*, Vol. XXVII, Pt. 2, pp. 440, 450, 459–61, 463–64, 477, 491.
10. *Ibid.*, 440–41, 461–63, 477.

The hill that Early captured at sunset commanded the main Federal works. Even though he expected Milroy to evacuate during the evening, Early prepared to resume his attack the next morning. When Gordon received orders to join in the assault, he was dumbfounded. His demonstration in front of the "frowning fortress" that afternoon had revealed the natural strength of the position and the abundance of defenders, both of which made a frontal assault almost suicidal. Gordon also believed that Milroy's forces could be either surrounded or forced to withdraw by Confederate maneuvering in the open country around Winchester; but orders were orders and he had to obey. Late that night, as he planned his attack, a vision of the slaughter of his brigade as it ascended the hill came to him, leaving him with the conviction that he had "not one chance in a thousand to live through it." With "a feeling that was akin to a presentiment," Gordon wrote what he believed would be his last letter to his wife and gave it to his quartermaster with instructions to deliver it to Fanny after his death the next morning. In the eerie predawn darkness of June 15, a grimly fatalistic Gordon led his men up the long slope. Fully expecting to be engulfed in a deadly storm of lead at any moment, he moved closer. But as he approached the fort, he discovered that Early's prophecy had come to pass—the Federals had withdrawn during the night—and he breathed a heartfelt sigh of relief.[11]

Gordon's brigade moved to Shepherdstown after Winchester and waited there until June 22 while the rest of the army advanced toward the Potomac. Gordon took advantage of the respite to write to his wife in Richmond and inform her that he had found suitable lodgings for her in Shepherdstown. The prospect of having Fanny much nearer greatly pleased him because physical separation had become increasingly difficult to bear after their constant companionship during his convalescence. However, Fanny failed to receive his letters at this time, for unbeknown to Gordon she had already left Richmond and was attempting to move as close to the Confederate army as she could. The people that Fanny had been staying with in the capital were uncertain of how to reach her, so rather than blindly forwarding the general's letters, they returned them to him—an act that sorely distressed the young brigadier.[12]

Even though most of Gordon's letters during June and July, 1863,

11. *Ibid.*, 463; Gordon, *Reminiscences*, 68–69.
12. *OR*, Vol. XXVII, Pt. 2, pp. 442–43, 464; Gordon to wife, June 21, June 23, July 10, 1863, all in Gordon Family Collection, UGA.

miscarried, their content reveals the profound sense of intimacy that had developed between Fanny and John. When Gordon realized that none of his letters had reached Fanny, he was bitterly disappointed and lapsed into a deep depression. Traveling "in an enemy's country," surrounded by hostile faces, knowing nothing of his wife or of her whereabouts—and she likewise ignorant of his—Gordon tearfully poured out his innermost feelings in his next letter to Fanny. For him to say simply that he loved her seemed "so tame" and woefully inadequate. He declared that "God only knows *how I love you*. Honor, reputation, money, ease and comfort could all now be gladly parted with if it purchase for me, the constant presence of my Fanny." Gordon professed his willingness to sacrifice "*every* other enjoyment of any description" just to be with his wife and "precious little family." Such depression was common among soldiers separated from their loved ones. Although distraught, Gordon sensed that Fanny might be unduly alarmed by his "*unmanliness*," so he quickly reassured her that his disconsolate condition was only momentary. Able to unburden his heavy heart only to her, he utilized the letter to tell of his unhappiness at their separation and to express his powerful love for her.[13]

In addition to this new closeness to Fanny, Gordon also exhibited an increasing spiritual awareness. Believing that only the grace of God had spared him in his earlier battles, Gordon committed his life to the Lord with the "hope he [sic] will protect me as He has done." He wrote to Fanny, "My confidence . . . is pretty strong. I trust in Him. Pray that I may trust Him more and pray with faith." Gordon nevertheless cautioned his wife to be prepared to accept his death. "My life is in the hands of a wise and good God. If He takes it, it is all right." Gordon repeatedly prayed that regardless of what happened, he and Fanny might always have God's spirit in their hearts and that they might strive to be "better and more consistent and more constant Christians." Gordon would remain committed to God and wife as the twin bastions of his life, but he never again articulated their importance to him so clearly as he did in these wartime letters to Fanny during Lee's second northern invasion.[14]

After crossing the Potomac, Gordon's brigade continued its northward march through Maryland and on into Pennsylvania. The beauty

13. Gordon to wife, June 23, 1863, in Gordon Family Collection, UGA.
14. Gordon to wife, April 30, June 7, June 23, July 7, July 10, 1863, all in Gordon Family Collection, UGA.

and bounty of the lush valleys of Pennsylvania, untouched by war, greatly impressed Gordon. Amid this "scene of universal thrift and plenty," the Confederates found food, especially milk and butter, to be abundant and cheap. Long after the Gettysburg campaign, Gordon vividly recalled the hot breakfast and cold milk he enjoyed with a Pennsylvania Dutchman and the cool serenity of lounging in the farmer's dining room, through which flowed a natural spring. Requisitioning food, supplies, and money were primary reasons for invasion, but Gordon saw to it that his men closely adhered to Lee's orders protecting people and private property. Gordon noted only a few "insignificant exceptions," one of which highlighted "adherence to the letter and neglect of the spirit" of his orders. While encamped one evening in open country where wood was at a premium, his men asked him for permission to use a few rails from a nearby fence for their campfires. He assented but stipulated that only the top layer of rails be taken. When morning revealed bare fence posts, Gordon had no choice but to admit that his enterprising men "had gotten the better of me." Each man who had taken a rail had in fact taken only the top one—all the way down to the last layer.[15]

Moving by a different route in advance of the rest of the division, a small force of infantry, artillery, and cavalry under Gordon's command neared York by nightfall on June 27. Gordon and Early conferred that night and made plans for a joint assault on the town if Union forces occupied it. In the event that York was undefended, Early ordered his subordinate to proceed to Wrightsville and attempt to seize intact the bridge over the Susquehanna. Later in the night, a committee of York's citizens visited Gordon and formally surrendered the town. The Georgians entered York the next morning amid the ringing of Sunday church bells. Having earlier found the people near the Maryland border to be "very indifferent as to the result of this war," Gordon was astonished "to see how much afraid of us" the residents of York were. His assurances of protection of life and property, given to the deputation the previous evening, had evidently failed to convince the "terror-stricken" inhabitants.[16]

Gordon, riding at the head of his brigade, found it difficult to move through the densely packed streets. Noticing a crowd of ladies, he

15. Gordon, *Reminiscences*, 140–41, 144–47; Gordon to wife, June 23, July 7, 1863, both in Gordon Family Collection, UGA; *OR*, Vol. XXVII, Pt. 3, pp. 912–13.
16. *OR*, Vol. XXVII, Pt. 2, pp. 466, 491; Gordon to wife, June 23, July 7, 1863, both in Gordon Family Collection, UGA; Gordon, *Reminiscences*, 142.

turned toward them to speak some words of reassurance when "a cry of alarm came from their midst" and a "young lady . . . ran from me as tho I had been a demon." Quite probably, it was the fearsome appearance of Gordon's dusty men—especially when contrasted with the attire of these crowds of churchgoers—that generated much of the concern. "Begrimed . . . from head to foot with the impalpable gray powder" from their rapid marches on the macadamized pikes, the Confederates, officers and privates alike, did indeed present a wild appearance. Nevertheless, Gordon employed his full oratorical powers and managed to convince the concerned populace that they and their property would be protected, maintaining that his men, "though ill clad and travel-stained," were gentlemen. He concluded his remarks by promising "the head of any soldier under my command who destroyed private property, disturbed the repose of a single home, or insulted a woman."[17]

As Gordon moved out of York toward Wrightsville, a little girl of about twelve rushed up to him and handed him a large bouquet of roses. He inspected the arrangement and discovered a note, "in delicate handwriting," hidden among the flowers. The tersely written, unsigned message described in great detail the Federal position at Wrightsville. It not only provided Gordon with the number and disposition of troops but also suggested how he might turn the Union line. As he marched toward the Susquehanna River, Gordon undoubtedly read and reread the note and pondered its accuracy as well as the identity of its author. He desperately wanted to seize the huge bridge between Wrightsville and Columbia. A mile and a quarter in length, the wooden superstructure built upon stone pillars served as a railroad bridge, a wagon bridge, and a towpath for barges that crossed the river at that point. If the bridge were to be captured, the Confederates could move to the eastern bank of the Susquehanna and attack Harrisburg or perhaps even Philadelphia.[18]

Despite the midday heat, Gordon's brigade marched swiftly, arriving at Wrightsville in the late afternoon. Gordon surveyed the Federal position from a high ridge that the note had suggested, and discovered that the particulars of his "mysterious communication" were accu-

17. Gordon, *Reminiscences*, 142–43; Gordon to wife, July 7, 1863, in Gordon Family Collection, UGA; John W. Daniel, "Address at Unveiling of Valentine's Recumbent Figure of Lee," *Southern Historical Society Papers*, XI (1883), 368, hereinafter cited as *SHSP*; Pollard, *Companions in Arms*, 540–41; Atlanta *Constitution*, January 15, 1904.

18. Gordon, *Reminiscences*, 143–44, 147; Gordon to wife, July 7, 1863, in Gordon Family Collection, UGA; *OR*, Vol. XXVII, Pt. II, p. 467.

rate in every detail. He advanced a line of skirmishers against the Federals guarding the approach to the bridge and at the same time moved three of his regiments down a deep gorge beyond the Union flank. Finding it impossible to cut the enemy off from the bridge, he opened fire on the Union troops with his artillery battery. After only a few well-placed shots, the militiamen hurriedly retreated across the bridge. Gordon's men pursued as rapidly as possible but were unable to seize the opposite end of the bridge because the Federals set fire to the structure "with the most inflammable materials." The head of Gordon's column reached the center of the bridge before being forced back by the flames.[19]

The fire quickly consumed the bridge and soon threatened the entire town of Wrightsville as flames spread to an adjoining lumberyard. Gordon's earlier pleas to the residents for aid in extinguishing the fire on the bridge had gone unheeded, but as the danger to the town increased, "buckets and tubs and pails and pans innumerable came from their hiding places." Gordon formed his men in a bucket brigade stretching from the river to the fire and back, and in this manner sought to contain the flames. In spite of "excessive fatigue" caused by their twenty-mile march and the skirmish earlier in the day, Gordon's men labored long into the night and finally checked the spread of the fire. Only by gallant exertions had the exhausted Confederates managed to preserve most of the town, but the northern newspapers, with "base ingratitude," mistakenly reported that Gordon's brigade had burned Wrightsville. The citizens of the town, however, realized that the Confederates had "labored as earnestly and bravely to save the town as they did to save the bridge."[20]

One particularly grateful homeowner, who had looked on anxiously as the Georgians fought the flames endangering her home, sought out the brigadier that evening. Learning that Gordon's brigade would depart Wrightsville early the next morning, Mrs. Luther L. Rewalt expressed her unwillingness to allow Gordon and his men to leave without a token of her appreciation. She insisted that the general and as many men as could be served in her dining room have breakfast with her prior to their departure. Gordon found the table so bountifully supplied, her welcome so gracious, and her demeanor so

19. OR, Vol. XXVII, Pt. 2, pp. 466–67, 491–92; Gordon to wife, July 7, 1863, in Gordon Family Collection, UGA; Gordon, Reminiscences, 143–44, 147.
20. Gordon, Reminiscences, 147–48; Gordon to wife, July 7, 1863, in Gordon Family Collection, UGA; OR, Vol. XXVII, Pt. 2, pp. 466–67, 492.

calm and kind that he thought she might be a "Southern woman." Perhaps suspecting that she had penned the helpful note he had received in York, he cautiously, and in a roundabout manner, inquired where her sympathies lay. In a firm voice, unshaken by the fact that she was surrounded by Confederates, she replied, "General Gordon, I fully comprehend you, and it is due to myself that I candidly tell you that I am a Union woman." Her husband's service in the Union army and her constant prayers for preservation of the Union permitted no misunderstanding of her position. But strong ties to the North did not release her from an obligation to the Confederates in her presence; simple courtesy dictated she show her gratitude for their saving of her home. Gordon, always an admirer of strong women, later called Mrs. Rewalt "one of the most superb women" he met during the war and fondly referred to her in his lectures after the war as "the heroine of the Susquehanna."[21]

Wrightsville had been saved, but the prized bridge had not. As it burned, energetic plans for a campaign east of the Susquehanna dissipated in the smoke. With no other means of crossing the deep, wide river, Gordon marched his command back to York on June 29 and rejoined the division for the first time since June 26. Gordon and his men had "penetrated farther . . . than any other Confederate infantry into the heart of Pennsylvania." Even if the bridge had been saved, the Confederate advance into Pennsylvania would have been at an end. Late in the evening of June 28, while Gordon's men rested on the western bank of the Susquehanna, General Lee received startling news at his headquarters at Chambersburg. The Federal army had crossed the Potomac and was moving northward. Realizing that this unexpectedly sudden threat jeopardized the Confederate communication and supply lines that stretched back to Virginia, the commanding general ordered the advance on Harrisburg abandoned and called for immediate concentration of the army. On June 30, Gordon marched his brigade from York to near Heidlersburg, where he received orders to move to Cashtown the following day. While on the march the next morning, new orders arrived; instead of turning west to Cashtown, Gordon was to continue south to a new destination — Gettysburg.[22]

21. Gordon, *Reminiscences*, 148–50; John Brown Gordon, "Last Days of the Confederacy," in Thomas B. Reed (ed.), *Modern Eloquence* (15 vols.; Philadelphia, 1900–1903), V, 474–75.

22. Gordon, *Reminiscences*, 147, 140; *OR*, Vol. XXVII, Pt. 2, pp. 467–68, 492, 307, 316.

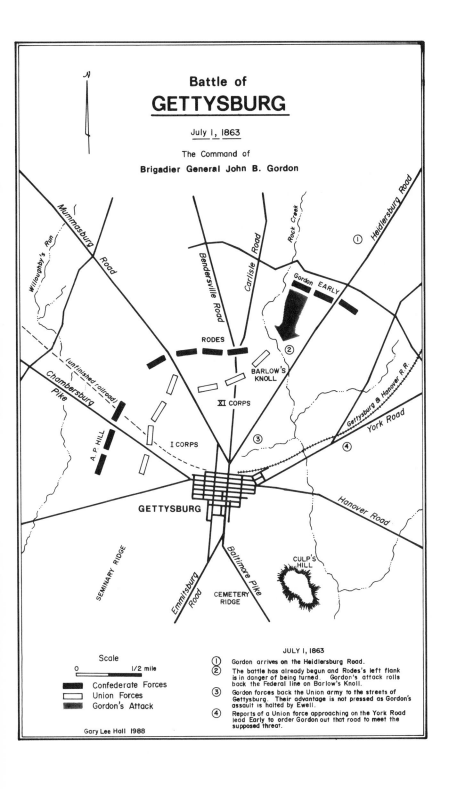

# Battle of
# GETTYSBURG

July 1, 1863

The Command of

**Brigadier General John B. Gordon**

N

Mummasburg Road

Willoughby's Run

Bendersville Road

Carlisle Road

Rock Creek

Heidlersburg Road

① 

Gordon EARLY

RODES

②

(unfinished railroad)

Chambersburg Pike

A. P. HILL

BARLOW'S KNOLL

XI CORPS

I CORPS

③

④

Gettysburg & Hanover R.R.

York Road

GETTYSBURG

Hanover Road

SEMINARY RIDGE

Emmitsburg Road

Baltimore Pike

CEMETERY RIDGE

CULP'S HILL

Scale

0        1/2 mile

▬ Confederate Forces
☐ Union Forces
▨ Gordon's Attack

Gary Lee Hall 1988

JULY 1, 1863

① Gordon arrives on the Heidlersburg Road.

② The battle has already begun and Rodes's left flank is in danger of being turned. Gordon's attack rolls back the Federal line on Barlow's Knoll.

③ Gordon forces back the Union army to the streets of Gettysburg. Their advantage is not pressed as Gordon's assault is halted by Ewell.

④ Reports of a Union force approaching on the York Road lead Early to order Gordon out that road to meet the supposed threat.

Marching at the head of Early's division, Gordon reached the Gettysburg battlefield at a most opportune time. Rodes's division had been heavily engaged north of the town for hours, and by 3 P.M., "affairs were in a very critical condition." A large Federal force had advanced against Rodes's left and threatened to turn that flank. Gordon immediately grasped the seriousness of the situation as he deployed his brigade on the right of the Heidlersburg Road. He cautiously moved his command forward, creeping to within three hundred yards of a wooded knoll that anchored the Union line. From there, Gordon's twelve hundred Georgians swept forward with "great impetuosity," despite heavy fire. After a short but fierce fight, Gordon's men drove the Federals back "in the greatest confusion" and "with great slaughter." Having uncovered the Union right flank, Gordon pressed on, rolling up the Federal line.[23]

As Gordon urged his men on, a Confederate artilleryman inquired, "General, where are your dead men?" Flushed with the fire of battle, Gordon retorted, "I haven't got any, sir; the Almighty has covered my men with his shield and buckler!" This same Confederate officer vividly remembered Gordon mounted upon a magnificent solid-black stallion as "the most glorious and inspiring thing" he had ever seen. The unforgettably "splendid picture of gallantry" of Gordon, "standing in his stirrups, bareheaded, hat in hand, arms extended, and, in a voice like a trumpet, exhorting his men," was "absolutely thrilling."[24]

The Federals fell back across the open fields to a low ridge just north of Gettysburg, where they attempted to rally. Seeing that this second Union line extended beyond Gordon's left, Early ordered the Georgian to halt while the other brigades of the division advanced against the Federal flank. When the Confederates renewed the attack, the right of the Union XI Corps again crumpled, precipitating a hurried retreat through the streets of the town and onto the commanding heights to the south.[25]

23. OR, Vol. XXVII, Pt. 2, pp. 445, 468–69, 492–93; Gordon to wife, July 7, 1863, in Gordon Family Collection, UGA; Gordon, Reminiscences, 151; Robert Stiles, Four Years Under Marse Robert (New York, 1904), 210.

24. Stiles, Four Years, 210–11.

25. OR, Vol. XXVII, Pt. 2, pp. 445, 469; General Jubal A. Early, "Review of the Whole Discussion (of the causes of Lee's defeat at Gettysburg)," SHSP, IV (July–December, 1877), 254, hereinafter cited as "Causes of Gettysburg Defeat"; James M'Dowell Carrington, "First Day on the Left at Gettysburg," SHSP, XXXVII (1909), 330.

While riding forward with his rapidly advancing men, Gordon came across a severely wounded Union officer. Having earlier seen this officer bravely trying to rally his retreating troops, Gordon dismounted and gave him a drink from his canteen. He soon discovered that he was aiding Brigadier General Francis C. Barlow, a New Yorker who commanded the division that the Confederates had just routed. Believing Barlow's wound to be fatal, Gordon had his paralyzed foe carried out of the merciless July sun, into the shade. As Gordon prepared to leave, Barlow asked him to take his wife's letters from his pocket, and destroy them, and then made a final request of the Confederate. If Gordon should ever meet Mrs. Barlow, would he tell her that her husband had died willingly while serving his country and that his last thoughts were of her? Gordon promised to fulfill Barlow's dying request. Learning that Mrs. Barlow was near Gettysburg, he resolved to deliver a message to her that evening and provide safe passage for her to join her husband. Painfully reminded of his separation from Fanny, Gordon was "especially stirred by the announcement that his [Barlow's] wife was so near him." Convinced that Barlow would soon be dead, Gordon bade farewell to his prostrated opponent and rejoined his brigade.[26]

Barlow, however, survived and returned to duty with the Army of the Potomac later in the war. When he learned of the death of a Confederate general J. B. Gordon at the Battle of Yellow Tavern, he assumed it was the Gordon who had aided him. Thus, each man believed the other to be dead. Some fifteen years later, during his second term in the Senate, Gordon received an invitation to dine with Clarkson Potter, a New York congressman, who had also invited a former Union general named Barlow. With the host knowing nothing of the incident on the first day at Gettysburg and Gordon expecting to

26. Gordon, *Reminiscences*, 151–52. I have drawn exclusively from Gordon's account of this incident as presented in *Reminiscences*, even though it is the least dramatic. Gordon never sought to minimize the drama of the Civil War, especially in the writing of his book, so I believe this account is closer to what might have happened. There is substantial doubt as to whether the famous Barlow-Gordon meeting ever took place at all. William F. Hanna, in "A Gettysburg Myth Exploded," *Civil War Times Illustrated*, XXIV (May, 1985), 42–47, contends that under his examination of all verifiable facts Gordon's account cannot stand up. Hanna's evidence that the alleged meeting between Gordon and Barlow at Gettysburg never occurred and that much, if not all, of Gordon's account of the incident was fabricated is hard to refute. Even so, I have chosen to include the story because it is one of the most enduring tales of the Civil War, and it nicely reflects Gordon's late-nineteenth-century efforts to reconcile the formerly warring sections. The first published account of this story that I have located

meet a kinsman of the Barlow he had encountered, the guests sat down at the table. Gordon inquired, "General, are you related to the Barlow who was killed at Gettysburg?" Barlow replied, "Why, I am the man, sir. Are you related to the Gordon who killed me?" "I am the man, sir," responded Gordon. The startled Georgian later remembered, "[N]othing short of actual resurrection from the dead could have amazed either of us more." The friendship that had begun on the field of battle at Gettysburg, now renewed, remained unbroken until Barlow's death in 1896.[27]

Gordon's late-afternoon attack on July 1 had yielded magnificent results. Arriving on the battlefield after a fourteen-mile march and finding Rodes nearly overwhelmed, Gordon's brigade delivered an attack styled "as brilliant as any charge of the war." Although he had no way of ascertaining the exact number of casualties his men had inflicted, Gordon believed the enemy's loss in men killed and wounded exceeded the number of Confederates he had carried into battle. Gordon's 1,200 men in fact disabled 1,200 to 1,500 Yankees and captured about 1,800—all in less than an hour and with fewer than 380 casualties. Ewell was quoted as saying that "Gordon's brigade that evening put *hors de combat* a greater number of the enemy in proportion to its own numbers than any other command on either side ever did, from the beginning to the end of the war." Gordon's claim that his brigade's devastating attack "gave relief on the whole line" was certainly true for action north of Gettysburg, where all Union troops began to yield after Gordon crushed the Federal right flank.[28]

With the enemy falling back toward Cemetery Hill in "perfect confusion," Gordon urged immediate pursuit. The disorganized condition of the Federals convinced him that "it was only necessary for me to press forward . . . [and] in less than half an hour my troops would have swept up and over those hills" to the south. Many years

---

is in *SHSP*, XXI (1893), 337–39, though it states that the article, "An Incident of Gettysburg," was drawn from the New Haven *Evening Register*. The exact same article appeared in *McClure's Magazine* (June, 1894), 68–70, the following year, under the authorship of T. J. Mackey. This account differs slightly in some details from the one in *Reminiscences*, as well as from another version presented in Gordon's lecture, "Last Days of the Confederacy" (*Modern Eloquence*, V, 476–79), but the basic story line remains the same.

27. Gordon, *Reminiscences*, 152–53.

28. Gordon to wife, July 7, 1863, in Gordon Family Collection, UGA; *OR*, Vol. XXVII, Pt. 2, p. 493; Stiles, *Four Years*, 211; Early, "Causes of Gettysburg Defeat," 253.

after the war, Gordon contended that he refused to obey orders to stop until a "fourth order of the most preemptory character" arrived; even then, he maintained, he would have risked the consequences of disobedience had not Lee's instructions to avoid a major engagement accompanied the order. Gordon rode to find Ewell and impress upon him the necessity for an attack on the heights. Gordon was with the corps commander when a staff officer from Johnson's division arrived and reported that General Johnson was nearing Gettysburg with his division "in prime condition" and ready to go into immediate action. "In the ardor of battle and the magnitude of the opportunity," the Georgian "broke disciplinary bounds" and announced that his brigade could attack with Johnson's division and together they could carry Cemetery Hill before nightfall. To the dismay of almost all of the surrounding officers, Ewell ignored Gordon and dispatched orders that Johnson's division continue its march to the front, then halt and await further orders. Ewell's remarks ended the discussion, and though crestfallen, Gordon could say no more.[29]

A short while later, Gordon and Ewell rode together into Gettysburg. Most of the fighting had ceased, but small pockets of isolated Federals continued to resist. One such group that remained near the outskirts of town opened a "brisk fire" upon the mounted Confederates. As a number of accompanying officers fell, Gordon "heard the ominous thud of a Minié ball" striking Ewell, who rode beside him. The concerned brigadier anxiously asked his commander if he was hurt. The crusty Ewell, who had lost a leg earlier in the war, replied "No, no, . . . I'm not hurt. But suppose that ball had struck you: we would have had the trouble of carrying you off the field, sir. You see how much better fixed for a fight I am than you are. It don't hurt a bit to be shot in a wooden leg." Despite his feistiness, Ewell was still not inclined to attack the heights south of Gettysburg.[30]

Any lingering hope that Gordon entertained about assaulting Cemetery Hill prior to sundown vanished when new orders from Early arrived. While looking for Ewell "for the purpose of urging an immediate advance . . . in order to get possession of the hills," Early received word from one of his brigade commanders stationed on the York Road that a Federal force was advancing on the Confederate left

29. Gordon, *Reminiscences*, 140, 154; Henry Kyd Douglas, *I Rode with Stonewall* (Chapel Hill, 1940), 247; Carrington, "First Day At Gettysburg," 333; Randolph H. McKim, *A Soldier's Recollections* (New York, 1910), 175.
30. Gordon, *Reminiscences*, 157.

flank. He did not believe the report but felt compelled to guard against the possible threat. Accordingly, he directed Gordon to move his men out the York Road and to take command of both brigades posted there. As rumors of an enemy advance from that direction continued to pour in after dark, Early retained the two brigades under Gordon in that sector.[31]

Even though his troops remained on the York Road where no serious activity took place, Gordon evidently spent much of the night roaming picket lines other than his own, probably those around Culp's Hill. There the ominous sounds of Federal activity drifted down to him. The sound of entrenchments being dug with picks and shovels, the shuffle of large bodies of troops marching about, and the deep rumble of artillery pieces being moved left no doubt that the heights were being fortified and steadily reinforced. Gordon was convinced that by dawn the Federal position would be virtually impregnable. Unable to suppress his anxiety any longer, Gordon rode to the headquarters of Ewell and Early at 2 A.M. He reported his observations and urged "a concentrated and vigorous night assault" against the heights, despite the lateness of the hour. Although a night attack involved considerable risk, Gordon considered it infinitely preferable to a daylight assault that he felt would cost the Confederates ten thousand men. Gordon sensed a "disposition [by his superiors] to yield to my suggestions, but other counsels finally prevailed." The attack would wait until the next day.[32]

The passage of years apparently colored Gordon's interpretation of the events at Gettysburg. Without question, he strongly urged that an attack upon Cemetery Hill be made late in the afternoon of July 1. His readiness to join Johnson's division in an attack is wholly consistent with Gordon's audaciously offensive spirit. Although his brigade had suffered more severely in the earlier action than the rest of Early's division, Gordon was capable of reorganizing his men and making the assault. Whether it would have been successful is a matter of conjecture and not under consideration here. What is open to question is Gordon's insistence in *Reminiscences* that the "fatal mistake" of July 1 occurred when he was ordered to halt by Early and Ewell, neither of whom, he maintained, understood the actual situation or appreciated the demoralized state of the Federals. Clearly, Gordon was wrong

31. *OR*, Vol. XXVII, Pt. 2, p. 469; Early, *Narrative of the War*, 271; Jubal A. Early, "Report of the Gettysburg Campaign," *SHSP*, X (1882), 546n.

32. Gordon, *Reminiscences*, 156–57.

with regard to Early, who was equally earnest in his insistence that the heights be taken immediately. At the heart of the issue is Gordon's effort to shift any of the blame for the failure of the Army of Northern Virginia at Gettysburg away from Lee and to disperse it among his subordinates—namely, Ewell on the first day and Longstreet on the second and third days. It is impossible to determine how much Gordon's participation in postwar controversies and the attempt to insulate Lee from critics shaped his view of the past. In his official report, he made no mention of his despair over being halted (later in the war, under somewhat similar conditions, he did officially express his displeasure with a superior's decision) and that portion of his letter to his wife detailing the Battle of Gettysburg has not survived. Although Gordon lobbied fiercely for an attack on the heights on July 1, he was probably not as distraught as *Reminiscences* intimates. The first day at Gettysburg had, in the main, been a great Confederate success, and with all of Lee's army closing in on the town, there was little reason not to believe that the next day would hold more of the same.

For all intents and purposes, however, Gordon's participation in the Battle of Gettysburg had already ended. On the second day, he and his brigade returned to Early and were placed in the rear of two of Early's other brigades. When these troops assaulted Cemetery Hill near sundown, Gordon moved to their original position in order to support them. His brigade did not advance up the hill because Early, seeing that the troops on his right had failed to attack, determined that such a move would be fruitless. Gordon's command occupied frontline positions throughout July 3 and, though exposed to artillery and sharpshooter fire, was never seriously engaged. At two o'clock the following morning, Gordon and the rest of Early's division withdrew from their positions and moved west of Gettysburg as Lee attempted to shorten his line.[33]

The long march back to Virginia commenced on the evening of July 4 in the midst of a severe storm. During the retreat on July 5, Gordon's brigade acted as the rear guard for the entire army. When Union pursuit threatened the Confederate rear near Fairfield, Gordon deployed a regiment as skirmishers and successfully checked the Federal advance while the army's trains moved to safety. The with-

33. *OR*, Vol. XXVII, Pt. 2, pp. 470–71, 481; Jubal A. Early, "Reply to General Longstreet," *SHSP*, IV (July–December, 1877), 297.

drawal continued relatively unhindered, and on July 14, Gordon and his brigade forded the Potomac near Williamsport.[34]

While encamped near Hagerstown during the retreat, Gordon wrote to Fanny—probably his first letter to his wife in over two weeks—to let her know that he had survived "the most terrific battle of the war." Earnestly praying for God "to fill my heart and my dear wife's with gratitude and praise," Gordon humbly gave thanks to the Lord for mercifully sparing his life while thousands had died. In a later letter, he noted that his brigade had been "greatly complimented in high quarters" and that he had "made without an effort to do it, some reputation as a commander." But he found such praise to be of little consequence. "My separation from you—the soul of my happiness on this Earth—the awful uncertainty as to the future—the seemingly endless blood shed that is to take place—the thousands of noble lives lost in the last horrid battle, all conspire to render every personal compliment and idle talk of *glory* as exceedingly worthless to me." Burdened with the uncertain "fate of our unhappy country" and continued separation from his wife, Gordon could derive little solace from personal accolades.[35]

Gordon saw almost no combat during the next ten months. After the titanic struggle at Gettysburg, the two great eastern armies moved back into Virginia, where they rested and regrouped. Gordon participated in all the operations of the II Corps during the final months of 1863, but no serious confrontations developed. By the end of December, both armies were securely established in their winter quarters along the Rapidan River.[36]

With active campaigning at an end until spring, fraternization between pickets on opposite sides of the river grew to proportions that alarmed both Union and Confederate officers. Gordon received instructions to put an end to it. Accordingly, he paid a number of surprise visits to his outposts, where on one occasion he discovered an unusual amount of commotion. His men nervously reported that all was in order, but Gordon noticed the high weeds along the riverbank shaking. He ordered the weeds broken down, whereupon a scantily clad soldier emerged. "'Where do you belong?'" queried Gordon. The soldier answered simply, "'Over yonder,'" motioning to the Union

34. *OR*, Vol. XXVII, Pt. 2, pp. 309, 322, 448, 471–72, 493; Gordon, *Reminiscences*, 172–74.

35. Gordon to wife, July 7, 10, 1863, both in Gordon Family Collection, UGA.

36. Gordon, *Reminiscences*, 188–91; *OR*, Vol. XXIX, Pt. 1, pp. 843–45.

side of the Rapidan. When the Georgian asked him what he was doing here, he forthrightly replied, "'Well General, I didn't think it was any harm to come over and see the boys just a little while.'" Gordon pointed out that the war had not ended and that these "boys" were the enemy, yet the unperturbed Yankee responded, "'Yes, General, but we are not fighting now.'" Suppressing an impulse to laugh aloud, Gordon assumed his sternest bearing and growled, "'I am going to teach you, sir, that we are at war. You have no rights here except as prisoner of war, and I am going to have you marched to Richmond and put you in prison.'" Gordon's horrified men immediately came to the defense of their visitor, pleading that they had invited him over and guaranteed his protection; if he were imprisoned, their honor would be ruined. Seeing that his threat had accomplished its purpose—frightening both his men and their "northern guest"—Gordon turned to the Yankee and inquired, "'Now sir, if I permit you to go back to your own side, will you solemnly promise, on the honor of a soldier, that—'" He never finished his sentence because the nearly naked soldier emphatically answered, "'Yes, sir,'" as he "leaped like a bull frog into the river and swam back."[37]

In the months of relative inactivity that followed the Pennsylvania invasion, Gordon took "an active interest in religious exercises and in the spiritual welfare of those under his charge." He frequently led prayer meetings in his brigade and, "with eloquent words and tearful eyes," made "powerful appeals to his men to come to Christ." In an impassioned letter to a high-ranking Confederate religious official, Gordon pleaded for more missionaries to be sent to the army. He felt that entirely too little attention was being paid to the spiritual needs of the soldiers, primarily because there were not enough chaplains or visiting ministers. In some cases, brigades of up to two thousand men went without even a chaplain. Gordon also chastised those "*good Christians*" on the home front who considered soldiers "too '*demoralized*' to be benefited by preaching." To the contrary, he believed that the ranks of the army provided a magnificent opportunity for ministers to obtain converts and undertake valuable Christian service. The great religious revival that swept through Lee's army in the winter and spring of 1864 revealed the truth of Gordon's observa-

37. Gordon, *Reminiscences*, 110–12; Gordon, "Last Days of the Confederacy," in Reed (ed.), *Modern Eloquence*, V, 482–83; Atlanta *Constitution*, March 25, 1881; General Gordon, "They Would Mix on the Picket Line. Anecdote of War," *SHSP*, X (1882), 422–23.

tions. At a time when interest in religious gatherings was widespread, numerous traveling missionaries reported that both the attendance at meetings and the number of converts in Gordon's brigade were extremely high. And as a leading Confederate chaplain later recalled, Gordon was "one of the most valuable and efficient workers" in these revival meetings.[38]

More important than the reputation he had earned as an "active friend and helper of his chaplains" was his rising status as a military leader. As a civilian volunteer in an army staffed by professionals, Gordon had succeeded in impressing the commanding general with his soldierly abilities—by no means an insignificant accomplishment. On two separate occasions in early 1864, Lee spoke very highly of Gordon in letters to President Jefferson Davis. He wrote in January, "[O]f the brigadiers, I think General Gordon, of Alabama, one of the best." Three months later, while considering the necessity of transferring one of his division commanders, Lee reported he could better spare Jubal Early than Edward Johnson "because I might get Gordon or Hoke of that division in his place." Clearly, Lee had a high opinion of the young citizen-soldier, who had, less than three years earlier, entered military service as a captain in command of the Raccoon Roughs. Now, Gordon might be ready for divisional command, if necessary. And the necessity might soon become a reality as spring was unfolding and the army across the Rapidan was stirring.[39]

38. J. William Jones, *Christ in the Camp or Religion in Lee's Army* (Richmond, 1887), 104–105, 341–42, 348, 351, 371, 373, 374; William W. Bennett, *A Narrative of the Great Revival Which Prevailed in the Southern Armies* (Philadelphia, 1877), 372; Gordon, *Reminiscences*, 229–30, 233; Gordon, "Last Days of the Confederacy," in Reed (ed.), *Modern Eloquence*, V, 488–89; Atlanta *Constitution*, December 19, 1877, January 15, 1904.

39. Jones, *Christ in the Camp*, 104; OR, Vol. XXXIII, 1124, 1321.

# IV · Evening Star of the Confederacy

On May 4, Lieutenant General Ulysses S. Grant opened his overland campaign in Virginia. He established his headquarters with the Army of the Potomac as it began crossing the Rapidan on the night of May 3. By rapid movement, Grant hoped to maneuver around Lee's right flank and bring him to battle under conditions favorable to the Union army; however, the Confederate commander discovered his opponent's action and took immediate countermeasures. He directed Ewell's II Corps and Lieutenant General Ambrose Powell Hill's III Corps to advance eastward on the Orange Turnpike and the Orange Plank Road, respectively, and to strike the Union army while it was in the dense, overgrown area known as the Wilderness. By bringing his adversary to battle in this wooded maze, Lee hoped to minimize the two-to-one manpower advantage of the Union army, as well as its artillery superiority. May 4 passed quietly as Gordon and his men moved from their winter quarters near Clark's Mountain down the old turnpike to Locust Grove.[1]

The march into the Wilderness resumed early on the morning of May 5. Lee had instructed Ewell to control his march so as to advance abreast of A. P. Hill on the Orange Plank Road and to avoid a general engagement until Lieutenant General James Longstreet's I Corps, still far to the rear, could arrive. Despite these orders, Ewell's two

1. Jubal Anderson Early, *Autobiographical Sketch and Narrative of the War Between the States* (Philadelphia, 1912), 344–45, hereinafter cited as *Narrative of the War*; John B. Gordon, *Reminiscences of the Civil War* (New York, 1903), 236–37; OR, Vol. XXXVI, Pt. 1, p. 1070, Pt. 2, p. 951; A. A. Humphreys, *The Virginia Campaign of 1864 and 1865* (New York, 1903), 18–19.

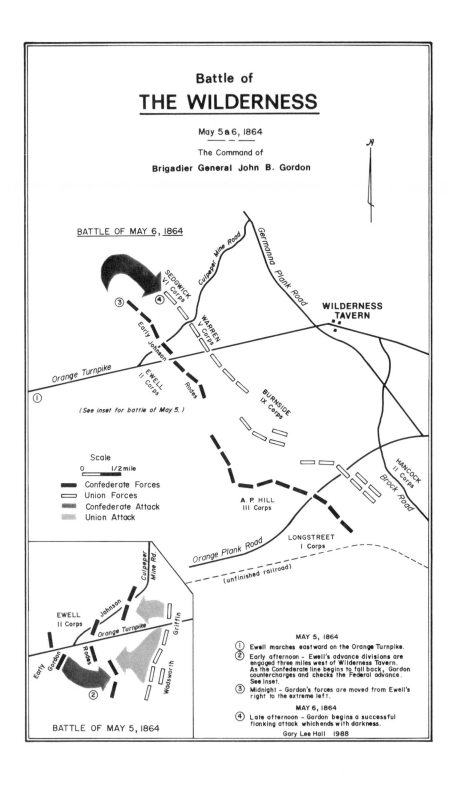

# Battle of
# THE WILDERNESS

May 5 a 6, 1864

The Command of

**Brigadier General John B. Gordon**

BATTLE OF MAY 6, 1864

SEDGWICK
VI Corps

Culpeper Mine Road

Germanna Plank Road

WILDERNESS
TAVERN

Early Johnson

WARREN
V Corps

Orange Turnpike

EWELL
II Corps

Rodes

BURNSIDE
IX Corps

(See inset for battle of May 5.)

Scale

0 ___ 1/2 mile

▬▬▬ Confederate Forces
▭ Union Forces
▨ Confederate Attack
▨ Union Attack

HANCOCK
II Corps

Brock Road

A. P. HILL
III Corps

LONGSTREET
I Corps

Orange Plank Road

(unfinished railroad)

EWELL
II Corps

Johnson

Culpeper Mine Rd.

Griffin

Early

Gordon

Rodes

Orange Turnpike

Wadsworth

BATTLE OF MAY 5, 1864

MAY 5, 1864

① Ewell marches eastward on the Orange Turnpike.

② Early afternoon – Ewell's advance divisions are engaged three miles west of Wilderness Tavern. As the Confederate line begins to fall back, Gordon countercharges and checks the Federal advance. See inset.

③ Midnight – Gordon's forces are moved from Ewell's right to the extreme left.

MAY 6, 1864

④ Late afternoon – Gordon begins a successful flanking attack which ends with darkness.

Gary Lee Hall  1988

advance divisions, under Johnson and Rodes, became heavily engaged in the early afternoon, approximately three miles east of Wilderness Tavern. A spirited Federal attack on either side of the turnpike struck Ewell's troops with such speed and force that the right center fell back in confusion. Alerted by "the steady roll of small arms" to the seriousness of the conflict well before he reached the front, Gordon had his brigade ready for immediate action. As he rode forward, he met Ewell galloping down the road in search of reinforcements. The corps commander, fully aware of the gravity of this penetration of his lines, excitedly told his young subordinate, "General Gordon, the fate of the day depends on you, sir." Gordon, in a voice loud enough that his troops could hear him, shouted, "These men will save it, sir."[2]

Gordon threw one of his regiments forward in a rapid countercharge to check the Federal advance, at least momentarily. "The sheer audacity and dash" of the single regiment's thrust bought Gordon the time he needed to wheel the rest of the brigade into line south of the turnpike at a right angle to it. As he moved his men forward into the threatening gap in Ewell's front, Gordon encountered a portion of his old command falling back in disorder. His words of encouragement as he passed—"Steady, 6th Ala."—undoubtedly brought a cheer from his old comrades, as well as a renewed determination to reorganize and reenter the fray. With a deafening "rebel yell" adding to their ferocity, Gordon's men advanced and struck a victorious yet tremendously confused and irregular Union line. Their "dashing charge" shattered the forces in their front; but as his troops pursued the retreating Federals, Gordon encountered what he styled "one of the strangest conditions ever witnessed on a battlefield."[3]

He had successfully checked the Federals on his immediate front; however, the enemy on both his flanks continued to advance. Faced with the prospect of total envelopment, Gordon had to discontinue his forward movement. Quickly realizing that this "unique and alarming" situation required "very unusual tactics," he halted his

2. Humphreys, *Virginia Campaign*, 25–26; *OR*, Vol. XXXVI, Pt. 1, pp. 1070, 1076–77; Gordon, *Reminiscences*, 237–39; J. William Jones, *Army of Northern Virginia Memorial Volume* (Richmond, 1880), 214; F. L. Hudgins, "38th Georgia Regiment at the Wilderness, 5th, 6th, 7th of May 1864" (MS in Confederate Veteran Papers, Duke).

3. Hudgins, "38th Georgia"; Gordon, *Reminiscences*, 239; Edward Steere, *The Wilderness Campaign* (Harrisburg, 1960), 163; *OR*, Vol. XXXVI, Pt. 1, pp. 610–11, 1071, 1076–77; E. M. Law, "From the Wilderness to Cold Harbor," in Robert Underwood Johnson and Clarence Clough Buel (eds.), *Battles and Leaders of the Civil War* (4 vols.; 1887–88; rpr. New York, 1956), IV, 121n.

men and attempted to make the best of his plight. While holding his front with two regiments, he advanced three others by the right flank and the remaining regiment by the left flank. This method of attack, though novel, proved devastatingly effective, and in conjunction with Gordon's movements, the rallied troops of Rodes's division advanced, driving the Federals back and restoring the front. Gordon's rapid, energetic attack, made in the midst of great confusion, had been delivered "just in time to prevent a serious disaster." As firing died away, the lines rested in approximately the same location they had occupied when the battle began. Gordon held this position on Ewell's right until near midnight, when he received orders to withdraw and move to the extreme left of the II Corps.[4]

Even before daylight on May 6, Gordon had his scouts out searching for the Union flank. About dawn, his men returned and reported that his line greatly overlapped the flank of the Army of the Potomac. The Union right ended abruptly in the woodland near Gordon's line and appeared to be completely unprotected. Unwilling to believe his good fortune, Gordon dispatched another party to reconnoiter. This second group not only corroborated the first report but found that there were no supporting troops within several miles of the exposed flank. Gordon had to be certain before he could report such a tremendous opportunity to his superior, so he undertook a personal reconnaissance. Guided by a cavalryman, he traveled almost two miles into the rear of Sedgwick's VI Corps and "found the reports correct in every particular." He even crept on his hands and knees to within hearing distance of the end of the Union line, where, for as far as he could see, blue-clad soldiers, oblivious to their vulnerable condition, lazily prepared their breakfast. Here, lying before him, was the flank of Grant's great army, totally exposed and wholly unsupported. Presented with an opportunity "rarely equalled in any war," Gordon visualized even greater success than that attained by Jackson's famous flank attack one year earlier at Chancellorsville, only a few miles away.[5]

4. Hudgins, "38th Georgia"; Atlanta *Constitution*, November 26, 1878; Gordon, *Reminiscences*, 239–42; Cadmus M. Wilcox, "Lee and Grant in the Wilderness," in *The Annals of the War* (Philadelphia, 1879), 492; J. W. Jones, *Army of Northern Virginia Memorial Volume*, 215; W. S. Dunlop, *Lee's Sharpshooters or the Forefront of Battle* (Little Rock, Ark., 1899), 388–89; Gordon to Lee, December 20, 1867, in Robert Edward Lee Headquarters Papers, VHS; *OR*, Vol. XXXVI, Pt. 1, pp. 1070, 1077; Jones to Daniel, July 3, 1904, in John Warwick Daniel Papers, Duke.

5. Gordon, *Reminiscences*, 243–47; T. G. Jones to Daniel, July 3, 1904, in Thomas Goode Jones Collection, ADAH; *OR*, Vol. XXXVI, Pt. 1, p. 1077.

As Gordon hurried back to his command, the method of attack almost planned itself. He would place his brigade, with whatever others could be spared, in line squarely on the flank and rear of the VI Corps. As he hit the flank, the Federals would inevitably be compelled to withdraw, and as they fell back, they would easily be captured by the Confederates rapidly moving into their rear. Coupled with his flank attack would be a frontal demonstration by all other Confederates in line, in order to hold the Union front in place until the flank had been crushed. Then, as Gordon proceeded down the constantly receding flank of the Union army, he would continually move to his left, allowing room for the Confederate units that had faced the recently disposed-of Federals to fall in on his right "thus swelling at each step of our advance the numbers, power, momentum of the Confederate forces as they swept down the line." Such an opportunity must not be permitted to slip away.[6]

Gordon immediately sent a member of his staff, Thomas G. Jones, to find either Ewell or Early and explain the situation to them. Young Jones located the corps commander first and was talking to him when Early rode up and joined the conference. Despite Jones's report that supporting troops were nowhere near the Union right, Early vigorously opposed an attack, contending that Major General Ambrose E. Burnside's IX Corps occupied Sedgwick's rear. Cavalry reports, which he accepted but had not investigated, led Early to believe that the enemy was, in fact, moving to turn the Confederate flank. With Burnside so near, failure by Gordon to achieve a striking success would leave the Confederate flank open to a Union attack. Since Ewell possessed no ready reserves, Early reasoned that a successful Federal counterattack would result in disaster for the II Corps and perhaps for all of Lee's army. Accordingly, Early instructed Jones "to tell Gordon to hold still, and later, they [Ewell and Early] would come over to the left and see what could be done."[7]

Moments later, Gordon galloped up and began to plead his own case fervently. Yet some fifteen or twenty minutes of "very earnest conversation" failed to convince either Early or Ewell. Moving away, a greatly disappointed Gordon told his staff officer, "General Early, evidently didn't believe a word of what I told him of what I had seen myself." Ewell apparently concurred with his division commander but told Gordon that he would make a personal examination "as soon

6. Gordon, *Reminiscences*, 245–48.

7. Jones to Daniel, February 29, July 3, 1904, both in T. G. Jones Collection; Early, *Narrative of the War*, 348.

as other duties permitted." It was barely 9 A.M., so Gordon's hopes might yet have been realized. Unfortunately, however, neither Early nor Ewell made their promised reconnaissance until late in the day, and Gordon's repeated requests for permission to attack went unfulfilled. A virtual stalemate continued on the Confederate left.[8]

In light of his unexplained delay in personally examining the Union right, Early's opposition to Gordon's proposed attack deserves little discussion except for his concern about the possibility of a disaster resulting from a Federal counterattack. The Confederate army simply did not possess the number of sufficiently fresh troops needed to institute a large-scale flanking movement. If Gordon had failed to turn the Union right, no reserves would have been available to bolster defenses against a countermovement. Despite the validity of this point, Early cannot be excused for his gross inattention to Gordon's findings, especially since on the basic point of conflict between Gordon and Early—whether Burnside's corps occupied the rear of the Union right, as Early insisted both on May 6 and in his writings after the war—the Virginian was, without question, in error. Numerous Union reports concerning the movement of the IX Corps on May 6, in the *Official Records* and other accounts of the battle, show that three of Burnside's four divisions had passed well beyond the Union right prior to 9 A.M. They were moving toward the Federal center, where they had been ordered to participate in the assault against the Confederate right. The other division remained in the vicinity of Germanna Ford to guard the crossing over the Rapidan, and posed little or no threat to Gordon's flank attack. To put it quite simply, Gordon's early morning reports were entirely correct.[9]

Both Early and Ewell had more responsibilities than did Gordon, but their front was comparatively quiet that day, undergoing only a limited number of easily repulsed attacks. The pressure on them should not have been so heavy as to prohibit throughout the entire day any substantial investigation of Gordon's reconnaissance. The fundamentals of military science demanded that Early and Ewell

8. Jones to Daniel, February 29, July 3, 1904, both in T. G. Jones Collection; Gordon, *Reminiscences*, 255–56; *OR*, Vol. XXXVI, Pt. 1, pp. 1071, 1077. Also see *OR*, Vol. XXXVI, Pt. 2, pp. 961–62 for messages between Gordon, Ewell's headquarters, and cavalry pickets in the area. Although the index to *OR* identifies this correspondence as cavalry Brigadier General J[ames] B. Gordon's, the nature of the messages indicates that they were those of infantry Brigadier General John B. Gordon.

9. Gordon to Lee, December 20, 1867, February 6, 1868, both in Lee Headquarters Papers; *OR*, Vol. XXXVI, Pt. 1, pp. 18, 190, 321, 906, 927, 942, 987–88.

consider Gordon's personal findings more seriously, especially given the tremendous possibilities involved. At a time when frontal assaults were the dominant mode of offensive warfare, an enemy's exposed flank was not to be ignored. Early must bear a large portion of the blame for this gross oversight. Even though he had received reports from cavalry scouts that the Confederate left might be threatened and that Burnside's corps rested in the rear of the Union right, he should not have summarily dismissed Gordon's early morning findings as false. The Georgian had personally verified his findings, but Early had done nothing to substantiate his reports and instead "acted on his apprehensions." Clearly, as Douglas Southall Freeman observed, "Early had been completely deceived as to the strength and dispositions of the enemy on his front." To the detriment of Lee's army, Early's basically unfounded arguments against Gordon's proposal succeeded in swaying the commander of the II Corps. "Perplexed or weary, or hypnotized for the moment by the confident insistence of Early, he [Ewell] permitted the fateful afternoon to pass without an offensive blow."[10]

Gordon finally received his long-sought order to attack shortly before sunset. Although it is generally accepted that this order emerged from a conference of Lee, Ewell, Early, and Gordon, at II Corps headquarters late in the afternoon of May 6, the only evidence for this meeting comes from Gordon's writings, long after the war. Gordon contended that Lee—whose full attention throughout the morning and afternoon had necessarily been devoted to the Confederate right, especially after Longstreet's fall—finally visited the left flank about 5:30 P.M. Meeting there with Ewell, Early, and Gordon, he inquired whether anything could be done on Ewell's front to relieve the heavy pressure on the army's right. In *Reminiscences*, Gordon wrote that he listened patiently for a few minutes but soon felt compelled to apprise the commanding general of Sedgwick's exposed flank. When Early renewed his argument that Burnside's corps lay behind Sedgwick's line, Gordon again asserted that he had personally ridden far behind the Union right and encountered no opposition whatsoever. Gordon maintained that after he had detailed his plan, Lee immediately concurred and ordered the attack. "His words were

10. Douglas Southall Freeman, *Lee's Lieutenants: A Study in Command* (3 vols.; New York, 1942–44), III, 443, 370; Douglas Southall Freeman, *R. E. Lee: A Biography* (4 vols.; New York, 1934–35), III, 297n; Jones to Daniel, July 3, 1904, in T. G. Jones Collection.

few, but his silence and grim looks . . . revealed his thoughts almost as plainly as words could have done." Such is Gordon's account.[11]

In all probability, however, the passage of years substantially distorted the general's recollection of the events; it is doubtful that Gordon attended such a conference or that Lee directly issued such an order. In correspondence with Gordon shortly after the war, Lee inquired whether they had met in the Wilderness before or after the attack of May 6. Gordon answered, "I am *positive* that I conversed with you on the morning of the 7th. Do not remember having seen you [on] that flank prior to that time. Indeed I was not aware of your desire to make a movement on that flank until after the 6th. I am glad to know that such was your wish." Given the recentness of the war and the respectful manner in which Gordon dealt with the paternal Lee, it is likely that this letter reveals the events of May 6 more accurately than does *Reminiscences*, written almost forty years later.[12]

It seems likely that Ewell or Early finally investigated Gordon's morning reconnaissance, and Ewell then ordered Early and his division to make the turning movement. This sequence of events is more plausible than Gordon's account, in which Lee directly orders the attack over the head of his lieutenant general. Lee did not normally overrule the commander on the scene; moreover, he had spent the entire day south, on the Orange Plank Road. It is extremely doubtful that he would have instructed Ewell, who would have (or should have) been better acquainted with the situation on his front, to make an attack that the corps commander opposed. And even if Lee had been present on the Confederate left at 5:30 P.M., it is improbable that he would have issued, in the presence of the brigadier's superiors, a direct order to Gordon to attack. In his official report, Gordon himself stated, "Late in the afternoon of 6 May I received orders from Major General Early to make the attack." Although it is difficult to excuse Gordon's "recollection" of a nonexistent conference, his mistake does not detract from his criticism of the actions of Early and Ewell. Their failure to investigate Gordon's morning report more conscientiously deprived the Army of Northern Virginia of an excellent opportunity for an attack that might have demolished the Union right and

11. Gordon, *Reminiscences*, 258.
12. Gordon to Lee, December 20, 1867, February 6, 1868, both in Lee Headquarters Papers; Lee to Gordon, February 22, 1868, in Gordon Family Collection, UGA.

that would certainly have relieved the intense pressure being exerted on the Confederate right.[13]

Late in the afternoon, Early placed Gordon in charge of the actual flanking maneuver, which would be made by Gordon's own brigade and that of Brigadier General Robert D. Johnston. After assembling his men in an open field to the north, Gordon positioned them squarely on the flank of the VI Corps and formed Johnston's brigade in a line facing the enemy's rear. As the sun reached the horizon, the Confederates moved forward. Surprise, confusion, and rout were complete. The Georgia brigade crumpled Brigadier General Alexander Shaler's flank and swept down a mile of the VI Corps front. The rapid advance carried the Confederates through camps where only moments before Union soldiers had been boiling their coffee and cooking their supper. Brigadier General Truman Seymour's command, to the left of Shaler's, was also driven from the field. Both brigadiers were captured, along with six hundred of their men. The Confederates, "literally revelling in the chase," drove onward, enjoying what was for many the "finest frolic" of the war. Gordon reported that despite frequent attempts by the enemy to change front and halt his progress, "the advance of my brigade was steady and uninterrupted until the approach of darkness in the dense woodland created confusion in my right two regiments." Over one-half of the mere fifty casualties suffered in the attack were sustained when confused Confederates, still facing the Union works, opened fire upon Gordon's right as it passed their front. By the time he straightened out the disorganization caused by the enfilading fire, darkness had brought a halt to his advance.[14]

The manner in which the battle ended convinced Gordon that one more hour of daylight would have resulted in the capture of a large

13. OR, Vol. XXXVI, Pt. 1, 1071, 1077; Early, Narrative of the War, 348–49.

14. Early, Narrative of the War, 348–50; Dunlop, Lee's Sharpshooters, 413–15; J. W. Jones, Army of Northern Virginia Memorial Volume, 238–39; Gordon to Lee, December 20, 1867, in Lee Headquarters Papers; Gordon, Reminiscences, 248–50; OR, Vol. XXXVI, Pt. 1, pp. 1071, 1077–78, Pt. 2, p. 966; Jones to Daniel, February 29, June 20, July 3, 1904, all in T. G. Jones Collection; Hudgins, "38th Georgia"; William W. Swan, "Battle of the Wilderness," in Military Historical Society of Massachusetts, The Wilderness Campaign, May–June 1864, Papers, IV (Boston, 1905), 161–63; Jedediah Hotchkiss Journal, May 6, 1864 (MS in Jedediah Hotchkiss Papers, LC). That portion of the Hotchkiss Journal covering the period between March 10, 1862, and April 18, 1865, has been published in Archie P. MacDonald (ed.), Make Me a Map of the Valley: The Civil War Journal of Stonewall Jackson's Topographer (Dallas, 1973).

portion of the VI Corps. He believed that "the rout was complete" because his troops had crushed all opposition before them. In his official report, he boldly expressed his displeasure with his superiors' lack of aggressiveness. Gordon averred that "had the movement been made at an earlier hour and properly supported, each brigade being brought into action as its front was cleared, it would have resulted in a decided disaster to the whole right wing of Grant's army, if not in its entire disorganization." Whether Gordon's attack would have yielded greater results had it been launched earlier in the day has long been a point of controversy. Unquestionably, the attack shattered the unprotected flank, rolling up both Shaler's and Seymour's brigades and generating considerable confusion and concern in the Union army. However, as darkness fell and the Confederate lines of battle moved through the tangled Wilderness, the attack became confused. What was at first a relatively simple advance at right angles to entrenched works grew disjointed almost immediately. Johnston's brigade pushed too far to the left and failed to maintain contact with the Georgia regiments; and the Confederate line, across whose front Gordon's assault moved, fired upon his advancing column, disorganizing its right. The density of this woodland that helped hide Gordon's movement toward the flank also contributed mightily to the confusion that beset his attack. According to one historian, "[A]ny prolonged advance against opposition in this wooded land sooner or later brought crippling disorganization. Troops thus disorganized were largely at the mercy of any compact column of attack whose ranks had not yet been disordered by an hour of blind fighting in the overgrown ravines." As all sense of cohesion faded, so too did the effectiveness of the Confederate assault.[15]

The positive steps taken to resist any further movement by Gordon were equally important in limiting the results of his attack. Exaggerated tales of disaster and rumors of the disintegration of the Union right—including the capture of General Sedgwick, the seizure of the army's entire wagon train, and the advance of large bodies of Confederates down the Germanna Plank Road—reached Grant's headquarters almost immediately after Gordon launched his attack. Such reports undoubtedly generated considerable concern among the Union high command, but swift actions to counter the movement

15. OR, Vol. XXXVI, Pt. 1, pp. 1077–78; Gordon, Reminiscences, 250–55; Bruce Catton, Grant Takes Command (Boston, 1968), 196; Early, Narrative of the War, 349–50.

against the right were already being taken. Most official accounts indicate that despite the uncontrollable panic that seized the troops of Shaler and Seymour, adjoining commands and other elements of the VI Corps rapidly established a defensive line across Gordon's path of advance. Many of the officers occupying this new front reported that they met attacks after dark and successfully repulsed them. Clearly, Gordon's attack threw a large portion of the Union right into substantial confusion; still, the Georgian underestimated the ability of Grant's army to resist a continued assault. Considering the confusion that beset Gordon's advance, as well as the Federal movements to meet the threat, it appears that the Confederate attack—organized with only two brigades because of the limited manpower of Lee's army—achieved all that it could have even if it had been launched earlier in the day. Darkness ended the immediate threat to the Union flank, but Gordon's dusk attack nevertheless forced Grant to draw back both the VI and the V Corps lines and strengthen his right flank.[16]

Amid the reorganization and regrouping of commands during the night, Gordon narrowly escaped capture and possibly death. He and a courier, William Beasley, rode forward into the darkness to check on the placement of his picket line. Annoyed by the seemingly careless deployment of a body of men that he suspected were his troops, Gordon was preparing to administer a stern rebuke when his aide whispered, "General, these are not our men, they are Yankees." Gordon replied, "Nonsense, Beasley," but the courier's sincere persistence forced him to notice that the uniforms of the soldiers did indeed appear to be blue. The two Confederates reversed their direction and were moving away when a Union officer called upon them to halt. Willing to risk death to avoid certain capture, Gordon and Beasley swung out of their saddles and clung to the sides of their horses as they made a run for safety through the surrounding Federals. Fortunately for the men on horseback, the Yankees were so

16. OR, Vol. XXXVI, Pt. 1, pp. 2, 18, 666, 719, 723, 732, 737, 742; Horace Porter, *Campaigning with Grant* (New York, 1897), 68–70; Theodore Lyman, "Addenda to the Paper by Brevet Lieutenant-Colonel Swan on the Battle of the Wilderness," in Military Historical Society of Massachusetts, *Wilderness Campaign May–June 1864*, p. 170; Hazard Stevens, "The Sixth Corps in the Wilderness," in Military Historical Society of Massachusetts, *Wilderness Campaign May–June 1864*, p. 202; Thomas Hyde, *Following the Greek Cross* (Boston, 1895), 186–87; U. S. Grant, *Personal Memoirs of U. S. Grant* (2 vols.; New York, 1885), II, 202; Humphreys, *Virginia Campaign*, 49–51; OR, Vol. XXXVI, Pt. 1, p. 926, Pt. 2, pp. 438, 448, 454, 455, 465.

closely bunched that it was almost impossible for them to fire at the Confederates without hitting their own men. A confused and scattered Union volley missed both the riders and their horses as they galloped away into the darkness. What had begun as "a cautious ride to the front" ended with "a madcap ride to the rear."[17]

The morning of May 7 revealed to the Confederates just how shatteringly effective Gordon's attack had been. At Lee's request, Gordon joined the commanding general in a ride over the field of the previous night's action. Large numbers of haversacks, knapsacks and muskets, discarded in precipitate flight, lay strewn about the field with more than four hundred Federal dead. Years later, Gordon recalled that Lee, speaking freely as they rode about, commended him for the vigilance and skill he had displayed the day before. Although Lee's biographer may be correct in questioning Gordon's memory of exactly what was discussed on this ride, Lee's actions the following day made clear one indisputable fact: Lee thought very highly of the young brigadier's actions in the Wilderness.[18]

On the evening of May 7, Gordon began his march to Spotsylvania Court House—Grant's next objective after pulling away from the Wilderness front—as a brigade commander. But when he arrived there, he was given command of Early's division, a temporary elevation resulting from a series of command manipulations that were accomplished by General Lee with skill and tact. A. P. Hill's illness had incapacitated him and forced Early's assignment as temporary III Corps commander. As the senior brigadier in Early's division, Harry Hays was by regulation the officer who should have assumed command. Instead, Lee raised Gordon to divisional command and added to Hays's prestige by consolidating his command with the Louisiana brigade of the late Brigadier General Leroy Stafford and placing it in Johnson's division. To replace Hays's brigade, Lee transferred R. D. Johnston's brigade from Rodes's division. Douglas Southall Freeman offered an insightful assessment of these shifts in command when he wrote, "[O]ld soldiers might have asked themselves whether so many changes ever had been made by Army Headquarters to give a Brigadier

17. Gordon, *Reminiscences*, 263–66; E. A. Pollard [A Distinguished Southern Journalist], *The Early Life, Campaigns and Public Services of Robert E. Lee, with a Record of the Campaigns and Heroic Deeds of his Companions in Arms* (New York, 1871), 544; Gordon to Lee, December 20, 1867, in Lee Headquarters Papers; Hudgins, "38th Georgia."

18. *OR*, Vol. XXXVI, Pt. 1, pp. 1077–78; Dunlop, *Lee's Sharpshooters*, 415; Gordon, *Reminiscences*, 267–70; Freeman, *R. E. Lee*, III, 302.

General a Division." Due to his "brilliant services" of May 5 and the vigilance and aggressiveness that he displayed the following day, Gordon's star was clearly on the rise as the armies shifted to the south.[19]

Arriving at Spotsylvania Court House on the afternoon of May 8, Gordon's division assumed the role of general reserve for the II Corps. Ewell's corps occupied "an awkward and irregular salient" north of the Court House, which the troops soon dubbed the Mule Shoe. Defense of such a prominent bulge might prove difficult, but the Confederates entrenched along this line in order to take advantage of the high ground that it covered. Rodes's division manned the western face of this roughly semicircular line, and Johnson's division controlled the northern and eastern sides. Gordon placed his three brigades in the rear of these commands and established a line running approximately east and west across the salient, forming the bar of the letter A. By positioning his men nearly equidistant from all the front-line works in the salient, Gordon conformed to his orders to be able to move "to support any portion of the line around the long salient which might be attacked."[20]

Late in the afternoon of May 10, a serious breach of the Confederate line occurred when Colonel Emory Upton of the Union VI Corps led a brilliant assault that penetrated Rodes's works. Upon hearing the sounds of the attack, Gordon rapidly moved his command toward the critical area. He deployed his leading brigade across the path of the enemy advance and ordered an immediate charge. With the help of adjoining elements of the II Corps on both right and left, Gordon forced the Federals out of the captured trenches and again secured the front. Lack of proper support guaranteed the eventual containment of Upton's attack, but Gordon's prompt action rapidly restored the Confederate line.[21]

Following the repulse of this attack, Gordon withdrew two of his brigades behind the incomplete line of works midway up the salient, slightly in front of the Harrison House. Fearing another attack on the

19. Early, *Narrative of the War*, 351; *OR*, Vol. XXXVI, Pt. 1, pp. 1071, 1078, Pt. 2, p. 974; Vol. LI, Pt. 2, pp. 902–903, 890; Freeman, *Lee's Lieutenants*, III, 391.

20. Freeman, *Lee's Lieutenants*, III, 394; *OR*, Vol. XXXVI, Pt. 1, pp. 1071–72, 1078; Gordon, *Reminiscences*, 272; Humphreys, *Virginia Campaign*, 66, 73–74; Gordon to Charles S. Venable, November 24, 1878, in Charles Scott Venable Papers, VHS.

21. Gordon, *Reminiscences*, 272–73; *OR*, Vol. XXXVI, Pt. 1, pp. 668, 1072, 1078; Dunlop, *Lee's Sharpshooters*, 446–47; C. S. Venable, "The Campaign from the Wilderness to Petersburg," *SHSP*, XIV (1886), 528; Humphreys, *Virginia Campaign*, 83–87.

# Battle of
# SPOTSYLVANIA COURT HOUSE

May 10 & 12, 1864

The Command of

**Brigadier General John B. Gordon**

BATTLE OF MAY 12, 1864

HANCOCK
II Corps

NY RIVER

East Angle

Bloody Angle

Rodes

Johnson

McCoull
House

MULE SHOE SALIENT

Gordon ③

Harrison
House

new trenches

④

BROCK ROAD

N

Upton

MULE SHOE
SALIENT

Rodes

Johnson

②

Gordon

①

Brock Road

BATTLE OF MAY 10, 1864

Scale

0                1/4 mile

▬▬▬  Confederate Forces
☐☐☐  Union Forces
▓▓▓  Union Attack

MAY 10, 1864

① Gordon positions his men as reserves.

② The reserves under Gordon promptly advance to
repel Upton's attack on the Mule Shoe salient.

MAY 12, 1864

③ Union forces break through the Confederate defenses
at the Mule Shoe. Gordon again summons his troops
to check the enemy. The command of Gordon helps
hold the salient until new fortifications are built at
the base of the Mule Shoe.

④ Gordon withdraws to the new trenches after midnight.

Gary Lee Hall 1988

northern part of the salient, he moved his other brigade—his old command, now under Colonel Clement A. Evans—to the rear of Rodes's right and Johnson's left, just in front of the McCoull House. Gordon's troops remained in these positions throughout May 11, as a hard daylong rain discouraged any major action; nevertheless, rumors of attack at various points along the salient abounded. Late that evening he received information from Johnson that the enemy seemed to be massing on his front and that an attack at dawn appeared certain. To meet this threat, Gordon advanced Pegram's brigade, now commanded by Colonel John S. Hoffman, to support Johnson, who placed the troops in the rear of his division's left flank, near Evans' brigade. As a cold drizzle continued on into the dreary predawn darkness of May 12, many of Gordon's men found sleep impossible, for, as one soldier remarked, "there was a nameless something in the air which told each man that a crisis was at hand."[22]

Just before dawn, at about 4:30 A.M., Major General Winfield S. Hancock's II Corps attacked Johnson's front, hitting the apex of the salient and completely crushing its defenders. Spreading quickly to the left and to the right, Hancock's men captured or disabled nearly all of Johnson's division in a matter of minutes. Resistance along the front lines "was so slight that no time was afforded for bringing into position the supporting force." Gordon, alerted by the initial firing and alarmed by the sudden silence thereafter, began moving up the salient without waiting for orders. Advancing at the head of his only remaining brigade, R. D. Johnston's North Carolinians, Gordon found visual observation of troops more than a few score yards ahead impossible owing to the darkness, heavy mist, and dense undergrowth. He had moved only a short distance beyond the McCoull House when he struck the Federal line; Hancock's assault had been delivered so quickly and so silently that Gordon's first indication of serious trouble came in the form of a volley from unseen Union troops. This "sudden and unexpected blaze from Hancock's rifles" seriously wounded Johnston and drove in his advance elements.[23]

22. Humphreys, *Virginia Campaign*, 96; *OR*, Vol. XXXVI, Pt. 1, pp. 1072, 1078, 1079–80; Gordon, *Reminiscences*, 274; J. Catlett Gibson, "The Battle of Spotsylvania Courthouse on May 12, 1864," *SHSP*, XXXII (1904), 200; William W. Smith, "The Battle of Spotsylvania Courthouse, May 12, 1864," *SHSP*, XXXII (1904), 210; Venable, "Campaign from the Wilderness to Petersburg," 529; M. S. Stringfellow, "The Bloody Angle," *SHSP*, XXI (1893), 245; Hotchkiss Journal, May 11, 1864; Robert Hunter, "Major-General Johnson at Spotsylvania," *SHSP*, XXXIII (1905), 336–38.

23. Hunter, "Johnson at Spotsylvania," 338–39; Humphreys, *Virginia Campaign*, 92–93; *OR*, Vol. XXXVI, Pt. 1, pp. 335, 358–59, 1072, 1078–79, 1080; Gordon, *Remi-*

Although still uncertain as to what had happened at the front, Gordon moved "with that splendid audacity which characterized him." He deployed Johnston's entire brigade as a long skirmish line and ordered it forward, in the hope that the daring charge would confuse the enemy and allow him time to "find out more of the situation." The North Carolinians were almost instantly over-whelmed by the advancing Federals, who overlapped both their flanks. As Johnston's men fell back, Gordon began to perceive the true nature of the impending disaster: Lee's army was being cut in two. With an entire division *hors de combat* and a large portion of the Union army pouring into the void, the very existence of the Army of Northern Virginia hung in the balance. Should the Federals succeed in maintaining the huge gap in the center of the Confederate line and continue to throw in reinforcements, Lee could be defeated in detail.[24]

The extraordinary gravity of the situation forced the immediate recall of Gordon's two detached brigades. The Federals, stunned by the unexpected advance of Johnston's brigade and confused by the semidarkness that concealed the weakness of Gordon's forces, halted, but only momentarily. As soon as Evans' brigade rejoined him near the McCoull House, Gordon sent three regiments forward to check the enemy. This bold action of once again throwing forth a thin line bought Gordon the time he needed for Pegram's brigade to re-turn. While his troops fell back to the works near the Harrison House in order to form a line of battle, Gordon rode forward to locate the exact position of the Federals but was still unable to see any consider-able distance due to the denseness of the fog. Only by ascertaining the direction from which the storm of bullets came could he determine the location of the enemy. A lively Union fire informed him that the Federals had moved far beyond his right and were continuing to advance.[25]

*niscences*, 274–76; Gordon to Venable, November 24, 1878, in Venable Papers; Venable, "Campaign from the Wilderness to Petersburg," 529.

24. Venable, "Campaign from the Wilderness to Petersburg," 529–30; Dunlop, *Lee's Sharpshooters*, 462; Gordon to Venable, November 24, 1878, in Venable Papers; *OR*, Vol. XXXVI, Pt. 1, pp. 1072, 1078–79; Humphreys, *Virginia Campaign*, 96; Gordon, *Reminiscences*, 276–78.

25. Gordon, *Reminiscences*, 277; Francis A. Walker, *History of the Second Army Corps* (New York, 1886), 472; Gibson, "Spotsylvania Courthouse," 201; Smith, "Spotsylvania Courthouse," 210–11; *OR*, Vol. XXXVI, Pt. 1, p. 1079; Humphreys, *Virginia Campaign*, 96; Dunlop, *Lee's Sharpshooters*, 462; Hunter, "Johnson at Spotsylvania," 339; W. W. Old, "Trees Whittled Down at the Horseshoe," *SHSP*, XXXIII (1905), 18.

As Gordon moved about, he was struck by a Minié ball that passed through the back of his coat just above his sword belt, barely missing his spine. When a concerned aide anxiously asked whether Gordon had been hit, the ramrod Georgian answered in his best martial manner, " 'No, but suppose my back had been in a bow like yours? Don't you see that the bullet would have gone straight through my spine? Sit up or you'll be killed.' " The young aide's straightening of his posture with a sudden jerk "probably brought a smile to Gordon's soldierly face, but the imminence of disaster left no room for banter."[26]

Gordon quickly returned to his men and found their deployment almost completed. He then prepared himself to lead the charge that might well decide the fate of the Confederacy. Riding down his line of battle, he met General Lee, whose manifest concern over the lack of information had brought him to the front. Gordon explained his plan of action; the concerned commanding general readily assented and ordered him to proceed. As he started away to complete the dressing of his line, Gordon noticed that Lee was riding to the center of the line. With hat in hand, Lee obviously intended to join the division's desperate charge. Gordon swiftly dashed back, crossing Traveller's path. Sensing his commander's stern resolve and deeply concerned by the increase in the intensity of fire from the approaching enemy, he appealed to the one source of influence that could compel Lee's immediate withdrawal. With his voice pitched above the roar of battle so that his men might hear, Gordon spoke more to them than to their commander when he shouted, "General Lee, this is no place for you. These men behind you are Georgians and Virginians. They have never failed you and will not fail you here. Will you boys?" Gordon's men, almost in unison, cried, "No, no, no; we'll not fail him," and took up the "Lee to the rear" chant that had been raised once before that week. Gordon seized Lee's bridle, turned the horse to the rear, and ordered two men to take Lee back. As others swarmed around Lee and led him away, the enemy crept to within sixty yards of the Confederate line. Gordon, knowing that the "hour of destiny" had arrived, rose up in his stirrups and roared, "Forward!"[27]

26. Stringfellow, "Bloody Angle," 246; Gordon, *Reminiscences*, 277; Freeman, *Lee's Lieutenants*, III, 405.

27. There are numerous versions of this "Lee to the rear" episode. Freeman considered W. W. Smith's account ("Spotsylvania Courthouse," 212) to be the most reliable, owing to the author's youth and closeness to the scene (Freeman, *R. E. Lee*, III, 319n). I believe Freeman was correct in his judgment, especially since Gordon's 1878

Gordon led his grimly determined men into "the center of a fire from hell itself." Carrying the colors and advancing at the head of his troops, Gordon was, remembered one of his soldiers, the "most superb looking soldier he ever saw." Even though his line, with Evans on the left and Pegram on the right, proved too short to span the width of the Mule Shoe, he drove his men onward. Inspired by Lee's presence and the Georgian's eloquent, impassioned appeal to their pride, Gordon's troops charged headlong up the right side of the salient with an almost irresistible fury. Despite desperate fighting, they steadily drove back the Union forces in their front and, with the aid of III Corps, forced the Federals completely out of the eastern portion of the salient. Some of Gordon's men even continued their spirited advance a quarter of a mile past the original lines before halting.[28]

While Gordon struggled to gain control of the trenches to the right of the apex, other elements of the II Corps on his left fought their way up the salient and succeeded in evicting the enemy from the western and northwestern trenches. Only the east and west angles at the apex of the salient, where there was a slight bend in the works a few

letter supports essentially the same wording and sequence of events (Gordon to Venable, November 24, 1878, in Venable Papers). Other accounts may be found in Gordon, *Reminiscences*, 278–80; J. William Jones, "General Lee to the Rear," *SHSP*, VIII (1880), 31–36; Charles S. Venable, "General Lee to the Rear," *SHSP*, VIII (1880), 105–10; W. W. Smith, "General Lee to the Rear," *SHSP*, VIII (1880), 562–66; Venable, "Campaign from the Wilderness to Petersburg," 530; Stringfellow, "Bloody Angle," 246–47; W. L. Goldsmith and R. D. Funkerhouser, "General Lee to the Rear," *SHSP*, XXIV (1896), 79–82; Gibson, "Spotsylvania Courthouse," 201–204; Felix Gregory DeFontaine [Personne] *Marginalia: or Gleanings from an Army Notebook* (Columbia, S.C., 1864), 229–30; John H. Worsham, *One of Jackson's Foot Cavalry* (New York, 1912), 214; Clement A. Evans (ed.), *Confederate Military History* (12 vols.; Atlanta, 1899), III, 451–52. Two other accounts of the action on May 12 involving Lee and Gordon, which wrongly identify it as taking place on May 10, are A. L. Long, *Memoirs of Robert E. Lee* (New York, 1886), 338, and Henry A. White, "Lee's Wrestle with Grant in the Wilderness 1864," in Military Historical Society of Massachusetts, *Wilderness Campaign May–June 1864*, p. 62. Despite minor discrepancies between all these accounts, the differences are not that important, for all agree on the basic story line. My narration draws heavily from Gordon's 1878 letter but can most accurately be described as a composite sketch.

28. Dunlop, *Lee's Sharpshooters*, 463–64; G. Moxley Sorrel, *Recollections of a Confederate Staff Officer*, ed. Bell Irvin Wiley (Jackson, Tenn., 1958), 242; Gordon to Venable, November 24, 1878, in Venable Papers; Stringfellow, "Bloody Angle," 246–50; Venable, "Campaign from the Wilderness to Petersburg," 530; Law, "Wilderness to Cold Harbor," 132; Gibson, "Spotsylvania Courthouse," 204–205; Smith, "Spotsylvania Courthouse," 212–13; Gordon, *Reminiscences*, 280–82; *OR*, Vol. XXXVI, Pt. I, pp. 336, 1072, 1079; Early, *Narrative of the War*, 355; H. A. White, "Lee's Wrestle with Grant," 64; Humphreys, *Virginia Campaign*, 96.

hundred yards long, remained in Union hands. Repeated assaults by both Federals and Confederates failed to dislodge either force from its holdings. At the west angle, some of the most severe and brutal fighting of the war took place. In the rain and mud, this struggle at the Bloody Angle raged throughout the day and night of May 12 and on into the early morning hours of the following day. Confederates all along the front of the salient were forced to continue their resistance until a new set of works could be constructed in the rear. Evans' and Pegram's brigades remained in line, holding the east face of the Mule Shoe, while Johnston's brigade and the remnants of Johnson's division, who had been placed under Gordon's command, labored on the new fortifications. Not until 3 A.M., May 13, did the exhausted Confederate troops withdraw to the new line spanning the base of the salient.[29]

Immediately after the titanic struggle at the Bloody Angle, Lee took steps to reward the man whose actions "in the estimation of many [gave] an additional lease of 12 months to the life of the Confederacy." On May 13, the commanding general telegraphed President Jefferson Davis requesting Gordon's promotion to major general with the commission to date from May 12, 1864. In spite of Lee's wish to recognize Gordon's outstanding services in this distinctive manner, "lack of consideration in Richmond" resulted in his commission being dated May 14, 1864, rather than the day of his invaluable actions. Gordon's conduct on that most critical morning had indeed been brilliant. His recall and deployment of his dispersed troops were effected quickly and always toward the correct end. Rather than passively awaiting the Union assault, he boldly and aggressively led his small command into the area where it was most needed. His skillful use of Lee's attempt to lead his charge, coupled with his own courage and "dauntless intrepidity," inspired Gordon's men to new heights of determination that enabled them to throw many of the Union forces out of the salient in only one hour's time. Gordon and his troops, though outnumbered, acted "with extraordinary valor equalizing ev-

29. Humphreys, *Virginia Campaign*, 96–101; Law, "Wilderness to Cold Harbor," 132–34; Walker, *Second Corps*, 466, 493; *OR*, Vol. XXXVI, Pt. 1, pp. 336–37, 359–60, 1072–73, 1079, 1094; Venable, "Campaign from the Wilderness to Petersburg," 530; Smith, "Spotsylvania Courthouse," 213–14; Hotchkiss Journal, May 12, 1864; Gordon, *Reminiscences*, 282–86; H. A. White, "Lee's Wrestle with Grant," 66; Venable, "Lee to the Rear," 107; Evans (ed.), *Confederate Military History*, III, 452–54; Gordon to Venable, November 24, 1878, in Venable Papers; John O. Casler, *Four Years in the Stonewall Brigade* (Girard, Kans., 1906), 212–14; Hunter, "Johnson at Spotsylvania," 339–40.

erything else." Bold, aggressive, courageous, hard-hitting—the Georgian had truly performed well during his first days as a division commander.[30]

The five days following the fight at the salient—May 13 to May 17—proved uneventful, but on the morning of May 18, the Army of the Potomac renewed its offensive by again attacking over Hell's Half Acre. Moving over the same ground where the terrible fighting of May 12 had occurred, the Federal advance encountered the new Confederate line that Gordon's troops had helped construct. Gordon, still temporarily in command of Early's division and the survivors from Johnson's division, held the right of the II Corps. His entire position was well concealed by forest, completely covered by artillery and musketry, and strongly entrenched with abatis. Consequently, when the Federals attacked, they met a withering fire and were easily and bloodily repulsed. The next day, Gordon participated in Ewell's mishandled reconnaissance in force but managed to escape without heavy casualties. He remained in command of Early's division until May 21, when A. P. Hill resumed his duties at the head of the III Corps, thus freeing Early to return to his division. Then, in order to give Gordon a command commensurate with his grade, Lee transferred Gordon's old brigade to Johnson's decimated division and placed the new major general in charge.[31]

While Gordon was earning his promotion in the desperate struggles around Spotsylvania Court House, his wife penned a letter that revealed a frightening understanding of the Union army's new-found tenacity. "The enemy is so obstinate. . . . He will never give up as long as he can get fresh troops to fight with." Despite increasingly gloomy reports, Fanny took heart in the realization that the "battle is not always to the strong," and continued to believe that God would deliver the Confederacy from the travails of its birth. "Surely there

30. John S. Lewis to General Trousdale, June 13, 1865, in William Trousdale Papers, TSLA; Gordon's Service File, in Military Service Records, NA; Military Records of John B. Gordon, in ADAH; Gordon to Venable, November 24, 1878, in Venable Papers; OR, Vol. LI, Pt. 2, p. 926; Henry Kyd Douglas, I Rode with Stonewall (Chapel Hill, 1940), 282; Venable, "Campaign from the Wilderness to Petersburg," 533; Captain Vaughan Sawyer, Grant's Campaign in Virginia, 1864 (New York, 1908), 81–82.

31. Porter, Campaigning with Grant, 122–23; Gordon, Reminiscences, 288–90; OR, Vol. XXXVI, Pt. 1, pp. 337–38, 361–62, 1073, 1082–83, Pt. 3, pp. 813–14; Humphreys, Virginia Campaign, 110–14; Hotchkiss Journal, May 13–19, 1864; Colonel W. E. Cutshaw, "The Battle near Spotsylvania Courthouse on May 18, 1864," SHSP, XXXIII (1905), 332–34; Stephen Dodson Ramseur to wife, May 30, 1864, in Stephen Dodson Ramseur Papers, SHC; Douglas, I Rode with Stonewall, 282–83; Early, Narrative of the War, 358–59.

are still righteous enough in the land for whose sake God will spare it. . . . May God bring her safely through, & O may He stay the flowing blood." Even as Fanny wrote, the sounds of artillery fire reached her. Fearful for her husband's safety, she repeated her constant prayer that the Holy Spirit would always abide in John's heart and that "His protecting wings may be spread over you & around you & that in the hour of battle you may be unharmed." Fanny knew well the horrors of war. During the previous week's fighting, she had often visited with and ministered to her husband's wounded. They were "extravegant [sic] in their expressions of admiration & love" for Gordon, and upon discovering that she was the wife of their commander, "they raised a tremendous shout" in her honor. The uncertainties of combat brought danger, but Fanny endeavored to remain as close as possible to John as the two armies moved nearer to Richmond.[32]

Gordon, though constantly active during the final days of May, saw little significant action until early June, at Cold Harbor. His command moved with the Army of Northern Virginia as it repeatedly countered Federal movements around its right flank—first at the North Anna River, then at Totopotomoy Creek, and finally near Cold Harbor. Following the bloody repulse of Grant's forces there, Gordon continued to hold his troops in a state of readiness but engaged in only minor skirmishing during the next ten days as room for maneuver north of the James dwindled. Being so close to Richmond, he did, however, avail himself of every opportunity to write or to see Fanny, who was boarding in the capital city. Although troubled by the bad news pouring in from the Shenandoah Valley—where a Federal force under Major General David Hunter had gained control of nearly the entire length of the valley—Gordon told his wife to take heart because "we will drive them back I hope in a few days." His presumption that troops would soon be detached from Lee's army to deal with this threat was borne out on June 12, when word reached Richmond that Hunter had occupied Lexington, Virginia, the day before. Convinced that he must strike Hunter immediately, Lee ordered the entire II Corps to prepare to move as quickly as possible. Gordon, perhaps the brightest star emerging from the devastation of the spring of 1864, was headed for the valley.[33]

32. Fanny to her husband, May 15, 1864, in Fanny Haralson (Mrs. John B.) Gordon Letters, AC. 68-432, GDAH.

33. Early, *Narrative of the War*, 361–64; Freeman, *Lee's Lieutenants*, III, 496–508, 523–24; Gordon to wife, June 3, 7, 8, 11, 1864, all in Gordon Family Collection, UGA; *OR*, Vol. XLIII, Pt. 1, p. 1018; Vol. XXXVII, Pt. 1, p. 346.

# V · In the Valley

Early on June 13, 1864, Gordon and the rest of Jackson's old corps began moving toward the Shenandoah Valley. Lee ordered Jubal Early, the new commander of the II Corps, to drive back the advancing Union force under David Hunter, destroying it if possible, and then to continue down the valley with the intention of menacing Washington. Marching first to Charlottesville and then moving by train to Lynchburg, Early's command arrived there too late to strike Hunter, who had hastily retreated "beyond the mountains toward the Ohio." Discontinuing his rapid pursuit, Early began a slow advance down the valley, gathering supplies and preparing his men for the rigors of another northern invasion. While in the valley, Early temporarily assigned Gordon's division to Major General John C. Breckinridge's command, in order to provide the Kentuckian with a force befitting his rank; the move was primarily for the sake of appearance, however, for Gordon continued under Early's overall command. By the first week in July, Early's small army, including his corps and Breckinridge's so-called corps, had crossed the Potomac and moved into Maryland.[1]

1. John H. Worsham, *One of Jackson's Foot Cavalry* (New York, 1912), 227–28; *OR*, Vol. XXXVI, Pt. 3, pp. 873–74; Vol. XXXVII, Pt. 1, pp. 346, 768; Vol. LI, Pt. 2, pp. 1028–29; John B. Gordon, *Reminiscences of the Civil War* (New York, 1903), 300–301, 309; Jubal Anderson Early, *Autobiographical Sketch and Narrative of the War Between the States* (Philadelphia, 1912), 371–86, hereinafter cited as *Narrative of the War*; Gordon's Report, July 22, 1864, in Robert Edward Lee Headquarters Papers, VHS.

The Diary of Captain W. W. Old, aide-de-camp to General Early, June 13, 1864, to August 12, 1864 (MS in Jubal Anderson Early Papers, LC), provides a brief sketch of Early's actions during this two-month period. A similarly succinct report of II Corps operations between May 3 and November 14, 1864, by Jedediah Hotchkiss, can be found in *OR*, Vol. XLIII, Pt. 1, pp. 1015–32. The best accounts of Early's Corps in 1864,

IN THE VALLEY · 83

After passing through Frederick on the morning of July 9, Early discovered a small Union force under Major General Lew Wallace blocking his advance near Monocacy Junction. Finding the Federals "strongly posted" behind the eastern bank of the Monocacy River and uncertain of how to proceed, Early paused to reconnoiter. As he examined the enemy's position, Brigadier General John McCausland's cavalry command forded the river about one mile below the Georgetown pike bridge and assailed the Federal left flank. This move resolved Early's dilemma; he ordered Breckinridge's nearest infantry division to cross at the same ford and move to support the cavalry's flanking movement.[2]

Gordon had reached the Monocacy about midday and had ordered his division "to stack arms and rest" while long-range probing took place. Stretched out on a hill overlooking McCausland's action, Gordon's men were enjoying their unique opportunity "to *look* at a battle" when a courier galloped up to their commander. Gordon read Early's message and immediately swung into action, ordering his division to take arms and cross the river. While his men scrambled up the Monocacy's slippery banks, he rode ahead to inspect the enemy's defensive arrangements. He found a Federal line running along a ridge some seven hundred yards away and a second one in the narrow valley just behind the first line. Gordon also observed that the fields through which he would have to advance were laced with "strong farm fences . . . [and] thickly studded with huge grainstacks . . . so broad and high and close together that no line of battle could possibly be maintained while he advanced through them."[3]

Nonetheless, placing Evans' brigade on the right, Zebulon York's brigade on the left, and holding William Terry's brigade in reserve, Gordon began his advance, moving en echelon from the right. Despite the temporary confusion wrought by heavy enemy fire and the obstacles in the fields, Gordon's men broke the first Union line and drove it back on the second. Halting only momentarily, the Confederates again advanced and, after a short but desperate struggle, suc-

---

however, are found in Jedediah Hotchkiss Journal (MS in Jedediah Hotchkiss Papers, LC), and Early, *Narrative of the War*, 371–458. Hotchkiss' Journal for the period August 4–December 31, 1864, is reprinted in *OR*, Vol. XLIII, Pt. I, pp. 567–88.

2. Gordon's Report, July 22, 1864; Early, *Narrative of the War*, 386–87; *OR*, Vol. XXXVII, Pt. I, pp. 347–48.

3. *OR*, Vol. XXXVII, Pt. I, pp. 350–51; Worsham, *One of Jackson's Foot Cavalry*, 235–36; Gordon, *Reminiscences*, 309–11.

ceeded in dislodging the Federals from their second position. In his official report, Gordon wrote, "So profuse was the flow of blood from the killed and wounded of both these forces that it reddened the stream for more than 100 yards below." Still, he drove his men onward.[4]

Pressing his advance, Gordon encountered a third Federal line, one longer and stronger than either of the first two. Increasingly obstinate resistance on his front and a galling fire upon his left flank forced him to commit his reserve brigade. Terry's Virginians moved to the left and quickly disposed of the Yankees nearest the river. Despite this success on the left, Gordon's other two brigades, weakened by their previous assaults, were still unable to make any headway against the enemy line. Realizing that reinforcements were necessary, Gordon called for another brigade but learned it would not arrive for some time. He resolved to continue the attack with the troops at hand and ordered Terry to change front to the right and move against the Federal right while Evans and York applied pressure to the front.[5]

When the head of Terry's column reached the top of the hill from which they would launch their attack, they found a solitary figure awaiting them. "There was Gordon," remembered one soldier, "sitting on his horse as quietly as if nothing was going on, wearing his old red shirt, the sleeves pulled up a little, the only indication that he was ready for a fight." He hurried his men into position as a new Federal line advanced toward them. When the Virginians caught sight of the approaching Yankees, they surged forward yelling, "At them, boys!" Gordon, however, restrained his troops and admonished them, "Keep quiet, we'll have our time presently!"[6]

After ordering his men to pull down a portion of a fence in his front, Gordon led them through the opening. He wanted to hold the Virginians back until a regular battle line could be formed, but when about one hundred of them had passed through the fence, a cry of "'Charge them! Charge them!'" rose. "It was useless for General Gordon to try and stop it now,—nothing but a shot through each man could have done it." Raising a chilling "rebel yell," Gordon's frenzied men charged forward and sent the enemy reeling back. When the rest of the brigade came up and was fully deployed, Gordon pushed on. With Terry's rolling up of the Federal right flank and the increased frontal

4. Gordon, *Reminiscences*, 311–12; *OR*, Vol. XXXVII, Pt. 1, pp. 351–52.
5. *OR*, Vol. XXXVII, Pt. 1, p. 351; Worsham, *One of Jackson's Foot Cavalry*, 237.
6. Worsham, *One of Jackson's Foot Cavalry*, 237–38.

pressure from Evans and York, the entire Federal line soon collapsed and the retreat degenerated into a complete rout. Cheered on and quickly joined by Confederates from the opposite side of the Monocacy, Gordon's men pursued the retreating Federals until Early sent word that no more prisoners should be taken; he simply did not know what to do with them all. For at least one of Gordon's men, it was "the most exciting time I witnessed during the war."[7]

Gordon had won a hard-fought victory. Fighting exclusively with his unsupported division, he had faced a major portion of Wallace's force and, in what he asserted was "one of the severest [battles] ever fought" by his troops, had routed the Federals. When Breckinridge found the Georgian after the battle, he exclaimed, "Gordon, if you had never made a fight before, this ought to immortalize you." As gratifying as such personal praise may have been, Gordon was distressed by his heavy losses at Monocacy. His division disabled almost seven hundred Federals and captured a similar number but at a cost of nearly seven hundred of its own—about one-third of Gordon's command. Numbered among the wounded Confederates were Clement Evans, the division's senior brigadier, and Gordon's brother Eugene, whose severe wound near the elbow threatened the loss of his right arm and possibly his life. Even more unsettling was the fall of his close friend Colonel J. H. Lamar of the 61st Georgia, whose death Gordon called "one of the saddest events to me of the war." Despite personal grief, Gordon devoted himself to the task at hand. Washington lay less than forty miles to the southeast and, as a consequence of his actions on July 9, the road to the Federal capital lay open to the invading Confederates.[8]

A day and a half of rapid marching brought Early's army closer to the national capital than any armed Confederates had ever been before. His advance elements reached the defenses of Washington shortly after noon on July 11. Early immediately ordered the formation of a battle line and prepared to attack, but it soon became obvious

7. *Ibid.*, 238–40; *OR*, Vol. XXXVII, Pt. 1, pp. 348, 351–52; Early, *Narrative of the War*, 388.
8. Early, *Narrative of the War*, 388; Gordon to Lee, February 6, 1868, in Lee Headquarters Papers; Gordon to wife, July 11, 1864, in Gordon Family Collection, UGA; Worsham, *One of Jackson's Foot Cavalry*, 240; E. A. Pollard [A Distinguished Southern Journalist], *The Early Life, Campaigns and Public Services of Robert E. Lee, with a Record of the Campaigns and Heroic Deeds of his Companions in Arms* (New York, 1871), 545, hereinafter cited as *Companions in Arms*; *OR*, Vol. XXXVII, Pt. 1, pp. 199–202, 348, 352; Gordon, *Reminiscences*, 312–13.

that the oppressive heat and choking dust of his two-day forced march had taken a heavy toll. Over two-thirds of his weary men were still straggling toward the front as the afternoon slipped away. Although convinced that the city could have been taken by the first Confederates who arrived, Gordon must nonetheless have concurred with Early's decision to halt and reconnoiter, especially in view of the condition of his men. Gordon's division "was stretched out almost like skirmishers, and all the men did not get up until night." That evening, Early conferred with his division commanders—Breckinridge, Rodes, Ramseur, and Gordon—at his headquarters in the home of Postmaster General Francis P. Blair to determine how best to proceed. A decision had to be reached quickly, for other Federal forces had already begun to close in on the Confederates' rear. All agreed they had come too far and were too close to the Union capital to retreat without a fight. Despite the exceedingly formidable fortifications facing them, they decided to attack at dawn.[9]

Daylight of July 12, however, revealed the Federal works bristling with newly arrived reinforcements. Any attack, even if successful, would prove prohibitively expensive. Stripped of alternatives, Early spent the day skirmishing in front of Washington and began quietly withdrawing after sunset. Moving as swiftly in retreat as it had in advance, Early's force crossed the Potomac and reentered Virginia on July 14. The remainder of the summer was consumed in "marching and countermarching toward every point of the compass in the Shenandoah Valley, with scarcely a day of rest, skirmishing, fighting, rushing hither and thither to meet and drive back cavalry raids."[10]

The seemingly endless routine of marching and fighting wore heavily upon discipline in Gordon's division. Heavy casualties, particularly in Evans' brigade, added to the problem, but in all probability, the most important factor contributing to lax discipline grew

9. Gordon, *Reminiscences*, 314–15; Early, *Narrative of the War*, 389–92; Hotchkiss Journal, July 10–11, 1864; Worsham, *One of Jackson's Foot Cavalry*, 241; Gordon to wife, July 11, 13, 1864, both in Gordon Family Collection, UGA; *OR*, Vol. XXXVII, Pt. 1, p. 348; Vol. XLIII, Pt. 1, p. 1021; Henry Kyd Douglas, *I Rode with Stonewall* (Chapel Hill, 1940), 294–95.

10. Early, *Narrative of the War*, 392–419; *OR*, Vol. XXXVII, Pt. 1, p. 348; Vol. XLIII, Pt. 1, p. 1021; Worsham, *One of Jackson's Foot Cavalry*, 242; Clement A. Evans (ed.), *Confederate Military History* (12 vols.; Atlanta, 1899), III, 482–84; Hotchkiss Journal, July 12-September 18, 1864, Douglas, *I Rode with Stonewall*, 295–96; Gordon, *Reminiscences*, 317.

out of the May reorganization of those units that formerly made up Johnson's division. York's Louisiana brigade incorporated what an inspector-general called "the discordant fragments of Hays's and Stafford's brigades." The fourteen Virginia regiments that prior to May 12 had comprised three famed fighting units—Steuart's, Jones's, and the Stonewall brigades—had been lumped together and placed under the command of Terry. In each case, "both officers and men bitterly object[ed] to their consolidation into one brigade," preferring to retain their old designations. Strange troops serving under strange commanders could be overcome, but the fierce pride and intense *esprit de corps* of the long-famous brigades seriously complicated matters. Although merely the inheritor of the problem, Gordon certainly labored tirelessly to correct it, for even as the inspector filed his critical report, he noted improvement. Perhaps more important than the conduct of Gordon's division in camp was its performance in battle, and it was stated that in every engagement, "in spite of all defects, the division has fought with conspicuous gallantry and constant success." Even under unfavorable conditions, Gordon demanded and received the utmost from the troops he commanded.[11]

As summer turned to autumn, Gordon and the rest of Early's army continued to maneuver and fight throughout the Shenandoah Valley, effectively holding the more numerous Union forces at bay.[12] Although generally engaged with cavalry, Gordon knew that the Federal infantry in the valley, now under the command of Major General Philip H. Sheridan, was merely biding its time. As the Union force gathered supplies and added to its numbers, Sheridan planned his campaign and waited to strike when success would be certain. At dawn on the morning of September 19, Sheridan's entire force began crossing Opequon Creek and moving on Winchester. While Ramseur's division struggled valiantly to hold Sheridan's main body at bay a few miles east of the town, Early ordered a rapid reconcentration of his dispersed command. Gordon, marching from Stephenson's

11. *OR*, Vol. XLIII, Pt. 1, pp. 609–10; Vol. XXXVI, Pt. 3, pp. 813–14, 873–74; Worsham, *One of Jackson's Foot Cavalry*, 222–23.

12. In a heavy skirmish near Shepherdstown on August 25, Gordon received a bloody head wound but was not incapacitated. Hotchkiss recorded that Gordon's wound resulted from a saber slash. Hotchkiss Journal, August 25, 1864; "Stories Told About Immortal Gordon," newspaper clipping in John B. Gordon Biographical File, AHS; "Letters of a Confederate Surgeon: Doctor Abner Embry McGarity, 1862–1865," *Georgia Historical Quarterly*, XXX (1946), 35.

Depot, four miles to the north, reached the field about 10 A.M.;
Rodes's division arrived shortly thereafter and filled in the gap between Gordon and Ramseur.[13]

Discovering a heavy Federal column moving to turn Ramseur's left
flank, Gordon and Rodes hastily conferred and decided to launch a
simultaneous charge by both divisions to outflank the column of
Federals. Scarcely had they concluded their discussion when Rodes
received a mortal wound. Despite his deep grief at the fall of his
comrade and friend, Gordon forced himself "to stifle sensibilities and
silence the natural promptings of his heart," for the situation at hand
demanded immediate action. Assuming temporary command of
Rodes's men in addition to his own, the Georgian directed both divisions to meet the Federal advance with a charge. At the extreme left
of his line, Evans' brigade gave way after being struck while in the act
of forming, but Gordon benefited from skillful artillery fire and met
this emergency by feeding into line the last brigade of Rodes's division, which had just arrived. That addition enabled him to break the
Union assault and resume his charge all along the line. Gordon's and
Rodes's men forced the Federals back with heavy losses, and at that
point, the battle appeared to be over. In fact, one of Gordon's soldiers
remarked that "we lay down to rest. We had been in action only about
an hour and we thought we had gained an easy victory." Such was not
the case.[14]

Early's army, once fully reassembled, formed a defensive perimeter
northeast of Winchester roughly in the shape of an upside-down L.
But as the afternoon wore on, it became increasingly clear that Sheridan had no intention of breaking off contact and that both Confederate flanks were in danger of being turned by the more numerous and
extremely aggressive Federal cavalry. Late in the day, an overwhelming force of blue-clad horsemen swept down on Early's left and gained

13. Gordon, Reminiscences, 319–21; OR, Vol. XLIII, Pt. 1, pp. 46–47, 554–55;
Early, Narrative of the War, 420–21; Douglas, I Rode with Stonewall, 309; "Diary of
Captain James M. Garnett," SHSP, XXVII (1899), 4–5; Thomas H. Carter to John W.
Daniel, November 28, 1894, in John Warwick Daniel Papers, Duke.

14. Gordon, Reminiscences, 321–22; "Diary of Captain Robert E. Park, of Twelfth
Alabama Regiment," SHSP, II (July–December, 1876), 25–26; William R. Cox, "Major
General Stephen D. Ramseur," SHSP, XVIII (1890), 248; Carter to Daniel, November
19, 28, 1894, both in Daniel Papers; Early, Narrative of the War, 421–23; OR, Vol.
XLIII, Pt. 1, pp. 47, 555; Worsham, One of Jackson's Foot Cavalry, 258; Wesley Merritt,
"Sheridan in the Shenandoah Valley," in Robert Underwood Johnson and Clarence
Clough Buel (eds.), Battles and Leaders of the Civil War (4 vols.; 1887–88; rpr. New
York, 1956), IV, 507–509; "Diary of Captain Garnett," 5.

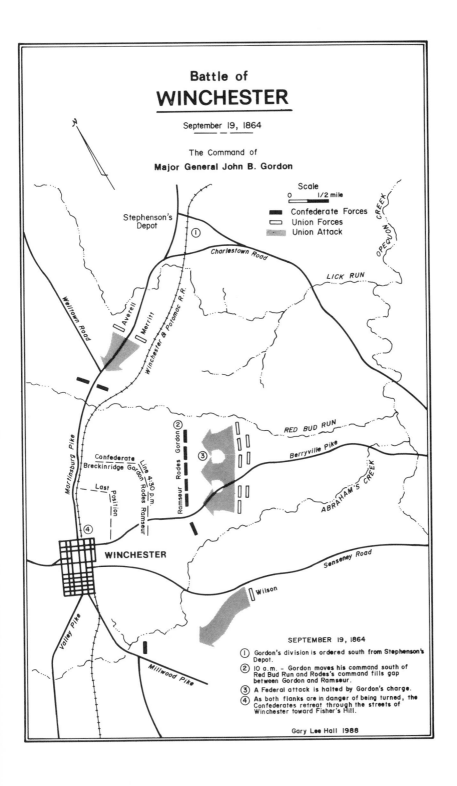

# Battle of
# WINCHESTER

September 19, 1864

The Command of
**Major General John B. Gordon**

Scale
0       1/2 mile

■■■ Confederate Forces
▢ Union Forces
▨ Union Attack

Stephenson's Depot

①

Charlestown Road

LICK RUN

OPEQUON CREEK

Welltown Road

Averell

Merritt

Winchester & Potomac R.R.

RED BUD RUN

②

Ramseur  Rodes  Gordon

③

Berryville Pike

ABRAHAM'S CREEK

Confederate
Breckinridge Gordon

Line 4:30 p.m.
Gordon Rodes Ramseur

Martinsburg Pike

Last Position

④

**WINCHESTER**

Senseney Road

Wilson

Valley Pike

Millwood Pike

SEPTEMBER 19, 1864

① Gordon's division is ordered south from Stephenson's Depot.
② 10 a.m. – Gordon moves his command south of Red Bud Run and Rodes's command fills gap between Gordon and Ramseur.
③ A Federal attack is halted by Gordon's charge.
④ As both flanks are in danger of being turned, the Confederates retreat through the streets of Winchester toward Fisher's Hill.

Gary Lee Hall 1988

the rear of the bent Confederate line. Even though rapid movement by Breckinridge's troops drove the enemy cavalry back and all other commands continued to repel Union frontal assaults, "noise accomplished what force had failed to do." "Hearing the fire in the rear, and thinking they were flanked and about to be cut off," the troops all along the front lines began falling back. A short stand behind a line of breastworks on the outskirts of Winchester momentarily held the enemy back, but the entire line gave way in confusion as darkness approached.[15]

As Gordon's troops streamed through Winchester in great disorder, the determined wife of their commander met them in the streets. Fanny had narrowly escaped capture that morning when her carriage broke down as she hurriedly crossed a stream, in flight before Federal cavalry. Only assistance from some of Rodes's men, who held off the enemy while repairs were made, allowed her to reach Winchester safely. Although Early's opposition to the practice of wives following their soldier-husbands was well known, Fanny had persisted in her efforts to remain as close as possible to John. She traveled in carriages, ambulances, a "rock-a-way," or almost any means of transportation available. In fact, "it had become a tradition in the Army that when she was seen on her way to the rear, action was about to open." Early, objecting to her almost constant presence, once muttered, "I wish the Yankees would capture Mrs. Gordon and hold her till the war is over." Fanny somehow learned of the Virginian's caustic remark and took the opportunity to good-naturedly tease him about it at a camp dinner. An embarrassed Early recovered after a moment and replied, "Mrs. Gordon, General Gordon is a better soldier when you are close by him than when you are away, and so hereafter, when I issue orders that officers' wives must go to the rear, you may know that you are excepted." Upon discovering Fanny's success in keeping up with the army in its movements around Winchester, Early exclaimed, "Well, I'll be ———! If my men would keep up as well as she does, I'd never issue another order against straggling."[16]

15. Early, *Narrative of the War*, 423–26; *OR*, Vol. XLIII, Pt. 1, pp. 47, 555, 557–58; Douglas Southall Freeman, *Lee's Lieutenants: A Study in Command* (3 vols.; New York, 1942–44), III, 580; Hotchkiss Journal, September 19, 1864; Cox, "Ramseur," 249; Carter to Daniel, November 28, 1894, in Daniel Papers; "Diary of Captain Garnett," 5–7; Gordon, *Reminiscences*, 322.

16. Gordon, *Reminiscences*, 318–21; Caroline Gordon Brown to Samuel Chiles Mitchell, May 24, 1934, in Samuel Chiles Mitchell Papers, SHC; clipping from Macon *Daily Telegraph*, May 7, 1912, in John B. Gordon Biography File, GHS; Freeman, *Lee's Lieutenants*, III, 328.

When Fanny found that a portion of the retreating Confederates belonged to her husband's command, "she lost her self-control, and rushed into the street, urging them to go back and meet the enemy." Believing that his wife had gone to the rear as she normally did whenever a battle appeared imminent, Gordon was indeed stunned to discover her still in Winchester and horrified to find her in the street, struggling to rally his troops, with shells and bullets flying about her. He immediately insisted that she enter the house of a friend where, though capture would be inevitable, she would, at least, be safe. But as her husband dashed on, Fanny took steps to avoid falling prisoner to the rapidly advancing Yankees. Finding that her driver had disappeared, she stopped some of Gordon's men who brought her carriage and horses to her. For the second time that day, she sped away only moments ahead of the enemy. This time, however, she joined in the general withdrawal of Early's army.[17]

"Drearily and silently," the dismal retreat dragged on throughout the night, stopping briefly at Newtown and then continuing to Fisher's Hill. There Early determined to make a stand and try to halt Sheridan's progress; however, the loss of over thirty-six hundred men at Winchester made it difficult for Early to maintain effectively the almost four-mile line that he chose to occupy. Consequently, when Sheridan attacked on the afternoon of September 22, he crushed Early's left and forced the discouraged Confederates to withdraw in disorder once again. Gordon remembered "the retreat (it is always so) was at first stubborn and slow, then rapid, then—a rout." Having sustained almost five thousand casualties and lost two major engagements in only four days, Early pressed his withdrawal well up the valley. He did not stop until he had fallen back to Staunton and Waynesboro, where his "very much shattered [and] . . . very much exhausted" troops enjoyed a period "of comparative rest and recuperation."[18]

Early's defeats aroused the ire of many disgruntled southerners

17. "Sketches of Stories and Family Matters" (MS in William W. Stringfield Papers, NCDAH); Douglas, *I Rode with Stonewall*, 311; clipping from Macon *Daily Telegraph*, May 7, 1912, in Gordon Biography File; Gordon, *Reminiscences*, 42, 322–23; "Diary of Captain Park," 28–29; Alex S. Paxton, "Sheridan's Bummers," *SHSP*, XXXII (1904), 92; Atlanta *Constitution*, June 24, 1871.

18. Gordon, *Reminiscences*, 324–27; Hotchkiss Journal, September 20–22, 1864; *OR*, Vol. XLIII, Pt. 1, pp. 48, 555–56, 557–58; Early, *Narrative of the War*, 429–30. Numerous Federal reports following the Battle of Winchester mistakenly stated that Gordon had been mortally wounded during the action on September 19. *OR*, Vol. XXXIX, Pt. 2, p. 423; Vol. XLIII, Pt. 1, p. 25; Vol. XLIII, Pt. 2, pp. 110, 118, 123–25, 137, 138, 153.

who saw the once brightly glowing spirit of independence fading noticeably in the last half of 1864. Grumbling undoubtedly surfaced in Early's army and, in all probability, Gordon likewise questioned the competency of his commander of the past year and a half. They had fought well together at Chancellorsville and during the Gettysburg campaign, but almost from the onset of campaigning in the spring of 1864, problems had developed. Early's refusal to believe, let alone investigate, Gordon's findings on the morning of May 6 quite possibly signaled a hardening of relations between the two men. When Early assumed temporary command of III Corps and Gordon took over his division at Spotsylvania Court House, the young Georgian burst upon the center stage of Lee's army, capturing the attention of many, both in and out of the military. Referred to by some as "the Stonewall Jackson of this [Lee's] army," Gordon, with his youthful dash and fiercely offensive spirit, supplanted his superior in the eyes and hearts of many Confederates, a fact that no doubt grated upon the normally ill-tempered Early. Problems multiplied once they were no longer under the directing hand of Lee. After Winchester, Gordon criticized Early's apparent overconfidence, which resulted in the delayed recall of the widely dispersed Confederate forces on the morning of September 19. He also noted his commander's failure to protect the army's left flank at Fisher's Hill, which again led to disaster. If Gordon entertained serious doubts about Early as an independent commander, actions in October were to confirm them.[19]

Buoyed by reinforcements from Lee's army and expressions of confidence from the commanding general, Early resolved to strike a blow at Sheridan if possible. By early October, when it began moving back down the valley, Early's force had been augmented by the arrival of Major General Joseph B. Kershaw's fine South Carolina infantry division, plus cavalry and artillery units. Early returned to Fisher's Hill on October 13 and found Sheridan's army encamped north of Cedar Creek between Strasburg and Middletown. Faced with the choice of falling back "for want of provisions and forage" or attacking immediately, Early undertook reconnaissance to see if either of the enemy's flanks could be turned. He sent Brigadier General John Pegram to investigate the Union right and dispatched Gordon to the Confed-

19. Millard Kessler Bushong, *Old Jube: A Biography of General Jubal A. Early* (Boyce, Va., 1955), 243–46; Richmond *Enquirer*, May 17, 1864; Gordon, *Reminiscences*, 319–20, 330, 326.

IN THE VALLEY · 93

erate signal station on Massanutten Mountain to examine Sheridan's left.[20]

Accompanied by members of his division and Captain Jedediah Hotchkiss, Gordon spent much of October 17 scaling the rugged mountain. Once on the summit of the so-called Three Top Mountain, he found that his observation post provided him with a magnificent view of the Federal army spread out below him. "Not only the general outlines of Sheridan's breastworks, but every parapet where his heavy guns were mounted, and every piece of artillery, every wagon and tent and supporting line of troops, were in easy range of vision." Sheridan obviously considered his left flank—anchored on the north fork of the Shenandoah River and protected by the apparently impassable Massanutten—secure and safe from attack, for he had taken few steps to guard it; however, the vulnerability of the virtually unprotected Federal left leaped out at the Confederates. Gordon and Hotchkiss immediately realized that a golden opportunity lay before them and quickly formulated a plan of attack before beginning their arduous descent to inform Early of their findings.[21]

That evening, Hotchkiss presented the plan to Early, and Gordon confirmed their findings when he conferred with his commander the next morning. Convinced beyond all doubt that adoption of the plan "would guarantee the destruction of Sheridan's army," Gordon offered to assume full responsibility if the attack failed. Although aware of the tremendous potential of the plan, Early first had to be sure of its practicality; accordingly, he sent Gordon and Hotchkiss out again to ascertain if a suitable route around the mountain existed. When they located a narrow path running between the river and the foot of the mountain, Early completely accepted the plan and prepared for action.[22]

In writings after the war, both Early and Gordon claimed to have planned the attack, and like so many other minor points, their con-

20. OR, Vol. XLIII, Pt. 2, pp. 878–81, 891–92; Early, Narrative of the War, 433–38; Jones to Father, October 21, 1864, in Thomas Goode Jones Collection, ADAH; Hotchkiss Journal, October 17, 1864; Douglas, I Rode with Stonewall, 316; Gordon, Reminiscences, 330–33.

21. Gordon, Reminiscences, 333–35; Hotchkiss Journal, October 17, 1864; Gabriel Wharton, "Battle of Cedar Creek" (MS in Jubal Anderson Early Papers, LC); OR, Vol. XLIII, Pt. 1, p. 1030; Vol. XLVI, Pt. 2, pp. 385–86.

22. Hotchkiss Journal, October 17–18, 1864; Gordon, Reminiscences, 335–36; Jones to Father, October 21, 1864, Gordon to Jones, June 11, 1902, both in T. G. Jones Collection; Early, Narrative of the War, 439–40; OR, Vol. XLIII, Pt. 1, p. 561.

flicting statements served to fuel postwar controversies. In truth, both could claim credit. In his journal, Hotchkiss recorded that "General Gordon and myself fixed upon a plan of attack to suggest to General Early, which we discussed fully as we came back. General Gordon was to propose it to General Early." Physically unable to climb Three Top Mountain, Early had to rely upon "the eyes and reports of others"; yet, even though the plan originated with his subordinates, Early could justifiably take credit. As commander of the Confederate forces, he had to make the final decision and dispositions, as well as bear full responsibility for the outcome of the attack. Early himself wrote, "I was not likely to permit any other to plan a battle for me . . . yet I was always willing to receive and adopt valuable suggestions from any of my officers." Although others seriously questioned his receptiveness to subordinates' suggestions, Early appears to have accepted Gordon's advice and planned the Battle of Cedar Creek accordingly. Perhaps the best analysis of the situation came from Thomas G. Jones after the death of both Early and Gordon. He observed that Early "was responsible for the plan, & he held on & would not turn back" even in the face of some troubling Federal movements on the day preceding the attack. "It is no impugnment of Early's glory, that he knowing he would have to move on one flank or the other, sent his best officers to look, and then after hearing them, determined which he would adopt. If the plan were adopted on Sheridan's left, the details of it must necessarily be shaped largely by what was seen from there." In sum, Gordon proposed the plan of attack; Early adopted it and implemented it.[23]

Early called all of his division commanders together on the afternoon of October 18 and carefully detailed each man's responsibility in the following morning's assault. The Virginian entrusted the entire II Corps to Gordon, who was to direct the major thrust of the attack. He would lead his three divisions around the foot of the Mas-

23. Hotchkiss Journal, October 17–18, 1864; Gordon, *Reminiscences*, 356; Jones to Daniel, July 3, 1904, in T. G. Jones Collection; Douglas, *I Rode with Stonewall*, 33; Pollard, *Companions in Arms*, 477; Jubal Anderson Early, *A Memoir of the Last Year of the War for Independence in the Confederate States of America, Containing an Account of the Operations of His Commands in the Years of 1864 and 1865* (New Orleans, 1867), 93n. Much of Early's *Narrative of the War* is based upon this *Memoir*. Although there are some differences between the 1867 work and the larger 1912 book, such as the omission of the lines quoted herein, the changes concerning the Battle of Cedar Creek are not of great significance.

sanutten after dark, deploy them on Sheridan's flank and rear, attack just before daylight, and drive the Federals back toward Belle Grove. Kershaw was to attack the enemy's front and left as soon as Gordon struck the flank and then join the Georgian in pushing the Federals across the valley pike. Brigadier General Gabriel C. Wharton's division would move up the pike, gain control of the bridge over Cedar Creek, and then take whatever position in line that circumstances dictated. Early directed the cavalry to occupy the enemy's horse, protect the army's flanks, and operate against the Federal rear. With their plans set, the Confederates departed Early's headquarters to prepare their individual commands for the attack. "All were very sanguine of success, believing the attack would be a surprise." On the eve of this battle, most of the veterans in Early's army probably shared thoughts similar to those of one of Gordon's staff officers. "Tomorrow is the 19th of October just one month from the defeat at Winchester. If by God's kindness we can whip Sheridan, it will be the greatest thing of the war."[24]

Gordon's command, faced with the longest and most circuitous march, began its move at 8 P.M. After crossing the river near Fisher's Hill, his men spent most of the night working their way around the mountain along the precarious path which often forced them to move in single file. Stripped of all unnecessary accoutrements that might arouse attention, "the long gray line like a giant serpent glided noiselessly along the dim pathway above the precipice." Having wisely posted guides at every fork along the route in order to prevent any mishap, Gordon reached Bowman's Ford without serious incident, about an hour before the time of attack. Waiting in the darkness within sight and hearing of Federal pickets stationed in the middle of the river, Gordon found the situation "unspeakably impressive. Everything conspired to make the conditions both thrilling and weird." The tense moments of anticipation finally gave way to the appointed hour. Accompanying cavalry units advanced and brushed aside the Federals at the ford. The horsemen dashed off in a futile attempt to capture Sheridan while Gordon's infantry crossed the river without opposition for the second time that evening. Once on the opposite

24. Early, *Narrative of the War*, 440–42; Wharton, "Cedar Creek"; Hotchkiss Journal, October 18, 1864; Thomas H. Carter to Samuel J. C. Moore, October 15, 1889, in Samuel J. C. Moore Papers, VHS; *OR*, Vol. XLIII, Pt. 1, pp. 1030–31; Jones to Eugene C. Gordon, October 18, 1864, in T. G. Jones Collection.

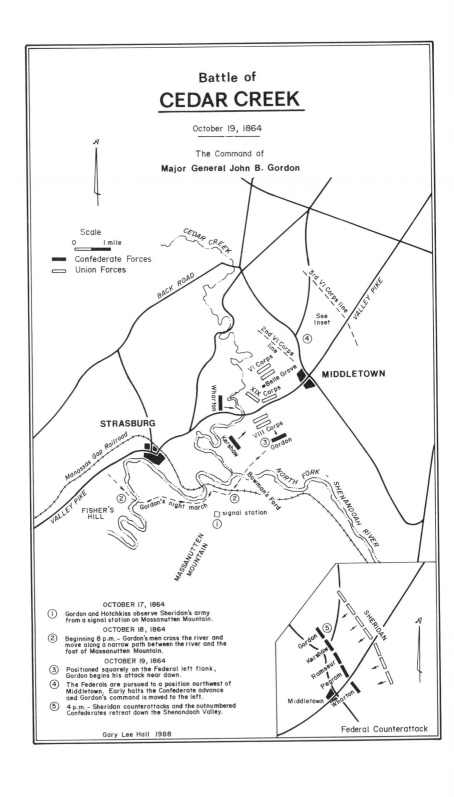

# Battle of
# CEDAR CREEK

October 19, 1864

The Command of
**Major General John B. Gordon**

Scale

0 ——— 1 mile

■ Confederate Forces
☐ Union Forces

CEDAR CREEK

BACK ROAD

3rd VI Corps line

VALLEY PIKE

See Inset

2nd VI Corps line

VI Corps

●Belle Grove

MIDDLETOWN

XIX Corps

Wharton

STRASBURG

Kershaw

VIII Corps

Gordon

Manassas Gap Railroad

NORTH FORK

SHENANDOAH RIVER

Bowman's Ford

VALLEY PIKE

FISHER'S HILL

Gordon's night march

☐ signal station

MASSANUTTEN MOUNTAIN

OCTOBER 17, 1864
① Gordon and Hotchkiss observe Sheridan's army from a signal station on Massanutten Mountain.

OCTOBER 18, 1864
② Beginning 8 p.m. – Gordon's men cross the river and move along a narrow path between the river and the foot of Massanutten Mountain.

OCTOBER 19, 1864
③ Positioned squarely on the Federal left flank, Gordon begins his attack near dawn.

④ The Federals are pursued to a position northwest of Middletown. Early halts the Confederate advance and Gordon's command is moved to the left.

⑤ 4 p.m. – Sheridan counterattacks and the outnumbered Confederates retreat down the Shenandoah Valley.

Gary Lee Hall 1988

SHERIDAN

Gordon

Kershaw

Ramseur

Pegram

Middletown

Wharton

⑤

Federal Counterattack

bank, Gordon rapidly pushed his men northward approximately one and a quarter miles and then deployed them squarely upon the Federal flank.[25]

As soon as Evans (who commanded Gordon's division) and Ramseur could wheel their divisions into line, Gordon attacked. Hitting the flank and rear of Sheridan's army, he completely surprised the sleeping Federals. "Thrown into the wildest confusion and terror by Kershaw's simultaneous assault in front," the Union VIII Corps stampeded into and through the camps of the adjoining XIX Corps. Confusion and disorder prevailed as the two surprised Union corps broke and fled without offering any real resistance. In a remarkably short period of time, two-thirds of Sheridan's army was routed and driven from the field. In addition, much of the Union artillery fell into Gordon's hands. Only the veteran VI Corps remained intact, and even it withdrew northward to a new position west of Middletown. While Gordon reorganized—bringing Pegram's division into line—and prepared to push on against the VI Corps, Colonel Thomas H. Carter brought the guns of the II Corps into action. The artilleryman exclaimed to Gordon, "General, you will need no infantry. With enfilade fire from my batteries I will destroy that corps in twenty minutes." Carter's heavy and extremely effective bombardment forced the Federals to fall back again, this time forming a line northwest of Middletown. Believing that the destruction of Sheridan's army was within his grasp, Gordon ordered his "three Divisions of Infantry and 39 pieces of Artillery to move rapidly down the Pike, mass on the enemy's left, and by one grand charge, sweep the 6th Corps to four winds."[26]

While Gordon completed preparations for this final advance, Early, aglow with the ecstasy of victory, joined him on the battlefield. Riding up to the Georgian, he declared, "Just one month ago, to-day

25. *OR*, Vol. XLIII, Pt. 1, pp. 561, 598, 1031; Samuel D. Buck, "Battle of Cedar Creek, Va., Oct. 19th, 1864," *SHSP*, XXX (1902), 105; Hotchkiss Journal, October 18, 1864; Wharton, "Cedar Creek"; Jones to Father, October 21, 1864, in T. G. Jones Collection; Early, *Narrative of the War*, 442–43; Gordon, *Reminiscences*, 336–39; Fanny Gordon to her husband, October 16, 1864, in Fanny Haralson (Mrs. John B.) Gordon Letters, AC. 68-432, GDAH.

26. Gordon, *Reminiscences*, 339–41; Buck, "Cedar Creek," 105–106; *OR*, Vol. XLIII, Pt. 1, pp. 561–62, 598–99, 1031; Early, *Narrative of the War*, 443–45; A. L. Long, "General Early's Valley Campaign," *SHSP*, XVIII (1890), 89; Hotchkiss Journal, October 19, 1864; Carter to Daniel, November 19, 1894, in Daniel Papers; Cox, "Ramseur," 253; Carter to Moore, October 15, 1889, in Moore Papers; Pollard, *Companions in Arms*, 545–46; Jones to Father, October 21, 1864, in T. G. Jones Collection.

General, we were going the other way." Alluding to the fact that
Sheridan had been promoted after Winchester and Fisher's Hill, Early
added, "I wonder what they will make of this Brigadier General in the
regular army, now." Confident that he had won a glorious victory,
Early asked Gordon to point out the VI Corps's exact location, as fog
and battle smoke continued to obscure his field of vision. Gordon
pinpointed the enemy's new position and explained the steps he had
taken to press the attack and destroy the VI Corps. To Gordon's
surprise, "Early said in substance, 'It will go to the rear with the rest.
They are all trying to get away now.' Gordon said he thought not, and
that it [the VI Corps] was in the best place we could get at it for attack
where it was." Early, for whatever reasons, refused to be swayed by
his division commander and held fast to his belief that the VI Corps
was acting as a rear guard, merely covering the retreat of the army.
Although Gordon persisted in arguing for a continuation of the attack, Early ignored his pleas for a final, massive assault. The conversation ended with Early instructing his subordinate, "General, you
had better look after your division."[27]

Although Gordon and Early may have met more than once during
the morning of October 19, this conversation occurred after the VIII
Corps and XIX Corps had been driven from the field and most likely
after the VI Corps had withdrawn to its last position northwest of
Middletown. Gordon related the meeting as follows: "Well, Gordon,
this is glory enough for one day. This is the 19th. Precisely one month
ago to-day we were going in the opposite direction." Gordon replied,
"It is very well so far, general; but we have one more blow to strike,
and then there will not be left an organized company of infantry in
Sheridan's army." As Gordon explained his dispositions and the need
for pressing the attack, Early exclaimed, "No use in that; they will all
go directly." Dumbfounded, Gordon answered, "That is the Sixth
Corps, general. It will not go unless we drive it from the field." Un-
moved by his subordinate's arguments, Early reiterated, "Yes, it will
go too, directly." Douglas Southall Freeman's assertion that Gordon's
account "scarcely can have been reported with literal accuracy" is
correct, but the essence of the conversation remains clear. Gordon
wanted to push the attack vigorously; Early, for reasons known only
to himself, decided not to press the immediate assault upon the VI
Corps.[28]

27. Jones to Father, October 21, 1864, Jones to Daniel, July 3, 1904, both in T. G.
Jones Collection; Pollard, Companions in Arms, 546.
28. Gordon, Reminiscences, 341; Freeman, Lee's Lieutenants, III, 603–604.

Years later, Gordon remembered that at that moment "my heart went into my boots. Visions of the fatal halt on the first day at Gettysburg, and of the whole day's hesitation to permit an assault on Grant's exposed flank on the 6th of May in the Wilderness, rose before me." Gordon bitterly recalled that the "concentration was stopped; the blow was not delivered. We halted, we hesitated, we dallied." Having reverted back to divisional command once Early arrived on the field, Gordon, under orders, moved his men to the left of the Confederate line. There he remained as Early's army spent most of the afternoon "firing a few shots here, attacking with a brigade or a division there." But in the main, the Confederates "waited— waited for weary hours."[29]

Although Early later wrote that he sent orders to Gordon to press the attack against the VI Corps, it is impossible to ascertain when or if these orders were issued. If such instructions were dispatched, it would appear that they were never delivered because a member of Early's staff, Lieutenant Mann Page, somehow determined on his own that Gordon's division was in no condition to move forward. Early's narrative, which suggests that the orders were issued prior to Carter's artillery bombardment, adds to the confusion and difficulty of reconciling the differences between the *Official Records* and *Reminiscences*. Gordon's assertion that he never received any orders to attack rings true, particularly in light of his steadfast condemnation of Early for "the fatal halt at Cedar Creek," a phrase that was used as a chapter title in *Reminiscences*. In it, Gordon supplied abundant documentation from both Union and Confederate officers to support his contention that Early's decision to suspend the attack, and not the "bad conduct" of the men, resulted in the disaster at Cedar Creek. Gordon and his men "were not only urgently anxious to advance, but were astounded at any halt whatever." Without question, Early stopped the attack during the morning; however, at some time in the afternoon, he ordered his left forward to probe the VI Corps position. Skirmishers made this move but fell back when they discovered the enemy's defenses were too strong. Early's forces made no full-scale assault after the initial attack had been halted.[30]

Early's decision not to attack the VI Corps with his entire force

29. Gordon, *Reminiscences*, 341–44.

30. Early, *Narrative of the War*, 445–47; *OR*, Vol. XLIII, Pt. 1, pp. 562, 599; Carter to Moore, October 15, 1889, in Moore Papers; Gordon, *Reminiscences*, 344–45, 354–63, 364–65; Jones to Daniel, July 3, 1904, in T. G. Jones Collection; Freeman, *Lee's Lieutenants*, III, 606.

deeply disturbed Gordon, but the situation that developed on his front signalled a new alarm. The Federals, seeing that vigorous pursuit had been abandoned, began to rally behind the VI Corps and, with their ever-growing numbers and Sheridan's return, prepared to assume the offensive. As the afternoon wore on, Gordon received increasingly ominous reports that both enemy cavalry and infantry were massing on his front and flank. Alert to the great danger, he sent several urgent messages to Early informing him of the situation on the left and appealing for assistance. Early, believing the right to be in much greater danger, seemed to attach little importance to Gordon's report and told Gordon that the Federal activity on his front was "only a demonstration in order to cover a retreat." He added that Gordon "must show a fierce front to the enemy, and hold on" for the Yankees would retire once darkness came. Even late in the afternoon, Early seems to have remained convinced that the enemy planned to retire after nightfall. Nevertheless, he did send some artillery to the left, which Gordon welcomed, though its arrival forced the Georgian to weaken his already thin lines by pulling troops out of line to support the guns. Seriously troubled by the gaps along his front, Gordon rode over to Early's headquarters and voiced his concern. His appeals were to no avail, so Gordon galloped back to the Confederate left just as Sheridan's rallied forces began attacking his line.[31]

Outflanked and grossly outnumbered, Gordon's division fell back. Effective covering fire by the artillery enabled Gordon to make a brief stand, but it proved only temporary; his division was soon fleeing to the rear. Almost as quickly as word of the retreat on the left spread down the line, adjoining divisions began to pull back. Despite immense exertions by officers to halt their men, the withdrawal rapidly became a rout and then a stampede as panic swept through the ranks when Federal cavalry descended upon the disintegrating left. Attempts to rally small bodies of troops and check the seemingly ceaseless pursuit "or at least delay it long enough to enable the shattered and rapidly retreating fragments [of Early's army] to escape" proved fruitless.[32]

---

31. Jones to Father, October 21, 1864, Jones to Daniel, July 3, December 25, 1904, all in T. G. Jones Collection; Gordon, *Reminiscences*, 345–47.

32. Gordon, *Reminiscences*, 347–48; Carter to Moore, October 15, 1889, in Moore Papers; Early, *Narrative of the War*, 448–50; Hotchkiss Journal, October 19, 1864; Wharton, "Cedar Creek"; Jones to Daniel, July 3, December 25, 1904, Jones to Father, October 21, 1864, all in T. G. Jones Collection; *OR*, Vol. XLII, Pt. 1, pp. 864–65; Vol.

While engaged in one of these delaying actions well after dark, Gordon barely escaped capture. Finding his hastily drawn position outflanked and about to be overwhelmed, he realized that his only avenue of escape lay down the steep banks of a nearby creek. "Wheeling my horse to the dismal bank, I drove my spurs into his flanks, and he plunged downward and tumbled headlong in one direction, sending me in another." Although knocked unconscious, Gordon soon recovered his senses and was able to mount his dazed horse and make good his escape in the darkness. "Lonely, thoughtful and sad," Gordon rode throughout the night, wondering how in the same day "a most brilliant victory [had been] converted into one of the most complete and ruinous routs of the entire war."[33]

Gordon had plenty of time to reflect upon the disaster at Cedar Creek, for Sheridan's victory there effectively ended serious campaigning in the Shenandoah Valley. The Confederates retreated all the way to New Market before the army finally halted and began to reorganize. On October 21, Early supplied Lee with a detailed account of his army's actions two days earlier. In it, Early stated that after great success in the early morning, many of his men stopped to plunder enemy camps. Their actions compelled him to suspend his attack and try to hold what he had gained. When the rallied enemy attacked late in the afternoon and drove the left back, Early reported that "an insane idea of being flanked" seized his other troops and turned the withdrawal into a rout "as thorough and disgraceful as ever happened to our army." He succinctly concluded, "We had within our grasp a glorious victory, and lost it by the unaccountable propensity of our men for plunder . . . and the subsequent panic of those who had kept their places." In this official report, he expressed his willingness to resign, but Early unmistakably sought to place the blame for his defeat upon the officers and men under his command.[34]

In the immediate aftermath of the disaster at Cedar Creek, relations between Early and Gordon, never very cordial after leaving the Richmond front, grew increasingly sour. Several days after the battle,

---

XLIII, Pt. 1, pp. 562–63, 599–600; Bryan Grimes, *Extracts of Letters of Major General Bryan Grimes to his Wife: Written while in Active Service in the Army of Northern Virginia, together with some personal recollections of the war written by him after its close*, comp. Pulaski Cowper (Raleigh, 1883), 77–78.

33. Gordon, *Reminiscences*, 348–51.

34. Hotchkiss Journal, October 19–20, 1864; Early, *Narrative of the War*, 450; *OR*, Vol. XLIII, Pt. 1, pp. 562–64, 1031.

Gordon received word that Early had stated that even though the Georgian was a good fighter, "he had stopped in the midst of success to look after plunder." Early reiterated this thought shortly thereafter in an address to his army, a "severe censure and reprimand" in which he denounced his command for plundering and bad conduct. Early asserted that "the officer who pauses in the career of victory to place a guard over a sutler's wagon, for his private use, is as bad as the soldier who halts to secure for himself the abandoned clothing or money of a flying foe; and they both soil the honor of the army, and the blood of their country for a paltry price." Gordon had in fact stopped a black-covered wagon that resembled an ammunition wagon shortly after the initial attack early in the morning. Fearing that it was carrying munitions away from the front, he instructed the driver to halt. When he learned that the wagon was another officer's headquarters wagon, he allowed it to move on. Early, however, accepted a grossly inaccurate account of this incident and "for a while, believed it, quite strongly." It was clear that the Virginian intended his comments as a slap at his subordinate.[35]

Early also charged Gordon with inspiring an unsigned letter that appeared in the Richmond *Enquirer* soon after the action. The detailed nature of this lengthy letter suggested that only a participant in Gordon's flank attack could have penned it. In fact, Captain Frank Muskoe, a II Corps signal officer, had written it as a private letter to a friend, who signed it with a nom de plume and published it. Even though Gordon knew nothing of either the writing or the publication of this detailed account of Cedar Creek, he apparently endured his commander's snide insinuations in relative silence until he learned the contents of Early's official report from a friend in the War Department. Charges that he had attacked late and that he had lost control of his division due to excessive plundering were too much for Gordon to bear.[36]

Incensed by these allegations, Gordon confronted Early on October 29. Hotchkiss recorded the "meeting" as a "contention between Generals Gordon and Early about the battle of Cedar Creek & c." In the

35. Jones to Daniel, July 3, December 25, 1904, both in T. G. Jones Collection; Edward A. Pollard, *The Last Year of the War* (New York, 1866), 113. The text of Early's October 22, 1864, "dressing-down" of his command can be found in Pollard, *Last Year of the War*, 112–14.

36. Jones to Daniel, July 3, December 25, 1904, both in T. G. Jones Collection; Early, *Narrative of the War*, 451; Carter to Daniel, November 19, 1894, in Daniel Papers.

"very 'fierce interview'" that ensued, both men spoke freely and often heatedly. Although the exact nature of the discussion is unknown, it would seem that all the "strongly controverted points"
between Gordon and Early grew from a similar source: the commander's attempt to blame the defeat on everyone but himself. His
insistence that he had wanted to press the attack but had been prevented from doing so because the men were plundering forced Gordon to protest and swept the Georgian into the center of the controversy. Some unauthorized looting unquestionably took place, but
substantial evidence exists that the stragglers and plunderers "were
not sufficient enough to prevent a vigorous and victorious pursuit."[37]

In all probability, Early sincerely believed that his morning success
had so shattered the two Union corps that Sheridan's entire army
would be forced to retreat and remained convinced of that idea at
least until the early afternoon. That does not in any way excuse his
failure to press onward and conduct an energetic pursuit if it was at all
possible. Even though his men were tired from their night march to
the field and their dawn assault, Early should have either pushed the
attack home or broken off contact. Once he suspended the attack, the
Virginian committed an almost equally grievous error by maintaining his thinly stretched line in the open country around Middletown
rather than retiring to a more defensible position. He compounded
this mistake in the afternoon by refusing to take adequate steps to
meet the gathering storm on his left.

Even Early realized his critical mistake and supplied the most
incriminating piece of evidence confirming it. His instruction to
Hotchkiss, who departed for Richmond shortly after the battle to
report on affairs in the valley, showed an almost childlike fear of

37. Hotchkiss Journal, October 29, 1864; Jones to Daniel, July 3, December 25,
1904, both in T. G. Jones Collection; Carter to Daniel, November 19, 1894, in Daniel
Papers; Gordon, *Reminiscences*, 352–72. It is indeed unfortunate that Gordon's official report of the Battle of Cedar Creek has never surfaced. Gordon wrote to Lee shortly
after the war and stated that he had been unable to find his account of the battle but
would continue to search. It is possible that he later located the report and sent it to his
former commander, because Gordon expressed surprise at its omission from the *OR*.
Discovering the "unexpected and unexplained absence" of his report, he endeavored to
vindicate the men of Early's army in *Reminiscences*. Believing that Early's charge of
bad conduct and plundering "so directly, so vitally concerns the reputation, the honor,
the character of Southern soldiers . . . as to demand the most exhaustive examination," Gordon devoted much of his discussion of the battle to countering Early's
critcisms. Gordon to Lee, February 6, 1868, in Lee Headquarters Papers; Gordon,
*Reminiscences*, 332–33, 354–56, 360, 363–72.

fatherly rebuke. He told the engineer "not to tell Lee that we ought to have advanced in the morning at Middletown, for, said he, we ought to have done so." Early also provided the most succinct evaluation of the battle when he stated, "The Yankees got whipped and we got scared." Less cryptic but equally illuminating are the comments of the II Corps artilleryman Thomas Carter. Although he criticized Early for allowing Sheridan time to recover and assume the offensive, he wrote, "It is true, as I believe, the Fickle Goddess proffered him [Early] as a miracle almost, an opportunity at Cedar Creek such as she gives only to one man in millions, and but once in a life to the one so favored; it was so dazzling as to blind, and he passed it by." Considering these and numerous other statements, plus the human penchant for covering up one's mistakes, Early's aggressively defensive behavior after Cedar Creek can best be described as an effort to justify his decision to halt by shifting the onus of defeat elsewhere.[38]

Few if any of the major points of controversy between Gordon and Early were adequately resolved at the time. Gordon considered asking for a court of inquiry to clear both himself and his men but dismissed the thought because of the harmful effect such open and bitter dissension between generals would have on the already sagging Confederate morale. Similarly, he rejected the option of seeking a transfer to another department because of his attachment to the men under his command. Even though Early's conduct at Cedar Creek and in the days that followed the battle unquestionably confirmed the worst of Gordon's suspicions about his commander, the Georgian resigned himself to continued service under the irascible Virginian. Finally in early December, after seven more weeks of minor skirmishing with Federal cavalry, Gordon received orders to return to the Army of Northern Virginia. Early would remain in the valley with a skeleton force while Gordon and the bulk of the II Corps rejoined Lee's army in the trenches near Petersburg. There they would endure the final winter of the war. Additional fighting lay ahead, but the end was drawing near—the death of the Confederacy was in sight.[39]

38. Hotchkiss Journal, October 23, 19, 1864; Carter to Moore, October 15, 1889, in Moore Papers.
39. Jones to Daniel, July 3, December 25, 1904, both in T. G. Jones Collection.

# VI · Toward Appomattox

On December 8, 1864, Gordon's and Pegram's divisions departed from Waynesboro, moving by train to Richmond and then on to Petersburg. Less than one week later, Rodes's old division, now under Brigadier General Bryan Grimes, also left the valley and joined Gordon on the Petersburg front. With Early remaining in the Shenandoah under orders from Lee, Gordon assumed command of these three divisions. Although serving as commander of the II Corps, Gordon did not receive a promotion to lieutenant general because Early might return to Lee's army and resume his old position; nonetheless, Gordon shouldered the responsibilities and exercised the authority of a corps commander—a position he held until the war's end.[1]

1. John B. Gordon, *Reminiscences of the Civil War* (New York, 1903), 373–74; Jedediah Hotchkiss Journal, December 8–9, 14, 1864 (MS in Jedediah Hotchkiss Papers, LC); Bryan Grimes, *Extracts of Letters of Major General Bryan Grimes to his Wife: Written while in Active Service in the Army of Northern Virginia, together with some personal recollections of the war written by him after its close,* comp. Pulaski Cowper (Raleigh, 1883), 92–93; A. A. Humphreys, *The Virginia Campaign of 1864 and 1865* (New York, 1903), 308; Henry Kyd Douglas, *I Rode with Stonewall* (Chapel Hill, 1940), 321; *OR*, Vol. XLIII, Pt. 1, pp. 582–87, Pt. 2, pp. 765, 772, 780, 911, 938; Vol. XLII, Pt. 3, pp. 1272, 1285, 1362–65; Vol. XLVI, Pt. 2, p. 1271.
Gordon, by virtue of his lengthy command of the II Corps, has frequently been referred to as a lieutenant general, but it is extremely doubtful that he was ever officially elevated to that rank. His signature as a major general at Appomattox provides the most convincing evidence to that effect. After the war, Gordon often spoke of a conference with Secretary of War John C. Breckinridge in early 1865, in which Gordon's former commander notified him that he had been promoted. Also, Alexander H. Stephens told Gordon that he had seen the Georgian's commission as lieutenant general on Jefferson Davis' desk. If such a recommendation did in fact reach the president, he probably never acted upon it during the final, confusing days of the Confederacy.

Upon reaching Petersburg, Gordon moved to the extreme right of Lee's army and occupied a position near Burgess' Mill along Hatcher's Run. There his corps suffered through the final winter of the war while struggling to protect the Southside Railroad. As Grant's intention to seize this vital supply and communication line became increasingly evident, Lee urged the new II Corps commander to "be more than usually vigilant in guarding our right flank." Gordon succeeded in maintaining the security of the railroad, but the physical condition of the army continued to grow more desperate each day. Food supplies, generally of poor quality anyway, were frequently cut, and many Confederate soldiers were forced to subsist on less than half rations. With hunger gnawing at the strength of his men and the cold of winter sapping their spirit, Gordon noted an alarming increase in the number of desertions; by the end of February, 1865, the strength of his II Corps had been reduced to barely eight thousand officers and men. He felt that the Confederate Congress dealt a particularly devastating blow to army morale during that month by refusing to pass a measure to arm slaves. Having found that his command decidedly favored the voluntary enlistment of blacks as soldiers, Gordon reported that such an act would greatly bolster the men's spirits, in addition to providing the army with badly needed reinforcements. He also wrote that defeat of the bill produced despondency within the ranks, further increasing the rate of desertion. Despite the growing specter of doom, Gordon was not yet ready to admit defeat.[2]

With Longstreet north of the James and A. P. Hill frequently indis-

---

Despite this oversight, Gordon served as a lieutenant general in every sense of the position. Gordon to C. C. Jones, July 28, 1875, in Georgia Portfolio II, Charles Colcock Jones, Jr., Collection, Duke; Gordon to Charles Edgeworth Jones, July 26, 1894, and newspaper clipping in unbound scrapbook, both in Charles Edgeworth Jones Collection, Duke; Gordon to M. J. Wright, August 13, 1892, in Marcus Joseph Wright Papers, SHC; Gordon's Service File, in Military Service Records, NA; Caroline Lewis Gordon, "De Gin'ral an' Miss Fanny" (MS in Gordon Family Collection, UGA); Atlanta Constitution, January 14, 1904.

2. OR, Vol. XLVI, Pt. 2, pp. 134, 1270–71, Pt. 1, pp. 388–89; Vol. LI, Pt. 2, p. 1063; Edward A. Pollard, The Last Year of the War (New York, 1866), 175–77; Gordon, Reminiscences, 376–85; R. E. Lee to Gordon, December 27, 1864, January 21, 1865, both in Gordon Family Collection, UGA; Douglas Southall Freeman, R. E. Lee: A Biography (4 vols.; New York, 1934–35), IV, 529–45; Gordon to Major, February 26, 1865, in Gordon Family Collection, UGA; Henry W. Thomas, History of the Doles-Cook Brigade (Atlanta, 1903), 36; Douglas Southall Freeman, Lee's Lieutenants: A Study in Command (3 vols.; New York, 1942–44), III, 619–24; John B. Gordon, "Last Days of the Confederacy," in Rossiter Johnson (ed.), Campfire and Battlefield (New York, 1978), 485.

posed, Gordon came to occupy "a special place" in dealings with his commander during the depressing winter months. In an army in which military training was vital not only to survival but to promotion as well, Gordon had risen rapidly. In spite of his lack of formal schooling in the science of war, he had displayed boldness, vigilance, aggressiveness, and sound military sense that both captured the public's attention and deeply impressed the army's commander. Thus, by virtue of his steady growth as a soldier, and "his temperament and propinquity to Lee, Gordon became," in the opinion of the Virginian's biographer, "Lee's principal confidant—as far as any man ever enjoyed that status." As a result, when the military outlook grew exceedingly bleak in the early months of 1865, Lee turned to his youngest corps commander.[3]

According to Gordon, the commanding general summoned him to headquarters and asked him for a candid opinion of what "was best to do—or what duty to the army and our people required" of them. Cognizant of Grant's ability to bring some 280,000 well-supplied troops to bear upon Lee and Johnston's 65,000 weakened Confederates, Gordon responded that he saw only three options, and he listed them in the order he thought they should be tried. First, negotiate with the enemy and secure the best terms possible; second, abandon the army's present lines, march rapidly to Johnston's command in North Carolina, and attack Sherman before he could unite with Grant; and third, strike Grant at once. Lee, in complete agreement with his subordinate's assessment, devoted the remainder of the night to what Gordon remembered as an "intensely absorbing, and in many ways harrowing" discussion in which they examined each of the alternatives in detail. Lee did not explicitly state which course he preferred, but Gordon came away from the conference with the impression that the paternal Virginian "thought immediate steps should be taken to secure peace." However, failure of the Hampton Roads Conference in February, 1865, had demonstrated the improbability of obtaining a satisfactory negotiated peace. With Confederate officials unwilling to evacuate Richmond and Petersburg until absolutely necessary, Lee decided he must attack; and to that end, he ordered Gordon to study the enemy lines around Petersburg.[4]

3. Freeman, *Lee's Lieutenants*, III, 628.
4. Gordon, *Reminiscences*, 385–97; Gordon, "Last Days of the Confederacy," in Rossiter Johnson (ed.), *Campfire and Battlefield*, 485–87; Gordon to General Lewis, August 21, 1886, in William Gaston Lewis Papers, SHC.

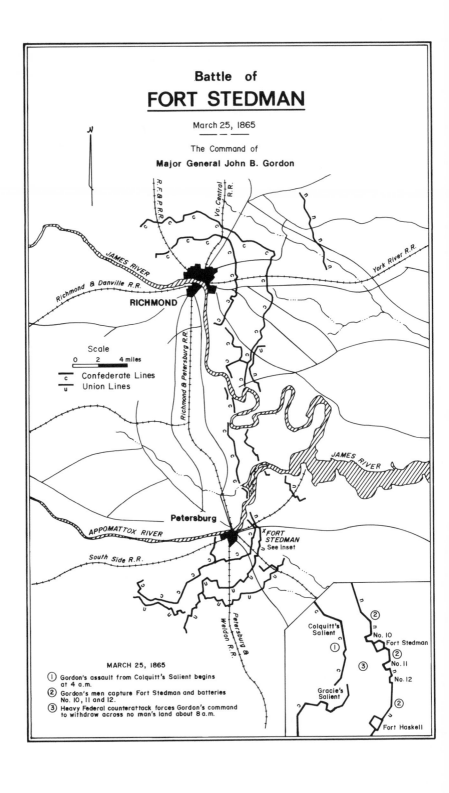

# Battle of
# FORT STEDMAN

March 25, 1865

The Command of

**Major General John B. Gordon**

RICHMOND

Scale

0   2   4 miles

c — Confederate Lines
u — Union Lines

Petersburg

ˣ*FORT
STEDMAN*
See Inset

Colquitt's
Salient

No. 10
Fort Stedman

No. 11

No. 12

Gracie's
Salient

Fort Haskell

MARCH 25, 1865

① Gordon's assault from Colquitt's Salient begins
at 4 a.m.

② Gordon's men capture Fort Stedman and batteries
No. 10, 11 and 12.

③ Heavy Federal counterattack forces Gordon's command
to withdraw across no man's land about 8 a.m.

The new corps commander found that the fortifications and obstructions all along the Union front were "as perfect as human ingenuity and labor could devise"; but after more than a week of extensive investigation, Gordon concluded that Fort Stedman offered "the most inviting point for attack." Built upon Hare's Hill, the fort lay less than two hundred yards from the opposing Confederate lines along Colquitt's Salient—"so close that you could almost see the whites of the Yankees' eyes." Given the proximity of Fort Stedman to his trenches and the belief that his men could silently disable Federal pickets before they could sound an alarm, Gordon felt that a surprise night or predawn attack on the fort could succeed. After the enemy's pickets had been silenced, fifty axmen would rush forward and rapidly chop a number of passageways through the formidable Federal abatis and chevaux-de-frise protecting the front lines. Then, aided by three hundred men carrying empty muskets with fixed bayonets, these axmen would push on into the fort, overwhelm its unprepared defenders, and quickly move into the trenches to the right and to the left.[5]

For Gordon, the "purpose of the movement was not simply the capture of Fort Stedman and the breastworks flanking it"; rather, he planned for a total breakthrough. In order to reach Grant's rear and turn on his flanks, Gordon specially selected three columns of one hundred men each to follow upon the heels of the leading elements of the assault force. Once Stedman fell, these sharpshooters, posing as the Federal defenders of the fort, would "flee" toward the rear and, in the darkness, pass through the line of supporting infantry by invoking the names of Union officers known to be serving on that front. In this manner, the three columns could advance approximately one mile into the rear, move behind the line of hills there, seize the three forts that Gordon believed commanded the main line of defense, and turn their guns upon the Federal rear. To employ this captured artillery

5. Gordon to General Lewis, August 21, 1886, in W. G. Lewis Papers; Thomas, *Doles-Cook Brigade*, 38–39; Gordon, *Reminiscences*, 397–403; *OR*, Vol. XLVI, Pt. 1, pp. 173, 316; Thomas G. Jones, "Last Days of the Army of Northern Virginia," *SHSP*, XXI (1893), 69; John F. Hartranft, "The Recapture of Fort Stedman," in Robert Underwood Johnson and Clarence Clough Buel (eds.), *Battles and Leaders of the Civil War* (4 vols.; 1887–88; rpr. New York, 1956), IV, 584; James A. Walker, "Gordon's Assault on Fort Stedman," *SHSP*, XXXI (1903), 19–23; Douglas, *I Rode with Stonewall*, 328; Grimes, *Letters to his Wife*, 98; Jefferson Davis, *The Rise and Fall of the Confederate Government* (2 vols.; New York, 1881), II, 650–51. Gordon's October 16, 1880, letter to the former president of the Confederacy, detailing the assault on Fort Stedman, is published in Davis, *Confederate Government*, II, 650–54.

most efficiently, Gordon arranged for Confederate artillerymen to accompany the advance elements of the attack. As the main body of infantry poured into the breach and moved forward, as well as against both exposed flanks, Confederate cavalry would proceed against the Union rear, disrupting communications and destroying supplies. If all went as planned, the Federal military railroad link to the west would be severed. With his army thus divided, Grant would be forced to abandon, or at least to curtail, a substantial portion of his lines. Either of these actions might allow Lee the opportunity to slip away and unite with Johnston.[6]

Gordon began moving his corps into the trenches surrounding Petersburg during the middle of March. From deserters and prisoners, he soon learned the names of Federal commanders on his front and, with Lee's assistance, secured guides who professed familiarity with the terrain around Fort Stedman to lead his three storming columns. Although he proceeded slowly and cautiously in order to ensure the utmost secrecy, Gordon had completed most of his preparations by March 23, when he met with Lee for the last time prior to the assault. Both men fully appreciated the desperateness of the proposed attack, but as the plan "seemed to give more promise of good results than any other hitherto suggested," the commanding general placed nearly one-half of his army at Gordon's disposal.[7]

Most of the following night was spent moving and concentrating troops in the rear of Colquitt's Salient and quietly removing the obstructions fronting the Confederate lines. To minimize confusion during the first stages of the attack, Gordon had strips of white cloth distributed among all of the leading elements. With these identifying markers tied across their chests, the Confederates could differentiate between friend and foe in the darkness. As the hour of attack approached, Gordon visited with his shock troops. He told them that if they succeeded in capturing the three rear forts, he would see that each man received a thirty-day furlough, as well as a silver medal.

6. Davis, *Confederate Government*, II, 652–53; Walker, "Gordon's Assault," 23, 30; T. G. Jones, "Last Days," 69–70; Gordon, *Reminiscences*, 403–405; Gordon to General Lewis, August 21, 1886, in W. G. Lewis Papers; Robert M. Stribling, *Gettysburg Campaign and Campaigns of 1864 and 1865 in Virginia* (Petersburg, Va., 1905), 298; Thomas, *Doles-Cook Brigade*, 38; Douglas Southall Freeman and Grady McWhiney (eds.), *Lee's Dispatches* (New York, 1957), 342–43; Gordon's Report, April 11, 1865, in Robert Edward Lee Headquarters Papers, VHS.

7. Gordon's Report, April 11, 1865; Gordon to General Lewis, August 21, 1886, in W. G. Lewis Papers; Hotchkiss Journal, March 21, 1865; Gordon, *Reminiscences*, 405–406; Davis, *Confederate Government*, II, 651–52.

One participant long remembered Gordon's "stirring and impressive speech" to the men "standing there in the night, with the awful task and eternity staring us in the face."[8]

At 4 A.M. on March 25, all was in readiness. Gordon, standing atop his breastworks, was supervising the removal of some scattered debris in his front when a Union picket, alerted by the activity, called out, "'What are you doing over there, Johnny? What is that noise? Answer quick or I'll shoot.'" As visions of disaster—"an alarm, picket firing, an awakened enemy, a repulsed charge"—flashed through Gordon's mind, a quick-witted private by his side answered, "'Never mind, Yank. Lie down and go to sleep. We are just gathering a little corn. You know rations are mighty short over here.'" The Federal, evidently satisfied, replied, "'All right, Johnny; go ahead and get your corn. I'll not shoot at you while you are drawing your rations.'" Moments later, when the last troublesome obstacles had been cleared away, Gordon ordered this same soldier to fire his rifle as a signal for the attack to commence. The conscience-stricken private hesitated. Unwilling to abuse the magnanimity of his generous counterpart, who had allowed him to continue his supposed search for food, the Confederate called out, "'Hello Yank! Wake up; we are going to shell the woods. Look out; we are coming.'" With that, he fired a single shot and the assault began.[9]

The attack, in its initial stages, could scarcely have proceeded more smoothly. Gordon's pickets quickly overwhelmed the Union sentinels, thereby allowing his axmen to cut their way through the menacing obstructions in front of Fort Stedman almost without opposition.[10] In the predawn darkness, surprise was complete; the fort

8. Davis, *Confederate Government*, II, 653; Gordon's Report, April 11, 1865; Hotchkiss to Gordon, April 28, 1893, in Hotchkiss Papers, LC; Gordon, *Reminiscences*, 406–407; Thomas, *Doles-Cook Brigade*, 39–41; Captain J. P. Carson, "Fort Steadman's Fall," *Confederate Veteran*, XII (1904), 461; Walker, "Gordon's Assault," 24–25.

9. Walker, "Gordon's Assault," 24; Gordon, *Reminiscences*, 407–10; Gordon, "Last Days of the Confederacy," in Rossiter Johnson (ed.), *Campfire and Battlefield*, 488–89.

10. A number of Federal reports complained that the Confederates used an additional ruse to overwhelm their pickets. By taking advantage of a recent order encouraging Confederate deserters to bring their weapons with them, whole squads of pretended deserters penetrated Union lines. Then, when Gordon's storming columns followed closely, the prisoners turned and overpowered their captors. Confederate accounts of the battle, however, make no mention of employing such a tactic. *OR*, Vol. XLVI, Pt. 1, pp. 317, 320; U. S. Grant, *Personal Memoirs of U. S. Grant* (2 vols.; New York, 1885), II, 432; George L. Kilmer, "Gordon's Attack at Fort Stedman," in Johnson and Buel (eds.), *Battles and Leaders of the Civil War*, IV, 580.

fell, and four to five hundred feet of the trenches on either side were seized. The sudden dash of Gordon's troops also captured artillery and more than five hundred prisoners. But problems developed as dawn approached. Although the three columns of "fleeing Federals" had successfully penetrated the Federal infantry supports and reached the rear, they were unable to locate— let alone capture— the three key forts. As a result, when daylight arrived and the surrounding Federals realized the limited extent of the breach in their lines, they were able to contain the attack and bring reinforcements to bear upon the Confederates. Murderous artillery fire and concentrated small-arms fire defeated several attempts by Gordon's men to seize adjoining forts and expand their holdings. By 7:30 A.M., heavy Federal reinforcements had counterattacked and successfully cordoned off a small area around Fort Stedman. With all available Federal batteries pouring a "consuming fire on both flanks and front," Gordon saw the futility of continued occupation of his toehold in Union lines. He notified Lee of the situation and soon received orders to suspend the attack, whereupon he withdrew his men at about 8:00 A.M. Most of Gordon's casualties occurred during the evacuation of Fort Stedman and the return across no-man's-land. The vicious Union crossfire sweeping the open ground between lines proved so deadly that many of Gordon's men surrendered rather than face almost certain death, "running the gauntlet" back to the Confederate trenches. Gordon's effort to break Grant's hold upon Petersburg had failed.[11]

Union forces attacked other portions of the long Confederate line that afternoon, but Gordon's immediate front remained relatively quiet. With a lull prevailing, Gordon requested and obtained a flag of truce to remove his dead and wounded who had fallen in or near the enemy works. Confederate losses in the assault upon Fort Stedman approached 3,500 men, including 1,900 prisoners. Gordon himself sustained a flesh wound in the leg while recrossing the open area

11. Kilmer, "Gordon's Attack at Fort Stedman," 580–83; Gordon, *Reminiscences,* 410–12; Gordon to Lewis, August 21, 1886, in W. G. Lewis Papers; Stribling, *Gettysburg Campaign,* 298–99; Walker; "Gordon's Assault," 25–29; T. G. Jones, "Last Days," 70–73; Gordon's Report, April 11, 1865; Thomas, *Doles-Cook Brigade,* 36, 40–42; Carson, "Fort Steadman's Fall," 461–62; R. D. Funkhouser, "Fort Steadman—'So Near and Yet So Far,'" *Confederate Veteran,* XIX (1911), 217–18; Gordon, "Last Days of the Confederacy," in Rossiter Johnson (ed.), *Campfire and Battlefield,* 489–91; Hartranft, "Recapture of Fort Stedman," 585–89; *OR,* Vol. XLVI, Pt. 1, pp. 173, 316–19, 320–21, 322–24, 331–32, 382–83, 391, Pt. 3, pp. 109–10; Freeman and McWhiney (eds.), *Lee's Dispatches,* 344–47; Humphreys, *Virginia Campaign,* 317–21; Davis, *Confederate Government,* II, 653–54.

between the opposing lines. He must have been bitterly disappointed by the failure of his attack, especially after its initial success. He thought that the failure to occupy the three forts in the rear had prevented him from breaking through and had thus severely limited the assault's success.[12] In his report to General Lee two days after the surrender of the Army of Northern Virginia, Gordon stated the "effort failed for want of proper guides and a knowledge of the ground upon which the officers selected for this purpose operated." Years later, he also maintained that because reinforcements from Longstreet's corps failed to arrive, he was prevented from carrying out his plan. However, the absence of these troops was probably of little consequence. Gordon knew on the previous evening that Longstreet's men would probably not reach him in time, and moreover, he was unable to use all the troops that were already at his disposal on the morning of the attack. He never expanded the breach of the Federal front sufficiently to allow for full deployment of the forces at hand. Even though Gordon placed a large portion of the blame for his defeat on his guides' inability to locate the forts and on the nonarrival of supporting troops, it is doubtful that this desperate attack could have yielded significant results. The Confederates were simply too weak and the Federals too strong.[13]

Gordon's responsibility for the defeat is difficult to assess. Without question, his failure to appreciate both the difficulty of locating the forts in the darkness and the destructive power of artillery fire from the carefully engineered Federal works contributed substantially to

12. Gordon was correct in believing that his inability to drive deep into the enemy rear and to carry the forts commanding the Federal main line doomed his assault. Although doubts concerning the actual existence of these forts have occasionally been raised, it appears quite certain that two of the redoubts were not only where Gordon thought they were but served as active Union artillery batteries as well. And though unoccupied at the outset of the attack, the third fort (a former Confederate battery in the 1864 Dimmock Line) was soon manned and used effectively by Federal artillery in repulsing Gordon's attack. O. F. Northington, Jr. (Superintendent of Petersburg National Military Park) to D. S. Freeman, December 4, 1943, in Petersburg National Battlefield Headquarters, Petersburg, Va.; Freeman, *R. E. Lee*, IV, 18; Freeman, *Lee's Lieutenants*, III, 653.

13. Freeman, *Lee's Lieutenants*, III, 650–51; *OR*, Vol. XLVI, Pt. 1, pp. 51, 318, 321, Pt. 3, pp. 152, 153, 156, 157; Brevet Colonel J. L. Van Buren to Gordon, March 25, 1865, in Gordon Family Collection, UGA; Stribling, *Gettysburg Campaign*, 304–305; Gordon to General Lewis, August 21, 1886, in W. G. Lewis Papers; W. Gordon McCabe, "Defence of Petersburg," *SHSP*, II (July–December, 1876), 300; T. G. Jones, "Last Days," 73–74; Douglas, *I Rode with Stonewall*, 329; Gordon, *Reminiscences*, 411–13; Gordon's Report, April 11, 1865; Davis, *Confederate Government*, II, 653–54.

his repulse. Gordon's unfamiliarity with the Petersburg front (he had not returned from the valley until December, and then he had occupied a position far to the west) helps explain his errors, but it does not excuse them. Nevertheless, one must be careful of criticizing Gordon too harshly for the Battle of Fort Stedman. By March, 1865, the physical deprivation and the attrition suffered by the Army of Northern Virginia had combined to rob it of efficiency at all levels of command. Douglas Southall Freeman observed, "[P]erhaps, in the misery of a dying cause, the usual care of competent soldiers [Gordon and others] weakened," and thus Gordon's mistakes may well have been shared by all. As Gordon later remarked, despite the hazardous nature of the assault, "it seemed necessary to do more than sit quietly waiting for General Grant to move upon our right, while each day was diminishing our strength by disease and death." Gordon's own description of the battle as "the expiring struggle of the Confederate giant, whose strength was nearly exhausted and whose limbs were heavily shackled by the most onerous conditions" is quite possibly the best assessment of his assault on March 25.[14]

In the days following the defeat at Fort Stedman, Gordon's physical and mental powers were supremely tested, for the ever-worsening situation of the Army of Northern Virginia afforded him little opportunity to rest. While intensifying its pressure on Confederate front lines, the Federal army continued to push westward toward the Southside Railroad. This increasing threat to Lee's right compelled Gordon to extend his already precariously thin line two miles farther, as adjoining troops slipped westward. Occupying a front more than six miles long with fewer than 5,500 men reduced the II Corps to little more than a long line of skirmishers. Forced to keep more than one-half of his entire command constantly on duty, Gordon painfully noted the alarming decrease in efficiency of both officers and men as physical exhaustion set in.[15]

On April 1, Union cavalry and infantry overwhelmed the Confederate forces at Five Forks, thereby turning Lee's right flank and rendering the Petersburg line untenable. Grant, realizing that this success would compel Lee to retreat, launched numerous heavy attacks against the Richmond-Petersburg line the next day. The II Corps front, stretching from the Appomattox River to Fort Gregg, was

14. Davis, *Confederate Government*, II, 654; Gordon, *Reminiscences*, 412; Freeman, *Lee's Lieutenants*, III, 652–54.
15. Gordon, *Reminiscences*, 415–17; Gordon's Report, April, 11, 1865.

broken at several points, but Gordon's skillful counterattacks—
made exclusively with his troops, for there were no reserves whatsoever—had restored most of his line when he received a fateful
message from Lee: Petersburg must be abandoned. Gordon was ordered to hold his position at all costs until nightfall, so that all other
commands might be withdrawn. This prevented the II Corps from
slipping away until well into the night of April 2. After crossing the
Appomattox and burning the bridges, Gordon's weary men set out on
a circuitous march that they hoped would lead them to Joe Johnston
in North Carolina. Evacuation from Petersburg proved particularly
distressing for Gordon because he was forced to leave his wife behind.
Fanny had given birth to their third son the day before and was in no
condition to travel. She had to remain and face the uncertainty of
occupation by Union forces while her husband fled the beleaguered
city.[16]

For the next four days, Gordon's command served as the rear guard
of the retreating army. Although hunger and exhaustion worked their
hardships upon Lee's veterans, the first three days passed with relatively little interference from the enemy.[17] However, April 6 wit-

16. Gordon's Report, April 11, 1865; J. L. Chamberlain, "The Last Salute of the
Army of Northern Virginia," SHSP, XXXII (1904), 356; Humphreys, Virginia Cam-
paign, 366–72; OR, Vol. XLVI, Pt. 1, pp. 54–55, 1061–63, 1263–65, Pt. 3, pp. 1378,
1379; T. G. Jones, "Last Days," 74–77; Gordon, Reminiscences, 417–23, 454–55;
Douglas, I Rode with Stonewall, 330–31; Gordon, "Last Days of the Confederacy," in
Rossiter Johnson (ed.), Campfire and Battlefield, 491–92; John Brown Gordon, "Last
Days of the Confederacy," in Thomas B. Reed (ed.), Modern Eloquence (15 vols.;
Philadelphia, 1900–1903), V, 487–88.
    17. On April 5, one of Gordon's scouts recognized two young men dressed in
Confederate cavalry uniforms as Union scouts. A thorough search of these "Jessie
scouts" uncovered an important message from Grant to Major General Edward O. C.
Ord—one that detailed marching orders for the following days and clearly showed that
Federal infantry already blocked Lee's chosen path of retreat—hidden in the lining of
one of the men's boots. Gordon told his captives that he had no choice but to adhere to
the rules of war and have them shot as spies the next morning. Despite this pronounce-
ment, Gordon had no intention of executing them with the end of the war in sight. So
when he informed the commanding general of the captured dispatch, Gordon also
included a recommendation that the spies' lives be spared. Lee assented and the
Yankees remained with the II Corps until after the surrender. Gordon, Reminiscences,
424–28; T. G. Jones, "Last Days," 97–98; Gordon, "Last Days of the Confederacy," in
Rossiter Johnson (ed.), Campfire and Battlefield, 493; T. M. R. Talcott, "From Petersburg to Appomattox," SHSP, XXXII (1904), 69. Lee's response to Gordon concerning the intercepted Union orders is located in OR, Vol. XLVI, Pt. 3, p. 1387. Gordon
believed that the original penciled order, dated April 6, 4 A.M., had been lost when his
home was destroyed in 1899, but somehow it survived and can be found in the Gordon
Family Collection, UGA.

nessed the devastating effectiveness of vigorous pursuit by a numerically superior foe. For nearly the entire length of its fourteen-mile march from Amelia Springs to Sayler's Creek, the II Corps fought to hold the closely pursuing Federal infantry at bay. Skillfully using his artillery and the surrounding terrain, Gordon continually formed his three divisions in successive lines and repeatedly withdrew the rearmost command through the other two, in an effort to safeguard the army's wagon train. Gordon's men trudged "on and on, hour after hour, from hilltop to hilltop, . . . alternately forming, fighting, and retreating, making one almost continuous battle." While Gordon had his hands full, fighting to protect the army's rear, Ewell, who commanded the infantry unit in front of the wagons guarded by the II Corps, diverted the army's wagon train from the main route and onto a more secure northerly road. For some unexplained reason, he failed to notify Gordon of the change, so that when the rear guard came to the fork in the road, it continued to follow the wagons as it had done the entire day. This oversight uncovered Ewell's rear and led to the well-chronicled debacle at Sayler's Creek.[18]

At the same time that Ewell and adjoining commands were being isolated and overwhelmed, Union forces continued to strike at Gordon's column as it neared another crossing of the stream. The maddeningly slow movement of the wagons and the increased pressure by the pursuing enemy forced Gordon "to make a determined stand or abandon the train." Despite his men's efforts "to push the ponderous wagon-trains through the bog, out of which the starved teams were unable to drag them," many of the heaviest wagons had to be left. Gordon's troops were fighting for their very lives. Both flanks were in danger of being turned and artillery ammunition was nearly exhausted when Gordon reported his critical situation to Lee. He had fought all day, lost heavily, and was still pressed closely. "I fear," wrote the Georgian, "that a portion of the train will be lost as my force is quite reduced and insufficient for its protection. So far I have been able to protect them but without assistance can scarcely hope to do so much longer." There would be no assistance for the men of the II

18. Gordon, *Reminiscences*, 423–24; T. G. Jones, "Last Days," 81; Humphreys, *Virginia Campaign*, 379–81; *OR*, Vol. XLVI, Pt. 1, pp. 651–52, 1107–1108, 1265–66, 1283–84, 1289–90, 1294–95, 1296–98, 1302, Pt. 3, p. 600; Gordon's Report, April 11, 1865. Christopher M. Calkins' *Thirty-Six Hours Before Appomattox, April 6 and 7, 1865* (N.p., 1980) is a thoroughly documented account of the Battle of Sayler's Creek and the actions of the following day.

Corps, however. Gordon managed to repulse two major attacks before intense pressure on three sides finally broke his line around sundown and sent his men fleeing in confusion.[19] The disasters of April 6 almost completely shattered what remained of the old command structure of the Army of Northern Virginia. The army had been reduced to two skeleton corps under Gordon and Longstreet, probably numbering fewer than 12,000 reliable armed men. Following the Battle of Sayler's Creek, Gordon rallied his survivors in the darkness and rejoined the main body of infantry. In the hasty reorganization that night and the following day, the scattered remnants of the commands of Richard H. Anderson, George E. Pickett, Bushrod R. Johnson, and Henry A. Wise were assigned to Gordon's decimated corps. On April 7, for the first time since leaving Petersburg, Gordon relinquished rearguard responsibilities; but he found little rest, for the march continued and action forced frequent deployment. Extraordinarily fine marching and a lack of Federal interference the next day enabled Gordon to reach the village of Appomattox Court House before halting.[20]

Late that evening Gordon was summoned to his commander's headquarters, where he conferred with Lee, Longstreet, and Major General Fitzhugh Lee about the fate of their commands—all that remained of the army. After learning that Lee was in correspondence with Grant and that Federal forces quite probably blocked the route of retreat, Gordon realized that this could be the last council of war. Years later he recalled this meeting around a low-burning fire. "[N]o tongue or pen will ever be able to describe the unutterable anguish of Lee's commanders as they looked into the clouded face of their beloved leader and sought to draw from it some ray of hope." Lee and his lieutenants, in spite of the hopelessness of their situation, made a decision to act in the finest tradition of the Army of Northern Virginia: attack and attempt to cut their way out. Fitz Lee's cavalry, closely followed by Gordon's infantry, would move at daylight while

19. *OR*, Vol. XLVI, Pt. 1, pp. 673–74, 681–82, 712, 779–80, 1266, Pt. 3, p. 600; Humphreys, *Virginia Campaign*, 381; T. G. Jones, "Last Days," 81–82; Thomas, *Doles-Cook Brigade*, 43–44; Grimes, *Letters to his Wife*, 113–14; Gordon, *Reminiscences*, 429–30; Gordon to R. E. Lee, April 6, 1865, in Lee Headquarters Papers; Carlton McCarthy, *Detailed Minutiae of Soldier Life in the Army of Northern Virginia, 1861–1865* (Richmond, 1882), 131–42; Gordon's Report, April 11, 1865.

20. Gordon's Report, April 11, 1865; *OR*, Vol. XLVI, Pt. 1, pp. 1266, 1290–91, 1292; Freeman, *R. E. Lee*, IV, 93; Grimes, *Letters to his Wife*, 116–17; Gordon to C. C. Jones, July 28, 1875, in Georgia Portfolio II, C. C. Jones, Jr., Collection.

Longstreet brought up the rear. If the advance encountered only cavalry, they were to drive the Federal horsemen away and open a path
for the rest of the army; if, however, they found heavy infantry supports, the game would be over. After riding away from the conference,
Gordon realized that he had not received specific instructions as to
where he should stop and camp the next evening, so he sent a staff
officer back to the commanding general. Lee's facetious response—
"Tell General Gordon that I should be glad for him to halt just beyond
the Tennessee line"—probably brought a smile to Gordon's scarred
face, for the Tennessee-Virginia border lay almost two hundred miles
away.[21]

At daybreak, Gordon's westward advance from Appomattox Court
House reached newly constructed Federal breastworks. Neither he
nor Fitz Lee could determine whether cavalry or infantry lay across
their path, so Bryan Grimes, one of Gordon's division commanders,
offered to attack. Gordon assented and placed his entire corps in line
with the cavalry on his right. Gordon's men attacked, carrying the
temporary Union works and capturing two pieces of artillery plus a
number of prisoners who turned out to be cavalry. The success proved
short-lived, because rapidly arriving infantry supports halted the advance and soon threatened to surround and crush Gordon's beleaguered veterans. "The appearance of these large bodies of the Enemy's
Infantry & the impossibility of Gen. Longstreet's moving up" convinced Gordon that "these circumstances rendered resistance for any
positive advantage useless & the loss of life by our brave men of no
avail." Gordon notified Lee that infantry, as well as cavalry, blocked
his retreat and grimly added, "I have fought my corps to a frazzle, and I
fear I can do nothing unless I am heavily supported by Longstreet's
corps." Then, as privately agreed upon at the previous evening's conference, he alerted Fitz Lee of the imminent possibility of a truce,
thereby allowing the cavalrymen to leave the field without being
surrendered. Gordon's troops continued "furiously fighting in nearly

21. Gordon, Reminiscences, 434–36; Gordon, "Last Days of the Confederacy," in
Reed (ed.), Modern Eloquence, V, 489; OR, Vol. XLVI, Pt. 1, pp. 1266, 1303; T. G. Jones,
"Last Days," 83; Gordon, "Last Days of the Confederacy," in Rossiter Johnson (ed.),
Campfire and Battlefield, 493; James Longstreet, From Manassas to Appomattox
(Philadelphia, 1896), 623; A. L. Long, Memoirs of Robert E. Lee (New York, 1886), 420;
Gordon to Bryan Grimes, May 6, 1872, in Bryan Grimes Papers, NCDAH; Gordon to E.
P. Alexander, March 27, 1888, in Edward Porter Alexander Papers, SHC; Atlanta Con-
stitution, April 9, 10, 1885. All of the messages between Lee and Grant during April 7
through 9 can be found in OR, Vol. XLVI, Pt. 1, pp. 56–58.

every direction" until word from Lee arrived. A truce now existed between Lee and Grant.[22]

Gordon took immediate steps to ensure a temporary cessation of hostilities on his front. He drafted a simple note—"'General Gordon has received notice from General Lee of a flag of truce, stopping the battle'"—and instructed Colonel Green Peyton to deliver it to Major General Edward O. C. Ord, the Union commander that Gordon believed was attacking his command. When he learned that the II Corps did not have a flag of truce and that his staff officer had no handkerchief, Gordon told Peyton to tear up his shirt and use it as a white flag. As if to delay the inevitable as long as possible, the colonel replied, "'General, I have on a flannel shirt, and I see you have; I don't believe there is a white shirt in the whole army.'" Thoroughly exasperated, Gordon thundered, "'Get something, sir; get something and go!'" With that, Peyton shrank away, found "a rag of some sort," and rode off to find the Federal commander.[23]

Although unable to locate Ord, Peyton found Sheridan and soon returned with a Union officer "of strikingly picturesque appearance." This superb horseman with long flowing hair galloped up to Gordon and proclaimed, "'I am General Custer, and bear a message to you from General Sheridan. The general desires me to present to you his compliments, and to demand the immediate and unconditional surrender of all the troops under your command.'" Gordon stiffened and replied, "'You will please, general, return my compliments to General Sheridan, and say to him that I shall not surrender my command.'" The brash Federal cavalryman informed the Confederate that if he showed any hesitation in surrendering, he would be annihi-

22. OR, Vol. XLVI, Pt. 1, pp. 1109–10, 1162–63, 1266, 1303–1304; Gordon's Report, April 11, 1865; Gordon to Grimes, May 6, 1872, in Grimes Papers; Grimes, Letters to his Wife, 117–22 (this account is also found in Bryan Grimes, "Appomattox Echo," SHSP, XXVII [1899], 93–96); J. William Jones, Army of Northern Virginia Memorial Volume (Richmond, 1880), 19–20; T. G. Jones, "Last Days," 84–86; Gordon to E. P. Alexander, March 27, 1888, in Alexander Papers; Walter A. Montgomery, "Appomattox and the Return Home," in Walter Clark (ed.), Histories of the Several Regiments and Battalions from North Carolina in the Great War 1861–1865: Written by Members of the Respective Commands (5 vols.; Raleigh, 1901), V, 259–60; Longstreet, From Manassas to Appomattox, 623–27; Long, Memoirs of Robert E. Lee, 420–22; Gordon, Reminiscences, 436–38.

23. Gordon, Reminiscences, 438–39; Gordon, "Last Days of the Confederacy," in Rossiter Johnson (ed.), Campfire and Battlefield, 493; Gordon to E. P. Alexander, March 27, 1888, in Alexander Papers; Gordon, "Last Days of the Confederacy," in Reed (ed.), Modern Eloquence, V, 490.

lated within an hour. Gordon bristled at this bald threat but calmly responded that he had nothing else to add to his earlier note and "if General Sheridan decided to continue the fighting in the face of the flag of truce, the responsibility for the blood shed would be his and not mine." Having failed to intimidate the Georgian, Custer rode off in the company of one of Gordon's staff.[24]

A short while later, another Federal under a white flag approached Gordon's line. In front of "a mounted escort almost as large as one of Fitz Lee's regiments" rode Gordon's nemesis in the Shenandoah Valley, Phil Sheridan. As the diminutive commander of the Union cavalry came within easy range of the sharpshooters who had gathered around Gordon, the Georgian had to physically restrain one of his marksmen, "a half-witted fellow," from shooting Sheridan. Gordon chided the private for even thinking about firing at a man under a flag of truce, but the unrepentant Confederate protested, " 'Well, general, let him stay on his own side.' " The discussion with Sheridan closely paralleled that with Custer because no official word of the temporary truce had arrived from Union headquarters. However, when Gordon showed him Lee's note, Sheridan immediately suggested a cease-fire and the withdrawal of both forces to less-exposed positions while they waited for word of the conference between Lee and Grant. Both commanders, after dispatching their staff officers to see that firing all along the line ceased, dismounted and conversed privately.[25]

Gordon found his adversary neither agreeable nor polite. Sheridan's "style of conversation and general bearing," though never overtly offensive, rankled Gordon. The Federal opened by saying, " 'We have met before, I believe, at Winchester and Cedar Creek in the Valley.' " Gordon acknowledged his presence there, but Sheridan snidely pressed the matter. " 'I had the pleasure of receiving some artillery from your Government, consigned to me through your commander, General Early.' " Detecting "in his manner a slight tinge of exultation," Gordon countered, " 'That is true; and I have this morning received from your government artillery consigned to me through General Sheridan.' " The Union cavalry leader evidently knew noth-

24. Gordon, "Last Days of the Confederacy," in Reed (ed.), *Modern Eloquence*, V, 490–91; Gordon, *Reminiscences*, 439, 440; Gordon to E. P. Alexander, March 27, 1888, in Alexander Papers.

25. Gordon to E. P. Alexander, March 27, 1888, in Alexander Papers; *OR*, Vol. XLVI, Pt. 1, p. 1110; Gordon, "Last Days of the Confederacy," in Rossiter Johnson (ed.), *Campfire and Battlefield*, 493; Gordon, "Last Days of the Confederacy," in Reed (ed.), *Modern Eloquence*, V, 491; Gordon, *Reminiscences*, 439–41.

ing of Gordon's early morning captures and started to object, but he abruptly dropped the matter when firing resumed on the Confederate left. Both commanders rose quickly, at which point Gordon realized that he had forgotten to notify an isolated brigade far to his left. He immediately sought a member of his staff to deliver the cease-fire order, but as none were available, Gordon had to borrow one of Sheridan's staff. Ironically, a Union captain protected by a ragged Confederate private bore Gordon's final combat order to his troops. Not long thereafter, word of the meeting between Lee and Grant arrived. The Army of Northern Virginia had surrendered.[26]

The end had come, but Gordon's soldierly responsibilities continued. As one of three Confederate commissioners appointed by Lee to complete the final details of the surrender agreement, Gordon spent much of April 10 in conference with Longstreet, Brigadier General William N. Pendleton, and their three Federal counterparts. He remembered long afterwards the "marked consideration and courtesy . . . [shown] by the victorious Federals, from the commanding generals to the privates in the ranks." The spirit of generosity and cooperation obviously impressed him, for as one Union officer recalled, Gordon "rose to his feet and made quite a speech, during which he said that . . . he considered his *personal honor* (with emphasis) required him to give the most liberal interpretation to every question which came up for decision." After completion of the agreement, Gordon devoted himself to writing a detailed report of the actions of his corps since the assault on Fort Stedman and to preparing his command for the surrender procession that must inevitably follow.[27]

The morning of April 12, "a chill gray morning, depressing to the senses," wore heavily on Gordon. What had been a brilliantly glowing star in 1861 was now no more than a faintly burning ember. The Confederacy, the dream of an independent nation, was dying. Despite his understandable depression, Gordon gathered his men together for their march to the formal surrender. The II Corps had been assigned the leading position in the surrender column and Gordon would ride

26. Gordon, *Reminiscences*, 441–42; Gordon to Major W. W. Parker, December 18, 1893, in Munford-Ellis Family Papers, Duke.

27. *OR*, Vol. XLVI, Pt. 3, pp. 666–67, 685–86; John Gibbon, "Personal Recollections of Appomattox," *Century Magazine* (April, 1902), 941; "Paroles of the Army of Northern Virginia," *SHSP*, XV (1887), 185; Gordon, *Reminiscences*, 443, 452; Atlanta *Constitution*, April 9, 10, July 31, 1885.

at its head. Had the final order of march been arranged to honor those who had fought the hardest and the best during the last year of the war, first place would have rightly gone to Gordon. As he rode with his famous corps, Gordon, "his chin drooped to his breast," appeared to one Federal "downhearted and dejected . . . almost beyond description." However, when he reached the drawn-up Union forces, a bugle sounded and the entire Federal line shifted from "order arms" to "carry arms," presenting their former foes with a marching salute. Gordon, startled by the "machine like snap of arms," looked up and immediately realized the significance of the Federal gesture. He

> instantly assumed the finest attitude of a soldier. He wheeled his horse . . . , touching him gently with the spur, so that the animal slightly reared, and as he wheeled, horse and rider made one motion, the horse's head swung down with a graceful bow, and General Gordon dropped his swordpoint to his toe in salutation. By word of mouth General Gordon sent back orders to the rear that his own troops take the same position of the manual in the march past as did . . . [the Federal] line. That was done, and a truly imposing sight was the mutual salutation and farewell.

Honor answered honor, salute answered salute as the Army of Northern Virginia marched out of existence and passed into history.[28]

With the painful surrender complete, Gordon rode among the shattered remnants of his corps. In an eloquent address, he bade an emotional farewell to the men who had served him so well under such trying conditions. Gordon reminded them of their heroic achievements, of their great sufferings, and of their selfless devotion to duty. More pointedly, however, he urged them to return to their homes in peace, to adhere to their paroles, to obey the laws, and to aid in rebuilding the South and in reuniting the country. As Gordon watched his veterans sullenly file away, his thoughts undoubtedly turned back to Petersburg and the wife and new baby boy he had left there when the retreat began. The question of what lay beyond his immediate return to his family must have been genuinely unfathomable for the thirty-three-year-old Georgian. Four years of total commitment to the cause of southern independence had come to an end. Now Gordon faced an uncertain, troubled future.[29]

28. Gordon, Reminiscences, 444–48; Freeman, Lee's Lieutenants, III, 745–46; Gordon, "Last Days of the Confederacy," in Reed (ed.), Modern Eloquence, V, 493; Chamberlain, "Last Salute," 361–63; Joshua Lawrence Chamberlain, The Passing of the Armies (New York, 1915), 258–62.

29. There is some confusion as to when—whether on April 10, 11, or 12—Gordon delivered his farewell address; it is quite possible that he spoke to various groups at

Even though Gordon's career as a soldier was concluded, the record
he made during the War Between the States permanently endeared
him to the people of his native state and section. As a soldier, Gordon
knew few peers. His rise from captain to corps commander was unmatched in the Army of Northern Virginia. Only five Confederate
soldiers rose to corps command without the benefit of previous military instruction; and of those, only the Georgian failed to receive his
deserved promotion to lieutenant general. Gordon, in spite of or perhaps because of his lack of formal military training, brought, in the
words of Douglas Southall Freeman, a "certain freshness, a boldness,
a freedom, an originality" to all of his battlefields. Yet he always
displayed the sound military sense of a natural soldier. Although
never tested by independent command, "his fearlessness and eager-
ness to assail the enemy . . . made him one of the most conspicuous
and popular commanders." Most southerners undoubtedly concurred
with Thomas Carter's assessment of the general. The artilleryman
believed that few, if any, of Lee's lieutenants were "so singularly
fitted for attack"; it was as if "the Creator moulded him for the risk of
the onset and put in him that subtle magnetic influence over his men
that strikes 'the electric chain wherewith we are darkly bound.'"[30]

A "soldier's soldier," Gordon possessed a rare combination of talents that set him apart from other military men. His "voice and mien
united to produce an almost unparalleled effect"; his outstanding
oratorical abilities, along with his physical and moral courage, often
inspired his men to almost inconceivable heights of valor and feats of
endurance; his martial appearance led one of his soldiers to remark,
"'He's most the prettiest thing you ever did see on a field of fight.
It'ud put fight into a whipped chicken just to look at him.'" Another
remembered Gordon as "the most gallant man I ever saw on a Bat-

different times. In all probability, he did address the remnants of his corps following
the stacking of arms and furling of flags. Henry Kyd Douglas, who heard Gordon's
speech, stated that he knew of no other general in the army who could have made a
speech to the troops at that time, or to whom the men would have listened so patiently
and intently. McCarthy, *Detailed Minutiae*, 154–55; A Private Soldier [pseud.], "Reminiscences of Lee and Gordon at Appomattox Courthouse," *SHSP*, VIII (1880), 39;
Douglas, *I Rode with Stonewall*, 333–34; Montgomery, "Appomattox," in Clark (ed.),
*Histories of the Several Regiments*, V, 263; Gordon, *Reminiscences*, 448–50; *Confederate Veteran*, XII (1904), 332.

30. Freeman, *Lee's Lieutenants*, III, xxxiv; John S. Wise, *The End of an Era* (Boston,
1900), 339; Thomas H. Carter to John W. Daniel, November 19, 1894, in John Warwick
Daniel Papers, Duke; Thomas H. Carter to Samuel J. C. Moore, October 15, 1889, in
Samuel J. C. Moore Papers, VHS.

tlefield. He had a way of putting things to the men that was irresistible, and he showed the men, at all times, that he shrank from nothing in battle on account of himself." Still another wrote, "it was the ringing name of John Gordon that most frequently thrilled the public ear" during the last year of the war. Idolized by the men he commanded, Gordon emerged from the war second only to Lee in distinction and belovedness, particularly in Georgia. The reputation that he earned while "wearing the gray" would significantly influence almost every aspect of his life during the next forty years. At war's end, he was one of the most popular men in the South. In little more than a decade, he would be one of the most well known and respected southerners in the United States.[31]

31. Lucian Lamar Knight, *Reminiscences of Famous Georgians* (2 vols.; Atlanta, 1907–1908), I, 338; Robert Stiles, *Four Years under Marse Robert* (New York, 1904), 212; John H. Worsham, *One of Jackson's Foot Cavalry* (New York, 1912), 228; Isaac W. Avery, *The History of the State of Georgia From 1850 to 1881* (New York, 1881), 323.

# VII · In Search of a Livelihood

Following the formal surrender of the Army of Northern Virginia on April 12, Gordon began making his way back to the wife and baby boy he had left behind ten days earlier. Riding on horseback with parole in hand, Gordon shared the road to Petersburg with Elihu Washburne, a northern congressman who had been present at Appomattox. Washburne commended the Georgian on the reconciliatory nature of his farewell address and assured him that the victorious North would deal generously with the defeated Confederates. An intimate friend and adviser of Abraham Lincoln, Washburne stated emphatically that the president desired, above all else, rapid restoration of the Union and would permit "no prosecutions and no discriminations" in his efforts to reestablish a normal relationship with the South as quickly as possible. Whatever optimism Gordon may have gleaned from these conversations with Washburne proved short-lived, for shortly after parting from him, Gordon learned of the assassination of Lincoln. From the outset, it was obvious that the road to reunion would not be a smooth one.[1]

Of more immediate concern for Gordon, however, was the safety of his family in Petersburg. When ordered to withdraw from the city on April 2, Gordon had been forced to leave behind his critically ill wife, who only hours before had given birth to their third son, John B. Gordon, Jr. His understandable anxiety over Fanny's condition and that of his son prompted him to telegraph her twice while en route, informing her that he was well and would soon return. Immediately upon reaching Petersburg on April 14, Gordon made his way through

---

1. John B. Gordon, *Reminiscences of the Civil War* (New York, 1903), 450–52, 457.

the rubble of the city to the home of J. Pinckney Williamson, where he had left Fanny. He found his wife and child improving in health and undisturbed by the occupying Federals. In his absence, "some knightly soldier with a blue uniform," as Gordon styled him, had considerately placed an armed guard around her home and prevented any intrusion. Gordon always credited General Grant with this magnanimous gesture, which he deeply appreciated.[2]

While Fanny recovered, Gordon prepared for the arduous journey back to Georgia. With his Confederate scrip "somewhat below par," he struggled to raise enough greenbacks to avoid making the trip south on foot. He had sold one of his finest horses to a Union officer at Appomattox, but he still found himself short of funds. Consequently, Gordon asked Williamson's assistance in selling two artillery horses that he had retained after the surrender. Thus he hoped to gain the three hundred dollars that he believed he needed to make the trip. Williamson located a buyer for the horses at the agreed price but only managed to obtain a thirty-day promissory note. This arrangement forced Gordon to utilize the services of a "curbstone broker," who exchanged the note for cash, less his 10-percent discount. Having secured these additional funds, Gordon and his family began the long homeward trek. Accompanied by Captain and Mrs. James M. Pace (Fanny's sister) and their family, the Gordons made the torturous journey "over broken railroads and in such dilapidated conveyances as had been left in the track of the armies." Despite the difficulties, they safely reached Georgia around the end of April and proceeded to the home of his parents. The Reverend Z. H. Gordon and his wife had been forced to move to Columbus when opposing armies maneuvered into northwestern Georgia in 1863.[3]

While there, Gordon learned of the capture and imprisonment of Jefferson Davis. Northern officials indicted the former Confederate president on charges of treason and initiated proceedings against other Confederate officials and high-ranking military officers. Then,

2. *Ibid.*, 454; Gordon to wife, April 12, April 13, 1865, both in Gordon Family Collection, UGA; John Brown Gordon, "Last Days of the Confederacy," in Thomas B. Reed (ed.), *Modern Eloquence* (15 vols.; Philadelphia, 1900–1903), V, 488; Gordon's Service File, in Military Service Records, NA; J. Pinckney Williamson, *"Ye Olden Times," History of Petersburg* (Petersburg, Va., 1906), 67; Caroline Lewis Gordon, "De Gin'ral an' Miss Fanny" (MS in Gordon Family Collection, UGA).

3. Williamson, *"Ye Olden Times,"* 67; Gordon, *Reminiscences*, 103–104, 454; Sarah Harriet Butts (comp.), *The Mothers of Some Distinguished Georgians* (New York, 1902), 2.

on May 29, 1865, the new president of the United States, Andrew Johnson, issued his Proclamation of Amnesty. A full pardon was offered to southerners who would swear an oath of allegiance to the United States, but Johnson excluded certain classes of former Confederates, including all military figures above the rank of colonel. Excluded individuals could not take the oath unless they had obtained an individual pardon from Johnson, and until pardoned and restored to full citizenship, they could neither vote nor hold office. Suddenly, that which endeared Gordon to his fellow southerners— his distinguished military record—now seriously clouded his future.[4]

Fear of imprisonment or even execution and the "prospect of the ills embraced in the exception to the Benefit of the Amnesty" led Gordon to consider leaving the country. Before seeking official permission from United States authorities to relocate abroad, he sought the assistance of Fanny's uncle, John Sutherland Lewis. In mid-June, 1865, Lewis wrote to an old friend and congressional colleague, General William Trousdale of Tennessee, and asked for letters of introduction for Gordon "to the Monarch, or some persons of the highest position" in Brazil, so that his nephew would not be viewed as an adventurer when he arrived in the South American country. Gordon evidently gave serious consideration to emigrating, despite later claims to the contrary. But in the last half of 1865, as the fear and uncertainty following the surrender gradually turned to tentative confidence and relative stability, he apparently abandoned such thoughts and resolved to remain in Georgia.[5]

Once he became reasonably confident of immunity from prosecution on charges of treason, Gordon began the difficult search for a new

4. Dunbar Rowland (ed.), *Jefferson Davis, Constitutionalist: His Letters, Papers, and Speeches* (10 vols.; Jackson, Miss., 1923), VII, 139–42; Charles M. Blackford, "The Trials and Trial of Jefferson Davis," *SHSP*, XXIX (1901), 59; C. Mildred Thompson, *Reconstruction in Georgia, Economic, Social, Political, 1865–1872* (New York, 1915), 144; Edwin C. Woolley, *The Reconstruction of Georgia* (New York, 1901), 12; *OR*, Ser. II, Vol. VIII, 578–80. Although numerous efforts were afoot in the North to bring formal charges against the civilian and military leaders of the Confederacy, few progressed much beyond the indictment stage. In May, 1868, a grand jury in the Circuit Court of the United States for the District of Virginia indicted Gordon for levying war against the United States. Although named as a co-conspirator, along with Davis, R. E. Lee, and some twenty other former Confederates, he was never at that late date in any real danger of being tried or convicted. Rowland (ed.), *Jefferson Davis*, VII, 179–95; Blackford, "Trials of Davis," 75–80.

5. John Sutherland Lewis to General Trousdale, June 13, 1865, in William Trousdale Papers, TSLA; Gordon, *Reminiscences*, 448; Atlanta *Constitution*, May 28, 1872.

livelihood. He retained his financial interest in coal mines located in the northwestern tip of Georgia, but extensive fighting there had seriously damaged the mines and forced them to close and Gordon lacked the capital to rebuild the railroads and the inclined planes that would enable the mines to return to productivity. The imposition of martial law in Georgia, under which the Federal army displaced all civil authority, precluded hopes of immediately reestablishing a law practice. Nevertheless, near the end of the summer of 1865, Gordon moved his family—Fanny, sons Hugh, Frank, and John, Jr., and daughter Frances—from Columbus to the more centrally located Atlanta, where he had practiced law in the 1850s. While in Atlanta, Gordon applied to President Johnson for a presidential pardon. On September 15, 1865, he signed an oath of allegiance and sent a letter to Johnson asking for removal of the political disabilities resulting from his participation in the war. Restored to full citizenship shortly thereafter, Gordon redoubled his efforts to find a new way to make a living.[6]

The abundant forests of Georgia, one of the state's few sources of wealth that remained relatively untouched by the war, soon attracted his attention. In the period immediately following the war, "cutting lumber with small sawmills," according to one southern historian, "afforded an easy road to setting up a modest business." Recognizing this economic opportunity, Gordon traveled to Savannah in November, 1865, with thoughts of developing a kindling trade with the North. He hoped to take advantage of the state's vast pine reserves by cutting the trees down to a manageable size and then shipping them by water to New York, where the bundles of wood would command a much higher price than they did in Georgia. Why Gordon never followed through on these plans is not known, but by late 1865, he had become involved in another timber-related enterprise. Gordon entered into a partnership with George Shorter of Brunswick, Georgia, a coastal town eighty miles south of Savannah. After securing financial backing from undetermined sources, they built two large sawmills near the Brunswick Railroad and established a lumber business that was eventually capitalized at between $80,000 and $90,000. Gor-

6. Gordon to Barlow, January 29, April 7, September 21, 1868, all in Samuel Latham Mitchill Barlow Papers, HL, by permission; Allen P. Tankersley, "Basil Hallam Overby, Champion of Prohibition in Ante-Bellum Georgia," *Georgia Historical Quarterly*, XXXI (1947), 17; Woolley, *Reconstruction of Georgia*, 10–15; Amnesty Records, United States State Department, NA.

don, Shorter and Company evidently enjoyed substantial success during its first year of operation because by the end of 1866, Gordon had also acquired a rice plantation along the coast. Moreover, a leading southern journal reported that all mills around Brunswick had "orders already in hand [that] cannot be filled for two years." And with Gordon as "the pioneer, and . . . the ruling spirit in this gigantic enterprise at Brunswick," it appeared to the editor of the periodical that many more mills would be erected in the near future. In addition to his own interests, Gordon also managed a number of other sawmills in the area, including those belonging to his friend Samuel L. M. Barlow of New York. Even at this early date, Gordon began establishing ties with northern businessmen—a fact that may have contributed to his commitment to reunion.[7]

Although business prospects appeared promising on the coast, Gordon found relations between the races particularly strained. Along the coastal belt, including the Sea Islands, blacks greatly outnumbered whites and, in the wake of the war, black troops frequently served as the occupation force. As he later reported to a congressional committee, Gordon discovered that "a very bad state of feeling between those negro troops and the citizens" of Brunswick already existed when he arrived in late 1865. Black soldiers, Gordon contended, reveled in verbally abusing former Confederate soldiers

7. E. Merton Coulter, *The South During Reconstruction, 1865–1877* (Baton Rouge, 1947), 270–71, vol. VIII of Wendell Holmes Stephenson and E. Merton Coulter (eds.), *A History of the South;* Willard Range, *A Century of Georgia Agriculture, 1850–1950* (Athens, 1954), 155–56; *De Bow's Review*, XXXV (August, 1866), 201; Jeremy Kilmer to E. P. Alexander, November 4, 1865, in Edward Porter Alexander Papers, SHC; *Testimony Taken by the Joint Select Committee to Inquire into the Condition of Affairs in the Late Insurrectionary States* (13 vols.; Washington, D.C., 1872), in *House Reports*, 42nd Cong., 2nd Sess., No. 22, Pt. 6, Georgia, Vol. I, pp. 304–305, this volume hereinafter cited as KKK Report; Gordon to Barlow, January 26, January 4, 1869 [i.e. 1868], Gordon to Finney, January 26, 1868, all in Barlow Papers; Atlanta *Daily Intelligencer*, January 20, 1866. It is difficult to determine from whom Gordon and Shorter received the money necessary to establish and operate their mills. Gordon's writings leave no substantial clues whatsoever. Rebecca L. Felton, a lady who would become the general's most persistent and vocal critic, years later maintained that he borrowed thousands from a southern cleric, using stock in his coal mines to secure the loan. Then when the lumber business failed, she claimed, Gordon welshed on his debt and left the clergyman holding worthless coal company stock. Gordon vehemently denied these charges. He asserted that he borrowed only three hundred dollars from Bishop Richard Wilmer of Alabama and that he satisfied that debt shortly thereafter. Mrs. William H. Felton, *My Memoirs of Georgia Politics* (Atlanta, 1911), 488, 493–94, 505–506; A. H. Stephens to Mrs. Felton, June 26, 1880, in Rebecca Latimer Felton Collection, UGA. See also Atlanta *Constitution*, March 8, 1879.

and in physically intimidating them by forcing whites off sidewalks when encounters occurred in the streets. In his opinion, the attitude of these troops contributed markedly to making the general black population "very obnoxious," heightening tensions, and alarming whites all along the coast. Concerned citizens of Brunswick and nearby Darien prevailed upon Gordon to go to the regional Federal headquarters in Savannah and request the removal of these soldiers. While in Savannah, Gordon met General Grant, who was in the midst of his inspection tour of the South. He traveled for three days with Grant through Georgia and attempted to impress upon the Federal commander the seriousness of the volatile situation on the coast. He made it clear that the patience of whites was wearing thin "and that very certainly there would be bloodshed unless these negro troops were removed." Alerted to the potential violence, the Union general ordered the removal of all black forces from that area of the coast. As soon as white units replaced the black commands, Gordon reported, the troubles subsided.[8]

In the months after the war, Gordon strove in other ways to ease racial tensions and improve relations between the two races in Georgia. In 1866, he and other members of the white community liberally contributed money and materials to help blacks build a church and schoolhouse in Brunswick. When trustees of the Brunswick Colored School asked for his opinions on black education, Gordon advised them "to educate themselves and their children, to be industrious, save money and purchase houses, and thus make themselves respectable as property holders, and intelligent people." He added, "With submission to the laws, industry and economy, with union among yourselves, and courtesy and confidence toward the whites, you will reach these ends, and constitute an important element in the community." As long as blacks agreed to remain in a subordinate position, Gordon pledged the cooperation of whites in black efforts at self-improvement. To that end, he supported pro rata distribution of Glynn County funds for separate educational facilities. He also introduced a resolution calling for the formation of a committee to solicit aid for education of blacks from northerners. He reiterated this call for white support at an educational convention when he endorsed "education of the negro population at the hands of our people, by direct taxation, putting the whites and blacks in that

8. KKK Report, 304–305, 309–10, 319.

respect upon the same footing." On another occasion, he asserted, "I am in favor of extending, by every possible means, every aid toward the moral and intellectual advancement of the colored race." Gordon repeatedly stressed the common interests of blacks and whites, for in his opinion, "[a]cquaintance, past association, in many instances mutual gratification and affection, as well as the mutual dependence of daily business relations, all conspire to bind" the two races together.[9]

Although he recognized the necessity for cooperation between the races, and appeared genuinely concerned with black education and self-improvement, Gordon clearly did not believe in racial equality. In a September, 1868, speech in Charleston, South Carolina, the Georgian took the opportunity to speak directly to blacks in the audience. "If you are disposed to live in peace with the white people, they extend to you the hand of friendship," but, he warned, "if you attempt to inaugurate a war of races you will be exterminated. The Saxon race was never created by Almighty God to be ruled by the African." In his mind, it was "heaven's unalterable decree" that "in all times and ages the white man has been God's chosen vessel and the superior race." Gordon, like most white southerners, particularly resented Republican efforts to make, in his words, "a recently servile race the political superiors of the educated classes of the South." Attempts, as he put it, to confer "upon the ignorant and vicious, rights,[?] or rather to place weapons in their hands to destroy the liberties and inalienable rights of the intelligent and virtuous" could have disastrous consequences. However, Gordon contended, if the "carpet-bagger" element—those whites who, he felt, agitated and inflamed the freedmen—were removed, and blacks and whites in the South were left to themselves, there would be no conflict because each knew and needed the other. Whites in Georgia needed the blacks, he asserted, for "the negro is the proper laborer for our State"

9. Ibid., 305, 307–308, 320, 340, 345; Savannah Daily News and Herald, April 10, 11, 1868; New York Times, April 30, 1867. Gordon provided college educations for several of the blacks with whom he was intimately associated. He sent Buddy Hampton, Wade Hampton's former slave who had helped nurse him back to health after Sharpsburg, to Atlanta University. Gordon also helped obtain college educations for the children of his manservant, Jim, and Fanny's chambermaid, Sarah, former slaves who took the Gordon name and continued to live with the family after the war. Black Gordons File, in Gordon Family Collection, UGA; C. L. Gordon, "De Gin'ral an' Miss Fanny"; Hugh H. Gordon, Jr., A Letter to My Sons about Their Forebears (Privately printed, 1954); KKK Report, 307. For more on the so-called Black Gordons who achieved prominence in their own right, see Black Gordons File, in Gordon Family Collection, UGA, and Gordon, Letter to My Sons.

and "we understand him and he understands us." Gordon may have been more benign in his approach to race relations than many southerners, but the peace and stability he hoped for required the continued subordination of the black race. The veins of traditional paternalism and white superiority ran deep in southern society.[10]

Despite his efforts to ensure a social harmony in which whites were in control, Gordon met with frustration on his own rice plantation. Violence broke out during the planting season of 1867, when black laborers refused to plant the rice in the manner that the overseer instructed. Preferring to cultivate the rice in their own particular way, the blacks armed themselves with guns, hoes, and other farm implements, threatened the overseer's life, and drove him away. Ultimately, Federal troops had to be called in to quell the disturbance.[11]

Outbreaks like the one on his plantation undoubtedly contributed to Gordon's willingness to leave the Georgia coast, but it was probably his failing business fortunes that finally convinced him of the need to look elsewhere for a new livelihood. Gordon's lumber business fell upon hard times in 1867. Although the reasons for the failure of the Gordon, Shorter and Company mills are uncertain, the company's collapse appears to have been part of a larger regional problem. As Gordon later explained, the tremendous fluctuation in lumber prices, which on one occasion fell by 50 percent in a single week, contributed mightily to his economic distress. By the end of that year, many mills along the coast around Brunswick "had broken down utterly" and had been forced to liquidate their assets by sheriff's sales. The Gordon, Shorter and Company mills fell victim to these public auctions. Gordon suffered heavily, estimating his losses in excess of $12,000. Determined not to declare bankruptcy, Gordon struggled in the years that followed to repay debts from the mills and probably from his plantation, as well. The burden often left him "utterly prostrated," and he complained to a friend that he felt bound by "an endless slavery to debt." It was to be a recurrent problem in Gordon's postwar years, for despite occasional spectacular successes, his more common failures in business kept him financially insecure. The specter of serious debt haunted him for the rest of his life.[12]

10. Columbus (Ga.) *Weekly Sun*, September 29, 1868, quoted in Alan Conway, *The Reconstruction of Georgia* (Minneapolis, 1966), 172; Atlanta *Constitution*, June 19, August 27, 1868, September 21, 1872; KKK Report, 306–308, 321, 334–35, 339, 341, 346.

11. KKK Report, 305–306.

12. Gordon to A. C. Holt, April 19, 1871, in Alexander Hamilton Stephens Papers I, Emory; James Gaston Towery, "The Georgia Gubernatorial Campaign of 1886" (M.A.

Stripped of available cash, Gordon sought to avoid bankruptcy by inducing his creditors to take as payment stock in the mines of the Castle Rock Coal Company of Georgia. The stock had no present market value and the mines remained under lease, but Gordon stressed their prewar productivity and prosperity. The company owned five thousand acres of "probably the best coal lands in the South," he claimed, and if the mines could be returned to production, they would "prove the best property in southern country." Although Gordon persuaded a number of creditors to accept this coal company stock—though at a discount—he remained hard pressed to ward off bankruptcy. Seeing no prospects for relief from financial distress in Brunswick, Gordon moved his family back to Atlanta near the close of 1867.[13]

"Struggling against adversity" imposed by his severe losses on the coast, Gordon also found himself "sorely perplexed" about how to handle his current expenses. He considered working as an agent "for one or two Locomotive Establishments," which would have enabled him to utilize contacts among his friends involved in various railroading ventures. However, Gordon soon discovered that his reputation as a military leader was of far greater value than he had imagined. In late 1867 or early 1868, two different companies interested in the South offered him important positions. Eventually, he accepted both and became the president of the Atlanta branch of the Southern Life Insurance Company and the vice-president of the publishing firm of Richardson and Company.[14]

The Southern Life Insurance Company provided Gordon with an excellent opportunity to capitalize on the name he had made for himself during the war. When the Memphis-based company named Gordon president of its new branch in Atlanta, his selection was clearly not justified by any proven business acumen but rather by his military fame. His name would act as a magnet to attract business and inspire confidence. Unlike many other former Confederates who were only nominally involved with the companies they headed, Gordon appears to have taken an active role in the management of the

thesis, Emory University, 1945), 64–65; Gordon to Finney, January 26, 1868, Gordon to Barlow, January 26, 29, April 7, September 21, October 19, 1868, January 4, 1869 [i.e., 1868], June 12, 1869, all in Barlow Papers.

13. Gordon to Barlow, January 29, April 7, September 21, October 19, 1868, all in Barlow Papers; Gordon to A. C. Holt, April 19, 1871, in Stephens Papers I, Emory; KKK Report, 304.

14. Gordon to Barlow, January 26, 29, 30, 1868, all in Barlow Papers.

Southern Life Insurance Company, and the Atlanta branch flourished under his direction. His leadership and his defense of the company against northern attacks enabled the Southern to grow rapidly. Reflecting upon its first year of operation, Gordon reported that the company had gained ground, but not as rapidly as he had hoped it would. For him, the insurance business represented much more than just a source of income. Gordon realized that as his business increased, the drain of capital from the South to the North would be effectively slowed. Perhaps in time, it would even be stopped. As more and more money remained at home in the South, vital funds would become available for developing southern business and industry. Thus, the Southern Life Insurance Company afforded Gordon the opportunity to improve his own economic well-being, as well as to promote the interests of the South. Gordon was, in the opinion of one historian, "another of those statesman, so prominent in his day, who combined a laudable desire to advance the common weal with large personal ambitions."[15]

As operations expanded in the following years, the Southern Life Insurance Company came under hostile attack from northern journals. These assaults compelled Gordon to defend the integrity of the company. In March, 1869, he bitterly objected to one particular sixteen-line article in *Insurance Times* that, he maintained, contained twelve *"wilful, malignant, unmitigated falsehoods."* Gordon refuted charges that the company was not a southern one, that it was not doing much business, and that it had both refused and failed to pay losses. He asserted that the Southern Life Insurance Company was "as safe an institution, as solidly founded, and as honestly managed as any in the United States." The Atlanta *Constitution* echoed his sentiments in August, 1869, when the newspaper strongly recommended the Southern to its readers, declaring it "fully entitled to the complete confidence of the people, for its solvency, and able and honest management."[16]

Even amid the mounting financial pressures in the country in the

15. Coulter, *South During Reconstruction,* 197–98; Atlanta *Constitution,* June 22, August 16, 1868, March 28, 1869; Savannah *Daily News and Herald,* May 18, 1868; Athens *Southern Watchman,* May 27, 1868; Atlanta *Daily New Era,* May 24, 1868; Gordon to Yancey, April 12, December 26, 1868, both in Benjamin C. Yancey Papers, SHC; Alex Mathews Arnett, *The Populist Movement in Georgia: A View of the "Agrarian Crusade" in the Light of Solid-South Politics* (New York, 1922), 29.

16. Atlanta *Constitution,* March 26, 28, August 7, November 5, 1869; J. H. Miller to John S. Bratton, August 6, 1869, in Bratton Family Papers, SCL.

early 1870s, the Southern continued to prosper. In an effort to make the company more attractive, Gordon offered its presidency to Robert E. Lee. Although Lee responded that he would derive great pleasure from once again associating with the many former Confederates then involved with the company, he declined the offer. Nevertheless, many other prominent men affiliated themselves with the Atlanta branch. Indeed, with Benjamin H. Hill, Wade Hampton, Robert Toombs, Alexander H. Stephens, Benjamin C. Yancey, C. H. Phinzy, A. Austell, William C. Morris, Alfred H. Colquitt, and H. V. M. Miller serving as officers or directors, or holding stock in the company, the Southern had broad appeal to Georgians. In April, 1871, the Atlanta *Constitution* praised its officers as "men of great ability and [who] number among them names that are dear to the Southern people." The paper also hailed the company's successful operation "with pleasure, for being a home interest, its success stimulates the progress of all other home interests." Two months later, after a patient and thorough examination of the books of the Atlanta branch revealed that "the business of the Company has been conducted by the officers with economy and fidelity," the paper announced that its "former confidence in the great success of the Company and its ability to furnish to policy-holders as perfect security as any in the country, has been strengthened." These were words of high praise for the young company under Gordon's management.[17]

The Southern Life Insurance Company, in addition to its standard life insurance business, was also the publisher of a weekly agricultural journal. The *Plantation*, "devoted to the interest of agriculture, rural economy, and the benefits of life insurance," was distributed free of charge to the Southern's policyholders. Serving "life insurance and agriculture with equal zeal," *Plantation* was both well received as a trade magazine and popular as an agricultural journal. Editors of the Atlanta *Constitution* testified, "We know of no agricultural periodical in which more taste is displayed in the make-up, or whose columns display more marked ability." Moreover, the jour-

17. Lee to Gordon, December 14, 1869, in Robert Edward Lee Letterbooks, VHS (original located in Gordon Family Collection, UGA); Lee to Gordon, March 1, 1870, in Gordon Family Collection, UGA; Atlanta *Constitution*, November 2, 1870, April 9, May 28, July 2, 1871. See also Gordon to Southern Stockholders, May 23, 1870, and statement of confidence, May 23, 1870, both in Yancey Papers. For statements of the continued prosperity of the Southern Life Insurance Company in the mid–1870s, see Atlanta *Constitution*, July 12, 1872, March 23, August 12, September 14, 1873, September 6, 1874.

nal provided a forum for southerners to air their views on any number of subjects. Gordon frequently used the pages of *Plantation* to answer what he considered the malicious accusations and puerile attacks of northern insurance companies on southern insurance ventures. He also heartily extolled the virtue and profitability of investments in the South.[18]

Building on the popularity of the journal, Gordon, B. C. Yancey, and W. C. Morris formed the Plantation Publishing Company in July, 1871. The copartnership continued to issue *Plantation* but also did general printing and bookbinding. Publication of *Plantation*, which brought in $300 a month from the Southern Life Insurance Company, remained the publishing company's major job until July, 1872, when the contract between the two companies expired. *Plantation* then became a subscription periodical rather than a free service for policy-holders. The format of the journal also changed substantially in the fall of 1872, when the sixteen-page weekly costing $3.00 per year was replaced by a fifty-page magazine published monthly at $1.50 per annum. Although *Plantation* continued to receive hearty endorse-ments, mismanagement and internal conflicts—particularly among later partners and Yancey—led to its rapid decline. During his asso-ciation with the publishing firm, Gordon never became deeply in-volved in its operations; instead, he left direction and control of the company to its president, Yancey. He severed his association with *Plantation* in October, 1873, when the Plantation Publishing Com-pany dissolved.[19]

In the meanwhile, Gordon had become much more actively in-volved with the New York–based publishing house Richardson and Company. Although he continued to direct the affairs of the pros-perous Southern Life Insurance Company, and remained devoted to it and to his vision of the benefits it held for the South, Gordon also worked to provide southern schools and colleges with what he con-tended were "unsectional, unpolitical and unpartisan" books. Early in 1868, the Georgian had accepted the vice-presidency of Richardson

18. Coulter, *South During Reconstruction*, 198; Atlanta *Constitution*, July 7, 1871, June 7, 1872.

19. Announcement, May 6, 1871, Contract of Copartnership, July 4, 1871, Notice, October 4, 1871, Testimony of E. D. L. Mobley, June 12, 1872, and C. R. Handleiter to Yancey, July 8, 1872, all in Yancey Papers; Atlanta *Constitution*, June 7, October 17, 1872, October 31, 1873.

and Company, and when it expanded and became known as the University Publishing Company, he retained his position. The company rapidly grew into "the most ambitious and best known" publishing house involved in the southern book business. The University Publishing Company claimed "to create a non-partisan school literature" that it hoped would help rid the nation, and especially the South, of works that sowed "the seeds of the religion of sectional hate." The Southern University Series of School-Books, later known as the University Series of School-Books, offered the South "a series of school books divested of the injurious reflections upon the Southern people and Southern history, which were usually found in Northern elementary works." Gordon insisted that southerners must steadfastly resist all efforts "to destroy the self-respect and character of Southern youth by teaching them . . . that they are descendants of *rebels* and *traitors* to the Constitution of the country." The South's heritage had to be preserved, and the motives that prompted southerners to go to war in 1861 must not be disparaged. Believing there could be no more noble or important cause, Gordon would devote much of his life to ensuring precisely these ends. Despite claims to the contrary, however, the books that he promoted obviously possessed a partisan (albeit southern) slant not unlike those that he so often criticized.[20]

From the beginning of his association with the University Publishing Company, Gordon labored tirelessly on its behalf. Like the Southern Life Insurance Company, it afforded Gordon the opportunity to recoup his financial losses while at the same time supplying what he termed "a long felt want in the South." In the late 1860s and early 1870s, working "with his characteristic energy and ability," Gordon addressed audiences throughout the South, penned countless letters—both public and private—and wrote numerous articles for newspapers and journals, in which he repeatedly stressed that the South must educate itself. He pleaded for southerners to remain united and ever-vigilant in their effort "to rid themselves of literary bondage to the North in the school room." Gordon felt he could not overemphasize the importance of this effort because, as he put it, "[o]ur self respect, our civilization, the character and manhood of our

20. University Series of School-Books Broadside, in Yancey Papers; Gordon to Barlow, January 30, 1868, in Barlow Papers; Coulter, *South During Reconstruction*, 329; Atlanta *Constitution*, June 1, 24, 29, July 14, 1871; Charles S. Venable to F. W. M. Holliday, May 23, 1878, in Frederick W. M. Holliday Papers, Duke.

children demand the introduction of . . . good Southern books into our schools."[21]

Gordon, however, had more in mind than merely a historical defense of the South, and the scope of the southern textbook series soon broadened to encompass a wide variety of subjects. The University Series of School-Books strove to provide books "of the highest order of scholastic and mechanical merits." In order to secure such works, the company contracted with several outstanding southern scholars to write its textbooks. Among "the ablest and most honored educators of the South" who contributed to the series were Charles S. Venable in arithmetic; Commodore Matthew F. Maury in geography; George F. Holmes in readers, spellers, grammars, and history; Basil L. Gildersleeve in Latin; Schele de Vere in French; and John and Joseph LeConte in science. This distinguished group of authors produced a series of texts that E. Merton Coulter found "as noteworthy and respectable as any in the country." The fine quality of many of the books led not only to their widespread use in the South but to their adoption in many northern schools as well.[22]

Nevertheless, the University Publishing Company encountered many of the same criticisms that were leveled against the Southern Life Insurance Company, for the firm was assailed from almost every conceivable angle. Enemies questioned its purpose and management, assaulted the motives and integrity of its officers, ridiculed the quality of the books, and impugned the ability of the authors. Criticized as a southern attempt to introduce strictly sectional books, the University Publishing Company also endured claims that it was a northern firm attempting to impose itself on the South. Gordon, just as he did with the Southern Life Insurance Company, shouldered much of the responsibility for combating what he viewed as the "unscrupulous assaults" on his company and the "virulent opposition" it encountered. He urged his readers not to be diverted by the attacks upon the

21. Venable to Holliday, May 23, 1878, in Holliday Papers; Gordon to P. G. T. Beauregard, May 10, 1872, in John Brown Gordon Papers, Duke; Gordon to R. D. Arnold, September 22, 1873, in Keith Morton Read Collection, UGA; Gordon to Charles Herbst, July 24, 1871, in Charles Herbst Collection, Kentucky Historical Society, Frankfort; Atlanta *Constitution*, November 12, 1870, June 26, July 14, August 12, 1871; R. E. Lee to Gordon, December 30, 1867, in Gordon Family Collection, UGA; Gordon to Barlow, January 30, 1868, in Barlow Papers.

22. Venable to Holliday, May 23, 1878, in Holliday Papers; University Series Broadside, in Yancey Papers; Gordon to Barlow, January 30, 1868, in Barlow Papers; Coulter, *South During Reconstruction*, 329–30; Atlanta *Constitution*, June 29, 1871.

company's honest efforts to publish and distribute "a just, unsectional and elevated school literature." Gordon pointed out that the University Publishing Company, though primarily concerned with southern education, also sought "to improve, to purify, to ennoble and to nationalize, the elementary works by which American children are to be educated." He also took great pains to defend the southern character of the firm. Even though the company utilized the services of a New York publishing house, he explained, financial considerations alone were responsible for that seemingly strange situation. As soon as a southern manufacturer could supply similar services at comparable prices, Gordon assured the public, operations would be shifted to the South because, "the purpose of the Company [is] to aid, in every way in its power, in the advancement of Southern interests."[23]

With Gordon as "its champion and friend," the University Publishing Company successfully furnished many southern children with a series of fine textbooks. Indeed, one historian has written, "[G]enerations of Southerners developed a debt of gratitude to these men" who wrote the texts. The publishing project would eventually fail, but Gordon took great pride in his contribution to the development and dissemination of these school books. By helping provide an alternative to the numerous textbooks that explicitly and implicitly denigrated southerners' role in American history, he assisted fellow southerners in their struggle to hold fast to their traditions. His devotion to national reconciliation would eventually emerge as a dominant theme in his postwar career; however, Gordon also labored with an unmatched zeal to preserve the heritage of his section and to defend southern participation in the Civil War, averring that southerners were guided by the same sincerity of purpose and purity of motive that had animated their northern brethren.[24]

Having committed himself to several businesses that enabled him to serve his state and section as well as himself, Gordon made Atlanta his permanent residence. In the late 1860s, he purchased land in Kirkwood, a sparsely populated community four miles outside the capital city. There, in 1869, in a dense woodland along the Central of

23. "Gen. Gordon's Reply to Certain Widely Circulated Slanders," April 27, 1872, University Series Broadside, in Yancey Papers; Atlanta *Constitution*, June 29, July 14, 25, 1871.
24. Venable to Holliday, May 23, 1878, in Holliday Papers; Coulter, *South During Reconstruction*, 329–30; Atlanta *Constitution*, July 14, 1871.

Georgia Railroad, Gordon carved out a place for his beautiful and beloved Sutherland estate. Built on a hill, his home provided a superb view of the surrounding countryside. The two-story white mansion, distinguished by its eight massive Ionic columns, became a local landmark. Its exceptionally high ceilings, spacious rooms, tall French windows, and elegant, ornate furnishings set Gordon's home apart from other Atlanta residences. Sutherland also became one of the premier social centers, as the Gordons soon established themselves as gracious and generous hosts. On the estate, which encompassed over two hundred acres, Gordon planted numerous varieties of trees, shrubs, and other plants, and raised various kinds of livestock. John and Fanny loved Sutherland so deeply that when it burned near the end of the century, they built an almost exact replica of the original. Sutherland not only served as a source of pride for Gordon but, more important, provided a comfortable refuge from the increasing responsibilities that kept him away from home more and more.[25]

Among those increasing responsibilities was Gordon's deepening involvement in politics. Even though his promotion of the Southern Life Insurance Company, the University Publishing Company, and the Plantation Publishing Company exerted tremendous pressure upon him, Gordon added to his burdens by entering the turbulent waters of Reconstruction politics. In the postwar period, Georgia Democrats, faced with Republican rule and the specter of black equality, appealed to the Gallant Gordon to aid them in their struggle to redeem their state. And just as he had done in 1861, when the Confederate call to arms was issued, Gordon responded. This time he rose to help restore white Democratic rule in Georgia.

25. C. L. Gordon, "De Gin'ral an' Miss Fanny"; Atlanta *Constitution*, June 22, 1899, January 12, 1904; Atlanta *Journal*, March 16, 1924, January 16, 1927, February 21, 1937, October 11, 1942; Paul W. Miller (ed.), *Atlanta: Capital of the South* (New York, 1949), 218–19; H. H. Gordon, Jr., *Letter to My Sons*. The real estate records of De Kalb County are full of transactions whereby Gordon both added to and sold portions of the Kirkwood property. See especially Real Estate Deeds and Mortgages, De Kalb County, Superior Court, Decatur, Ga. Photographs of Sutherland and its interior can be found in Gordon Family Collections, UGA and AHS.

# VIII · Emerging Politician

Passage of the Reconstruction Act of March 2, 1867, had begun anew the governmental reconstruction of the South. By early March of the following year, Georgia had conducted a second registration of voters—this one including blacks and disqualifying additional whites under the terms of the Fourteenth Amendment—and had drafted a new constitution more in line with Republican dictates. All that remained for Georgia to do in order to end military occupation and resume its normal place in the Union seemed to be the ratification of the constitution and the election of state and congressional officers. Accordingly, Major General George G. Meade, military governor of the Third District, which included Georgia, Alabama, and Florida, called for a four-day state election to be held from April 20 through April 23. Georgia Republicans quickly selected Rufus B. Bullock as their standard-bearer, but Democrats— or Conservatives, as they were also known—had a more difficult time choosing a candidate. The Democratic Committee's first two choices, Judges Augustus Reese and David Irwin, had both sworn oaths to the Constitution before the war, so Meade declared them ineligible under the officeholding terms of the Fourteenth Amendment. As a result, Georgia Democrats turned to a political novice. They called upon the Hero of Appomattox—John B. Gordon.[1]

1. Kenneth Coleman (ed.), *A History of Georgia* (Athens, 1977), 210–13; C. Mildred Thompson, *Reconstruction in Georgia, Economic, Social, Political, 1865–1872* (New York, 1915), 171–201; Charles G. Bloom, "The Georgia Election of April 1868: A Reexamination of the Politics of Georgia Reconstruction" (M.A. thesis, University of Chicago, 1963), 30–34; U.S. Army, Department of the South, *Report of Major General Meade's Military Operations and Administration of Civil Affairs in the Third Military District and Department of the South for the year 1868, with Accompanying Documents, in Senate Documents* (Atlanta, 1868) hereinafter cited as *Meade's Report;*

Although he had never held political office, Gordon was not ignorant of Georgia politics, nor were Georgians ignorant of his views. He
had been vitally involved in the events of the secession crisis in both
Alabama and Georgia and had been urged to run for office in the
Confederate Congress while he was recuperating from wounds during the winter of 1862–63. Only one year after the war, friends had
"strongly urged" him to seek the nomination for governor of Georgia.
He declined the honor yet took the opportunity to offer advice to his
fellow southerners on the political climate of the nation. "Let us
demonstrate to these enemies to truth, to principle and sound policy
(the Radicals of the North)" that the same southerners who had
fought the war "are most reliable in their observances of plighted
faith and truest to the principles of the constitution." Also in 1866, he
had presided over a meeting at Blackshear, Georgia, called to select
delegates to the National Union Convention in Philadelphia. In his
address, he stressed the importance of the Philadelphia meeting of
moderates from all parts of the country by comparing it to the Constitutional Convention of 1787. Unless a determined stand against
Radical policies could be made, he argued, equality between the
states would be destroyed, and with it, the South and liberty for all
would be lost. Gordon scored those Republicans whom he called
Radicals, "that pusillanimous battalion of warriors who, lest they
should be engulfed in it, gazed at the red tide of war from afar, and
who, now that we have surrendered, are incapable of magnanimity to
a brave and honorable and fallen foe." He urged the audience to send
"our best and wisest—our representative men," so that the Radicals'
"wicked and selfish designs against constitutional Government and
against liberty" could be thwarted. As one of these "representative
men," Gordon was selected as a delegate to the convention. In August, he attended the Philadelphia meeting, but he did not play a
prominent role.[2]

---

Lucian Lamar Knight, *Reminiscences of Famous Georgians* (2 vols.; Atlanta, 1907–
1908), I, 319.

2. E. A. Pollard [A Distinguished Southern Journalist], *The Early Life, Campaigns
and Public Services of Robert E. Lee, with a Record of the Campaigns and Heroic
Deeds of his Companions in Arms* (New York, 1871), 547–48; New York *Times*, July
12, August 5, 10, 1866; Isaac W. Avery, *The History of the State of Georgia From 1850
to 1881* (New York, 1881), 358; Atlanta *Constitution*, June 8, 1880. For an excellent
discussion of the South and the politics of Reconstruction from 1865 to 1868, see
Michael Perman, *Reunion Without Compromise: The South and Reconstruction,
1865–1868* (Cambridge, Eng., 1973). See also Perman, *The Road to Redemption:
Southern Politics, 1869–1879* (Chapel Hill, 1984).

Even before Gordon actively entered Reconstruction politics, the dual loyalties that would influence and shape his postwar career were apparent. Gordon, as an American, ardently desired national reconciliation, a reuniting of the former warring sections. Yet at the same time, Gordon, as a southerner, was equally, if not more, determined to oppose the policies of the Radicals in order to preserve what he thought of as traditional southern liberties. During Reconstruction, the conflicting obligations of these two identities manifested themselves most clearly when Gordon stood before different audiences. When addressing northerners or speaking in a national forum, the Georgian dwelt upon pacification. When speaking to southerners, he also stressed moderation and sectional accord, but he often castigated the Republican party just as vehemently as its members assailed the Democratic party. Before meaningful national reconciliation could begin, the politically pragmatic Gordon insisted, the South had to be redeemed and Reconstruction ended on southern terms. By 1868—if not before—when moderate reconciliatory efforts had given way to the harsh reality of Radical Reconstruction, Gordon was convinced that the Democracy offered the best means of achieving both reunion and redemption.

As early as February 1, 1868, while the constitutional convention debated the new constitution, Gordon's name had been bandied about as a gubernatorial candidate. A Republican paper declared that it would "take a strong man to beat . . . a man of Gordon's popularity." The same paper later speculated that even though Gordon had no plans to run for governor, the Democracy could not get along without him. And when Meade ruled that neither Reese nor Irwin could hold public office, the Democratic Committee turned to Gordon. In spite of his strong beliefs, he seems to have had little desire to enter politics, and only weeks before his selection as the Democratic candidate, he had confided to a friend, "I am too poor to give much time to politics." Nevertheless, Gordon accepted the nomination, asserting that only "the peculiar circumstances" that surrounded his nomination and the political situation in Georgia persuaded him to make the race.[3]

The gubernatorial contest between Bullock and Gordon lasted just over two weeks, but it proved to be "a bitter and vituperative campaign." Democratic newspapers and Conservative leaders imme-

3. Atlanta *Daily New Era*, February 1, 18, March 6, April 5, 1868; Savannah *Daily News and Herald*, April 10, 1868; Gordon to Barlow, January 29, 1868, in Samuel Latham Mitchill Barlow Papers, HL.

diately accepted Gordon and rallied behind him. When Meade issued a statement authorizing Gordon's eligibility and laid to rest lingering fears that the general might yet be prevented from running, the battle began in earnest. Democrats appealed to "men of *all parties, names and faith* to unite" behind "that gallant man whose name should be a tower of strength." Gordon concentrated upon the "aggressions of radicalism, the character of the men composing that party," and particularly urged his fellow Georgians to reject the "infamous constitution" being foisted upon them. Focusing upon what he thought were the more objectional measures of the document, he cautioned, "Have nothing to do with them, like the fabled tree of India, they have already filled the air with poison . . . [and] are dethroning all that is wise and good, and enthroning all that is ignorant and bad." This general Democratic policy of calling for the defeat of the constitution and for the election of Gordon placed Georgia Democrats on the horns of an unresolvable dilemma. Rejection of the constitution would prevent reestablishment of a civil government, thereby nullifying a Gordon victory and insuring a continuation of military occupation. Gordon would have done well to heed the advice of one prominent Georgian who counseled adoption of the constitution. "If the Radicals retain power, it [the constitution] is the best we can get—if the Dem'ts get in, we can make it what we desire." But Gordon persisted in his opposition to the constitution. The heated campaign drew to a close when balloting commenced on April 20.[4]

Charges of fraud and violence surfaced immediately, with each party vigorously condemning the practices of its opponent. On the final day of the election, Gordon expressed his conviction that the Radicals would win because they had "the entire management" of the electoral process and controlled the black vote. He referred to the election as "farcical for the reason that any negro can vote, upon his oath that he had registered in another county and had been in the county ten days." He contended that the Republicans had made full use of the black population by passing them from county to county during the four days of the election. Neither side, however, had a monopoly on election irregularities. Republicans abused their con-

4. Coleman (ed.), *History of Georgia*, 213; *Meade's Report*, 65–68; Augusta *Daily Constitutionalist*, April 7, 8, 1868; Atlanta *Daily New Era*, April 7, 10, 1868; Avery, *History of Georgia*, 383–84; Athens *Southern Watchman*, April 8, 15, 1868; Gordon to B. C. Yancey, April 12, 1868, in Benjamin C. Yancey Papers, SHC; Thompson, *Reconstruction in Georgia*, 202.

trol of electoral machinery and Democrats, noted one historian, "widely employed the weapons of economic coercion and outright terrorism." The combination of these excesses render a definitive assessment of the fairness of the election impossible. Regardless of the irregularities, when official results were reported, Gordon had lost by 7,171 votes—83,527 to 76,356—but Georgia voters had approved the new constitution by a vote of 88,172 to 70,200. A student of this contest concluded that the large differential between the two votes probably meant that some moderate Republicans, though they preferred Gordon to Bullock, still favored adoption of the constitution. Despite his belief that "wholesale fraud" had been employed to steal the election from him, Gordon accepted the outcome. He may have failed in his first venture into politics, but Gordon's activities on behalf of southern whites were only beginning.[5]

Beyond his energetic promotion of southern business and educational interests, Gordon lent his support to efforts by southern whites to maintain their social order. Specifically, when whites in the South felt threatened during Reconstruction by the Republican-led movement to provide blacks with social, economic, and political equality, Gordon endorsed restriction of freedmen and even sanctioned violence when necessary to preserve white-dominated society. While there is little doubt that the general became involved with the Ku Klux Klan—he was often referred to as the Grand Dragon of the Klan in Georgia—it is virtually impossible to penetrate the shroud of secrecy surrounding his association with it. Most of what is known about his role in the organization is contained in his testimony before a joint select congressional committee in July, 1871. Although they questioned the Georgian for five hours on conditions in his native state, the committee learned few specifics.[6]

When asked directly what he knew of illegal organizations known

5. Thompson, *Reconstruction in Georgia*, 204–208; Gordon to Barlow, April 23, 1868, in Barlow Papers; Augusta *Daily Constitutionalist*, April 21, 23, 1868; Bloom, "Georgia Election of April 1868," 41, 86; Coleman (ed.), *History of Georgia*, 213.

6. Thompson, *Reconstruction in Georgia*, 382; Stanley F. Horn, *Invisible Empire: The Story of the Ku Klux Klan, 1867–1871* (Montclair, N.J., 1969), 170–72; Susan Lawrence Davis, *Authentic History of the Ku Klux Klan 1865–1877* (New York, 1924), 228; Allen W. Trelease, *White Terror: The Ku Klux Klan Conspiracy and Southern Reconstruction* (New York, 1971), 20, 74; *Testimony Taken by the Joint Select Committee to Inquire into the Condition of Affairs in the Late Insurrectionary States* (13 vols.; Washington, D.C., 1872), in *House Reports*, 42nd Cong., 2nd Sess., No. 22, Pt. 6, Georgia, Vol. I, 304, this volume hereinafter cited as KKK Report; New York *Times*, July 28, 1871; Atlanta *Constitution*, July 23, 30, 1871.

as the Ku Klux, Gordon denied all knowledge of any combination by that name, except what he had read in the papers or heard second-hand. He did, however, reveal his association with a secret organization whose sole purpose, he maintained, was the preservation of peace. Gordon stated that when approached by some of Georgia's most respected men, he joined this "brotherhood of property-holders, the peaceable, law-abiding citizens of the State, for self-protection" from the threat posed by the black population that he thought was largely ignorant. Although he asserted that he had personally "never entertained toward the negro race anything but the very kindliest feelings," Gordon again explained that it was the influx of "carpet-baggers" and their seditious influence upon blacks that forced whites in the South to act. The introduction of this "class of men whose object seemed to be to stir up strife among the people, and to create animosity," in his opinion, disrupted the normally harmonious relations between the races. Organizing blacks into Union or Loyal Leagues, these unprincipled whites attempted to convince the former slaves that their interests "were in direct conflict with those of the white men at the South." Gordon also blamed these "carpet-baggers" for reinforcing the commonly held notion among blacks that all of the lands in the South really belonged to the freedmen, and not to the whites.[7]

Fearful that such incendiary preachings might well incite blacks to violence, native white southerners had little choice but to act on their own, Gordon contended. Thus they formed what he called a "peace police organization" to protect themselves, their families, and their property from outrage. "We would have preferred death," he asserted, "rather than to have submitted to what we supposed was coming upon us." Gordon testified that the whites of Georgia, facing what they saw as the "entire organization of the black race on the one hand, and the entire disorganization of the white race on the other hand," acted "purely in self defense, to repel the attack in case we should be attacked." He did not deny the possibility that abuses and outrages may have taken place in Georgia, but he declared that any attempt at intimidation by native whites paled in comparison with that used by Republicans who forced blacks to vote their party ticket. Similarly, Gordon admitted that individuals of all parties and all colors throughout Georgia occasionally resorted to violence; how-

7. KKK Report, 306–10, 320–21, 339, 341, 345.

ever, he claimed that no crimes had been committed by the association of which he spoke. He naturally concentrated on portraying this organization as an agency of peace rather than racial control.[8]

Even though Gordon styled his association "purely a peace police—a law-abiding concern"—he explained that native whites felt compelled to remain in the shadows because any attempt at public organization would be misconstrued by Federal authorities as a move antagonistic to the government. To the contrary, Gordon said, "the organization was in entire accord with what we believed to be the spirit of the white soldiers of the United States," that being "to maintain the peace, and keep down . . . anything that would tend to produce a war of races." Gordon even asserted that his organization would gladly have united with Federal troops to quell racial disorders, but, as he pointed out, "we apprehended that the sympathy of the entire Government would be against us." So long as conditions remained unsettled in the South, he believed the existence of such a self-defense association to be imperative.

> I want it distinctly understood that this organization was intended, by peaceable means, not by violence, to prevent a collision of the races. We did not want to have in our State a war of races—to have property and our lives destroyed. We feared the peril to our women and children. We felt that we must have some means of bringing to bear in an emergency a sufficient moral force in any particular neighborhood . . . to suppress anything of that sort by the power of influence and of numbers, and, in case of absolute necessity, by actual force.

To bear out his contentions, Gordon noted that once civil courts were reestablished and "a general protection" was extended to all, the necessity for this protective body ceased, and the organization disbanded. But he also added that it was generally understood among the organization's members that if similarly disruptive circumstances again arose, they would reunite to meet the threat.[9]

The investigative committee pushed Gordon for details about the structure, membership, and leadership of the organization, but his masterfully vague responses only further frustrated the congressmen. Pointed questions on the workings of the organization—oaths, disguises, signs, chain of command, means of control and mobilization—were met by professions of ignorance or forgetfulness. Despite

8. *Ibid.*, 308–10, 321, 325, 329, 341–44.
9. *Ibid.*, 308–10, 324–25.

his evasiveness, Gordon testified that if anyone in Georgia would have known the details of the organization, he would have been the one. "Nobody knows anything more about it than I do; I think I know all about it." Statements to this effect only strengthened the committee's resolve to determine if Gordon did, in fact, preside over the Klan in Georgia; but Gordon continued to deny the existence of a central authority capable of supervising all of the organization's movements and opined that such a tightly controlled, well-structured system had never been established. The organization "was a very temporary thing," he explained, and it had passed from the Georgia scene some two years earlier. Asked if it might still be operating and questioned about why local units reported to him, he simply answered that his frequent correspondence with former soldiers and his travel throughout the state made it "almost impossible for the organization to have existed recently without my knowledge." Unconvinced by Gordon's denials, the committee vigorously pressed him to elaborate on his position in the organization. Gordon repeatedly refused, but finally admitted, "I was spoken to as the chief of the State. I said very emphatically that upon that line I could be called on if it was necessary. But the organization never was perfected, and I never heard anything about it after that time." This was the closest he came to acknowledging leadership of the Georgia Klan.[10]

Unquestionably, Gordon occupied a prominent position within the Klan. The origin of the Klan in Georgia is generally dated from the first public reference to it in an Atlanta newspaper in March, 1868, when the recognized Grand Wizard of the Klan "coincidentally" visited Atlanta on insurance business. Even if Nathan Bedford Forrest had come to Atlanta to discuss insurance matters, it is quite likely that he conferred with the new president of the Atlanta branch of the Southern Life Insurance Company about a different kind of insurance. One student of the Klan, personally acquainted with Gordon, wrote that the general first learned of the Ku Klux Klan when visiting his brother Eugene, in Athens, Alabama, in the fall of 1866. This same authority reported that Gordon began organizing in Georgia shortly thereafter and, as leader of the Georgia Klan, often conferred with national Klan headquarters and actually directed the whole organization when Forrest's health failed.[11]

10. Ibid., 321–26, 341–42.
11. Horn, Invisible Empire, 170–72; Atlanta Daily Intelligencer, March 14, 1868; S. L. Davis, Authentic History, 227–30.

It is exceedingly difficult to determine Gordon's exact role in the Klan, but given the nature of his testimony, his almost constant travel throughout Georgia and the South, and his desire to maintain peace, social order, and white supremacy, one can conclude with reasonable certainty that he was at least titular head of the Georgia Ku Klux Klan. Even so, he probably had little knowledge of and little control over the local klaverns, as this terrorist association was never fully organized. Although it is remotely possible that Gordon was unaware of the threats and violence southern whites so often employed against southern blacks, it seems more plausible that Gordon simply "looked the other way" and countenanced such excesses as the price that had to be paid if social peace—a peace determined and defined exclusively by southern whites—was to be regained and preserved. Gordon may not have condoned the violence employed by Klan members, but he did not question or oppose it when he felt it was justified. In this sense, Gordon typified the upper levels of southern society: he would do what had to be done to assure a white-controlled social order, but he hoped it could be accomplished without violence.[12]

Gordon's testimony reveals more than merely his social and racial views. He also articulated the sense of betrayal that he and many other southerners felt because of the actions of the Federal government in the years following the war. The considerate treatment of southerners by the Union army at Appomattox Court House, argued Gordon, "led our people to feel that a liberal, generous, magnanimous policy would be pursued toward them." Although the Confederates who surrendered to Grant had no written pledge, except that embodied in their paroles, the Georgian asserted that he interpreted the magnanimity of the victors as a moral obligation to respect the "rights which we have inherited—which belonged to us as citizens of the country." Instead of pursuing Grant's liberal lead and restoring normal relations, the government, Gordon maintained, had adopted a vindictive policy of humiliation and subjugation. Disfranchisement, prohibitions that denied government office to many of the most respected whites in the South, and the concomitant elevation of former slaves to political equality had inflamed southerners. "The burning of Atlanta and all the devastation through Georgia never created a tithe of the animosity that has been created by this sort of treatment

12. Trelease, *White Terror*, 74–79.

of our people." Although plainly overstated, Gordon's assertion expressed the belief of many southerners that had they been dealt with
in the same spirit that existed at Appomattox, most of the postwar
difficulties could have been avoided.[13]

In addition to charges of bad faith, Gordon again related his conviction that the southern actions that led to the war should not be con-
strued as treasonous. For him, the war resulted from "a conflict of
theories, a honest difference of opinions as to our rights under the
General Government." He maintained that southerners, convinced
of the constitutionality of secession, attempted to leave the Union,
"boldly, fairly and squarely, staking our lives upon the issue." Just
like their northern counterparts, they wholeheartedly believed in the
correctness of their cause. For Gordon, four years of bloody combat
vindicated the sincerity of efforts by both sides and resolved the constitutional issues at the heart of the conflict. "We had fought the
contest; we had been defeated; and we thought that ought to be the
last of it." Instead, Gordon contended, the government had impugned
southerners' honor, stripped them of their rights, and in essence, said
to most whites in the South that they were unworthy of citizenship.
Understandably alienated and outraged, white southerners expressed
their indignation. While Gordon found no sentiment in Georgia for
again taking up arms against the government, he sadly concluded
that southerners' "affection for the Government, in virtue of old associations . . . has been diminished by the course which has been pursued toward them."[14]

Gordon's obvious dissatisfaction with relations between the South
and the national government in the midst of Radical Reconstruction
fueled his desire to work for the removal of the Federal troops still
garrisoned in his section. Although he chose not to enter the race for a
United States Senate seat two months after his defeat in the April,
1868, gubernatorial contest, Gordon nevertheless remained close to
the political scene. He would not hold an important political office
until 1873, but as one Georgia newspaper commented, "he can afford . . . to wait and bide his time." His interest in both Georgia and
national politics prompted correspondence both in and out of the
state. Trying to generate enthusiasm for the fall elections of 1868,
Gordon struggled to overcome what he viewed as the depression
afflicting many southerners who felt nothing "we may say or do, is of

13. KKK Report, 316, 318–19, 332–33, 342–44.
14. *Ibid.*, 316, 332–34, 342–43.

real importance in the approaching pres'l election." He preferred a candidate with "a first rate war record," but he assured a northern Democrat that the South would loyally support any candidate that the northern wing of the party nominated. Gordon also attempted to put the central issue clearly in focus. "The South can't afford to go into the contest with the sole object of saving *honor*." It was more important to "get rid of Military Government [but] without bringing upon us a worse one." Gordon attended the National Democratic Convention in New York in the summer of 1868 as a Georgia elector-at-large and then devoted much of the fall to stumping his home state on behalf of the Democratic standard-bearer, Horatio Seymour. His efforts helped the Democrats carry the state in November, but the resounding presidential triumph of U. S. Grant meant continued Republican control of the executive branch of the national government.[15]

Gordon never lost touch with Georgia politics during the next three years, even though he devoted the majority of his time to developing his business enterprises. He played no direct role in the actual "redemption" of his state from Republican rule in late 1871, but the restoration of white Democratic home rule in Georgia deeply gratified him. Gordon did not move to the forefront of Georgia and southern politics until faced with "the peculiar political situation" surrounding the presidential election of 1872. Horace Greeley's nomination by the liberal wing of the Republican party presented the Democratic party, and particularly southern Democrats, with a vexing problem. If the Democratic National Convention selected a candidate other than Greeley, many of the Liberal Republicans might be driven back into the Republican fold. If, on the other hand, the Democrats endorsed Greeley as their own candidate, they might jeopardize the principles of the party by placing a man with such an anti-Democratic past at its head. The Democratic party in Georgia fractured precisely along these lines, as many older, well-established antebellum politicians refused to accept Greeley. Gordon, on the other hand, took the lead in supporting Greeley once the national Democratic party nominated the New Yorker. Gordon clearly understood the dilemma and struggled to remind members of his party of the priorities involved. For him, the removal of troops from the South

15. Atlanta *Constitution*, June 19, July 24, August 1, 5, 14, 18, 27, September 6, 22, 30, 1868; Gordon to Barlow, January 29, April 6, 23, May 19, June 5, 1868, all in Barlow Papers; Avery, *History of Georgia*, 390.

and the full restoration of home rule were the paramount objectives. These could only be accomplished if the Republican party remained disunited. Although his impulses dictated "a Democratic ticket, a Democratic fight under Democratic banners, even though we might not win a Democratic victory," Gordon realized the folly of pursuing a course of action that would almost certainly result in the triumph of Grant and Radicalism. Given this alternative, he saw no choice.[16]

Greeley was—as he claimed—a Republican, but Gordon believed "that all southern Democrats can support him as a Republican without lowering their banners or staining their honors, and without any *abandonment of principle.*" Admitting that Greeley's record could be neither defended nor ignored, Gordon cautioned Democrats not to "confuse *ends* with *ways* and *means*" when dealing "with the stern inexorable present." Principles themselves could remain inviolate, even though the methods for safeguarding them changed. A temporary alliance between Liberal Republicans and Democrats to defeat "the arch enemies of justice and of freedom," he stressed, would sacrifice neither personal nor party principles. The removal of political disabilities that hindered many of the South's leading citizens, the peaceable overthrow of the militarily supported governments that still existed in the South, and the ouster of "the enemies of the Constitution and of good government" might all be accomplished with a Greeley victory, thus hastening the eventual triumph of Democratic principles, or so Gordon maintained. He made no attempt to paint Greeley as the ideal candidate, but he pointed out that the Liberal Republicans at least proposed "to shake hands across the bloody chasm"—a chasm that Grant and the Radicals would work to keep wide open. For all who would listen, he boldly proclaimed, "I'm willing to shake hands." And with such statements, Gordon established himself among the New Departure Democrats. He was willing to accept many of the political changes wrought by the war, in order to get on with the business of rebuilding the South. Once white southern Democrats were restored to supremacy in their section, an effective national reconciliation could be realized.[17]

Gordon, as he had done in 1868, attended the Democratic conven-

16. Atlanta *Constitution*, August 4, November 8, 1871, May 14, June 15, August 24, 1872; Gordon to Bryan Grimes, May 6, 1872, in Bryan Grimes Papers, NCDAH; Fanny to John, May 10, 1872, in Gordon Family Collection, UGA; Gordon to Barlow, August 22, 1872, in Barlow Papers; Gordon to W. L. Broun, December 3, 1872, in William Leroy Broun Papers, Department of Archives, Auburn University.

17. Atlanta *Constitution*, June 15, August 24, 1872. See also Perman, *Road to Redemption*, 57–86, 108–31.

tion and then went on the stump in Georgia, where he campaigned vigorously for the Liberal Republican–Democratic ticket. At some point during the late summer, Gordon met with Greeley and received assurances that if victorious, the New Yorker would not turn his back on those who had helped elect him. In essence, Greeley promised that he would recognize southern Democrats when making appointments and assembling his cabinet. Gordon not only spoke often in his native state but traveled into the North on Greeley's behalf. In Indiana, where he made his first speech north of the Ohio River, his remarks were so well received that one prominent Democrat declared, "If General Gordon will make a dozen such speeches at prominent points in Indiana we will carry the State for Hendricks and Greeley BY FORTY THOUSAND MAJORITY." Despite such claims, Gordon's efforts went for naught, as Grant retained the presidency, virtually assuring continued military occupation in portions of the South.[18]

Even as he canvassed the state during the fall of 1872, calls for sending Gordon to the United States Senate were heard. By early November, it became obvious that friends would press for his nomination when the General Assembly met in January, 1873. Many believed that his election would serve to unite the Georgia Democracy recently divided by the presidential election. Accordingly, they began working in all sections of the state for him. Gordon himself wrote letters to numerous prominent Georgians, soliciting their support. As 1872 drew to a close and the number of candidates for the Senate seat increased almost daily, the contest appeared to take on the characteristics of a struggle between generations. On one side were many of Georgia's older politicians, men who had been prominent in antebellum southern politics and who had opposed the Liberal Republican–Democratic fusion supporting Greeley. On the other side were men of the younger generation, like Gordon, who had made their reputations either in or since the war. As the opposing forces gathered for battle, Alexander H. Stephens, one of Georgia's most respected leaders, privately wrote, "Georgia is now really in the crisis of her fate. Events incalculable in their consequences will depend upon this senatorial election." The swirling turbulence of this crisis drew Gordon inexorably to its center.[19]

18. Atlanta *Constitution*, August 16, 22, 24, 25, September 3, 5, 21, 1872; New York *Times*, September 4, 6, 8, 1872; Avery, *History of Georgia*, 501–502; "Gordon's First Speech North of the Ohio," *Confederate Veteran*, XII (1904), 183–84.

19. Atlanta *Constitution*, October 29, November 7, 20, 22, December 7, 29, 1872, January 8, 1873; Gordon to A. R. Lawton, October 28, November 6, 1872, both in Alexander Robert Lawton Papers, SHC; Gordon to L. N. Trammell, November 6, 1872,

Alexander H. Stephens, Herschel V. Johnson, Henry L. Benning, and H. V. M. Miller, all spokesmen from the antebellum period, came to Atlanta to engage the emerging voices of "Young America," such as Gordon, Benjamin H. Hill, and Herbert Fielder. Supporters of Gordon, attempting to avoid the apparent generational conflict, portrayed their nominee as the ideal candidate behind whom Georgia Democrats could unite. Moreover, they maintained that Gordon could best serve the state's interests in the Senate. They argued that the opposition of the "Old Guard"—particularly that of Stephens—to Greeley's nomination, even after endorsement by the national Democratic party, would certainly detract from their national influence. Gordon's boosters also contended that B. H. Hill, the general's most serious opposition among the younger men, could wield little power because of his inconsistent political course. Only Gordon, "fresh and free from all political treachery," could go to Washington unencumbered by burdensome political baggage.[20]

The call to cast aside the old leadership in favor of "new men, against whom no political prejudices exist" was frequently heard throughout the short campaign. One letter to the editors of an Atlanta newspaper declared that the entire country would benefit if all older politicians were summarily dropped and replaced by the thousands of young men who had fought in the war. These youthful veterans, according to the correspondent, had "learned more of human nature, of the management and wants of the government in that four year struggle and calamity than they would have learned in a lifetime of peace and prosperity." And of this new, war-tempered breed, many considered Gordon the most gifted and most representative man in the state. "Gordon is young, vigorous, brilliant and popular," wrote one Georgian, and "has a hold upon the affection and confidence of the people of Georgia that nothing can shake." In addition to possessing an "eminently pure" war record, he had also demonstrated his political sagacity with his well-reasoned support of Greeley in the fall presidential election, an act that "made him many friends all through

---

in L. N. Trammell Letters, Emory; Gordon to H. V. Johnson, November 11, 1872, Alexander H. Stephens to H. V. Johnson, December 29, 1872, both in Herschel Vespasian Johnson Papers, Duke; Gordon to J. H. Hewitt, November 26, 1872, in John Hill Hewitt Papers, Emory.

20. Atlanta *Constitution*, December 29, 1872, January 8, 14, 16, 19, 1873; Atlanta *Daily Herald*, quoted *ibid.*, December 29, 1872; Avery, *History of Georgia*, 501–502.

the West." Supporters claimed that Gordon was keenly aware of the problems confronting the South and, equally as important, possessed "a mind fertile enough to devise and suggest a remedy."[21]

Most of the senatorial aspirants were well qualified to serve Georgia; ironically it was Gordon's relative inexperience that made him a particularly attractive candidate. Unfettered by old alliances and biases, he could grapple with the practical political questions of the day "without bitterness, without prejudice, and without enmity." As one newspaper proclaimed, since Gordon "belonged to the new era which began in 1861, . . . he can go into the Senate free from political prejudices of years, but full of the traditions of his people." This positive point concerning Gordon's qualifications for the office seems unmistakably correct. His deep-seated respect for the traditions of his native state and section would permit him to work effectively at healing the wounds still festering from the war while at the same time maintaining the honor and interests of the South.[22]

As the election approached, many political observers believed that Gordon commanded the most widespread support. His extensive letter writing, especially to newly elected members of the General Assembly, garnered for him a large number of first-ballot pledges. Zealous efforts by his supporters in all parts of the state also enhanced his prospects. Indeed, the organized effort on his behalf proved so effective that accusations of political manipulation began to surface. H. V. Johnson, despairing of both his and A. H. Stephens' chances of success, gloomily predicted an "unequal contest with a ring formed to elevate General Gordon and control legislation and animated by no principles save those of personal aggrandisement." This was the first time that cries of an "Atlanta ring" working to control Georgia politics arose in connection with Gordon, but it was only the beginning of a storm of protest that would frequently rage during his political career. At this point, specifics concerning the leadership of this "machine" centered in Atlanta are vague, but without question a large majority of the so-called pawns of the ring were former Confederate soldiers, veterans who idolized Gordon as "the gallant boy who bore their flag so proudly." Given the magnetic appeal of his war record and the increasing willingness to elevate young men of the war gener-

21. Atlanta *Constitution*, November 7, 12, 22, December 3, 7, 1872, January 8, 14, 16, 19, 1873; Atlanta *Daily Herald*, quoted *ibid.*, December 29, 1872.

22. Atlanta *Constitution*, January 8, 14, 16, 19, 1873; Atlanta *Daily Herald*, quoted *ibid.*, December 29, 1872.

ation to positions of authority, it appeared that Gordon had an excellent chance of winning the Senate seat.[23]

The General Assembly began balloting on January 21. Gordon, as anticipated, won a plurality in both houses on the first ballot, receiving a combined total of 93 votes; Stephens received 56, Hill 30, Fielder 18, and Amos T. Akerman, a Republican, 12. With none of the candidates possessing a majority, the legislature suspended balloting and adjourned until the following day. At noon on January 22, the Senate and the House reassembled in joint session for the purpose of electing a Senator. The first three ballots failed to produce a winner and witnessed only minor shifts in voting patterns—a slight decline in Gordon's votes, a somewhat greater increase in Stephens' strength, and a gradual erosion of Fielder's support. On the fifth ballot, however, as Fielder dropped out of the contest, support for Gordon began a surge that carried over into the succeeding ballot. When results of the sixth vote were first announced Gordon's total stood at 101 votes, still 6 votes short of a clear majority. Then "amid as wild an excitement as ever existed in a deliberative body," members began to change their votes as Hill's support disintegrated. Following a recount, Gordon emerged from "the torrent of confusing changes" triumphant with 112 votes. Against what one observer styled "an unparalleled array of competitors, the most popular, gifted and veteran public leaders in Georgia," Gordon had won his first triumph on the political field of battle. As a chronicler of Georgia history observed, none could "withstand the plumed knight of Appomattox."[24]

Even though Gordon's victory represented a significant step in the "changing of the guard" and, consequently, a transformation of Georgia politics, it also exerted a more immediate and dramatic impact upon his own life. In a very short period of time, he had to arrange for the management of both his business and personal affairs in Georgia and to complete preparations for his move to Washington. But Gordon's election proved to be of far greater importance than perhaps even he realized at the time. It provided him with his first

23. Atlanta *Constitution*, December 28, 1872, January 8, 21, 1873; H. V. Johnson to A. H. Stephens, December 9, 27, 1872, January 1, 1873, all in Alexander Hamilton Stephens Papers, LC; A. H. Stephens to H. V. Johnson, December 29, 1872, in H. V. Johnson Papers; J. Henley Smith to A. H. Stephens, January 3, 1873, in Stephens Papers, LC; Avery, *History of Georgia*, 390.

24. Avery, *History of Georgia*, 505–506; *Georgia House Journal*, 1873, pp. 134–36, 144–56; *Georgia Senate Journal*, 1873, pp. 96–97, 104; Atlanta *Constitution*, January 22, 23, 24, 1873; Knight, *Reminiscences of Famous Georgians*, II, 873.

national platform from which he could both preach his message of reconciliation and actively work at reuniting the former warring sections. Gordon would go to the Senate with this mission in mind, but southerners could still rest assured that he would safeguard and promote their interests. He was, one Georgian believed, "one of a very few of those men, like Washington, and Lee, and Stonewall Jackson, that you can shut your eyes and go it blind on."[25]

25. Atlanta *Constitution*, January 14, 1873.

# IX · Southern Spokesman

The special session of the Forty-third Congress assembled on March 4, 1873; however, John B. Gordon did not occupy his Senate seat until March 11. He was appointed to the standing committee on commerce, the standing committee on education and labor, and the select committee on levees on the Mississippi River. During this short three-week session, Gordon made no notable contributions; nevertheless, he served as the central figure in a minor though highly symbolic gesture of national reunification. On March 25, the day before Congress adjourned, Vice-President Henry Wilson called upon the Georgian to preside over the Senate for a short time. Gordon thus became the first former Confederate to be so honored. On the following day, Gordon visited the White House, where he obtained from President Grant a promise to remove those Federal officers in Georgia who had secured their nominations through fraud or corruption. In a sense, these two incidents typified the dual allegiance under which Gordon would labor for the remainder of his life. Although many other forces would be instrumental in determining his actions, it was these often-conflicting responsibilities—Gordon as a southerner and Gordon as an American—that most prominently molded his life in the postwar period.[1]

Wherever Gordon traveled, even at this stage of his public career, he carried these twin responsibilities with him. In May, 1873, in Charleston, South Carolina, Gordon assured his hosts that he would not rest until the state had been relieved of Republican domination and military occupation. Yet, almost within the same breath, he spoke of his sincere longing for the day when passions would fade,

---

1. *Congressional Record*, 43rd Cong., Special Sess., 1, 38, 48; Atlanta *Daily Herald*, March 26, 27, 1873; Atlanta *Constitution*, March 26, 27, April 1, 1873; Gordon to H. P. Farrow, April 14, May 3, 1873, H. P. Farrow to Gordon, April 18, May 7, 1873, all in Henry P. Farrow Papers, UGA.

sectional prejudices would be put aside, and there would be "genuine peace and co-operation for good government all over the country." By the fall of 1873, even northern newspapers were beginning to recognize the articulate Georgian. The New York *Herald* regarded him as "the leader of the new and young class of democratic States' rights politicians that have sprung up in the South since the close of the war." Furthermore, despite his congressional inexperience, the paper found that he "is looked upon as the representative Southerner, not only of Georgia, but of this entire section in the United States Senate."[2]

Even so, when Congress reconvened in December, 1873, Gordon did not immediately assert himself. At the outset, he contented himself with introducing minor bills, resolutions, and memorials, intended to relieve or aid the citizens and businesses of Georgia. Gordon also presented a number of petitions to remove political disabilities from those southerners still disfranchised as a result of their participation in the war. In the years that followed, Gordon would lead the fight for restoration of full citizenship to all former Confederates. Soon after the Christmas recess, Gordon began to take an active role in Senate affairs. On January 8, 1874, he spoke at length for the first time, when he urged rejection of a bill concerning salaries of Federal officers and officials. He found the retroactive nature of the "Salary Grab" bill repugnant to public sentiment, but what particularly troubled him was the gross inequity between civilian and military salaries. In the debate that followed, Gordon sought to reduce military salaries that, he contended, had grown exorbitant since the war. He argued that remuneration for military officers of all grades should never exceed that of a United States senator or the Chief Justice.[3]

Although Gordon's remarks on official salaries focused generally upon economy in government and specifically upon "the relative dignity of the different departments" of the national government, some congressmen chose to misinterpret his points. "Greatly surprised and not a little pained" by the failure of a number of senators to accept his "disclaimer of any intention to disparage" the soldiers of the Federal army, Gordon felt compelled to answer Republican accusations regarding the spirit of his comments. Even though he had

2. Atlanta *Constitution*, May 14, 15, 1873; New York *Herald*, quoted *ibid.*, September 12, 1873.

3. *Congressional Record*, 43rd Cong., 1st Sess., 479–81, 572–73.

been extraordinarily careful in selecting his words, he reluctantly admitted that "the passions of the past and the prejudices engendered by the war" had obviously not yet sufficiently subsided to allow a representative of the South to discuss such matters frankly without fear of misapprehension. So he took this opportunity to declare "in the most public manner, here at the capital of the nation . . . that had the questions which have so disturbed the country been left to the soldiers of the two armies after the surrender we should have had less ill-will between the sections." Indeed, his regard for the soldiers in blue who had dealt so generously with the defeated Confederates at Appomattox would permit no misunderstanding of his sentiments. Rather than casting aspersions upon a military calling, Gordon proclaimed that he had only the utmost respect for all true soldiers and their profession.[4]

In this, his initial sortie onto the Senate floor, Gordon overcame attempts by Radical Republican congressmen to twist his arguments and did not allow them to draw him into partisan controversy. Meeting their innuendos and attacks with forbearance, Gordon created from the outset a favorable impression. For him the war was over, and both sides, particularly the men in uniform, could take pride in their causes and their actions. Now was the time to join hands in rebuilding a stronger, more united country. Not surprisingly, many of Gordon's congressional colleagues were not so willing to bury the bitterness of the war.

Gordon delivered his first major prepared speech on January 20, 1874, when he argued against a bill proposing a return to specie payments. With the severe economic dislocations of the panic of 1873 as a backdrop, Gordon discussed the financial question as it related to the country's agricultural interests, which he regarded as "the foundations of all other interests." He began by declaring that when farming ceased to be profitable, when nonproducers absorbed the profits from cultivation of the soil, and when wealth increasingly concentrated in the hands of a few, "*then* there is a fundamental evil, a *radical wrong*, either in the financial system or the legislative polity, or both, of such agricultural country." After briefly considering the various reasons generally cited for the panic and the most commonly proposed remedies, Gordon pointedly asked the question facing Congress. "Shall we constrict; or shall we give the country more cur-

4. *Ibid.*, 573.

rency?" Personal preference and his own historical research convinced him that the latter offered "the shortest, surest, easiest, and best" way to relieve the country's financial woes. By no means a stout advocate of inflation, Gordon nevertheless found inflation preferable to insufficiency because "[c]heap money is the one thing needful for the agricultural and productive interest of the country."[5]

High interest rates had left agriculture prostrate, particularly in the South, which Gordon asserted "is even poorer to-day than she was the day Lee surrendered." He agreed that the end of slavery and the subsequent disorganization of labor significantly contributed to the South's plight, but he held that the constricted money supply and high interest rates—generally hovering around 20 percent—were the primary reasons for financial distress. "Give us the means," he pleaded, "give us a sufficiency of circulation to make interest cheap, and we will diversify our labor. Give us the means, and we will seize upon all the advantages nature has given us. . . . Give us the means." Even though an increase in the circulating medium could not cure all ills, he maintained, it would go a long way toward alleviating the heavy burdens under which the farmers of the South and the West labored. Gordon also cautioned his colleagues to heed the "already ominous . . . murmurs of discontent" arising among agricultural interests. "In their right to regulate wrong by the ballot the producers, despising party lines and party associations, will, sooner, or later, rid the country of a system which, by its discriminations, but perpetuates their bondage to poverty." In this, Gordon anticipated the nation's agrarian revolt of the 1890s, a movement that would threaten even his own political future.[6]

Gordon's maiden effort, according to one Georgia writer, "made a profound impression upon the whole country." Many senators of both parties "warmly congratulated" him on his treatment of the financial question. Even Republican Oliver P. Morton—an archenemy of the South who would soon be a frequent tormentor of Gordon—called it "the ablest effort made on the subject." One of Georgia's Washington correspondents reported that "Gordon's graceful delivery, his enthusiasm, his courteous bearing, and the line of argument pursued by him, all combined to make it an impressive and telling effort." In spite of its favorable reception, Gordon's speech failed to sway the Senate, which eventually passed the Specie Re-

5. *Ibid.*, App., 12–15.
6. *Ibid.*, 834, 1676; App., 15–17.

sumption Bill. Nevertheless, in this and ensuing debates, Gordon proved himself as an intelligent, forceful speaker, particularly on financial matters. During the next six years, many of his major speeches, both in and out of Congress, would deal with the nation's economy. His ability and labors so impressed the Republican New York *Times* that it pronounced him "the ablest man from the South, in either House of Congress." Clearly, by the end of the session, Gordon had established himself and was "working up a fine reputation in the Senate." Regarded by some as "the coming man of the South," the Georgian was even mentioned as a possible national Democratic vice-presidential candidate in the elections still two years away.[7]

Rumors also began circulating during the summer of 1874 that Gordon planned to associate with President Grant and endorse the Republican's attempt at a third term. Realizing that his personal friendship with Grant, which dated back to Appomattox Court House, was being misconstrued by some as a political endorsement, Gordon took immediate steps to quash such talk. In a number of letters to various southern newspaper editors, Gordon declared in unequivocal terms that nothing could ever persuade him to forsake the principles of the Democratic party. He had no intention of backing "any other than a purely Democratic candidate, with a Democratic platform." Even if he could advocate a third term for any man, under no conditions whatsoever would he support Grant—a man whose success, he said, "would continue in power, for four years longer, the party whose pitiless measures have brought sorrow and ruin to our people and irreparable damage to our free institutions." In any event, as the Baltimore *Gazette* pointed out, Gordon's declaration of principles put "the slander at rest, at once and forever." It is inconceivable that Gordon, even in the interest of speeding national reconciliation along, ever entertained any thoughts at all of switching parties or of endorsing Grant for president.[8]

Gordon further demonstrated his Democratic loyalties by campaigning extensively in his native state. In the fall elections, Demo-

7. Isaac W. Avery, *History of the State of Georgia From 1850 to 1881* (New York, 1881), 559; Atlanta *Constitution*, January 21, 25, February 25, 1874; Calhoun *Times*, quoted in Atlanta *Constitution*, April 2, 1874; Wilmington *Star*, quoted in Atlanta *Constitution*, April 5, 1874.

8. Atlanta *Constitution*, July 14, 17, 29, August 2, 1874; New York *Herald*, quoted *ibid.*, July 19, 1874; Baltimore *Gazette*, quoted *ibid.*, July 31, August 2, 1874.

crats won an overwhelming victory in Georgia and, for the first time since the war, captured a majority in the national House of Representatives. The ending of complete Republican control of Congress understandably heartened Gordon, as well as most of his fellow white southerners. At a massive rally of Fulton County Democrats, two nights after the election, a deeply moved, but ebullient Gordon likened the Democratic victory to deliverance by Almighty God. In his moment of rejoicing, he boldly forecast the demise of the Republican party and the end of Federal support for southern governments composed of "carpet-baggers, scalawags, thieves and usurpers." He predicted that the triumph over the Republicans would soon lead to a return of home rule and everything that attended it. White Democrats would control their own affairs, particularly the race question, without the ominous specter of Federal bayonets.[9]

Obviously, Gordon was premature in his declaration of an end to Republican rule in the South. Although northern willingness to use the military to buttress Republican governments in the South appeared to be dissipating, several southern states remained in the hands of the Republicans. Between 1875 and 1877, Gordon devoted the bulk of his energies to restoring southern home rule in these states. And it was the question of the use of troops in the South that afforded Gordon the opportunity to make his greatest speech and, in doing so, to enhance his position as spokesman for the South.

In the almost two years that he had served in the Senate, Gordon had scrupulously refrained from confronting Republican congressmen when they launched their frequent, vitriolic harangues against the South. When former Confederates rose to speak, Radical Republicans persistently diverted Senate debate away from the question at hand—regardless of what it was—and began a "discussion" of sectional issues, including the war, the South's culpability, and the state of affairs in the postwar South. Northern Radicals—among whom the most outspoken senators were Oliver P. Morton, Roscoe Conkling, and George F. Edmunds—repeatedly assailed southern whites, calling them traitors, murderers, and barbarians. In January, 1875, during an extended debate over the use of Federal troops in Louisiana, Radicals again unfurled and "waved the bloody shirt." Edmunds, harping upon the southern proclivity for violence and intimidation, openly implied that southern whites were little more than thugs and assassins. Furthermore, he referred to "our southern brothers, who it seems have not yet forgotten the old manners and ways of semi-barbarous times." Murder had become so commonplace in the South, Morton added, that an unparalleled system of false reporting had been established to conceal the outrages committed by southern Democrats. Warning northern Democrats that a political union with southerners required acquiescence to murder and intimidation, Morton thundered, "[Y]ou cannot handle pitch without being defiled." One indignant northern Democrat, Senator Allen G. Thurman of Ohio, stood to challenge these Radical assertions that he had heard so often before. He acknowledged that crimes took place in all sections of the country, but he endeavored to keep the discussion focused upon what was for him the real issue—that the army's intervention in Louisiana "to determine who are the rightful members of a State Legislature and to organize it not by the law but by the bayonet" was clearly in violation of the Constitution. But the hour grew late and the debate ended abruptly with adjournment. Gordon had once again sat in silence while Morton, Edmunds, and Thurman—all northerners—heatedly discussed southern affairs. It was to be the last time. He and his section had passively endured too much too long; the South must respond.[10]

When the Senate resumed its consideration of the Louisiana question on January 6, Gordon rose to reply to what he styled "the charges . . . [and] gratuitous insults offered to the white people of the South." Bristling with indignation grounded in a long-suppressed urge to reply to Radical assaults upon his section, Gordon carefully measured his words. He professed that he had desired to avoid such partisan disputes because "I felt that my duty to the people I represent required that I should suffer in silence the insults which Senators on the other side of this Chamber deemed themselves authorized to utter here." But on this occasion, the Radicals had gone too far.

> When the people of my section are held up to the gaze of the civilized world as murderers, assassins, and semi-barbarians, I feel that further silence will subject them to a more cruel misconstruction than can be extorted from any perversion, however gross and unjust, of my utterances here. And if my voice now betrays, as I fear it does, undue excitement, it is not the excitement of anger, but that of a man aggrieved at the unjust

10. *Congressional Record*, 43rd Cong., 2nd Sess., 247–52.

assaults upon the reputation of his people, conscious that they deserve a vindication which he feels himself inadequate to make.

Distressed by the existence of so much "hate and vindictiveness and of the spirit of vengeance," Gordon expressed his fear that the republican form of government in America was at an end if the Radicals accurately reflected the sentiments of most northerners. He did not believe, however, that they did. Rather, he remained convinced "that an overwhelming majority of the American people, North and South, East and West, utterly abhor the spirit of animosity, of hate, and oppression manifested in this debate."[11]

Having reaffirmed his conviction that most Americans wished to bury the sectional bitterness of the past and to foster a more fraternal feeling between sections, Gordon proceeded to defend the honor and integrity of southern whites. He flatly denied charges that murder had become "an everyday occurrence in the South" and that innocent blood flowed in the streets. Murder and outbreaks of violence did take place, Gordon admitted, but he added that "these rare and isolated instances" did not, in his opinion, justify Radical accusations. He declared "that wherever in the Southern States people of intelligence, integrity, and honesty have control of public affairs, property and life and rights, political and personal, are as secure as in . . . any State of this Union." Then, echoing his testimony before the Ku Klux committee, Gordon asserted that southerners had exhibited remarkable forbearance in the face of the overthrow of state governments, of usurpation of constitutionally guaranteed rights, of military occupation, of social disruption, and of incitement of the black population by a class of men who wanted neither peace nor harmony. Gordon questioned, however, how long the people of his section could endure such treatment. Indeed, he proclaimed, "no people in the history of the world have ever been so misunderstood, so misjudged, and so cruelly maligned" as the people he represented.[12]

During the course of his speech, he sparred verbally with Edmunds, but even though tempers flared, Gordon refused to be led astray from his defense of the South or drawn into a controversy about the war. If, as he declared, Edmunds and others desired fuel to feed the fires of sectional animosity, they would have to look elsewhere.

11. *Ibid.*, 269–70.
12. *Ibid.*, 270–72.

I am heartily sick of all this stirring up of bad passions. I was sent here for no such purpose. Nothing was further from my anticipation than that I should ever be forced into such a conflict. I came here with my heart full of good-will to all men of all sections of this country. . . . I have not lost faith in the *right* and in the American people. . . . Fraternity and good-will shall be restored to our divided country, and, despite efforts to prevent it, shall grow and strengthen until its final consummation in a united people, united to build up a common country and not to desolate one portion for the benefit of the other.

Despite "a deep and broad gulf between the sentiments of the people and the spirit of hate" often evident on the floor of the Senate, Gordon concluded, "the day of better feeling is dawning."[13]

Gordon's masterful speech, wrote a Georgia chronicler, "was the first time anything like an elaborate vindication of the South had been made by a Southern man" since the war. His eloquent defense of his fellow white southerners captivated the galleries, who frequently interrupted the Georgian with ringing outbursts of applause. Even Edmunds testified to the marked effect of the speech, when he cynically observed that he must wait to speak until "the solemnity that has fallen upon us on account of the sermon of the Senator from Georgia shall have been sufficiently relieved." The most impressive aspect of the speech, besides its moderate tenor, was the spirit of nationalism that pervaded it. Gordon, for the first time on the Senate floor, eloquently expounded his commitment to national pacification and to reconciliation of the formerly warring sections. Obviously aggrieved by the verbal assaults upon southern whites, Gordon responded forcefully to Radical charges and defended his section ably but without resorting to the bitter partisan polemic generally employed by the Radical Republicans. Although some southerners might have wished that Gordon had been even more outspoken in his defense of the South, one newspaper observed that "his judgment was superior to his personal feelings." Pacification and reconciliation had to triumph over anger and alienation if the South was to be redeemed and a meaningful reunion achieved.[14]

Still, Gordon must have been troubled by the disruptive effect that his verbal battle with Edmunds could have on the nation. On the following day, he sought to extinguish any smoldering embers of sectional hatred that his words and actions might have rekindled by

13. *Ibid.*, 271–74.
14. *Ibid.*, 272; Avery, *History of Georgia*, 559; Atlanta *Constitution*, January 9, 13, 1875; Louisville *Courier-Journal*, quoted in Atlanta *Constitution*, January 9, 1875.

apologizing to the Vermont Republican in the Senate. He did not back away from his defense of the South, but he did publicly profess his "sincere regrets" for uttering anything during their harsh exchange that could have been considered a personal assault. "Believing that under the impulse of the moment [he might have] done injustice" to his fellow senator, Gordon explained that he meant no disrespect. Edmunds graciously thanked the Georgian "for the handsome way" he had apologized and expressed his own regrets for any perceived impugnment of Gordon's character or personal conduct. Moderate, conciliatory gestures such as these did not go unnoticed in the North.[15]

Despite a sincere desire to hold passions in check, Gordon did not always successfully override his own sense of outrage. On January 13, Senator John A. Logan accused the Georgian of "uttering denunciatory sentences against the republicans and against the Government of the United States." Instantly, Gordon erupted, angrily defying "the Senator to find one solitary word in any utterance of mine against the Government of the United States or against any man in authority except the miserable people who are plundering mine." Gordon then indignantly challenged the former Union general to make good the charge or withdraw it, whereupon Logan qualified his accusations and avoided further controversy.[16]

Deeply imbued with the traditions of the South, Gordon displayed on this occasion, as on others when he perceived a personal affront, a particular sensitivity to matters of personal honor. His sense of honor, however, would prove to be a flexible, somewhat contradictory one. He could easily lie to the Ku Klux congressional committee, repeatedly refuse to repay his financial debts, and carefully conceal secret—perhaps illegal—dealings from the public he represented, all without feeling he was compromising his honor. Yet whenever he believed that his word was being questioned or his character impugned, Gordon reacted vigorously. He was rarely the one to throw down the gauntlet, but when an opponent did so, he unhesitatingly picked it up. This fierce sense of pride—often strangely twisted—compelled Gordon to respond to all challenges to his personal honor, real or imagined, justified or unjustified.

When, in January, 1875, he determined that he could aggressively

15. *Congressional Record*, 43rd Cong., 2nd Sess., 301; Atlanta *Constitution*, February 4, 1875; S. L. M. Barlow to T. F. Bayard, February 4, 1875, in Thomas Francis Bayard Collection, LC.

16. *Congressional Record*, 43rd Cong., 2nd Sess., 424.

defend his section without damaging its efforts to regain complete control of local affairs, Gordon served notice that he would regard all future attacks upon the South as personal assaults. In doing so, he assumed the role of spokesman for the South—a responsibility he would not take lightly and one for which he was eminently qualified. Gordon's defense of the honor and integrity of southern whites unquestionably won him their confidence, for whenever Republicans assailed the South, Gordon could be counted upon to rise to its defense. Southerners could trust him to safeguard and foster their interests in the national forum.

But of equal if not greater importance was the recognition that Gordon was a southerner with whom northerners could confidently deal. Keenly attuned to the sentiments of his native section, he accurately represented the feelings of most white southerners when matters of national importance were discussed. Moreover, with his sincere desire to bury the passions of the past and his commitment to a stronger, more united country, Gordon could also be counted upon to reflect these sectional views through the prism of a nationalism that embraced both the North and the South. Thus, in addition to becoming a spokesman for and of the South, Gordon emerged as a national statesman as well.

An obvious manifestation of his national reputation came almost immediately. Answering a call from the New Hampshire Democratic Executive Committee to make speeches on behalf of the party, Gordon and L. Q. C. Lamar, a congressman from Mississippi and a relative of Gordon, traveled to the Granite State in March, 1875. Their purpose was to solicit Democratic votes in the upcoming election, but even more, they wanted to present to northerners their views of the true conditions under which the South still labored. Earlier, in April, 1874, Lamar had delivered an eloquent eulogy of Charles Sumner of Massachusetts, long a bitter foe of the South, in the House of Representatives. In a private letter to a close friend, he explained his seemingly strange action as an attempt "to speak to the North on the condition and status of the Southern people." Lamar realized soon after he arrived in Washington that what southern congressmen were saying in Congress "*never reached the masses of the North*"; their efforts to correct frequent misrepresentations and distortions about the South were simply not being heard. Lamar believed that Sumner's death provided him with a unique "*occasion* on which they [northerners] would *listen* and listen with something of a feeling of *sympa-*

*thy . . . especially among those classes who have never given us a hearing."* Gordon, who shared Lamar's view of the situation, under-took the speaking tour with the same purpose in mind.[17]

In their speeches in New Hampshire, the two southerners stretched the truth somewhat when they declared that peace and harmony between races existed wherever local control had been returned to whites. They dismissed as political hatemongering the Republicans' portrait of a violent and murderous South. Although pleased with their opportunity to speak directly to at least a small portion of the northern public, Gordon and Lamar had little political effect. Re-publicans increased their overall majority in the state and the Dem-ocrats only managed to gain one additional congressman—a victory that many credited to the two southern Democrats. Still, the Wash-ington *City Herald* reported, "If the sincere and eloquent words of these honest and earnest men, pleading for peace and good will be-tween the sections, could have been listened to by every voter in the Granite State, the result might have been as we firmly believe, an overwhelming conservative triumph."[18]

Gordon and Lamar stopped in Boston on their return trip to Wash-ington. Although fatigued by their travels and labors, they consented to speak informally to the members of the city's Marshfield Club, a solidly Yankee assemblage dedicated to the constitutional principles espoused by Daniel Webster. Gordon again recited the woes still visited upon the South. He concluded, however, on a note designed to warm all the commercial hearts in attendance, predicting that once real peace between the sections had been attained, the South "would again turn towards the north the golden currents of commerce." Both his and Lamar's remarks were well received and often interrupted by enthusiastic applause. "The pleasant gathering" ended only when the southerners were compelled to leave in order to meet their train.[19]

Gordon, despite the broadly nonpartisan position he adopted when speaking to northern or national audiences, chose a vastly different approach when addressing his fellow southerners. In Congress he refrained from pointedly attacking the Republican party, but he often

17. Edward Mayes, *Lucius Q. C. Lamar: His Life, Times, and Speeches. 1825–1893* (Nashville, 1896), 217; Atlanta *Constitution*, March 5, 1875; L. Q. C. Lamar to C. C. Clay, September 5, 1874, in Clement Claiborne Clay Papers, Duke.

18. Mayes, *Lucius Q. C. Lamar*, 217–23; Atlanta *Constitution*, March 12, 1875; Boston *Advertiser*, quoted in Atlanta *Constitution*, March 12, 1875.

19. Atlanta *Constitution*, March 12, 16, 1875; New York *Herald*, quoted *ibid.*, March 16, 1875; Mayes, *Lucius Q. C. Lamar*, 223–24.

delivered withering assaults upon the opposing party when canvass-
ing the South. And the tactics he employed in assailing the Radicals
generally differed little from those used by the enemies of the South.
While campaigning for Lamar in Mississippi in the fall of 1875, Gordon spoke at great length on the "fruits" that ten years of Republican
misrule had borne: "a violated constitution, broken laws, the overthrow of long and wisely established local self-government, the
squandering of public revenue, and the prostitution of a brave and
generous army to partisan purposes." He also roundly denounced the
carpetbagger element still present in the South, which, he maintained, persisted in its efforts to turn the races against each other.
During the course of his tour, Gordon often spoke directly to those
blacks in attendance. In the traditional southern manner, he told
them that white southerners, not transplanted Yankees, had their
best interests at heart. Gordon's speeches contributed in part to the
resounding Democratic victory in November, which swept the Republicans out of office and enabled the Democrats to gain a majority
in both chambers of the state legislature. But as was common in all
southern states still dominated by Radical regimes, fraud and violence proved a more effective means of displacing the Republicans
than was mere rhetoric. Nevertheless, while the state rejoiced, one
Mississippi paper praised the Georgian whose "clarion tones" during
the "time of need" aroused Mississippians "in their struggles against
a wicked and unscrupulous government." As that newspaper grate-
fully reported, Gordon "has endeared himself to the people of Mississippi in ties that will never be broken."[20]

Gordon continued his criticism of the Republican party in February, 1876, when he discussed national politics in a speech in Atlanta.
Having returned home—probably to deal with the desperate financial problems that had beset the Southern Life Insurance Company—
he took the opportunity to address the Georgia General Assembly
and emphasize the importance of the upcoming presidential election.
He again dwelt upon the incompetency, the corruption, and the tyranny that, he asserted, characterized Republican control of the national government. To retain in power a party whose "exhibitions of
insatiate vengeance, of unconquerable prejudice and of undying hate"
had prevented sectional reconciliation would, in Gordon's words,

20. Mayes, *Lucius Q. C. Lamar*, 259–60; Atlanta *Constitution*, August 29, September 3, 12, November 2, 1875; Holly Springs *Reporter*, quoted in Atlanta *Constitution*,
November 9, 1875.

"surely endanger, if it does not destroy, the governments of these states [of the South], and of consequence, your liberties under them." Clearly, the tone and thrust of Gordon's comments varied depending upon his audience. While he exuded moderation and the spirit of reconciliation in national forums, Gordon generally took a much more partisan position in his native section. In his opinion, white southern Democrats must first displace the Republicans in the South; only then, with the southern states redeemed, could national reconciliation become paramount.[21]

Believing that the prospect for a Democratic victory in the fall was extremely favorable, Gordon also urged southerners to remain calm and to refrain from any inflammatory statements that might cause apprehension among their friends in the North. "Wild and unreasoning declarations"—like those recently uttered by the unreconstructed Robert Toombs, who announced his desire " 'to put the nigger where he will never be heard from again' "—had to be avoided, or northern apprehensions concerning the South would prevent an overthrow of the Republicans. He stressed that silence, even in the face of repeated partisan attacks upon the South, would prove to be the wisest policy. Only "when our self respect and the cause of truth demands that the south shall answer" would he respond in the Senate. If the South followed this rule of conduct and supported a high-principled platform as well as a qualified candidate, he believed that a Democrat would soon occupy the White House.[22]

Before Gordon could wholeheartedly devote himself to the fall elections, he had to resume his duties in the Senate. Almost immediately upon his return to Washington, he introduced a revenue bill that he had been working on for some time. In the wake of the Whiskey Ring scandal, Gordon sought to amend the laws relating to the whiskey tax and, more important, to establish a nonpartisan excise corps to collect revenues more efficiently. His own investigation of the collection system convinced him that since the war upwards of one million dollars in taxes had been lost to dishonest distillers and corrupt government officials. The central flaw in the system, Gordon maintained, was that the collection process remained in the hands of untrained, inexperienced officers whose only qualifications were allegiance to the party in power and the benefits they could bestow

21. Atlanta *Constitution*, February 18, 1876.
22. *Ibid.*

upon that party. As long as these partisan-appointed officials controlled the system, the revenue service would continue to be, as he styled it, "the shame of the people and the disgrace of the country." Utilizing Great Britain's custom system as a model, Gordon proposed creating "a corps of excise exalted above the exigences of party supremacy and removed from the temptations of party support." Appointment of officers for life or good behavior would separate the revenue service from partisan politics. Although Gordon averred that "it would be almost impossible for any party to do worse," he stopped short of blaming all the evils of the present system upon the Republicans; rather, he contended that the potential for abuse had become so great that even the Democrats might succumb to the temptation to use government funds to perpetuate themselves in power. So, Gordon argued, civil service reform offered the best solution.[23]

Despite Gordon's disclaimer of any partisan purpose in the introduction of his bill and his specific plea that both Democrats and Republicans "rise above party considerations in order that we may obtain honesty at least in the collection of our revenues," several Republicans immediately branded the Georgian's proposal "a party speech for party purposes." They resorted to their common tactic of converting discussion of almost any measure into a partisan debate that always managed to return to the war and the passions it engendered. Morton agreed in substance with Gordon's assertion that a sense of demoralization had beset the nation after the war, but he laid the blame for such a state of affairs upon the southerners who had precipitated the conflict. Similarly, he dismissed Gordon's right to propose remedies for the whiskey frauds, by declaring that "those who made the war are perhaps the last persons who have a right to complain of its consequences." Morton also distorted the Georgian's remarks, claiming that Gordon had stated that only bad men belonged to the Republican party, whereas the Democratic party was composed exclusively of good men. Defending his party against the misperceived and misconstrued indictment, the senator from Indiana chastised Gordon, asserting that the mere presence of former rebels in the Senate clearly demonstrated the magnanimity of the Republican party. Senator John Sherman continued the Radical onslaught, but devoted at least a portion of his diatribe to criticizing

23. *Ibid.*, February 29, March 2, 1876; Avery, *History of Georgia*, 560; Gordon to Manton Marble, March 12, 1876, in Manton Marble Papers, LC; *Congressional Record*, 44th Cong., 1st Sess., 1502, 1579–81.

Gordon's proposition, which he labeled "totally impractical and totally absurd." Nevertheless, he, like Morton, assailed Gordon primarily for the partisanship exhibited in his speech.[24]

In the face of this criticism, Gordon, as on other occasions, expressed his amazement at Republican tactics. He complained that his attempt to address a grievous wrong in government had once again been met with a "high-sounding bombast about anti-republicanism" designed exclusively to provoke partisan debate and to conceal the magnitude of the whiskey frauds. Sadly he asked, "Has it come to this, that whenever a southern Senator makes reference to crime perpetrated against the Government, he is to be insulted with the reminder that he sits here by the clemency of the republican party, and must, therefore, refrain from all reference to their delinquencies?" Gordon's fellow Democrat from Virginia, Robert E. Withers, answered him moments later when he sternly rebuked the Radicals for their diversionary tactics and their tiresome professions of sufferance. "When the beneficiary is constantly taunted with it," the Virginian declared, the magnanimity and clemency of the Republican party "ceases to be a benefit." The time when southerners in Congress would passively endure Republican abuse had most definitely passed away.[25]

Despite Gordon's refusal to be drawn into a "passionate discussion of those war issues . . . which [he hoped] have been buried never to be resurrected," the Republicans managed to turn the debate away from the issue at hand. Their success in distracting the Senate from an extended discussion of his reform proposal, however, did not prevent Gordon's speech from creating "a genuine sensation." One correspondent believed the address "attracted more attention than any speech . . . since the war." Gordon's call for civil-service reform elicited a wide variety of responses, with most of the nation's leading newspapers reacting favorably. The New York *Tribune*'s assessment of the speech and the ensuing debate accurately reflected the true situation. In spite of the "great display of that partisan rancor which breaks out in Congress nowadays upon the most trivial provocation," Gordon's speech was "not a political harangue" but a suggestion for a badly needed reform.[26]

24. *Congressional Record*, 44th Cong., 1st Sess., 1580–86.
25. *Ibid.*, 1586–88.
26. Atlanta *Constitution*, March 12, 14, 15, 17, 18, 26, August 3, 1876; New York *Herald*, quoted *ibid.*, July 30, 1876; New York *Tribune*, March 10, 14, 1876.

Gordon may have won new laurels for his reform efforts, but he had little time to enjoy them. The unusually long first session of the Forty-fourth Congress—from December, 1875, to August, 1876— occupied much of Gordon's attention during 1876, but the desperate financial condition of the Southern Life Insurance Company also made heavy demands upon his time and energy. Almost a decade of growth and prosperity came to an end when, in late 1875 or early 1876, overextension on the part of the parent company forced the entire life insurance enterprise into bankruptcy. In February, Gordon explained in a public letter to the people of Georgia that the Memphis-based parent company had committed a grievous error two years earlier when it absorbed the Carolina Life Insurance Company. Acting upon the advice of "the wisest counsels," Southern Life Insurance Company officials had assumed the "live" policies of the Carolina, along with the assets they believed were necessary to secure those policies. However, creditors of the Carolina brought suit against the Southern and succeeded in enjoining the use of its assets. Soon thereafter, death claims dramatically increased as a result of epidemics of cholera and yellow fever. The contract between the two firms did not protect the Southern from these devastating claims, so in an effort "to save the assets from utter sacrifice" and possibly provide time for working out a compromise measure, the Southern filed for bankruptcy.[27]

Although Gordon explained the failure as an honest mistake on the part of the Memphis directors, he also took great pains to point out that the operation of the Atlanta branch in no way contributed to the company's collapse. "Had it been possible, under the charter, to separate from the company," Gordon asserted, "this department would not have suffered from these complications." He proudly spoke of "the economy and care" that characterized the Atlanta branch and that would have led the department to even greater success had not "unexpected calamity" befallen the parent company. Despite his pride in the soundness of his office, Gordon had to inform his policyholders that it would be impossible to return any portion of the money paid in premiums. He vowed to do everything possible to relieve the effects of the disaster, but he candidly expressed his skepticism about the company's survival. Hopes that the Southern Life

27. Atlanta *Constitution*, February 20, 1876. See also *ibid.*, August 10, 12, September 14, November 21, 1873, September 6, 1874, July 31, 1875, March 12, 1876, March 8, 1879.

Insurance Company might reach a compromise with creditors that would enable it to resume business soon dissipated completely, and the failure proved to be "a very bad one."[28]

The collapse of the Southern Life Insurance Company added to Gordon's enduring financial woes. Having decided at the beginning of the 1875–76 congressional session to buy a house in Georgetown rather than rent or live in a hotel, Gordon had assumed this added financial burden just prior to the Southern Life Insurance Company debacle. Maintaining two homes, one near the nation's capital and another in Georgia, and trying to provide for Fanny and their five children threatened to overwhelm him. By May, Gordon found himself in immediate need of money. He wrote to Samuel L. M. Barlow in New York apprising him of his fiscal embarrassment and seeking the names of parties who might consent to a one- or two-year loan, which he would secure with his house and property in Kirkwood. Although Gordon received a number of offers, he refused them because he felt they might put him in a compromising position. But as the summer dragged on, Gordon again wrote that he would "be in a bad way if the session adjourns soon unless I secure help." How Gordon managed to resolve his pecuniary crisis is unknown, but it is possible that his acute financial discomfiture may have made him susceptible to the intense lobbying efforts of railroad magnate Collis P. Huntington. Indeed, it would later be alleged that Gordon, at about this time, began accepting money from Huntington. In any event, this episode was symptomatic of his chronic and often serious financial difficulties.[29]

As if his congressional responsibilities and financial burdens were not enough to tax his resources, Gordon increased his involvement in the affairs of the national Democratic party. Realizing that Democratic prospects for capturing the White House appeared brighter than they had at any time since 1856, he devoted much of his attention to the upcoming fall elections. In a letter to a Georgia delegate to the national convention, Gordon stressed the necessity of selecting an honest man who could carry the key northern states. Although Gordon himself probably preferred Thomas F. Bayard, he urged the South to go to the convention unpledged and to choose a standard-

28. Atlanta *Constitution*, February 20, March 12, 1876; Charlotte *Observer*, quoted *ibid.*, March 12, 1876.

29. Atlanta *Constitution*, December 1, 4, 28, 1875; Gordon to Samuel L. M. Barlow, May 19, 31, July 10, 1876, in Samuel Latham Mitchill Barlow Papers, HL.

bearer only after extensive discussion with northern Democrats, who could better assess the relative strengths of the various candidates in the North. When Samuel J. Tilden of New York received the nomination, Gordon assured northern Democrats that even though southern party members had some reservations about the New Yorker, they would rally behind him. Gordon probably wanted to begin actively campaigning for Tilden when Congress adjourned in August, but worn down by his exhausting pace during 1876, he chose to return to Georgia for a period of much "needed rest and recreation." By mid-September, however, he was back on the stump.[30]

Gordon spoke frequently at many points in the South in the weeks before the election, but he concentrated upon South Carolina, one of the three formerly Confederate states still under Republican control. As the November elections approached, Gordon seemed more committed than ever to achieving the restoration of home rule to Georgia's sister state and the removal of the Federal troops garrisoned there. He wrote a lengthy letter to the New York *Tribune* in which he attempted to correct what he perceived as misrepresentations about affairs in South Carolina that had reached the North. Even though most South Carolinians were wholeheartedly committed to ousting the present "corrupt and irresponsible State Government," Gordon assured northern readers that they were going about it peacefully. Clearly this was not always the case, but Gordon sought to portray South Carolina and the South in the most favorable light, so that the Federal troops would at long last be withdrawn. He dismissed reports of violence and intimidation of blacks as politically motivated distortions intended to alarm the North and perpetuate the Republican party in power. Gordon also advised the people of South Carolina to remain calm, even as their day of deliverance neared: "Stand by! Stand firm! Keep the peace! Under no stress of circumstances offer resistance to law, right or wrong. Keep the peace always; but while you do that, vote for Tilden and reform; and Hampton and home rule, and in one brief week you shall see this grand old commonwealth rise from the pit of degradation proud, grand and free."[31]

30. Atlanta *Constitution*, May 30, August 15, 19, 1876; Augusta *Chronicle*, quoted *ibid.*, August 30, 1876; New York *Times*, June 2, 1876; Gordon to Barlow, May 31, June 7, July 10, 1876, all in Barlow Papers; Gordon to T. F. Bayard, June 8, 1875, in Bayard Collection.

31. Atlanta *Constitution*, September 23, 26, November 2, 1876; Charleston *News and Courier*, quoted *ibid.*, November 2, 1876; New York *Tribune*, November 2, 1876.

The November election seemed to be the Democratic victory that Gordon so desired. Tilden clearly won the popular vote and also received 184 electoral votes, only one short of the majority needed to win. Confusion prevailed, however, over twenty disputed electoral votes that both parties claimed to have won. The returns from the three southern states still controlled by the Republicans—South Carolina, Louisiana, and Florida—plus a single electoral vote from Oregon, were contested. Rutherford B. Hayes, the Republican nominee, needed all twenty votes to win; Tilden needed only one. Confusion gave way to tension and consternation as Americans discovered there was no readily apparent constitutional guide to resolve the electoral impasse. A crisis of the first order developed, with the presidency hanging in the balance.

When it became apparent that the voting returns of South Carolina, Louisiana, and Florida would be contested, numerous national politicians descended upon these states. Gordon hurried to Columbia to monitor the canvass by the state returning board. He labored tirelessly, investigating returns, conferring with local leaders, and corresponding extensively with national figures and northern newspapers in an effort to promote the Democratic cause in the Palmetto State. In a November 27 letter to President Grant, Gordon and Bradley T. Johnson, another southern "visiting statesman" in South Carolina, protested incumbent governor Daniel H. Chamberlain's request for Federal troops. They asserted, "There is not the remotest danger of disturbance of the peace by the Democrats." Gordon also wrote numerous letters to the editor of the New York *Tribune*, attempting to inform the people of the North of what he maintained was the true state of affairs in South Carolina. Gordon insisted that even after soldiers initially denied admittance to some of the newly elected Democratic state legislators and then later, after allowing them to enter, expelled them from the State House, South Carolinians remained peaceful and content to protest "in the law abiding, liberty-loving spirit of the American people." When he left Columbia on December 2, the Atlanta *Constitution* regarded his departure as "an omen that the democrats in South Carolina will have fair play."[32]

32. New York *Tribune*, December 29, 1, 1876; Atlanta *Constitution*, November 15, 23, 28, 29, December 1, 3, 1876; J. B. Gordon and Bradley T. Johnson to U. S. Grant, November 27, 1876, in Ulysses S. Grant Papers, Hayes Memorial Library, Fremont, Ohio; Francis Butler Simkins, *South Carolina During Reconstruction* (Chapel Hill, 1932), 514–25.

Although it is impossible to determine the exact nature of Gordon's actions behind the scenes, it is certain that national Democratic leaders looked to him for information concerning their cause in South Carolina. In October and November, 1878, the New York *Tribune* published a series of cipher dispatches between Democratic managers—among them Smith Weed, Manton Marble, and William T. Pelton, Tilden's private secretary—and persons in Columbia. In their attempt to uncover a massive conspiracy to "purchase" the election in South Carolina, the editors of the *Tribune* accused Gordon of sending and receiving a number of these telegrams in an effort to secure money to buy the cooperation of the returning board. Gordon adamantly denied the charges and stated that he had never sent any dispatches in code. No evidence of illegality on Gordon's part has ever been unearthed, but the heavy volume of correspondence between Gordon, in Columbia, and Democrats in New York clearly shows that Gordon was deeply involved in South Carolina affairs. And, as a Georgia Republican astutely observed, even "if it were found that Genl *Gordon* was in a conspiracy to bribe the returning board of South Carolina to falsify the vote, in favor of the Democratic party, his popularity would be thereby increased."[33]

While at home in Kirkwood for a few days, preparing for his return to Washington and the new congressional session, Gordon granted an interview on the political situation to an Atlanta newspaper reporter. Although he was undoubtedly aware of the violence, intimidation, and outright fraud that surrounded the election, Gordon expressed his "conviction" that the Democrats had "honestly and peacefully" carried South Carolina. He also feared that the Republicans intended to defraud the Democrats of their victory if the administration in Washington could be convinced to "give the coveted support of troops even to the disgraceful end of this melancholy farce." Gordon revealed that he and others had been approached by parties who claimed intimacy with the present administration, with an offer to recognize Democratic victories in state elections if he and his fellow Democrats would cease their efforts to carry the state for Tilden. As attractive as the bargain may have been, Gordon reported that South

33. New York *Tribune*, November 26–30, 1878; Atlanta *Constitution*, November 23, 1878, February 1, 1879; Amos Akerman to W. H. Felton, December 21, 1878, in Rebecca Latimer Felton Collection, UGA; *House Miscellaneous Documents*, 45th Cong., 3rd Sess., No. 31, Vol. IV, reports on a congressional investigation into such charges that attempts were made to buy the election in South Carolina.

Carolina Democrats rejected it, believing they had triumphed in both state and national elections. He feared, however, that unless the magnitude of the developing Republican conspiracy could be conveyed to the honest inhabitants of the North—Republicans and Democrats alike—South Carolina would be lost, and with it the causes of liberty and truth. Thus, in Gordon's mind, the result of the national contest, as well as South Carolina's, depended on public opinion, on "how far the northern people mean to see this conspiracy go without arresting it, and how much of a protest they mean to make against the overthrow of republican government."[34]

Once back in Washington, Gordon continued his efforts on behalf of South Carolina while becoming more involved in the larger national electoral controversy. On December 29, he submitted a resolution in the Senate declaring that the Hampton government represented the legitimate, lawful government of South Carolina. When rumors of armed resistance to the inauguration of Hayes surfaced—despite repeated expressions of confidence by leaders of both parties that the election dispute could be peacefully resolved—Gordon addressed such fears. In an interview, he stated that southerners would not resort to violence "unless the integrity of their states should be threatened." Whether continued military support of Republican governments in the South constituted such a threat, Gordon did not spell out, but he did declare that "it would take a great deal to get them to fight again." He contended that history had witnessed few other examples of a people "so sick of war as the people of the south."[35]

For Gordon, the gnawing fear that the Democrats "were being robbed of our victory by our own supineness" loomed more ominously than the threat of violence. To help prevent such an occurrence, he traveled from Washington to New York expressly to confer with the party's candidate. Although he came away from a December 23 dinner-party conference with Tilden and other prominent Democrats with "a very good impression," he felt compelled to impress further upon the New Yorker the need for action. Returning to New York near the end of the year, Gordon maintained that he spoke for the South when he pronounced the southern Democrats to be of one mind in believing that Tilden had been fairly and constitutionally

34. Atlanta *Constitution*, December 5, 7, 10, 1876; New York *Tribune*, December 11, 1876.

35. *Congressional Record*, 44th Cong., 2nd Sess., 388–89; Chicago *Inter-Ocean*, quoted in Atlanta *Constitution*, December 22, 1876.

elected and that only gross illegality could defeat him. To ensure Tilden's rightful inauguration, Gordon stressed that Democrats must let the country know "through speeches, resolutions, the press and mass meetings" that they would persist in their efforts to inaugurate duly elected officials. "If we announce by our silence beforehand that we intend to acquiesce in any outrage they [the Republicans] may perpetrate," he warned, "we only invite aggression from them and prepare our own friends for a degrading submission." Gordon feared that unless the Democratic party took a bold stance and demonstrated its determination to resist efforts to force Hayes's inauguration, "the more daring leaders of the Republican party" would "ruthlessly proceed to carry out their purposes." Despite Gordon's warnings and those of other southern Democrats, Tilden continued his passive approach to the electoral controversy.[36]

As it became increasingly clear that Tilden would not deviate from his chosen course, Gordon realized that the presidency might be slipping away from the Democrats. In a January letter to Barlow, he emphasized the necessity of firmly confronting Republican "aggressions" but concluded "that any compromise is better than an ignominious surrender of the Government to Hayes and his advisors at Washington." He may have been referring to the possibility of a settlement determined by an electoral commission that Congress had recently established to rule on each of the disputed votes. However, it is quite probable that Gordon, even at this early date, had already seriously begun examining alternative means of resolving the struggle. He never placed much faith in a special electoral commission; instead, he believed that each house of Congress should independently determine the validity of the disputed votes. Even though Gordon knew that the deadlock would probably continue—partisan politics would preclude any objective evaluation—he thought that Congress might make "some decent republican acting president" until a new election could be held in November, a prospect far less objectionable than Hayes's immediate inauguration. And in the event of Tilden's defeat, Gordon was also determined to salvage what he could for the South, namely the removal of troops and reestablishment of self-government.[37]

36. Gordon to Barlow, January 2, 1877, in Barlow Papers; Atlanta *Constitution*, December 30, 1876; August Belmont to Manton Marble, December 24, 1876, in Marble Papers; Perry Belmont to T. F. Bayard, December 31, 1876, in Bayard Collection; New York *Tribune*, January 8, 1877.
37. Gordon to Barlow, January 2, 1877, in Barlow Papers; T. Harry Williams (ed.),

By late February, a Democratic defeat appeared certain. The proceedings of the Electoral Commission definitely indicated that Hayes would be awarded all the disputed votes and thus be elected president. Distraught Democrats, primarily those from the North, began threatening to filibuster in the House of Representatives until after the scheduled day of inauguration. This move could delay the electoral count and, quite possibly, throw the country into chaos. But for Gordon and other southerners who realized that the time to act had come, alternate courses of action appeared more promising.

Although the details of the compromises of 1876 and 1877 are reasonably well known and well documented, Gordon's role during the preinaugural turmoil has largely been overlooked. Despite being ill much of February, Gordon labored in the shadows, particularly when the filibuster threat reached its height. On February 26, at the request of Congressman John Young Brown of Kentucky, he met with Charles Foster of Ohio, one of Hayes's closest advisers, in a House committee room. There Gordon and Brown asked for written statements from Foster regarding Hayes's plans for the South if he were elected president. On the following day, Foster presented Brown with two similarly worded statements, one signed only by himself and a second bearing his signature and that of Stanley Matthews. Foster had originally presented his own unsigned letter to Brown in the House that morning, and the Kentuckian had made some corrections to it. About an hour later, Foster returned with a slightly "fuller and stronger" statement written by Matthews and signed by both Foster and Matthews. Brown, at that time, prevailed upon Foster to sign the original letter, as well. Both written pledges assured the southerners that Hayes would adopt "such a policy as will give to the people of South Carolina and Louisiana the right to control their own affairs in their own way." Although the letters made no mention of the withdrawal of troops, Gordon later maintained that "it was of course understood that this would follow." The basic content of these letters, though general in character, pledged the new Republican administration to restore home rule to the South.[38]

--------

*Hayes: The Diary of a President, 1875–1881* (New York, 1964), 52–53; Atlanta *Constitution*, February 27, 1877.

38. John Young Brown's account in Louisville *Courier-Journal*, quoted in Atlanta *Constitution*, March 31, 1877; *Congressional Record*, 44th Cong., 2nd Sess., 107, 1137; Atlanta *Constitution*, February 8, 27, March 28–31, 1877; Cincinnati *Enquirer*, quoted in Atlanta *Constitution*, March 31, 1877; New York *Tribune*, March 26–29, 1877; Jno. Ellis to T. F. Bayard, February 27, 1877, in Bayard Collection; *House Mis-*

These written statements and the verbal pledges secured at the more famous Wormley Hotel Conference in no way personally committed Hayes to abide by their terms. Yet, they clearly demonstrated the president-elect's unwillingness to retain troops in the South to support questionable Republican governments.[39] If, as his most intimate advisers pledged, he withdrew the troops and allowed the Democrats to assume control of the governments of South Carolina and Louisiana, then Hayes, in real terms, offered much more to southerners than did Tilden. The Democratic candidate would unquestionably bring a rapid, albeit possibly temporary, end to Federal occupation of the South, but this action on Tilden's part would not be as meaningful or significant as that of his Republican counterpart. Removal of the troops and reestablishment of local control by the party that initiated and administered Reconstruction would be tantamount to declaring an end to that process. Thus, Republicans would be unable to use the ending of Reconstruction as a campaign issue against the Democrats.

Gordon undoubtedly realized this. Firmly convinced that whites in the South desired above all else the restoration of home rule and an end to military occupation, he had devoted much of his energy, both in Georgia and in the Senate, to securing these ends. Although there is convincing evidence that a second—and perhaps more important— economic compromise was made, the political compromise in which Gordon played a leading role lay much closer to the hearts of southerners. His machinations during the winter of 1876–77 were exclusively devoted to that struggle and helped bring about an end to the Reconstruction process.

Gordon could take solace in the knowledge that his actions

---

*cellaneous Documents*, 45th Cong., 3rd Sess., No. 31, Vol. III, 624; John Young Brown to J. D. Head, December 9, 1878, in R. L. Felton Collection; H. J. Eckenrode, *Rutherford B. Hayes, Statesman of Reunion* (New York, 1930), 216–21.

39. Most studies of the electoral controversy have treated its resolution as a political compromise. These works range from Paul L. Haworth, *The Hayes-Tilden Election* (Indianapolis, 1906), to Keith Ian Polakoff, *The Politics of Inertia: The Election of 1876 and the End of Reconstruction* (Baton Rouge, 1973). C. Vann Woodward, in *Reunion and Reaction: The Compromise of 1877 and the End of Reconstruction* (Boston, 1951), uncovered additional compromises in which, he contends, economic considerations played a major role. Although the existence of these additional discussions cannot be disputed, one can argue whether Woodward's economic compromise, which primarily dealt with future considerations, was as important as the political compromise, which focused on immediate concerns.

seemed certain to hasten the redemption of South Carolina and Louisiana, but he must have looked on with disgust as the inauguration of Hayes drew near. He remained convinced that Tilden would have been elected by the House without resort to unconventional means had the Democratic party "but presented an unbroken front to the republicans." Instead, "the uncertain policy of the democrats, the reported divisions in the ranks and their alleged willingness to submit to any usurpation" so encouraged the Republicans that the Electoral Commission proved necessary, assuring the eventual victory of Hayes. Gordon believed that Tilden and the Democrats "lost by want of action prior to the passage of the electoral bill." Dismayed by the imminent Republican triumph, Gordon foresaw a future fraught with even greater peril. He anticipated that the Hayes administration would make "herculean efforts to capture southern democrats and debauch the southern party" by claiming credit for the recognition of Democratic governments in Louisiana and South Carolina. For Gordon, the division of the southern Democratic party and the inauguration of a "deadly struggle" for the black vote—a "most horrible result"—was more frightening than another four years of Republican "fraudulent and usurpatory administration." And four more years it would be: on March 5, Rutherford B. Hayes became president.[40]

Near the end of March, the details of Gordon and Brown's dealing with the Republicans were published, bringing forth immediate criticism in both the North and the South. In an interview with the Cincinnati *Enquirer*, the paper in which the story first appeared, Gordon explained his actions as an attempt "to try a little bull-dozing on Foster." During the following weeks, he constantly maintained that in spite of his inability to prevent completion of the Electoral Commission's count, he felt compelled to act in some manner because of his "responsibility of protecting, as far as he could, the government of Governor Hampton and the people of South Carolina." Gordon denied that he struck a bargain with the Republicans to work for the defeat of the filibuster once he received assurances from Foster, Matthews, and others; but it seems reasonable to assume that the filibuster threat must have contributed significantly to the decision by Foster and Matthews to provide written pledges. If this was the case, Gordon in fact played for stakes with cards he did not hold. He fervently desired home rule for South Carolina and Louisiana and

40. Atlanta *Constitution*, February 27, April 20, 1877.

bargained for it by offering something he never really possessed: the ability to control the actions of congressmen in the House. Despite denials by all parties involved, it appears almost certain that a deal—or agreement if one prefers—was made during the final days of February. As one Georgia newspaper wrote, Gordon and Brown "secure[d] half a loaf when they could not apparently get more." Skillful bluffing, Gordon believed, had helped him win important gains.[41]

Still, Gordon's actions were roundly criticized by some in his native state. In a letter published in the Atlanta *Constitution* on April 7, "Citizen" chastised Gordon and Brown because "they sold us too cheap." Branding the two Democrats as "very unfortunate and unskillful traders," the writer accused them of foolishly bargaining away four years of Democratic administration in return for mere promises to remove troops from the South. Instead of properly supporting Tilden, whose election would have guaranteed such action, Gordon and Brown entered into a deal—or as he mockingly called it, a "VERY CAPITAL UNDERSTANDING"—whereby they worked to end the filibuster, to allow the count to continue, and ultimately to elect Hayes. Thus "Citizen" alleged that Gordon and Brown bore the responsibility for Tilden's defeat. Defenders of the general and his actions immediately replied. On the following day, "Truth" labeled the attack "venomous" and "malicious" because it attempted to place the blame for breaking the filibuster upon Gordon, and to a lesser degree Brown, when in fact every southern senator and representative except one adopted the same course. "Truth" concluded that when Gordon realized that Hayes's election had become "a foregone conclusion," he "secured the only alleviation of the outrage" by getting all that he could under the circumstances: "He rendered certain the redemption of Carolina and Louisiana."[42]

The dispute dragged on for almost a month, during which time Joseph E. Brown eventually revealed himself to be "Citizen."[43] His criticisms of Gordon, probably motivated by jealousy and resentment of Gordon's immense popularity and his own corresponding fall from grace, deeply offended the general. In the main, however, Gordon

41. *Ibid.*, March 27, 30, 31, April 20, 1877; Cincinnati *Enquirer*, quoted *ibid.*, March 31, 1877; New York *Tribune*, March 26, 27, 1877.

42. Atlanta *Constitution*, April 7, 8, 1877. Examples of criticism of Gordon and praise of Brown can be found in the Joseph Emerson Brown Papers, Felix Hargrett Collection, UGA.

43. The controversy raged in the pages of the Atlanta *Constitution* between April 7 and May 6. See, in particular, the issues for April 7, 8, 15, 20, 22, May 2, 6, 1877.

managed to remain apart from the public controversy. Only when he consented to the publication of a private letter in which he explained his compromise course did Gordon personally enter the fray. Shocked by the efforts being made in Georgia to make him "in some way responsible for the defeat of Mr. Tilden's inauguration," Gordon sought to correct the record. He proclaimed, "No greater wrong or outrage was ever perpetrated upon any man in public life," a phrase he would often use when his honor or record was assailed. Not being a member of the House, Gordon could not vote on the count; he disclaimed any responsibility for its completion and denied any attempt to influence anyone's vote. He had opposed the electoral bill from the moment of its suggestion, but once it became law, he resolved to stand by it in good faith and resist all dilatory motions. Even though he rejected all charges that he "made any bargain of any sort" as being *"basely false in every syllable and in every sense,"* Gordon repeated that once he saw Tilden's case was "hopelessly lost," he determined to do everything in his power "to save from the wreck, local self-government in South Carolina and Louisiana, which was the great end of our endeavors in the last campaign." Willing to stand or fall on his record, he announced, "[I]f that be treason to principle, to party or to country, let my personal enemies make the most of it." Although Joe Brown and a few others persisted in their criticism, the vast majority of Georgia Democrats either acquiesced in or praised Gordon's actions. And most would probably have echoed B. H. Hill's thought that it was "a pity that such a patriotic record as he [Gordon] made on principle and for the peace of the country should be *smirched* by even the *smell* of a *trade.*"[44]

In South Carolina, universal and unqualified praise greeted Gordon's actions. Following the inauguration of Hayes, Gordon met almost daily with either the president or members of his cabinet in an effort to press for the prompt withdrawal of troops. Even before redemption, a South Carolina newspaper warmly praised Gordon as the man who, throughout the state's struggle, "has made it the business of his political life to secure justice and peace for South Carolina." On April 2, when the troops were finally ordered out of South Carolina,

44. Joseph H. Parks, *Joseph E. Brown of Georgia* (Baton Rouge, 1977), 492–95; Atlanta *Constitution*, March 27, 31, April 20, 1877; New Orleans *Democrat*, quoted in Atlanta *Constitution*, May 10, 1877; Gordon to L. N. Trammell, April 14, 1877, in L. N. Trammell Letters, Emory; B. H. Hill to Doctor Felton, April 13, 1877, in R. L. Felton Collection.

Gordon proudly declared, "Day breaks at last. South Carolina is free." And eight days later, governor-elect Wade Hampton wired a message to Gordon. "Perfect peace prevails. The troops are withdrawn, and Chamberlain surrenders South Carolina. Thank you."[45]

Gordon's efforts on behalf of the Palmetto State were not forgotten in the joy of triumph. In the wake of the restoration of home rule, the man who wrote that he considered the "liberation of South Carolina . . . dearer to me than any other matter in my public life" was deluged with letters of thanks and profound gratitude. On the day Federal troops received orders to leave South Carolina, a daughter was born to the Gordons, and friends of the general prevailed upon him to name her Carolina because of his services to the state. John and Fanny assented to the request, even though another daughter already bore the name Caroline. More "visible and tangible evidence" of the love and appreciation with which the people of South Carolina regarded Gordon came later in the year, when the women of Columbia presented to him a magnificent silver service bought with funds raised through popular subscription. On each of the six pieces of the service was engraved the following inscription: "Presented to General John B. Gordon of Georgia / By some of his many friends in South Carolina / In grateful remembrance of his sympathy and aid / In restoring to their State the rights of Self-Government 1876–1877." As his aid to Mississippi had won him its citizens' affections, so too Gordon's assistance to South Carolina "in the time of her distress and humiliation" endeared him to its inhabitants. Indeed, his political activities on behalf of the South endeared him to most white southerners. John B. Gordon was properly recognized as one of the foremost southern spokesmen.[46]

45. Atlanta *Constitution*, March 20, 21, April 3, 11, November 10, 1877; Charleston *News and Courier*, quoted *ibid.*, March 14, 1877; Gordon to Paul H. Hayne, March 20, 1877, in Paul Hamilton Hayne Collection, Duke.

46. Atlanta *Constitution*, April 4, 15, 1877; Charleston *News and Courier*, quoted *ibid.*, April 15, 1877; Gordon to Mrs. Grace Elmore, November 28, 1877, in Franklin Harper Elmore Papers, SCL; Caroline Lewis Gordon, "De Gin'ral an' Miss Fanny" (MS in Gordon Family Collection, UGA). The handles of the pieces of the ornate silver service resemble the trunk of a palmetto tree with its overlapping bark, and the cover of each piece is crowned by a solid-gold miniature palmetto tree. A monogram in raised gold, bearing the initials J.B.G., appears on the side opposite the inscription. To symbolize the bond between the sister states, the box that held the service was made of Georgia walnut and Carolina palmetto. Although the silver was divided among the various branches of Gordon's family after his death and has not been reassembled, a picture of the complete service can be found in Gordon Family Collection, UGA.

# X · Post-Reconstruction Politics

Although John B. Gordon entered
the United States Senate in 1873 as a relatively young man with little
political experience, he quickly assumed a position of importance far
beyond his years and training. In fact, during the turbulent years from
1873 through 1877, it seemed as if the more tumultuous the events,
the more involved he became. Yet, as exciting and eventful as these
years unquestionably were, the second half of his senatorial tenure
was quite different. To be sure, tremendous activity continued; however, for Gordon, gone was that sense of urgency and tension that had
been present while troops remained stationed in the South. Once
Reconstruction had ended, the need to defend the South was not
nearly so acute, and Gordon's activities became less clearly focused.
As a result, petty political squabbles and an increased concern with
affairs in Georgia dominated in the years between 1877 and 1880, a
period during which Gordon grew increasingly disenchanted with
political life.

Even while deeply involved in the behind-the-scenes actions that
culminated with the resolution of the electoral controversy, Gordon
continued to serve in his official senatorial capacity. In January, 1877,
he introduced a bill at the behest of Collis P. Huntington to create a
sinking fund for the liquidation of government bonds advanced to the
Central Pacific Railroad Company of California, the Western Pacific
Railroad Company, and the Union Pacific Railroad Company under
the Transcontinental Railroad Act of July 1, 1862. Although the bill
received little support from his fellow senators, Gordon's proposal
plus his steadfast opposition to the counterproposal that was eventually enacted would, years later, subject him to charges of corrup-

tion. In addition to his frequent introduction of bills to remove political disabilities from the few still-encumbered southerners, Gordon lobbied for the release of a large number of North Georgians charged with the illicit sale and distribution of spirituous liquors. Despite the evidence of gross abuse of the revenue laws in Georgia, he managed to convince President Grant that governmental clemency toward these small-time offenders—many of whom Gordon felt were not guilty—would "relieve the innocent from oppressive litigation, without demoralizing the revenue service and prove to be judicious and wholesome." Georgians naturally lauded Gordon's "generous interest in the welfare of his constituents" and at least one newspaper, however grudgingly, also praised the outgoing president for "one of the few debts of gratitude" Georgians owed him.[1]

Gordon quickly came to occupy a favorable position with the new Republican administration that assumed the reins of government in March, 1877. His refusal to resist Hayes's inauguration, his almost constant contact with the administration while working on behalf of South Carolina, and his backing of Hayes's cabinet nominees convinced many presidential advisers that the Georgian was a man with whom they could work. Hayes himself recorded his belief that only "the resolute support of the Southern Senators like Gordon, Lamar, and Hill" prevented formidable opposition to his cabinet appointees. And Gordon, despite his earlier fears that Hayes and the Republicans might make substantial inroads in the South, began to view the president in a more positive light. He believed Hayes would strive to eliminate "the Southern questions from American politics, by giving to the South all her rights of local self-government." As these rights included appointment of southerners to federal positions, as well as complete control of domestic affairs, Gordon chose to remain in Washington well after Congress adjourned. In frequent conferences with administration officials, he constantly pressed for immediate withdrawal of troops in the South, for unqualified restoration of home rule, and for selection of "good men" for southern offices.[2]

1. *Congressional Record*, 44th Cong., 2nd Sess., 589, 615; Gordon to H. P. Farrow, March 3, 1877, in Henry P. Farrow Papers, UGA; Attorney General Alphonso Taft to Gordon, March 4, 1877, in L. N. Trammell Letters, Emory; Atlanta *Constitution*, March 3, 7–9, 1877.

2. Atlanta *Constitution*, March 8, 20, 25, May 16, 1877, January 25, 1878; Charleston *News and Courier*, quoted *ibid.*, March 21, April 15, 1877; New York *World*, quoted *ibid.*, May 16, 1877; New York *Tribune*, March 30, April 24, 1877; New York *Herald*, quoted in New York *Tribune*, April 27, 1877; T. Harry Williams (ed.), *Hayes: The Diary of a President, 1875–1881* (New York, 1964), 81.

Gordon returned to Georgia in mid-May to rest following his strenuous exertions in South Carolina and in the nation's capital. As relaxing as his respite may have been, it was tragically interrupted in August, when his youngest daughter, Carolina, died. The infant's death left the Gordon family nearly prostrated with grief. A convention assembled during the summer of 1877 to write a new state constitution, but Gordon played virtually no part in it. He explained that his "protracted and very painful domestic affliction" prevented him from maintaining the close contact with the convention that he desired. Gordon may not have really emerged from his depression until late September, when he and other prominent Georgians entertained President Hayes in Atlanta on his tour of the South. During the course of after-dinner remarks, Gordon issued a new challenge to the North "to compete with the south in devotion to the constitution and to the union of the states under the constitution." Then, expressing his hope that all the obstacles that had held the two sections apart since the war would quickly be removed, Gordon extended "a cordial support in all rightful constitutional measures" to his former military foe.[3]

Following his return to the Senate in October, Gordon continued his close relationship with the Hayes administration. In fact, he seemed more like the "compromisers" described by historian C. Vann Woodward that did Woodward's actual compromisers. Some observers considered Gordon "the recognized official leader of the administration" during the fight over New York customs nominations. Although that was perhaps an overstatement, Gordon's closeness to and frequent support of the Hayes wing of the Republican party earned him the undying enmity of the Stalwart Republicans, particularly Roscoe Conkling, already a longtime opponent. In an executive session of the Senate on December 14, Gordon and Conkling exchanged verbal blows when Gordon chose to interpret a rather flippant remark by the New Yorker as an attempt by the Republican to give orders to the vice-president. Conkling, whose comment had been a routine call for a continuation of the Senate's calendar, vehemently denied such intent and announced that anyone who placed such construction upon his words distorted the truth. Ever-

3. Atlanta *Constitution*, May 12, 16, August 28, September 25, 1877; Caroline Lewis Gordon, "De Gin'ral an' Miss Fanny" (MS in Gordon Family Collection, UGA); Gordon to James P. Hambleton, August 20, 1877, in James Pinckney Hambleton Collection, Emory; Fanny Gordon to Mrs. Felton, August 27, 1877, in Rebecca Latimer Felton Collection, UGA.

mindful of his personal honor, Gordon immediately responded. A heated exchange took place during which the Georgian stated in effect that the matter would be settled elsewhere. To many, this "sharp altercation" harked back to an earlier time when impugnment of one's honor frequently led to violence. Soon after the Senate opened its doors late that afternoon, rumors of a duel swept through Washington.[4]

Close friends of both participants, however, quickly began working on a compromise. Although Gordon withdrew into a private conference with fellow southerners and refused to comment on the matter, he did allow Senators Matt W. Ransom and Joseph E. McDonald to represent him in discussions with Conkling's "seconds," Senators Hannibal Hamlin and Timothy O. Howe. In secret conversations that night and the next morning, these men effected an arrangement acceptable to both Gordon and Conkling, though neither corresponded with the other. In essence, the statement explained that the harsh words used by both Gordon and Conkling during the previous day's session were "the outgrowth of misapprehension." Consequently, "whatever was felt to be unkind and offensive in the remarks of either should be treated as if never uttered, and . . . [the remarks] are mutually and simultaneously withdrawn." The Senate, behind doors closed specifically for consideration of this matter, accepted this unique statement and ordered it entered into the *Congressional Record*.[5]

Despite its peaceful resolution, the incident nonetheless demonstrated a number of salient points. In the past, Gordon had generally avoided such confrontations and ignored similar slaps; now he appeared less inclined to tolerate them. In the wake of his vigorous support of Hayes's customhouse nominations and their subsequent defeat at the hands of Conkling, Gordon quite probably harbored a grudge. When he lashed out at Conkling, his outburst, though probably motivated by a blow to his pride, may well have been a manifestation of his increasing sense of political security, as well. Gordon was

4. Atlanta *Constitution*, December 15–20, 1877, January 9, 25, April 20, 1878; New York *Times*, December 15–16, 1877; New York *Tribune*, December 15–16, 1877; H. J. Eckenrode, *Rutherford B. Hayes, Statesman of Reunion* (New York, 1930), 270–75.

5. Alfred R. Conkling, *The Life and Letters of Roscoe Conkling* (New York, 1889), 560–62; New York *Times*, December 16, 24, 1877; New York *Tribune*, December 17–18, 1877; *Congressional Record*, 45th Cong., 2nd Sess., 237; Edward Mayes, *Lucius Q. C. Lamar: His Life, Times, and Speeches, 1825–1893* (Nashville, 1896), 379.

confident of his home base, his position in the national Democratic party, and the comfortable working relationship he had established with the present Republican administration. Abundantly secure in his political status, he displayed less willingness to suppress his impulses when matters of pride were involved. And yet, despite his momentary loss of control, Gordon quickly recovered and, through the efforts of go-betweens, brought an immediate end to the incident and the passions and sectional feelings it engendered. His pride may have gotten him into trouble, but his commitment to national reconciliation guided him out of it.

The excitement surrounding the tiff in the Senate had hardly subsided when reports that Gordon might accept a commission to go to Europe as an agent on behalf of southern business surfaced. L. Q. C. Lamar had earlier informed him that the latest reports from Europe indicated a desire on the part of European capitalists to turn away from northern and western investments. Although eager to invest in southern cotton, Europeans, according to Lamar, still feared the unsettled conditions in the South, particularly "political perturbations and the supposed liability of our Southern communities to arbitrary interference of Federal authority." If a respected public man from the South could go to Europe and provide the necessary assurances of opportunity and stability, Lamar believed that capital would immediately begin to flow into the South. Many considered Gordon to be that man. Although little is known of this proposition, Gordon evidently expressed his willingness to go to Europe the next year if so commissioned by "Boards of Trade and businessmen of the South." He offered to act without compensation, save the simple defraying of his expenses. The mission, with Gordon as the special agent, did not materialize at this time, but southerners did not forget the idea. Six years later, when southern businessmen were again soliciting foreign capital, he was selected as the man who could induce and encourage investment from Europe.[6]

Gordon's desire to cement commercial as well as political and emotional bonds between the sections carried him north again in 1878. Late in April, he headed a delegation of southern congressmen that visited Boston at the invitation of the city's Commercial Club. Acting as principal speaker when the Bostonians feted the southerners, Gordon informed his hosts that the delegation had come not

6. New York *Times*, December 13, 21, 1877.

only as friends and countrymen but as observers of northern industry, as well. He served notice that "we of the south intend to enter the race with you" because the development of a business and industrial rivalry between the North and the South would benefit the material interests of the nation as a whole. Gordon also pleaded for the eradication of sectional animosity and the establishment of a new sense of national unity. A terrible internecine war had been fought, but it had been, he maintained, a conflict of constitutional theories and "in another sense a war over slavery." Both issues, however, had indisputably been settled with the defeat of the Confederate army. By offering their lives on the battlefield, Union and Confederate soldiers alike had proven the strength of their convictions during the war. Now, Gordon contended, another standard of loyalty existed—one that called citizens of all sections into competition to see who could best serve the interests of the whole country. He concluded his hopeful assessment of the nation's future by proclaiming to his enthusiastic audience that the "causes that divided us are gone, and gone forever. The interests which now unite us will unite us forever."[7]

While Gordon promoted national unity in Boston, political factionalism in Georgia forced him to devote much of his energy during the fall of 1878 to affairs in his home state. The Conservative Democrats, or New Departure Democrats, had dominated Georgia politics since they had seized control from the Republicans, but the "germs of insurgency and independency" spread quickly. The emerging Independent movement was centered in Georgia's northern counties where Unionist sentiment had remained strong even during the Civil War. Protests against single-party control of the state in this region with "a long-standing tradition of opposition to the political leadership of the black belt" took tangible form in 1874. Dr. William H. Felton of Bartow County, running as an Independent, won a seat in the Seventh Congressional District, a fourteen-county district in northwestern Georgia. Felton became the major spokesman for insurgents who split from the Democratic Party because they believed it no longer served the best interests of the people. The Independents argued that the Georgia Democracy was controlled by political rings

7. *Ibid.*, April 30, 1878; Atlanta *Constitution*, April 28, 30, May 3, 7, 1878; Gordon to Barlow, April 21, 1878, in Samuel Latham Mitchill Barlow Papers, HL; E. H. Watson to Mrs. Gordon, May 11, 1878, in John Brown Gordon Papers, Emory. See also Paul H. Buck, *The Road to Reunion 1865–1900* (New York, 1959), 108–10.

that used the party to consolidate their hold on the state and to further their own selfish ends.[8]

Felton's victory and the growing strength of the Independent movement deeply troubled the regular Democrats, and in 1878, they determined to make an all-out effort to crush the insurgents. The resulting campaign proved to be one of the most bitterly contested off-year elections in Georgia history. To help defeat the Independents, the Democratic party prevailed upon the man often considered the most prominent Georgian. Gordon promptly answered the call. During the fall of 1878, he campaigned extensively on behalf of the regular Democratic party but especially hard in the "Bloody Seventh," where George N. Lester opposed Dr. Felton. This was not the first time he had taken the stump in opposition to Felton. In 1874, Mrs. Rebecca Latimer Felton heard that Gordon would speak in the Seventh and wrote to the general, inquiring about his plans. His evasive reply, indicating that previous commitments in south Georgia would probably prevent any campaigning in her husband's district, coupled with his appearance at a mass meeting in the Seventh exactly one week later provoked the combative Mrs. Felton. This incident was the opening act of a long and bitter political drama involving the general and the lady.[9]

College-educated and exceptionally articulate, Mrs. Felton was truly an unusual individual. At eighteen, she married William H. Felton, a physician and ordained Methodist minister twelve years her senior. The early years of her marriage were devoted to raising a family, but when her husband entered politics, she avidly joined his fight against the Democratic party. She had no intention of remaining apart from the fray, even though contemporary attitudes dictated that politics be left to the men. At the outset, Mrs. Felton labored in

8. E. Merton Coulter, *A Short History of Georgia* (Chapel Hill, 1933), 363–65; Kenneth Coleman (ed.), *A History of Georgia* (Athens, 1977), 216–20; Judson Clements Ward, Jr., "Georgia Under the Bourbon Democrats, 1872–1890" (Ph.D. dissertation, University of North Carolina, 1947), 73–74. See also George L. Jones, "William H. Felton and the Independent Democratic Movement in Georgia, 1870–1890" (Ph.D. dissertation, University of Georgia, 1971).

9. Ward, "Georgia Under the Bourbons," 95–105; John E. Talmadge, *Rebecca Latimer Felton: Nine Stormy Decades* (Athens, Ga., 1966), 40–41; Gordon to Mrs. Felton, October 24, 1874, in R. L. Felton Collection; Gordon to Doctor Hambleton, October 9, 1874, in Hambleton Collection; Mrs. William H. Felton, *My Memoirs of Georgia Politics* (Atlanta, 1911), 150–52; Atlanta *Constitution*, September 29, October 3, 8, 17, 31, November 1–3, 7, 1878.

the background; nevertheless, she was soon acknowledged as her husband's campaign manager and press secretary. Her pen became her most powerful and indefatigable weapon as she wrote countless speeches and letters for the doctor. Unquestionably, Gordon's apparent duplicity in 1874 angered her, but relations between the Gordons and Feltons seemed to have remained cordial until 1878. In August of the preceding year, Mrs. Felton, who had endured the heartbreak of the death of several of her own children, sent a very touching letter to Fanny after learning of Carolina's death. And correspondence that year between the general and the doctor does not evince any of the bitter animosity that would later characterize their relationship.[10]

But as the 1878 election neared and Gordon increased his efforts against the doctor, the Feltons' antipathy intensified. The general pleaded for party loyalty by reminding the voters that "party organization was the means of our rescue; party dissension would insure our overthrow." Asserting that the Independents were "uniting with the worst elements of the Rad. [Radical Republican] party & threatening us [Democrats] with the loss of our state," Gordon enlisted the talents of other prominent Democratic senators. He called upon Lamar of Mississippi and Ransom of North Carolina to speak at Democratic rallies and help destroy Independentism in Georgia. Gordon also employed the particularly effective tactic of appealing to the sentiments of Georgians by drawing attention to the doctor's failure to enter the Confederate military. Even though Gordon frequently excoriated Republicans for using the war for their partisan purposes, he had no qualms whatsoever about calling forth the "gray ghosts" when it was to his political advantage. Parading back and forth on numerous campaign stages with "his fine head held high, his scarred face alive with the joy of battle," Gordon often accentuated the Democratic candidate's contribution to the war as "he lifted Lester's empty sleeve and smiled down at the tumult." One can almost see the livid, enraged Mrs. Felton glaring back at the beaming general. The lavish praise by Democratic publications of Gordon's willing-

10. John E. Talmadge, "Rebecca Latimer Felton," in Horace Montgomery (ed.), Georgians in Profile (Athens, 1958), 277–302; Josephine Bone Floyd, "Rebecca Latimer Felton, Political Independent," Georgia Historical Quarterly, XXX (March, 1946), 14–34; Talmadge, Felton, passim; Fanny Gordon to Mrs. Felton, August 27, 1877, Gordon to Doctor Felton, February 25, 1876, both in R. L. Felton Collection; Gordon to Dr. Felton, April 29, 1877, in Doctor William Harrell Felton and Mrs. Rebecca A. Latimer Felton Collection, UGA.

ness to "throw himself into the breach . . . at this critical juncture to come to the rescue of the party of peace, property and safety" undoubtedly compounded her anger. While criticizing other prominent Democrats for refusing to enter the contest in the Seventh, the Atlanta *Constitution* glowingly reported the general's labors on behalf of the "true democracy." Nevertheless, despite the pressures brought to bear on them, Felton and another Independent won congressional seats.[11]

Immediately upon the heels of the early November contests, Gordon faced his own battle as he sought a second term as United States Senator. Although prospects for his reelection appeared bright, Gordon had been cautioning his supporters for over a year not to be misled: "I don't want too great confidence in my success to create apathy on the part of my friends." Recent "threats of vengeance" from Independents and warnings that "they would 'beat him for the senate'" may have given Gordon cause for concern, but almost all of Georgia's newspapers confidently predicted an easy victory for the general, perhaps by the largest majority ever received by a senatorial candidate. That was exactly what happened on November 19, 1878, when the Georgia General Assembly met and reelected Gordon by a nearly unanimous vote.[12]

In a magnificent speech at the state capitol on the night after the election, Gordon humbly thanked his fellow citizens for their expression of confidence in him. Somberly reflecting upon his almost six-year struggle against Republican opponents in the Senate, he tried to describe the grave burdens of responsibility that he believed he had borne while in their service. "No man but those who served you then can ever know the agony of that awful suspense nor fully appreciate the dangers that surrounded your liberties." Even now, at a time when much of the deep-seated sectional hatred had abated, Gordon cautioned his listeners that the danger persisted. Radical Republicans, he insisted, now "seize again the faded bloody shirt, plunge it in

11. Talmadge, *Felton*, 51–55; Atlanta *Constitution*, September 29, October 3, 17, November 7, 1878; Willie D. Halsell (ed.), "Some Correspondence Between Lucius Q. C. Lamar and John B. Gordon," *Georgia Historical Quarterly*, XXVIII (March, 1944), 46–47; Gordon to Ransom, October 7, 1878, in Matt W. Ransom Papers, SHC.

12. Atlanta *Constitution*, October 17, 23, November 12, 19, 20, 1878; Gordon to L. N. Trammell, September 14, 1877, in Trammell Letters; New York *Tribune*, November 20, 1878; *Georgia House Journal*, 1878, pp. 143–45; *Georgia Senate Journal*, 1878, pp. 86–87.

the chronic crimson vat, run it up the party staff and fly it as the symbol of a new civilization and a 'restored union.'"[13]

As disturbing as these renewed efforts "to reopen the wounds that were healing and to revive the passions that were dying" were to Gordon, he found the increasing rift in the ranks of the Democratic party in Georgia even more alarming. Any attempt to establish a third party could only work to the detriment of the Democratic party by allowing the Republicans to "rush through the breach and seize the governments, state and federal." Gordon's plea for loyalty to the Democratic cause took on an almost evangelistic tenor. Speaking directly to the men who had so bitterly berated both him and his party only days earlier, Gordon stressed that despite their differences, the Independents and the Democrats must work within the confines of the organized Democracy. Only the Democratic party, Gordon asserted, served as the true repository of the ideals and principles upon which America had been built; the Republican party, on the other hand, had been "conceived in passion, born of fanaticism and baptized in blood." As he neared the end of his speech, he whipped the audience into a frenzy by dramatically reaffirming that it had been the Democratic party that had, state by state, redeemed the South from Republican tyranny. And it would be, he concluded, the Democratic party that would continue to fight for the principles of true democracy. Although he couched his appeal for party unity in terms of preventing Republican rule, it is obvious that Gordon wanted to beat back the Independents because of the challenge they represented to leaders of the Democratic party, among whom he was the most prominent.[14]

Gordon's appeal for an end to party disloyalty and for a return of the insurgents to the Democratic fold fell upon deaf ears in much of northern Georgia. Dr. Felton had retained his congressional seat by a comfortable margin, but his wife was not content merely to bask in the glory of victory; rather, she launched a vicious assault upon the Georgia senator who had campaigned so intensely against her husband. As Mrs. Felton's biographer observed, "[F]ate could not have harassed Gordon with a more formidable opponent: a lady who insisted on being considered a lady even while she was employing all the bare-knuckled tactics of a belligerent man." Mrs. Felton opposed and hated many prominent Georgians but "none so long and wholeheart-

13. Atlanta *Constitution*, November 22, 1878.
14. *Ibid.*

edly" as Gordon. His active political opposition to her husband was the genesis of her resentment; however, it was the Confederate hero's emotional appeal to Georgians to vote against a man who had failed to support the Confederate cause that earned him the lady's everlasting enmity. "She could never put from her mind," wrote her biographer, "the picture of Gordon smiling triumphantly from the platform while the 'Rebel yell' echoed around him." Mrs. Felton's contempt for Gordon's business failures only reinforced her belief that the general was "at best . . . a charlatan with limited capabilities." Gordon truly had an enemy with whom he had to reckon.[15]

To avoid being put in the difficult position of attacking a southern woman, Gordon tried to ignore Mrs. Felton's barbs. But that proved impossible as her efforts to destroy his reputation became frenetic. In a series of letters and articles in early 1879, especially in the pages of the Feltons' own Cartersville *Free Press*, she waged a sustained and bitterly personal campaign against Gordon. She dwelt upon the failure of his various business ventures, which she claimed defrauded numerous Georgians of their investments; she accused him of borrowing money from Richard Wilmer, Episcopal bishop of Alabama, and using worthless securities as collateral; she charged him with using convict labor for personal gain and with housing the prisoners in a camp she called "a disgrace to civilization"; and she alleged that Gordon had enriched himself while in the Senate, through political and financial corruption. Mrs. Felton reiterated all these denunciations in a February letter in which she replied to charges that Independents in the Seventh had solicited funds from the Republican party in the last election. Although Anderson W. Reese, correspondent of the Macon *Telegraph*, had made the accusation, she ignored him and assailed Gordon as "the master in this attack." And lastly, as was her habit, she chided Gordon and other "shifty politicians" for their "resolve to attack women."[16]

Gordon usually allowed his friends and the Democratic newspapers to act in his defense, but by March, 1879, he felt compelled to respond personally to Mrs. Felton's charges. He did so in a forceful letter to the Augusta *Chronicle and Constitutionalist* in which he maintained that he had not entered the canvass in the Seventh by

15. *Ibid.*, November 22, 23, 1878; New York *Tribune*, November 22, 1878; Talmadge, *Felton*, 55–57.

16. Talmadge, *Felton*, 56–59; Atlanta *Constitution*, February 25, 28, 1879. For more information on the 1879 clash, see Felton, *Memoirs*, 479–96.

198 · JOHN BROWN GORDON

choice but rather at the behest of the Democratic party. He asserted that he "made no assaults upon Doctor Felton's character" until the "wanton and reckless" nature of the slanders against his own character "made it proper for me to repel them." In addition to denying all of Mrs. Felton's charges, Gordon also turned the tables on her by denying that she was the true slanderer and—wisely though unfairly—concentrating on her husband as "the author and circulator of the calumnies" heaped upon him. Employing some of the most bitter invective he ever issued for publication, Gordon assailed Felton for hiding "behind his wife, his grey hairs and the robes of a minister of Christ." Felton had proven himself, in Gordon's words, "false to his people in the war; false to the political organization which served his people in peace; false to the teachings of Him who he professes to follow; [and] begrimed with a wicked and corrupt alliance with the enemies of his party, section and people." Gordon acknowledged that these were extremely "strong words," but he concluded that for the sake of his children and the people who had elected him, he must publicly denounce "these foul and atrocious calumnies" in such a manner as to leave no doubt of their falsehood.[17]

By making the doctor the object of his attack, Gordon managed to cut Mrs. Felton out of the public portion of the controversy, and as neither man wished to persist in violently assailing the other, the feud soon faded from the public's eye. The hatred it engendered, however, lived on long afterward. Little material of a personal nature, which would provide a definitive answer about how Gordon regarded Mrs. Felton, has survived. Nevertheless, he must have detested the woman. With her intrusion into what almost everyone considered the masculine arena of politics, she, in Gordon's mind, forfeited her immunity from attack as well as the abiding admiration and respect he always entertained for women. And yet, in spite of her unladylike actions, Mrs. Felton insisted that she be treated with the full deference due her sex. This woman and her peculiar prejudice would trouble Gordon for the remainder of his life. Until her death in 1930, she seized every opportunity to assail him on any grounds whatsoever. Much of *My Memoirs of Georgia Politics*, her autobiography published in 1911, was devoted to her unrelenting obsession to expose Gordon and to chip away at his popularity—to harry the general even beyond the grave.[18]

17. Atlanta *Constitution*, February 26, 28, March 8–10, 1879.
18. Talmadge, *Felton*, 55–56. Following this bitter fight in 1879, Mrs. Felton began collecting material she deemed damaging to the general. Her efforts filled numerous

During the course of his controversy with the Feltons, Gordon remained in Washington, where he had taken on new responsibilities. Democratic victories in the fall of 1878 enabled Gordon's party to gain control of the United States Senate and with it, the chairmanships of the various Senate committees. As the senior Democratic member of the Committee on Commerce, Gordon was elevated to its head. Despite his advancement, Gordon accomplished little of note in 1879 because of a severe attack of inflammatory rheumatism. In fact, Gordon became so "very desperately sick" during the last two weeks of March that Fanny thought he would die. One visitor to Gordon's bedside reported that public interest in his condition was "something phenomenal"; he received over two hundred cards in one day. Gordon did not entirely recover until near the end of April. Although generally robust and vital, Gordon, as he grew older, experienced considerable problems with his health. Undoubtedly, his wounds and his immense physical exertions during the war contributed to his increasingly frequent periods of painful debility.[19]

Following a pleasant summer of family life at his home near Atlanta, Gordon resumed his senatorial duties and his efforts at national reconciliation. In interviews with a number of northern newspapers in late 1879, Gordon advised southern members of Congress not to be lured into the partisan debates that he felt had damaged the Democratic cause in the last session. Continued "indulgence of excited oratory and the discussion of sectional issues," he averred, would only detract from national pacification and, in the process, harm the South. Gordon told southerners that "silent contempt" was the best way to meet Republican charges: "When the people of the north see that we endure all that they [the Republicans] can say without reply and are only here for the purpose of attending to the business of legislation, they [northerners at large] will take us for what we really are and trust us." The Philadelphia *Times* concurred with Gordon and heartily praised his continued "efforts in behalf of the peace that is based upon mutual good will, a thorough acceptance of the results of the war and the national sentiment, which is the natural outgrowth of these conditions."[20]

---

scrapbooks and provided the basis for much of her memoir, almost one-third of which touches upon Gordon's actions or Mrs. Felton's accusations against him. Felton, *Memoirs*, 631, *passim*.

19. Atlanta *Constitution*, March 8, 18–20, 25, April 2, 3, 10, 23, 1879; *Congressional Record*, 46th Cong., 1st Sess., 1, 136; 2nd Sess., 19.

20. New York *Journal of Commerce*, quoted in Atlanta *Constitution*, October 16,

Although Gordon steadfastly worked "to prevent the keeping alive of sectional animosities, [and] the stirring up of sectional strife," he became embroiled in an acerbic dispute within his own Georgia delegation in early 1880. Rumors of a rift between Gordon and Alexander H. Stephens over the appointment of a supervisor of the census for the first district of Georgia surfaced in January. In what quickly became "a personal conflict," Gordon violently opposed Stephens'— and Dr. Felton's—nominee, Thomas J. Simmons, "on the ground of utter incompetency and bitter malignity to the best people of the state, branding them as . . . 'secesh traitors.'" During a private three-hour meeting between the Senate committee on the census and the Georgia congressional delegation to consider Simmons' nomination, "an exceedingly spirited, and at times very personal, colloquy" between Gordon and Stephens took place. Gordon exploded when Stephens, who had earlier charged that the general's negligence had resulted in the defeat of a Georgia river-and-harbor appropriation bill, accused him of favoring a Republican, former marshal Thomas Smyth, for the census supervisor's job. Gordon later explained that "my indignation was so great that I used to you [Stephens] language which, in view of your age and our long established friendship, I deeply regret." Although letters of apology were exchanged, the Gordon-Stephens feud continued, eventually attracting national attention. Most Georgians, dismayed by the profitless war between two of their most respected representatives, probably concurred with the sentiments of the Macon *Herald*: "Private controversies should be fought out in private. Besides all this, these gentlemen were not sent to Washington to wage war on each other; and the fact is worthy of their consideration."[21]

Disputes such as this one may well have helped sour Gordon on politics. In his seven years in the Senate he had achieved much.

---

1879; Baltimore *Sun*, quoted *ibid.*, December 4, 1879; Baltimore *Gazette*, quoted *ibid.*; Philadelphia *Times*, quoted *ibid.*, December 5, 1879.

21. Atlanta *Constitution*, January 27, February 5, 7, 8, March 10, 14, 19, 20, April 25, 27, 1880; Philadelphia *Times*, quoted *ibid.*, December 5, 1879; Macon *Telegraph*, quoted *ibid.*, April 25, 1880; New York *Times*, February 12, 15, April 12, 1880. In addition to the specific dates cited, almost every issue of the Atlanta *Constitution* between February and April, 1880, made some mention of the controversy. Numerous letters dealing with the Gordon-Stephens imbroglio in February can be found in Alexander Hamilton Stephens Collection LC. See also Felton, *Memoirs*, 297–301; and Ulrich B. Phillips (ed.), *The Correspondence of Robert Toombs, Alexander H. Stephens, and Howell Cobb* (Washington, D.C., 1913), 741.

Beyond the personal reputation he had earned as a southern spokesman, he had also established himself as a strong proponent of national reconciliation. More tangible was the major role he had played
in bringing Reconstruction to an end and restoring self-government
to all the states of the South. Perhaps the Senate no longer held the
attraction it once had for Gordon because he had accomplished all
that he could at the present time. He had successfully met the challenges that had confronted him in both his military and political
careers. But as a businessman, he could only look back upon a record
of disappointment and failure. Given his feelings about this record
and his disgruntlement with politics—or at least with affairs like the
Stephens conflict and the bitter contests against the Independents—
Gordon began to look for a new challenge beyond the Senate. Like a
good general who regroups his forces following a successful campaign
in anticipation of the next one, Gordon looked to the future.

Just as the Gordon-Stephens controversy retreated from the headlines, a shocking announcement "like a bolt out of the blue" reached
Georgia. On May 19, 1880, unheralded by rumor, Georgians learned
that Gordon had resigned from the Senate. He had tendered his resignation in a May 15 letter to Governor Alfred H. Colquitt. Having been
in public service, either at war or in politics, almost constantly for
nearly twenty years, Gordon explained that he was "simply carrying
out a long cherished desire to retire from public life." He contended
that hitherto he had subordinated that desire to his sense of duty,
which made him reluctant to leave the service of his fellow southerners. However, the rights of self-government and full representation had now been restored to all southern states, and Gordon felt
"free therefore to consult my inclinations and the imperative interests of my family, without the least detriment to the public service."
Colquitt appealed to Gordon to withdraw his resignation or at least
delay it until the Georgia General Assembly met, but the general,
"though anxious to oblige," replied, "I feel constrained to decline."
Reluctantly, Colquitt acceded to Gordon's request. Gordon was leaving the Senate.[22]

22. Atlanta *Constitution*, May 20, 1880; Colquitt to Gordon, May 18, 20, 1880, both
in Governor's Letterbooks, January 1877–April 1881, Records of the Executive Department, Record Group 1, GDAH.

John Brown Gordon at age twenty-two, as he appeared when he met and married Fanny

*Courtesy of the Hargrett Rare Book and Manuscript Library, University of Georgia Libraries*

Fanny Rebecca Haralson Gordon (center) and two of her sisters, Mrs.
Logan E. Bleckley (left) and Mrs. Basil H. Overby (right), who all married
members of the same law firm

*Courtesy of the Hargrett Rare Book and Manuscript Library, University of Georgia Libraries*

Major General John Brown Gordon, looking every inch a soldier

*Courtesy of the National Archives*

Fanny Rebecca Haralson Gordon, as she appeared during the Civil War
while she accompanied her husband on his campaigns
*Courtesy of the National Archives*

Gordon in the late 1860s, ready for new challenges after the Civil War
*Courtesy of the Library of Congress*

Gordon began building Sutherland, his home in Kirkwood, in the late
1860s; it burned in 1899.

*Courtesy of the Hargrett Rare Book and Manuscript Library, University of Georgia Libraries*

The portico of Sutherland, with its eight massive Ionic pillars

*Courtesy of the Hargrett Rare Book and Manuscript Library, University of Georgia Libraries*

The dining room of Sutherland, with the silver service given to Gordon by South Carolinians, in "grateful remembrance of his . . . aid [i]n restoring to their State the rights of Self-Government"

*Courtesy of the Hargrett Rare Book and Manuscript Library, University of Georgia Libraries*

Caroline Lewis Gordon, daughter of John and Fanny, and author of "De Gin'ral an' Miss Fanny," an unpublished manuscript that provides valuable information on the Gordons' home life

John Brown Gordon as United States senator in 1896—a fire still burns in the eyes of the old warrior

*Courtesy of the Hargrett Rare Book and Manuscript Library, University of Georgia Libraries*

Fanny Gordon in her later years, probably while John was serving as
senator in the 1890s

*Courtesy of the Hargrett Rare Book and Manuscript Library, University of Georgia Libraries*

Gordon at Beechwood Plantation, about 1900—in war and in peace,
straight as a ramrod

*Courtesy of the Hargrett Rare Book and Manuscript Library, University of Georgia Libraries*

Gordon lying in state in the Georgia State Capitol, where tens of
thousands would file by in final review of the general

*Courtesy of the Hargrett Rare Book and Manuscript Library, University of Georgia Libraries*

The Gordon Monument on the state capitol grounds in Atlanta, dedicated and unveiled May 25, 1907

*Courtesy of the Hargrett Rare Book and Manuscript Library, University of Georgia Libraries*

# XI · A Breath of Scandal

Gordon's unexpected resignation profoundly shocked and saddened people in all sections of the country. National newspapers, unstinting in their praise of Gordon's senatorial services both to his state and to the nation, lamented his decision to leave the national forum. The St. Louis *Post Dispatch* acknowledged that Gordon's desperate financial plight was well known and declared that a "senatorship with $6,000 a year and a family means poverty in Washington." Recognizing that such a paltry sum forced many senators to lead a "dog's life," the Boston *Post* expressed surprise "that his example is not more frequently followed." Praise of the Georgian also cut across party lines: the New York *Tribune* recalled "few parallels in the history of the senate" of a man retiring at the peak of his power and acclaim. This Republican paper, often a severe critic of Gordon, nevertheless noted that Republicans and Democrats alike respected and trusted the Georgian, whose "fairness and moderation . . . made him personally one of the most influential members of the Senate." The Baltimore *Gazette* knew of "no man in public life who in so short a space of time has made a deeper or broader impression upon national affairs." And in probably the most glowing tribute to Gordon, the Washington *Post* expressed its deep regret at the loss of a man whose "mere presence has been so serviceable in bringing about a constantly improving feeling" between the formerly warring sections. The *Post* added that it had "yet to read or hear of the northern man who has met him who does not heartily respect him, and who does not, as a consequence, entertain a higher respect for the people whom he represents."[1]

1. Quoted in Atlanta *Constitution*, May 23, 25, 1880; New York *Tribune*, May 21, 1880. During the last days of May, the daily issues of the *Constitution* are laced with favorable editorials from numerous newspapers throughout the country. See also Gordon Family Collection, UGA.

Although Georgia newspapers echoed similar expressions of disappointment and praise, their comments had barely reached print when a second, more electrifying jolt rocked the citizens of the state. On the same day that Gordon's letter of resignation was published, Georgians learned that Governor Alfred H. Colquitt had appointed that political chameleon Joseph E. Brown—the same man who less than a decade earlier had been a prominent figure in the Republican party—to succeed Gordon in the Senate. Outrage and indignation instantly replaced the surprise and regret that had greeted Gordon's announcement. This appointment of the thoroughly detested Brown shook Georgia politics to its very core. It had, in the words of one contemporary, "something like the effect that the explosion of a powder magazine would have in a fortification." Gordon's resignation coupled with Colquitt's selection of Brown spawned a political whirlwind of "more sudden and uncontrollable fury" than Georgia had ever before witnessed.[2]

First reports from Washington concerning Gordon's decision to step down cited the same reasons that he had provided in his letter of resignation, namely, his desire to leave public life and the necessity of devoting himself to a full-time, more-lucrative business enterprise. Henry W. Grady, managing editor and correspondent of the Atlanta *Constitution*, reported from the nation's capital that though the general had "several flattering offers," he would do nothing until he had "a few weeks rest." Georgia editorials written immediately following the announcement of Gordon's resignation praised the native son's brilliant record of service on the state's behalf. Having defended Georgia's liberty first on the battlefield and then in the Senate, Gordon could now, in one Atlanta paper's opinion, put "off a toga that is as stainless as the sword he surrendered at Appomattox." However, the announcement of Joe Brown's appointment as Georgia's interim senator cast a wholly different light upon Gordon's action. Rumors immediately began to circulate that Gordon would assume the presidency of Brown's Western and Atlantic Railroad. To many Georgians, it appeared that all the elements of a corrupt bargain were present: Brown, using his money and influence to assist Gordon in business and Colquitt in politics, gained a seat in the Senate; Colquitt, anticipating immense difficulty in retaining his gubernatorial chair in the

2. Atlanta *Constitution*, May 21, 1880; Isaac W. Avery, *History of the State of Georgia From 1850 to 1881* (New York, 1881), 558.

fall elections, secured the support of two influential Georgians; and Gordon, desiring to leave politics in order to make money, obtained the prominent business position he had long sought. Cries of "bargain," "sale," "trade," and the "calumny of understanding between the three" reverberated from virtually every section of Georgia.[3]

The source of the political storm that swept over the state was obviously Colquitt's appointment of Brown to Gordon's vacated Senate seat. Although Brown had risen meteorically in prewar politics and had ably led the state as governor during the Civil War, his acceptance of Republican rule and ready conversion to that party in the postwar period had earned him the everlasting enmity of most white Georgians, especially Democrats. Commenting upon Brown's remarkable political career, one Georgia historian styled him "first in secession, first in reconstruction, and very nearly first in the restoration of Democratic home rule." In spite of his reconversion to the Democratic party in the early 1870s, Joe Brown remained probably the most widely detested native-born public figure in all Georgia. His brilliant success in various postwar business endeavors brought him immense wealth, but all his money could not buy him the political vindication that he sought from the people of Georgia. One biographer contends that it "is doubtful that Brown really wanted to go to Washington as a Senator, leaving behind all his business interests, yet he thought the honor due him." More than merely believing the Senate post was an honor he had earned, Brown yearned to emerge from under the dark cloud of political ostracism that shadowed him at all times in the postwar period. In light of the complex railroad dealings in which he was involved in May, 1880, it is unlikely he would have accepted Colquitt's offer had he not truly wished to return to public life. But without a helping hand, Brown had virtually no chance of again holding high political office. Now, as the result of Gordon's resignation and Colquitt's appointment, Brown was politically resurrected.[4]

Reaction to the resignation and appointment, though varied, was swift and forceful. Throughout the entire controversy, the Atlanta *Constitution* denied any wrongdoing on the part of Gordon, Colquitt,

3. Atlanta *Constitution*, May 20–23, 1880; Avery, *History of Georgia*, 558–59.
4. Joseph H. Parks, *Joseph E. Brown of Georgia* (Baton Rouge, 1977), 19–506, especially 518; C. Mildred Thompson, *Reconstruction in Georgia: Economic, Social, Political, 1865–1872* (New York, 1915), 223; Avery, *History of Georgia*, 563; Louise Biles Hill, *Joseph E. Brown and the Confederacy* (Chapel Hill, 1939), 311.

or Brown and was the most vocal defender of the general. On May 25, it delivered a blistering editorial that castigated those who were impugning Gordon's motives and denouncing his actions. How could—and why would—residents of Gordon's own native state assassinate his character, the paper incredulously inquired; he was "a senator who is too poor to maintain his family and meet the demands made upon him with the salary of his office." Although some papers, like the *Constitution*, recognized Brown's selection "as a proper appointment and as good as could have been made," numerous other newspapers in the state unleashed a withering assault upon all the involved parties. Brown, as might be expected, bore the brunt of the tirade. Characterized by the Savannah *Record* as "venal, mercenary, mediocre, vindictive, ever veering his sails to suit the wind," Brown was denounced not only for his prior political transgressions but also for his central role in the current controversy. Colquitt also came under intense fire for his alleged complicity in the "Senatorial deformity." At a large public meeting, residents of Columbus adopted resolutions severely condemning the governor for "the shameful and disgraceful manner" in which he had foisted Brown upon the people. Most Georgians conceded Gordon's right to resign but, like the Columbus *Enquirer*, found "the rewarding of Brown, the bitter pill" given them by Colquitt, outrageous and unpalatable. "Base and treacherous conduct," "eternal infamy," and "a stench in the nostrils of honest men" were but a few of the blistering insults showered upon Brown and Colquitt by Georgians who felt betrayed by the apparent conspiracy.[5]

Gordon, of course, did not escape his share of abuse. The Columbus *Times* believed that unless he could provide a more complete and more satisfactory explanation for his sudden retirement, Gordon deserved even greater censure than Colquitt. Some charged Gordon with willingly and purposefully exchanging his Senate seat for favors from Brown. If this proved to be the case, it was asserted that Gordon would forever forfeit his special place in Georgians' hearts. A more commonly heard criticism, and the one stated by the Atlanta *Daily Post*, pictured Gordon "more as the unfortunate victim of an unholy conspiracy than as the architect of his own misfortune." That paper further speculated that Gordon, having become "financially involved

5. Atlanta *Constitution*, May 21, 25, 1880; Savannah *Record*, May 24, 1880, quoted in Parks, *Brown*, 510; Columbus *Enquirer*, quoted in Atlanta *Constitution*, May 21, 1880; Avery, *History of Georgia*, 560–61.

beyond hope of disenthralment . . . listened to the words of the seducer [Brown] and bartered his position, if not his honor, for personal gain." Many Georgians probably concurred with a similar proposition, put forth in a letter to the editors of the *Constitution*, that Gordon as well as Colquitt had "been made the dupes of the artful and sagacious arch-political traitor, Joseph E. Brown." The former governor, according to this letter signed "Pro Bono Publico," used his wealth and influence, both in railroading and in politics, as "a mighty lever" to secure the position of United States Senator that he so greatly desired. Realizing that election to the post was impossible, Brown offered financial assistance to Gordon and political support to Colquitt, the benefits of which neither could resist. Regardless of the varied forms the condemnations of Gordon, Brown, and Colquitt took, the swell of protest assumed frightening proportions within a matter of days.[6]

Public outrage grew so intense that all the accused parties felt compelled to respond to the grave allegations being leveled against them. Colquitt and Brown published accounts of their involvement in the resignation and appointment process only three days after the announcement of Gordon's decision. Colquitt indignantly denounced rumors of a bargain or understanding between Gordon, Brown, and himself as "utterly, wantonly false" and branded anyone who made such accusations "a liar or a thief." He explained his swift selection of Brown by revealing that he had known for several months that Gordon wanted to resign. This knowledge had allowed him "to look about for a successor" before Gordon actually stepped down. Convinced that the former governor was "the fittest appointment," Colquitt approached him about the Senate post. According to the governor, Brown initially refused the offer, urging instead that he redouble his efforts to dissuade Gordon from resigning; however, when convinced that Gordon's decision was final, Brown reconsidered and accepted the appointment, an act that the governor maintained "surprised and gratified" him. As that was the extent of his role in the controversy, Colquitt declared that he had "nothing but loathing and contempt for the man who hints of corruption or questionable methods."[7]

6. Columbus *Times*, quoted in Atlanta *Constitution*, May 22, 1880; clipping of Atlanta *Daily Post*, May 23, 1880, in Felton Scrapbooks, Scrapbook No. 17, p. 51, in Rebecca Latimer Felton Collection, UGA; Atlanta *Constitution*, May 25, 26, 1880.
7. Atlanta *Constitution*, May 23, 1880.

Brown, in a separate interview, similarly denied the charge of a prearranged understanding, calling it "an infamous falsehood." His explanation substantiated the governor's account in every detail. According to Brown, there was never even the suggestion of "any bargain or understanding or condition" at any time before or after he accepted the Senate offer. "I was simply urged to take the place, and finally agreed," he averred. "There never had been the slightest hint of a condition." Brown denied any contact whatsoever, in person, by mail or telegraph, or through an intermediary, with Gordon about anything vaguely related to the matter at hand. He also flatly rejected the rumor that Gordon would replace him as president of the Western and Atlantic Railroad. To the contrary, Brown reported that the only suggestions that he had received in this connection were from stockholders who strongly urged him to continue as head of the road. Like Colquitt, he concluded by emphasizing that the strength of his denial of all charges could not possibly be overexaggerated.[8]

A full-fledged explanation by Gordon of his actions was not immediately forthcoming; he remained in Washington attending to Senate duties until his successor arrived. Nevertheless, Georgians learned through additional articles by Grady that Gordon had already received a number of attractive business offers. The first came from one of his old soldiers, T. Egenton Hogg, who wanted the general to move to Oregon and take charge of his large railroad and mining interests there. Another proposal offered Gordon the presidency of the Great Southern Railway of Florida. But Grady maintained that Gordon had yet to accept any position. And in an effort to quash pernicious rumors, Grady stated positively that Gordon had not been and would not be offered the presidency of the Western and Atlantic Railroad. In the same issue of the *Constitution* that carried Grady's report, Gordon authorized the paper "in the strongest sense to deny in his name that there was any trade or suspicion of a trade." Early dispatches reported that Gordon would soon return home from Washington "to discuss face to face with the people the issues" that had grown out of his resignation; however, his wife's serious illness forced him to postpone the trip until she improved. But when the rumblings of discontent in Georgia grew audible even to Gordon in the nation's capital, it became apparent that he had to comment directly on the charges being leveled against him. Consequently, on

8. *Ibid.*

May 25, he granted an interview to Charles Howard Williams of the *Constitution*.[9]

Apprised that universal regret and surprise had greeted his resignation, Gordon corrected the journalist, stating that the surprise was far from universal. "Many of my intimate friends have known of my disinclination for public life and of my purpose to resign for a long time." Although he reiterated his ardent love for the South and his willingness to bear almost any hardship on behalf of its people, Gordon explained that he longed for the quietude of domesticity more than the honors of political life. He also expressed fear that his health, which had recently broken twice under the "constant work and trials" of the Senate, might again fail and leave his family financially distressed. "The case is this: I love my home and family, and am forced to neglect the one and do injustice to the other as long as I remain in public life." Further, "pressing and increasing pecuniary demands . . . and my decreasing ability to meet them" convinced him that he had little choice but to seek a more remunerative position.[10]

When asked about the suddenness of his resignation and his unwillingness to wait until the Georgia assembly again met, Gordon explained that the nature of his business arrangements simply would not allow him to continue at his Senate post until the end of the session. Although he did not expand upon these business considerations, he did inform the interviewer that he had accepted a position as general counsel with the Louisville and Nashville Railroad Company. Gordon carefully pointed out that this offer from H. Victor Newcomb, president of the railroad, "was the consequence and not the cause" of his resignation, in that he had already resigned in order to take the Oregon job. But, Gordon stated, when Newcomb learned of his resignation and tendered him a position that would not carry him far from home, he accepted the less lucrative offer so that he might remain in Georgia. Responding to claims that he had deserted his post while the South remained in danger, Gordon asserted that the exact opposite was true. With the South fully restored and his greatest goal in political life thereby accomplished, he predicted that he might be of even greater service to his section as a private citizen. Gordon assured Williams that in spite of his resignation, he would remain active in public affairs, particularly "on all proper occasions

9. *Ibid.*, May 23, 27, 28, 30, 1880.
10. *Ibid.*, May 27, 1880.

to restore good will between the sections and advance the cause of good government in the state and the union." At the close of the interview, Gordon emphatically denied all charges of a trade between Brown and himself, not only denouncing the accusation as "a base calumny and falsehood in all its length and breadth and depth" but also labeling it preposterous because Brown had nothing to offer him.[11]

Several letters to the editors of the *Constitution*—though perhaps written at Gordon's request—supported many of his contentions. A correspondent from the Augusta *Chronicle* wrote that Gordon had personally informed him three months earlier of his desire to retire from public life. Gordon's father also told residents of Georgia that during a visit in March, his son had confessed, "Pa, I am tired of public life. I crave the peace and quietude of my own home and home affairs; besides, I can't save up any money out of my salary; and this idea of dying and leaving my family without a competency troubles me no little." The Reverend Zachariah Gordon was only surprised that his son's resignation had not come sooner. A letter from "Observer" similarly revealed that Gordon, in a private conversation in January, had expressed his disappointment with public life and his haunting fear of "premature breaking down, physically and mentally." So even though Gordon's resignation caught most Georgians off guard, he had, it would seem, spoken of his desire to retire from public service on a number of earlier occasions.[12]

Gordon personally took his case to the people of Georgia on June 4. On the evening following his return to Atlanta, he delivered a stirring public address at DeGive's Opera House. Looking, in the opinion of the Atlanta *Constitution*, "more erect, more soldierly, more graceful, more commanding" than he had at any other time in his life, Gordon strode to center stage amid "a storm of applause which fairly shook the building." After briefly recounting his twenty years of service to Georgia, Gordon proudly proclaimed, "[N]o word or act of mine has ever been quoted by political foes to your detriment." In spite of his devotion to what he considered the best interests of the people of the state, Gordon admitted, he had made a number of enemies in Georgia who would never be satisfied with any explanation he might give for any of his actions. He mockingly dismissed most of the rumors about his resignation before turning to the charge that he, Brown, and Col-

11. *Ibid.*
12. *Ibid.*, May 22, 26, 27, 1880. See also September 3, 1880.

quitt had been party to a corrupt deal. Displaying a sense of righteous indignation, he announced, "[I]f my life, if my character, if my record as it stands now completed, in war and in peace, in public and private, does not answer that [charge], [then] it will go unanswered forever so far as I am concerned." Despite his willingness to stand on his record, Gordon continued. He did so, however, not on his own behalf, but rather, he contended, in the interest of the "cause of truth and justice" and with the purpose of exonerating his friend Governor Colquitt of all charges of impropriety.[13]

Gordon proceeded to elaborate upon the reasons that he had earlier cited for his resignation. Having "long since decided to retire from public life," Gordon explained, he "had only waited for time and opportunity to do so consistent with my own honor and your interests." Both conditions were satisfied early in 1880. Convinced that southern rights and liberties had been safely secured, he accepted the offer from Colonel Hogg to join him in his enterprises in Oregon. Hogg guaranteed him compensation that more than doubled his salary as a senator and also promised business opportunities that would enable him "to accumulate a fortune in a comparatively brief space." Gordon asserted that he had every intention of holding his Senate seat until Congress adjourned and the Georgia General Assembly could convene in regular session, but on May 1, he had received a letter from Hogg, pressing him for an immediate decision. Gordon determined that the few additional weeks he might spend in the Senate would not materially benefit Georgia or the South, yet they would work a great hardship upon him. Faced with the prospect of losing this lucrative opportunity, as well as another he was negotiating in the interest of his sons, Gordon decided to resign.[14]

The other business venture that the general spoke of involved his long-term negotiations with the Bowker Fertilizer Company of Boston and New York. Keenly interested in southern agriculture, Gordon resolved "to do whatever I thought would benefit that interest, and, at the same time, furnish my sons, who are now growing up, a legitimate business." Gordon reported that consequently, during the previous year, he had sought to induce large fertilizer manufacturers to locate in the South; but failing in that, he concluded an agreement with the Boston firm to supply high-grade fertilizer for Georgia. As the fertilizer business was still in its infancy in the South, Gordon proposed to "get in on the ground floor." He would sit as

13. *Ibid.*, June 4, 8, 1880.
14. *Ibid.*, June 8, 1880.

president of the southern branch of the firm, while leaving the actual operation of the agency to his sons. In this manner, Gordon hoped to enrich himself as well as provide a badly needed product for southern farmers.[15]

It was these business ventures that, Gordon maintained, convinced him to step down as Georgia's senator. As he had explained earlier, it was not until he had sent in his resignation and was conferring with Hogg in New York that he learned of Newcomb's offer, one that he accepted because it allowed him to remain close to home. According to Gordon, this account, verified by letters from Hogg and Newcomb and substantiated by the stories of Colquitt and Brown, was the whole truth of the matter.[16]

In addition to detailing his own actions, Gordon also defended Colquitt's selection of his successor. He admitted that most Georgians would have preferred almost any other man rather than Brown, but Gordon recognized that present political conditions made Brown the best possible choice. The former governor's greatest source of political strength in Georgia lay in the northern section of the state where Independents most seriously threatened the Democratic party. In Gordon's opinion, "the hardy yeomenry of the mountains dissatisfied and ready to break with the organization" might well desist from their independent course now that one of their favorites had been recognized and honored by the Democracy. Moreover, Gordon believed that the time had come either to "cease hostility to Governor Brown or cease to ask his time and talents and money for the benefits of our party." Even though he and Brown had never been on friendly terms, Gordon acknowledged that during the past decade the former governor had provided invaluable, unfaltering service to the Democratic party, on both the state and national levels. All things considered, Gordon concluded that Colquitt's—and therefore by implication his own—handling of the resignation and appointment process was beyond reproach.[17]

The *Constitution*—the most ardent supporter of the general—immediately proclaimed Gordon's address "one of the noblest speeches" ever to grace its columns and euphorically declared that it would effectively "dispel every vestige of the clouds that have been conjured about the names of Gordon and Colquitt, and let in the sunshine." And as the speech circulated through Georgia, the Atlanta

15. *Ibid.*, June 4, 1880.
16. *Ibid.*, June 8, 1880.
17. *Ibid.*

paper also predicted, "it will confirm not only the title that Gordon wears undisputed as the best loved of Georgians, but will add to his fame as an orator and statesman." Other papers, believing that their staunch support of the former senator and the governor had been vindicated, made proud announcements like that of the Savannah *News*, which declared that the "breath of slander cannot tarnish the bright escutcheon of such true men as Gordon and Colquitt."[18]

Although such assessments probably reflected the predominant sentiment in Georgia, where the intense furor attending the controversy had begun to abate by mid-June, questions concerning Gordon's resignation persisted. The vast majority of Georgians stood solidly behind their beloved Hero of Appomattox; but had they known all the details of the negotiations surrounding his resignation, their support might well have been less enthusiastic.

Although Gordon, Colquitt, and Brown remained steadfast in their denials of any prearrangements, material has recently been uncovered that casts a new light on the affair. The central figure, or middleman, in these newly revealed behind-the-scenes machinations appears to have been the brilliant and ambitious Henry W. Grady, an aspiring spokesman for an industrialized South. Grady was convinced that railroads were essential to the economic betterment of the South. Early in 1880, he undertook a special assignment, traveling to various transportation centers so that he might observe firsthand the workings of major railroads. Grady envisioned Atlanta as the railroad hub of the Southeast and hoped to lure additional lines into it and into the rest of Georgia, as well. Accordingly, he spent much of his time in the company of H. Victor Newcomb, who was soon to be the president of the massive Louisville and Nashville Railroad Company. Newcomb, the thirty-six-year-old son of a former L & N chief executive, ascended to the company's presidency in March, 1880. Well-respected for his financial expertise, he had been vitally involved in formulating the railroad's policy for years. Although he would mysteriously resign after only eight months in office—and never again occupy such a prominent position—Newcomb's energetic, brilliant leadership tremendously expanded the L & N network.[19]

Fascinated by the remarkable abilities of this young railroad mag-

18. *Ibid.*; Savannah *News*, quoted *ibid.*, June 16, 1880.

19. Raymond B. Nixon, *Henry W. Grady: Spokesman of the New South* (New York, 1943), 166–68; Maury Klein, *History of the Louisville & Nashville Railroad* (New York, 1972), 85–86, 126, 150–51, 167–70.

nate, whom he styled "the Napoleon of the railroad world," Grady developed a hearty respect and admiration for Newcomb. The feeling was obviously mutual; Newcomb offered the newspaperman a job as his private secretary, but Grady declined so that he might remain in journalism. During their months of travel together, Grady met numerous influential men in all parts of the country. While in New York, the ambitious editor was introduced to Cyrus W. Field—one of the city's most prominent brokers—by Gordon, who frequently traveled to New York. Field's decision in May to loan Grady twenty thousand dollars so he could purchase a one-quarter interest in the Atlanta *Constitution* was probably influenced by Newcomb's offer to help the young Georgian repay the loan by guiding him in stock speculation. The ties between Grady and Newcomb were clearly well established by early May, when the emerging "spokesman of the New South" became part owner of the *Constitution*.[20]

Newcomb shared Grady's desire to develop railroad interests in Georgia. He labored incessantly to gain control of or establish favorable working relationships with many of Georgia's railroads. One of the roads that the L & N sought to control was Joe Brown's Western and Atlantic; its 138 miles of track served as the only direct link between Chattanooga and Atlanta. A major competitor of the L & N in the Southeast was Edwin W. "King" Cole's Nashville, Chattanooga, and St. Louis Railroad. Rumors surfaced in late 1879 that Cole had gained control of the Western and Atlantic, and in early 1880 that Cole and Brown together had leased the Central of Georgia, which ran from Atlanta to Savannah. Newcomb reacted decisively to meet the threat to the L & N's plans. Maneuvering with dazzling speed and finesse, he quietly undercut Cole by purchasing a controlling interest in the "King's" road. Hopeful that his coup had netted him control of the W & A, as well as a favorable relationship with the Central of Georgia, Newcomb soon learned that the earlier rumors were just that—rumors. Undismayed, he persisted in his attempt to develop a united railway system that would link Chattanooga with Savannah, on the coast. A major part of his plan involved the strategic W & A.[21]

20. Nixon, *Grady*, 167–69; Joel Chandler Harris, *Life of Henry W. Grady, including his Writings and Speeches* (New York, 1890), 77, 608. See also Atlanta *Constitution*, August 12, 1880.

21. Klein, *History of the L & N*, 153–57; Parks, *Brown*, 507–508; Nixon, *Grady*, 166–68; John F. Stover, *The Railroads of the South 1865–1900: A Study in Finance and Control* (Chapel Hill, 1955), 224–27.

During the course of his efforts, Newcomb acquired ownership of the charter of the Georgia Western Railroad. This charter called for the building of a railroad from Atlanta to Birmingham, into and through the rich and relatively untapped coal and iron fields of northeastern Alabama. It also included a provision granting trackage rights over a portion of the Western and Atlantic. During the following months, Newcomb used the acquisition of the Georgia Western charter—which would later take on particular significance for Grady and Gordon—as an effective point of leverage in his discussions with the presidents of competing Georgia railroads. Finally, in early April, 1880, after a week of conferences, it was announced that the Western and Atlantic and other Georgia railroads had merged into a combination headed by Newcomb. It is impossible to unravel the intricacies of these complicated railroad dealings because most of the negotiations were carried on in secret. Nevertheless, during the first five months of 1880, while Newcomb skillfully maneuvered his way into Georgia, Grady was often by the side of the man whom he described as "the Moses that leads Atlanta out of bondage."[22]

At some point prior to the middle of May, Grady entered directly into the negotiations between Newcomb and Brown. Utilizing the services of W. H. Pittman of the Nashville, Chattanooga, and St. Louis Railroad, Grady delivered what was apparently a personally devised code to Brown. This code allowed the involved parties to use the telegraph, thus offering them speedy communication while still maintaining the utmost secrecy. On the back of the undated envelope in which he received the code, Brown wrote "private papers," the names Grady, Newcomb, and Brown, and "the envelope did not pass through the mails." Although it is impossible to determine exactly when Grady first brought Gordon into the secret discussions, it is clear that by May 15 the general's name figured prominently in the negotiations. On that date, while in New York, Grady sent his first—or at least the earliest surviving—telegram to Brown in Atlanta. The translated message reads: "Gordon will send in resignation certain. Newcomb highly pleased with Brown's assurances & anxious to do all wanted. He would like you to make Ravill vice prest if agreeable to you with no increase in duties while you hold senatorship. He wants all roads be interested in pool Gordon's salary & will fix at twenty thousand if your road will pay three to five thousand. Please do this. It fixes everything precisely as wanted. Answer."[23]

Although Brown's answer has not survived, Grady sent a second telegram to Brown on May 17.The decoded version reads: "Everything is fixed. Gordon's resignation sent in to Colquitt & Newcomb agrees that Brown shall hold presidency and senatorship but says in adjusting Gordon's salary four thousand should come from Brown's road. He begs that Brown come to New York on tomorrow's train as he wishes to have conference with him for better understanding. He is anxious. Can't Brown come. Newcomb says Brown must guarantee that Cole who is bitterly opposed to him shall not have charge of road while Brown is in Washington. Answer tonight." Brown's deciphered reply of the same date reads: "Brown cannot come to New York. Important engagement in Nashville Thursday prevents. General manager under Brown's instruction will control in his absence. Vice President will have nothing to do with it. Brown cannot speak positively about four thousand. Directors under rules control that. He will urge three thousand. Thinks that would be certain. He wants to meet Newcomb soon. When could he come here or meet Brown at some other agreed point."[24]

Although a number of other telegrams—both in cipher and in plain English—between Grady and Brown, and between Brown and a representative of Newcomb were sent on May 18 and 19, only one other bore any real reference to Gordon's salary. Exasperated by Newcomb's insistence that he come immediately to New York to confer, Brown sent an angry reply, not in code. "I have twice stated I cannot come to New York. After the assurances I have given, if distrust is shown by delays I shall decline to go to Washington and confine myself to my duties here. In that case we will assume no part of the salary of any one. I have acted frankly and in good faith with the most ready intentions and can say no more." The content of these and other telegraphic messages sent between May 15 and May 19, plus the fact that many were sent in code, clearly indicates that deals were being negotiated at the time of Gordon's resignation. The major focus

23. Grady to Brown, May 15, 1880 in Joseph Emerson Brown Papers, Felix Hargrett Collection, UGA. All the telegrams involved in the negotiations surrounding the resignation and appointment are located in Brown Papers, Hargrett Collection. Photocopies of the originals and the deciphered messages (typescript) can also be found in the Joseph E. Brown Papers, AHS.

24. Grady to Brown, May 17, 1880, and Brown to Grady, May 17, 1880, both in Brown Papers, Hargrett Collection.

of the correspondence that passed between Brown and Newcomb (or his representative) through Grady appears to have centered on railroad matters. The precise nature of the negotiations between Newcomb and Brown is difficult to discern because of their complicated and secretive maneuverings. Yet it is clear that Gordon's salary with the L & N railroad was a major point of discussion. It is intriguing to consider why Brown's road would provide funds for the employee of another railroad, certainly not a usual practice. One contemporary, who did not know conclusively that deals had been made but nevertheless suspected their existence, believed Gordon would act as general counsel for both the L & N and the W & A. Such an arrangement may have been the case, but the telegrams indicate that all the roads involved in the April, 1880, agreement were to contribute to his salary. Even so, it is entirely possible that Brown's road did not contribute at all, because when it was announced, Gordon's annual salary was only fourteen thousand dollars. Although it is impossible to determine who contributed what amount to Gordon's salary and why they did so, it is obvious that details vitally important to the general's future were being negotiated by Grady.[25]

Grady, as the central figure in these discussions, may have been the "prime mover" who introduced Gordon into the behind-the-scenes transactions. A multitalented man of vision, Grady had rapidly established the contacts he needed to realize many of the ambitions he had for Georgia and for himself. It is plausible to assume that he was the common acquaintance who drew Gordon, Newcomb and Brown together, perhaps in the following manner. Grady, as a friend and admirer of all three men, was privy to each man's private aspirations and desires. Having traveled extensively in Newcomb's company, Grady knew of the railroad man's displeasure at learning that in spite of the April, 1880, merger, Joe Brown still retained firm control of the W & A because of technicalities in its charter.[26] Cognizant of the strategic importance of the W & A, Newcomb really wished to oust Brown as its head but was willing to settle for getting him out of Georgia. Brown, on the other hand, was exceedingly wary of New-

25. Brown to Grady, May 19, 1880, *ibid*; Atlanta *Constitution*, May 26, 1880.

26. According to Brown's biographer, Newcomb's intense desire to confer with Brown in New York stemmed from his discovery that despite its purchase of a majority interest in the W & A, the L & N had virtually no control of the road. Brown would later explain before a railroad investigatory committee that no matter who owned the company's shares, "only the original lessees could sit at board meetings and participate in the management of the road." Parks, *Brown*, 517–18.

comb's covetous designs; nonetheless, he longed for the political success that had eluded him for almost fifteen years. Gordon, far removed from and perhaps even unaware of these railroad considerations, had already informed Grady that he would soon leave the Senate in search of the financial security he had never known.

Perhaps, recognizing an opportunity to satisfy all three parties plus himself, Grady began to deal. Knowing that Gordon preferred to remain in the South, he informed Newcomb of the general's desire to resign and his need for a remunerative job. He also mentioned that since the Georgia Western charter had lost its tactical value to the L & N in light of the April, 1880, merger, the charter could be offered to Gordon as an inducement to join the L & N. If Gordon stepped down and Brown could be persuaded to replace him in the Senate, then Newcomb would be in an advantageous position; he was convinced that he could outmaneuver the former governor once Brown moved to Washington. For Newcomb, the proposition appeared even more attractive for three additional reasons: the L & N could draw upon Gordon's tremendous popularity as it sought to expand in Georgia; the Georgia Western charter, which had earlier served its purpose, could now be used to additional benefit; and Gordon's salary could be spread among the other railroads, or shared at least with Brown's road. Brown also liked the arrangement; it offered him the chance for political vindication that he could not otherwise hope to achieve. Firmly convinced that regardless of Newcomb's brilliance he could maintain control of the W & A and ward off all assaults, he was willing to pay part of Gordon's salary providing Newcomb's terms did not delay his replacement of Gordon while Congress was still assembled. Even though less than a month remained in the current session, Brown was confident that he could reestablish himself as an able representative in the minds of Georgia's legislators, who would have the opportunity to vote on his continued service in the fall. Gordon, too, saw an ideal opportunity for the long-delayed achievement of financial goals. Having already decided to resign, he could now bow out of politics and step into a business situation that would more than double his Senate salary and would also provide the potential for much greater wealth. That potential, of course, lay in eventually building the Georgia Western railroad, a project foremost in Grady's mind. These considerations, in forms more complex than the simplified version presented here, quite probably contributed to Gordon's resignation and Brown's appointment.

Grady had apparently formulated his plans before May 10, because on that date, while traveling back to Atlanta on the train from Washington, he discussed the matter with friends from Athens, Georgia. According to the Athens *Southern Watchman*, Grady spoke freely about Gordon's impending resignation, Brown's probable appointment, and the general's association with the L & N. Among those Georgians who were aware of the journalist's "indiscretions," many probably joined Mrs. Rebecca Latimer Felton in dismissing such talk as an example of Grady's "careless handling of facts." A second reference to prearrangements came from Judge D. G. Candler, who revealed the details of a May 10 conversation with Colquitt. The governor later denied discussing such matters, but Candler contended that he learned on May 10 that Gordon had resigned to take a railroad job and that Brown would replace him in the Senate. Even though he personally rejected the notion that "any moneyed consideration passed between the parties," Candler did believe "that the matter was well understood for several days before Gordon's resignation was accepted." Thus, there were some rents in the veil of secrecy surrounding the negotiations that preceded Gordon's resignation.[27]

While very few people in Georgia suspected the extent of Grady's involvement in these discussions, virtually no one would have guessed the vitally important role played by the Georgia Western. This railroad had long been a dream of many Georgians. Considering Grady's great desire to provide Atlanta with immediate access to the mineral wealth of northeastern Alabama, it is quite likely that the possible sale of the old Georgia Western charter was considered in these negotiations. Perhaps viewing Gordon as the man best suited to breathe life into this oft-begun yet never completed enterprise, Grady probably laid the groundwork for the actual sale at this time; but at the very least, he aided Gordon in attaining a position from which the general could act whenever the opportunity presented itself. That opportunity came almost one year to the day after Gordon's resignation from the Senate, when he gained clear title to the Georgia Western charter. By the end of 1881, Gordon, with others, had begun construction of the long envisioned railroad linking Atlanta with Birmingham. This project would soon net the enterprising general

27. Columbus *Enquirer-Sun*, June 11, 1880; Cartersville *Free-Press*, June 17, 1880; Mrs. William H. Felton, *My Memoirs of Georgia Politics* (Atlanta, 1911), 303, 530; clipping of Atlanta *Journal*, in Scrapbook No. 19, p. 89, in R. L. Felton Collection; Atlanta *Constitution*, June 1, 5, 1880.

several hundred thousand dollars plus large blocks of railroad stock.[28] In setting the stage for this notable success, it is possible that Grady— trying to secure a lucrative position for a man whom he greatly admired while at the same time struggling to work out a railroad arrangement between Newcomb and Brown that would benefit Atlanta—acted on his own, and not at the behest of Gordon; however, it seems improbable that these negotiations were conducted without the general's knowledge. In spite of the difficulty in determining the exact nature of Gordon's involvement in the negotiations, it appears that he was not only aware of the discussions but probably a party to these "understandings," which were concealed from the public.

Grady's biographer, though he lacked access to the Newcomb-Brown correspondence, may have been very close to the truth in his assessment of the affair. He concluded that "undoubtedly there were understandings of the kind that friends reach everyday in business and politics, but on the basis of available evidence the transaction must be described as 'a deal, not a steal.'" Gordon and the others misled Georgians by denying any contacts or arrangements prior to his resignation and Brown's appointment. Yet, despite their secretive nature, these discussions do not appear to have violated the law; business and political agreements were often handled in this clandestine manner. Even so, all the involved parties fully comprehended the wisdom of concealing both the existence and the details of these prearrangements from the people. An unsophisticated public would simply not understand the purpose or the intent of these discussions and consequently would draw only the most negative of conclusions. Thus Gordon, and the other participants, withheld many of the facts surrounding the resignation and appointment in order to avoid implications of impropriety.[29]

As all the parties seemed to come away from the negotiations happy, there was no need to enlighten the public. Newcomb obtained the services of a man whose name alone might prove invaluable to his railroad enterprises in the South, especially in Georgia. Also, he established a more intimate—though, as time would prove, not neces-

28. Avery, *History of Georgia*, 635–36; Stover, *Railroads of the South*, 240; Klein, *History of the L & N*, 174, 183. References to Gordon's efforts to secure the Georgia Western charter are found in most issues of the Atlanta *Constitution* between February and May, 1881. See especially February 17, 23, March 2, 18, 26, May 18, 21, 22, 24, 25, 29, June 8, 28, July 28, 1881.

29. Nixon, *Grady*, 172.

sarily advantageous—relationship with Brown, his railroad rival. Brown continued as president of the W & A, but reentered politics, securing a position that afforded him the opportunity to redeem himself in the eyes of white Georgians. Grady aided all his friends and took giant strides toward the building of a railroad he deemed vitally important to Atlanta. Colquitt gained the badly needed support of two influential Georgians for his upcoming campaign to retain the governorship. And Gordon fulfilled his desire to leave politics and obtain a position that would enable him to overcome his financial woes.

An interesting epilogue to this controversy comes from the correspondence between Joe Brown and Herbert Fielder in 1882 and 1883. In the late 1870s, Brown persuaded the Georgia lawyer to write a life-and-times biography of him. The former governor was then "under a long-subsisting and heavy cloud in political matters," according to Fielder, and "took a deep interest" in the publication of a favorable biography, so that his image might be improved. However, writing to Brown, Fielder noted that "that interest ceased when your object was accomplished by an executive appointment." In the two years following the resignation-appointment controversy, relations between the two soured. Fielder charged that his subject withheld money owed to him and reneged on promises to help him get the manuscript published. Implicit in the letters he wrote to Brown demanding satisfaction was the veiled threat to rewrite portions of the biography including facts that had purposely been omitted. Fielder referred specifically to the appointment as "a startling alliance" that "brought men together who had stood at a cold and selfish distance—men who up to that time sought honors by different and opposing currents." He later wrote that his friendship with Brown at the time made him "willing to pass in silence the criticisms it was in my power, from personal knowledge and authentic data, to make." But when their friendship significantly cooled, Fielder subtly applied pressure to the former governor. "It is quite probable that few if any living know more of these [public figures] who flourished, and how they rose than I do, the incorporation of which may impart more truth to history even if not so flattering to successful men." Brown, unshaken as always, brusquely rebuffed the threat, daring the author to publish whatever he pleased. However, Brown insisted that if Fielder attacked him with materials that he had provided, then the author, as an honorable man, must return the three thousand dollars earlier paid to him. Brown eventually purchased the manuscript from Fielder for an additional one thousand dollars and had it published 1883 under Fielder's name. Gordon's name never entered into the correspondence, and Fielder's references to the appointment controversy seem to focus primarily on Colquitt and Brown. Nevertheless, these letters, always by indirect reference, provide additional evidence that the public knew very little about the details surrounding the resignation and appointment.[30]

Since Gordon was a central figure in the controversy, his motives and actions warrant a more thorough examination. There was no man more widely loved or respected in Georgia than Gordon. In all probability, he could have retained his Senate seat indefinitely, but it appears he sincerely yearned to leave politics. Disillusioned by the petty political squabbles that frequently dominated his post-Reconstruction political life and convinced that Georgia and the South were secure in their relationship to the national government, Gordon sought to retreat from public life. Despite his concern that Georgia have first-rate representation in Congress, Gordon probably believed that he had certainly done his part on behalf of his native state and section. And he had done so at substantial cost to himself, both in physical and financial terms. Deeply affected by his two serious illnesses, Gordon was genuinely concerned about his health and the crippling financial effect his death or disablement would have upon his family. Although never totally overwhelmed by his debts or the specter of economic ruin, Gordon had long endured the fears and doubts associated with financial insecurity. His senatorial salary and outside income had often failed to keep pace with the increasing demands of his family. These factors combined to exert a powerful force upon Gordon by 1880.

But of perhaps equal if not greater importance than these financial and family concerns was Gordon's deep-seated desire to prove himself in the business world. His history of failure in business stood in stark contrast to his brilliant successes in military and political endeavors and must have caused him considerable anxiety. His almost daily association with men of wealth and influence could only have strengthened his resolve to erase this record of failure. Both in the

30. Fielder to Brown, August 23, October 3, 30, 1882, July 30, 1883, Brown to Fielder, October 16, 1882, July 6, 1883, all in Hargrett Collection; Herbert Fielder, *A Sketch of the Life and Times and Speeches of Joseph E. Brown* (Springfield, Mass., 1883).

Senate and in New York, where he spent an increasing amount of time, Gordon saw tremendous fortunes being made. Envious of and possibly even piqued by the enormous success of many men whom he quite probably considered less able than himself, Gordon desperately wanted to make money and experience a sense of financial independence that he had never known. It seems likely that all these considerations—disillusionment with political life, health concerns, financial worries, and business ambitions—contributed to Gordon's decision to leave the Senate.

Although some Georgians continued to insist that specific inducements from Brown had persuaded him to step down, Gordon steadfastly maintained that he had simply waited for the right time and the best opportunity to leave politics. He did not apologize for his desire to devote himself to business full time. Hogg's lucrative offer and the pressure to commit to the Oregon enterprise were probably sufficient to convince Gordon to resign. Only after he had already determined to send in his letter of resignation did the L & N opportunity materialize, and it came primarily as a result of the negotiations Grady handled between Newcomb and Brown. Gordon claimed that he accepted the L & N position because it allowed him to remain in the South, but the Georgia Western charter was probably the lure that drew him to Newcomb's railroad. For it was the acquisition of this charter in 1881 that launched him into the high-stakes world of railroad building, where fortunes were made and lost in a remarkably short period of time. Certainly, Gordon did not have to resort to illegal deals to secure employment. In reality, he was highly marketable as an executive, especially in light of the national reputation he had gained in the Senate. Finding a job could not have posed a critical problem for the man whose name still held the magical allure it had first won in combat with the Army of Northern Virginia.

In any event, Gordon's popularity suffered very little, despite the widespread circulation of charges that he had sold his office. Most Georgians either believed his explanation or were willing to accept the assessment offered by "Pro Bono Publico," which concluded that the controversial situation "requires no direct bargain or sale, but it does involve a general understanding of the parties when the resignation of General Gordon, the offer of a lucrative railroad position and the appointment of Brown are so intimately connected." Perhaps they agreed that Gordon's twenty years of faithful service to them entitled him to the chance to seek his own fortune. Moreover, they may have realized that his activities as a private citizen might well aid Georgia and the South even more than had his actions as a public servant. Gordon saw the opportunity, as he had earlier with the Southern Life Insurance Company and the University Publishing Company, to link his own needs with those of Georgia. By accepting the job of general counsel for the L & N railroad, Gordon placed himself in a position that would eventually enable him to earn a great deal of money. His own financial success proved only temporary, but the strides he made, particularly in the field of transportation, had significant and long-lasting effects upon his native state.[31]

Although Gordon resigned from the Senate in order to enter the business world, political considerations prevented him from devoting his full attention to financial concerns for some time. His commitment to the cause of the Democracy did not end with his departure from the national forum, so during the summer and fall of 1880, Gordon remained active in politics on both the national and state levels. After addressing the charges leveled against him in the aftermath of his resignation, he traveled north to attend the national Democratic convention in Cincinnati. There he watched the prospects of his presidential hopeful, Thomas F. Bayard, fade as the Democrats turned to an old military foe of Gordon's, General Winfield Scott Hancock. Gordon did not attend the Georgia state Democratic convention in August; however, the divisiveness that marked that assemblage provided the backdrop for the equally bitter fall gubernatorial contest—a fray into which he would enter wholeheartedly.[32]

Even if Governor Alfred H. Colquitt had entertained thoughts of not running for reelection in 1880, he found himself honor-bound to stand for another term. The steady stream of abuse and criticism heaped upon him for his appointment of Joe Brown called his reputation into question. Colquitt, a wealthy planter who had risen to the rank of major general during the war, felt compelled to seek vindication in the eyes of the people of Georgia. Not surprisingly, the man chosen to direct his campaign for reelection was the same man who had played such an integral role in the resignation-appointment affair, Henry Grady. From the outset of the Democratic convention in August, Colquitt held a clear majority; but more than a week of

31. Atlanta *Constitution*, May 26, 1880.
32. Atlanta *Constitution*, June 20, 23, July 7, 1880; Perry Belmont to T. F. Bayard, April 24, 1880, John Hunter to T. F. Bayard, May 11, 1880, T. F. Bayard to Snowden Andrews, June 3, 1880, all in Thomas Francis Bayard Collection, LC.

236 · JOHN BROWN GORDON

intense wrangling failed to gain for him the two-thirds majority vote necessary for nomination. The deadlocked convention adjourned, presenting Colquitt to the voters as the "recommended" candidate rather than the Democratic nominee. The anti-Colquitt minority selected another prominent Democrat, former United States senator from Georgia, Thomas M. Norwood, as their candidate. As the opposing camps marshaled their forces for the October general election, the second, more vitriolic phase of the campaign opened. Colquitt's record during his first administration—a four-year term marked by controversy and charges of unethical and illegal activity—provided major points of attack for the opposition, but "the event around which the entire contest was to revolve" was the appointment of Brown. The vilification of the governor that had begun in May raged anew in the fall. And once more, the whirlwind of controversy drew Gordon into the center of the storm.[33]

In Gordon's opinion, indictments against Colquitt necessarily impugned his honor as well. Unwilling to endure renewed censure, Gordon took the stump to defend the governor and himself. Much of the shock and anger at Gordon's and Colquitt's actions in May had worn off, but the lingering bitterness made this gubernatorial campaign, in the words of one chronicler, "the most intense and desperate political contest of Georgia history." Alexander H. Stephens feared that "the old Democracy of Georgia [was being] sundered almost in her vitals," so he publicly avoided what he called "the present unfortunate embroglio." During September and early October, Gordon became Colquitt's greatest asset as he canvassed the state on behalf of his friend, neighbor, and frequent partner in business. He delivered what was perhaps his most forceful speech before a frequently disruptive crowd at Columbus. Rather than assailing the governor's opponent, Gordon concentrated on explaining why he resigned from the Senate, on detailing the positive accomplishments of Colquitt's first term, and on praising the incumbent's virtues. As he had often done before, Gordon professed amazement that despite his sincere desire to retire from politics, vicious attacks from within his own home

33. Avery, History of Georgia, 555–58, 563, 569; Atlanta Constitution, August 4–12, 1880; New York Times, May 21, 1880; Kenneth Coleman, "The Georgia Gubernatorial Election of 1880," Georgia Historical Quarterly, XXV (June, 1941), 92, 95. For treatments of the 1880 contest, see Coleman, "Georgia Gubernatorial Election," 89–119; Avery, History of Georgia, 568–601; and Carl M. Logue, "Gubernatorial Campaign in Georgia in 1880," Southern Speech Communication Journal, XL (Fall, 1974), 12–32.

state again forced him to defend both himself and the governor. He furiously denounced the opposition's assault upon the reputation of Colquitt, a man who, like himself, had proudly and honorably borne the Confederate standard. The "Hero of Olustee," as Colquitt was frequently styled, must be returned to the governor's mansion.[34]

The combined efforts of Gordon, Colquitt, Grady, and Brown completely overwhelmed the Norwood forces. In the October election, Colquitt scored a resounding victory, capturing 65 percent of the votes. This triumph alone may have represented a satisfactory repudiation of all charges growing out of Gordon's resignation and Colquitt's appointment of Brown; however, one more victory was necessary before complete vindication could be claimed. Brown still faced the task of winning in his own right the Senate seat that he had been appointed to under such dubious circumstances. Although Gordon did not like Brown, he had little choice but to support him. When the General Assembly officially selected Brown as his successor, Gordon could claim that the last spot of tarnish had successfully been removed from his armor. As a supporter of Brown's opponent believed, "Colquitt and Gordon having been saved by the management and money of Brown will be compelled even if averse to do so, to stand up" for him. Opponents put forth a worthy candidate, General Alexander R. Lawton, but he stood little chance because Brown had restored his reputation, primarily by several speeches he had made in the Senate during the last three weeks of the session. Most Georgians still did not like him, yet a clear majority of the General Assembly recognized him as an able representative of the state. Thus in November, Brown, too, won convincingly. Vindication of the three men who had been vilified and cursed so unmercifully at the end of May appeared complete by year's end.[35]

In the resignation-appointment controversy and its turbulent aftermath, the interests of these three men for the first time clearly

34. Avery, *History of Georgia*, 555–56, 571, 589, 593–95; Coleman, "Georgia Gubernatorial Election," 113; Alex Mathews Arnett, *The Populist Movement in Georgia: A View of the "Agrarian Crusade" in the Light of Solid-South Politics* (New York, 1922), 40–42; A. H. Stephens to Mrs. A. R. Lawton, September 20, 1880, in Alexander Robert Lawton Papers, SHC; Atlanta *Constitution*, August 26, 28, September 1, 3, 7, 17, 1880.

35. Parks, *Brown*, 523–31; Avery, *History of Georgia*, 564–67, 600–604; Atlanta *Constitution*, October 6, 7, 10, November 16, 17, 1880; A. R. Lamar to A. R. Lawton, October 9, 1880, in Lawton Papers; *Georgia House Journal*, 1880, pp. 37, 120–21; *Georgia Senate Journal*, 1880, p. 78.

coalesced. Gordon and Colquitt had long been friends and business associates; Brown and Colquitt had enjoyed a friendly relationship; Gordon and Brown, however, had never been very cordial. Perhaps Brown's refusal to accept Gordon's Raccoon Roughs into Georgia military service had been the origin of their troubles. In any event, the separate paths they followed after the war precluded the development of a friendship between the two. Gordon found it impossible to countenance the former governor's defection from the Democratic party during Reconstruction. His antipathy increased substantially when the public controversy between Gordon and the pseudonymous "Citizen," who was in fact Brown, erupted in the wake of the election of 1876. Yet, as the storm of public vituperation thundered down upon these three, they locked arms to repel charges of misconduct. As one Georgian observed, "[T]he alliance of the three in a battle where their coalition was intensified by a reciprocal interest and a common defamation of their conduct, was the junction of the most ponderous agencies of our Georgia leadership." Truly, he concluded, this "strong trio," became "an irresistible coalition" when assailed. An even more succinct appraisal of their combined strength came from a Georgia newspaper long before the fall elections demonstrated its validity: "Brown with his money, Gordon with his buttons, and Colquitt with his religion will make a combination that can not be beaten." In the end, even though Gordon, Colquitt, and Brown were all touched by the breath of scandal, each escaped relatively unscathed.[36]

36. Avery, *History of Georgia*, 558–59, 563–64; Atlanta *Constitution*, June 8, 1880; A. R. Lamar to A. R. Lawton, October 9, 1880, in Lawton Papers; Columbus *Daily Times*, May 25, 1880, quoted in C. Vann Woodward, *Tom Watson: Agrarian Rebel* (New York, 1938), 72.

# XII · New South Businessman

The controversy surrounding the resignation and appointment of May, 1880, died down by year's end, but the association between Gordon, Colquitt, and Brown endured. Gordon, Colquitt, and Brown dominated Georgia politics in the 1880s in much the same manner as Howell Cobb, Robert Toombs, and Alexander H. Stephens had dwarfed their rivals in the antebellum era. And, like the earlier trio, they were recognized as a ruling body of three, the so-called Bourbon Triumvirate. This term, like the one often applied to white southerners who reestablished home rule by ousting Republican regimes in the South—Bourbon Democrats—has become so historiographically encumbered that it tends to confuse rather than clarify. As C. Vann Woodward observed in the 1930s, "[S]ince the American aborigines were called *Indians* there has probably been no more fallacious misnomer in our history than this term *Bourbon*—at least when applied to the men who governed Georgia." Gordon, Colquitt, and Brown were unquestionably the most conspicuous figures in the political arena, yet it was Henry Grady who personified the economic spirit that they espoused. He may have remained in the political shadows, but Grady was as important a component in the Bourbon Triumvirate as were its recognized members. None of these men, however, held so tenaciously to the ideas and institutions of the past that they longed for a restoration of the prewar order. Although they often capitalized on southerners' reverence for the past by appealing to memories of the Confederacy, they were active spokesmen for and participants in the New South, a more industrial, commercially oriented South. That is not to say that industry did not exist in the antebellum South or that there were no prewar proponents of industrialization. To the contrary, on the eve of the Civil War, a solid industrial base had already been established. There was a thriving, though limited, industrial sector, but agriculture—staple crop agriculture—overwhelmingly dominated the southern economy. Nor is it to say that in the post-Reconstruction period, adherents of the New South credo turned their backs on southern agriculture. Indeed, on numerous occasions, Gordon stressed the necessity of fully developing the agrarian potential of his region, and he became personally involved in a wide variety of agricultural activities. Nevertheless, he and other New South leaders recognized that the South had to industrialize if it was to compete with the North. Seeking a more balanced economy, these spokesmen championed the cause of industrialism in the South and eagerly courted Eastern capital.[1]

Any examination of the course of each man's postwar career demonstrates a commitment to industrialism; yet their political views and policies reflected traditional southern social and political values. They cut taxes, checked government spending, limited government services, and kept the forces of social change at bay. These conservative policies were crucial to the maintenance of their power. In the eighteen years following the Democrats' recapture of state control from Republicans, from 1872 to 1890, either Gordon or Brown held one of Georgia's United States Senate seats, and after 1883, Colquitt occupied the other. For ten of those years, Gordon or Colquitt served as governor of Georgia. Although they held the key political offices, these three men did not in any sense collectively "rule" Georgia. A recent historian has noted that "the truth is that the three men who composed the Triumvirate seldom consulted one another on political matters, [and] often found themselves at odds on specific issues." Even so, Gordon, Colquitt, and Brown, with the less visible but equally influential Henry Grady, were the dominant powers in Georgia politics. So in spite of the confusion surrounding the term,

1. C. Vann Woodward, *Tom Watson: Agrarian Rebel* (New York, 1938), 56–66; C. Vann Woodward, *Origins of the New South, 1877–1913* (Rev. ed.; Baton Rouge, 1971), 14–17, 75; Alex Mathews Arnett, *The Populist Movement in Georgia: A View of the "Agrarian Crusade" in the Light of Solid-South Politics* (New York, 1922), 20–33; Mrs. William H. Felton, *My Memoirs of Georgia Politics* (Atlanta, 1911), 629–30; E. Merton Coulter, *A Short History of Georgia* (Chapel Hill, 1933), 363–65; Kenneth Coleman (ed.), *A History of Georgia* (Athens, 1977), 217–24; Judson Clements Ward, Jr., "The New Departure Democrats of Georgia, An Interpretation," *Georgia Historical Quarterly*, XL (September, 1957), 227–36; C. Vann Woodward, "Bourbonism in Georgia," *North Carolina Historical Review*, XVI (January, 1939), 23–25.

Bourbon Triumvirate can be used because it evokes the image of single-party, Conservative Democratic rule that did in fact exist in Georgia during much of the final third of the nineteenth century.[2]

In 1880, with Brown in the Senate and Colquitt in the governor's chair, Gordon turned his full attention to making money. Even while serving in the Senate, he had never been very far removed from the speculative mania rampant in New York City. He spent a great deal of time there and corresponded extensively with his friend and adviser, the successful corporate lawyer Samuel L. M. Barlow. The New Yorker supplied trusted counsel for the general, joined him in a number of investments, and even loaned him money on occasion. Although compelled to use most of his salary to meet his everyday needs, Gordon was as financially active as his duties and limited resources permitted. In spite of frequent economic distress, he always seemed to have enough money for the 10 percent advance necessary to speculate on stocks, bonds, or some other moneymaking enterprise.[3]

Gordon's letters to Barlow during his latter years in the Senate reveal a myriad of financial dealings, some of which raise questions about the possible misuse of his privileged position for personal pecuniary gain. In confidential letters—which often instructed Barlow not to let the information go any further or to destroy the missive— Gordon frequently wrote of his desire or his efforts to obtain inside information on bond and debt matters in several southern states. It appears that Gordon attempted to capitalize on information that he gained as a result of his prominent political position, information that was not readily available to the public. Whether he illegally sought unauthorized material cannot be determined from his letters,

2. Lewis N. Wynne, "The Bourbon Triumvirate: A Reconsideration," *Atlanta Historical Journal*, XXIV (Summer, 1980), 39–55. Although somewhat dated, Judson Clements Ward, Jr., "Georgia Under the Bourbon Democrats, 1872–1890" (Ph.D. dissertation, University of North Carolina, 1947) remains a very useful study of Georgia during the period in question. See also Steven Hahn, *The Roots of Southern Populism: Yeoman Farmers and the Transformation of the Georgia Upcountry, 1850–1890* (New York, 1983), Barton C. Shaw, *The Wool-Hat Boys: Georgia's Populist Party* (Baton Rouge, 1984), and Harold E. Davis, "Henry W. Grady, Master of the Atlanta Ring— 1880–1886," *Georgia Historical Quarterly*, LXIX (Spring, 1985), 1–38.

3. In comparison with the general dearth of Gordon manuscript material, the extant letters to Barlow in the period between 1877 and May, 1880, are numerous. Gordon sent six letters in 1877, eight in 1878, eleven in 1879, and thirteen during the first five months of 1880. Although some deal with national political questions, the vast majority concentrate almost exclusively on speculative and other financial matters, thus providing some insight into Gordon's economic status. Letters in Samuel Latham Mitchill Barlow Papers, HL.

but one point is clear. Gordon actively solicited advance notice of confidential matters that could tremendously benefit him. Similarly, whenever his own financial interests were involved, he lobbied extensively to protect those concerns. Many of his fellow senators successfully utilized similar methods to accumulate substantial fortunes. During an era in which political office offered enormous opportunities for wealth—beyond that gleaned from bribery or other illegal activities—Gordon seems to have occasionally used his political prominence for personal advantage; however, he appears to have enjoyed only limited success, at best.[4]

Even as Gordon eased away from politics, he was actively pursuing his business career. It is difficult to ascertain what services, if any, he performed for the Louisville and Nashville Railroad as its general counsel. His perennial critic, Mrs. Felton, charged that when later pressed to explain the nature of his job, Gordon admitted that he did not serve "as a lawyer, but *as counsellor and adviser* to the president, Newcomb." To her, that meant he operated as a lobbyist. Regardless of what his exact duties may have been, it is apparent that while in the railroad's employ, he was steadily organizing and developing another railroad company and working to secure the charter of the Georgia Western. In June, 1880, Gordon, A. H. Colquitt, and the general's two brothers, Walter S. and Eugene C. Gordon, formed a company to build a railroad running eastward from Columbus or Aberdeen, Mississippi, to either Birmingham or Blount Springs, Alabama. These four men, who frequently pooled their resources and talents in various business ventures, envisioned much more than just the construction of a short stretch of track. Seeing the tremendous opportunity lying before them, Gordon and his partners, ambitiously planned to build a railroad joining Atlanta directly to the Mississippi River.[5]

Due west of Atlanta was what the *Constitution* called a "railroad desert," a vast, relatively undeveloped area not penetrated by any east-west line. It seemed unimaginable that a straight-line connection between the railway hub of Atlanta and the railroad systems in

4. Gordon to Barlow, May 5, 17, June 13, September 3, 1877, May 31, 1878, January 28, undated [probably January or February], February 28, 1879, January 18, March 31, April 8, 16, 20, 1880, Thomas L. Snead to Gordon, August 25, 1877, A. C. Haskell to Gordon, September 10, 1877, J. L. Robertson to Gordon, December 16, 1877, all in Barlow Papers. See also Syracuse *Courier*, quoted in Atlanta *Constitution*, June 10, 1880; Thomasville *Times*, quoted in Atlanta *Constitution*, September 29, 1881.

5. Felton, *Memoirs*, 304, 529–30, 536, 638–39; Atlanta *Constitution*, May 23, July 20, February 17, March 26, May 22, August 26, 1881.

Texas leading to the Pacific had not already been established. Also, a railroad running through Georgia, Alabama, and Mississippi would traverse some of the richest coal fields in America. The virtually untapped mineral wealth of these states, especially northern Alabama, would be opened up as never before. Grady, and many others, had earlier seen the seemingly limitless potential for development offered by such a road, yet the line had never been built. Gordon and his partners set out to rectify that situation.[6]

In his effort to obtain the financial backing necessary for this enterprise, Gordon traveled extensively and spent much of his time in New York City. There he successfully enlisted the support of several noted capitalists eager to invest in such a promising venture. Hugh J. Jewett, president of the Erie Railroad, Joseph Anderson, president of the Tredegar Iron Works, C. H. Phinzy, president of the Georgia Railroad, and U. S. Grant, Jr., were among those prominent individuals who bought stock in Gordon's project. While Eugene Gordon controlled operations on the western end, Gordon concentrated on securing the right to build the most crucial portion of the proposed road, from Atlanta into northeastern Alabama.[7] Gordon began negotiations with L & N officials almost immediately upon joining the company—if not in fact even before he resigned from the Senate—for the purchase of the charter of the long-awaited Georgia Western Railroad. Although a tentative agreement was reached in December, 1880, a dispute over future traffic arrangements with the L & N and instability within that railroad's leadership—three different presidents in the space of three months—contributed to the delay of the sale. Grady, in the *Constitution*, had confidently been predicting the signing of the final contract since February, 1881; however, the actual transfer did not take place until May, 1881, when Gordon gained clear title to the Georgia Western charter for $50,000.[8]

Having acquired the Georgia Western, Gordon immediately proceeded to formalize the organization of the Georgia Pacific Company.

6. Atlanta *Constitution*, February 23, May 18, 25, 31, August 30, 1881; Maury Klein, *The Great Richmond Terminal: A Study in Businessmen and Business Strategy* (Charlottesville, 1970), 91.

7. On Eugene C. Gordon's prominent role in development of the Georgia Pacific, especially at the western end of the line, see Atlanta *Constitution*, May 23, July 20, 1880, February 17, March 26, June 7, July 30, 1881, June 14, 1882.

8. Isaac W. Avery, *History of the State of Georgia From 1850 to 1881* (New York, 1881), 635; Gordon to Barlow, May 18, August 11, 1881, in Barlow Papers; Maury Klein, *History of the Louisville & Nashville Railroad* (New York, 1972), 174, 183; Klein, *Great Richmond Terminal*, 92; John F. Stover, *The Railroads of the South, 1865–1900: A Study in Finance and Control* (Chapel Hill, 1955), 240.

As a parent company, the Georgia Pacific consolidated the results of all Gordon's efforts and all his claims so that a single, united road between Atlanta and the Mississippi could be built. By June, Gordon and his partners had secured promises for $350,000 from several Mississippi communities vitally interested in the construction of the road; they had obtained grants to over one hundred thousand acres of prime coal land in Alabama, deliverable upon completion of the railroad; they had solicited sufficient financial backing primarily from northern investors; and, in addition to the Georgia Western, they had obtained the charters for several other roads integrally involved in the overall scheme. The Georgia Pacific was eventually capitalized at $12.5 million, and when all available stock in the company was rapidly taken, prospects appeared extremely promising. Even a threat by the Richmond and Danville Railroad Company to build a second, competing road into the coal fields failed to deter the June organization of the Georgia Pacific.[9]

Gordon's plunge into high finance and railroad building vividly demonstrates his commitment to the economic philosophy of the New South. Even before he had completed arrangements for the purchase of the Georgia Western charter from the L & N, Gordon had entered into additional discussions that illustrate both the expansiveness of his business mind and his deepening involvement in New South economics. The actual transfer of title to the Georgia Western had scarcely taken place when Gordon sold a half-interest in a seventeen-mile stretch of the yet to be built road. He sold it to a competitor of the L & N for $50,000, thereby regaining the purchase price of the charter within a matter of days. More important, however, were Gordon's negotiations, during the first half of 1881, with the sprawling Richmond and Danville syndicate. Gordon wanted to strike a deal whereby the Richmond and West Point Terminal Railway and Warehouse Company, a holding company for the R & D, would absorb the emerging Georgia Pacific into its network. His hopes had repeatedly been frustrated, primarily because of monetary considerations. Gordon and his associates valued the properties and possessions that formed the basis of the Georgia Pacific at $700,000; the R & D, on the other hand, offered to pay only $250,000.[10]

9. Atlanta *Constitution*, May 29, June 4, 7, 8, July 28, August 26, 1881, April 1, 1882; Avery, *History of Georgia*, 635.
10. Stover, *Railroads of the South*, 240; Klein, *Great Richmond Terminal*, 90, 92; Atlanta *Constitution*, May 29, June 7, August 26, 1881.

But as the Georgia Pacific developed into a going concern, one capitalized soundly enough to begin actual construction of an Atlanta-Mississippi River road without depending on a major company, the R & D agreed to the merger on Gordon's terms. In return for the charter of the Georgia Pacific, all the lands and properties belonging to Gordon and his partners, and a controlling interest in the Georgia Pacific, the R & D paid them a reported $700,000 in cash. The founders of the Georgia Pacific (the Gordons and Colquitt) also received $1,000,000 worth of stock in the Richmond and Danville extension company—the construction firm contracted to take over and complete the building of the road—and stock worth two and one-half times that amount in the Georgia Pacific. Although they had sold their interest in the Georgia Pacific, the Gordons remained active in its operation. John continued as the company's president, Eugene served as president of two Mississippi railroads that extended the line from Birmingham to the river, and Walter became a director in the Richmond and Danville extension company. Thus, Gordon and his associates became very wealthy in a remarkably short period of time. Moreover, with the general as the guiding force, the Georgia Pacific was being built, and the coveted opening of Atlanta to the West was at last being realized.[11]

Atlantans were overjoyed as work all along the line of the Georgia Pacific commenced and progressed smoothly. Gordon personally drove the first spike at the eastern end of the road in Atlanta in November, 1881, and within three years, trains were running regularly between Atlanta and Birmingham. Henry Grady, more than any other man, deserved the credit for keeping the Georgia Western vision before the public eye. He had for years extolled both the virtue of building a road into Alabama and the necessity of opening the region's mineral wealth to the Georgia capital. Still, it was Gordon who received the most effusive praise from his fellow Georgians for bringing to completion the railroad project. The Atlanta *Constitution* lauded "the man who in New York was fighting alone and almost without resource, a battle—and few men know how bitter and stubborn a battle—for the practical development of his section." In June,

11. Atlanta *Constitution*, June 7, 8, August 16, 26, November 23, 1881, January 3, February 9, April 1, August 25, 1882; Avery, *History of Georgia*, 635–36; clipping of Charleston *Sunday Times*, July 3, 1887, in Scrapbook III, p. 37, in Francis Warrington Dawson I Collection, Duke; Stover, *Railroads of the South*, 240; Klein, *Great Richmond Terminal*, 92.

shortly after he returned to Atlanta with the title to the Georgia Western in hand, leading businessmen of the city tendered him a banquet at the Kimball House. During an evening replete with toasts and compliments, Gordon promised the commercial elite of Atlanta that he would push to finish the railroad as quickly as was humanly and financially possible. Asserting his pride in his recent business success, he declared, "It has been my fortune to do what I could in various fields for my country, but I had rather be in the van of this great enterprise than to bear all the political honors that could be heaped upon one." Gordon seemed to have finally gained the financial success he had longed for since the end of the Civil War.[12]

Gordon was more financially secure than at any earlier time in his life. As a consequence of the sale of the Georgia Pacific to the R & D, Gordon personally realized upwards of $350,000. In addition to this cash payment, he held large blocks of stock in both the Georgia Pacific and the R & D extension company. Earlier in 1881, Gordon had also sold his interest in the Belmont coal mines in Jackson County, Alabama, for perhaps as much as $100,000. Atop all his success and monetary gain, Gordon occupied a secure position as president of the Georgia Pacific, with an annual salary of $10,000. He probably could have lived comfortably on this competency that he had gained so rapidly, but as he would demonstrate throughout his business career, Gordon always looked to parlay whatever stake he had into something much grander. Success only whetted his appetite for more.[13]

The most common theme running through Gordon's financial correspondence during the last two decades of the nineteenth century was his unbounded optimism. Whether publicly offering stocks and bonds or privately encouraging a friend to invest in his numerous enterprises, Gordon repeatedly spiced his endorsements with promises of an immense return in a short period with a minimum of risk. Shortly after selling the Georgia Pacific, he tried to interest a New York capitalist in "a large body of first class pine land on the line of the Georgia Pacific." "There is an enormous speculation and quick returns," he wrote. "But to make the speculation a great success we

12. Atlanta *Constitution*, May 18, 22, June 8, 9, August 30, November 19, 1881.
13. Newspaper clipping, in Scrapbook III, p. 37, in Dawson I Collection; Atlanta *Constitution*, March 26, April 6, June 28, August 26, September 27, 29, 1881, February 9, August 25, 1882; Felton, *Memoirs*, 513, 535. Ferdinand Ward, of (U.S.) Grant, Ward & Company, believed Gordon bilked him on the Belmont deal. For his interesting account of the transaction, see also Atlanta *Constitution*, October 11, 1885.

ought to purchase 100,000 acres, so as to monopolize & C." Certainly, as a friend once explained, Gordon's mind "ran on large schemes." It was as if he believed that everything he undertook was guaranteed to succeed. To be sure, Gordon's Georgia Pacific venture proved a spectacular success that netted him tremendous wealth in little over a year after his resignation from the Senate. Still, Gordon continued to push ahead. He was not content to rest on his economic laurels, for indeed, he longed for something more than mere financial success. Unquestionably, he coveted riches, and he must have been gratified by the beneficial effects his labors had upon Georgia and the South; but above all else, Gordon yearned for recognition as a titan in the world of business and finance. A Georgia newspaper, commenting on his expansive mind in the wake of his recent success, reported that Gordon "has projects right ahead of him even larger than those that have engaged his attention for the past year. When these projects are unfolded and developed the people will understand that he could not afford and would not think of wasting any more of his life in politics." For now, Gordon as a businessman had more to offer the South.[14]

While continuing to serve as president of the Georgia Pacific, Gordon became involved in several other businesses. He invested heavily in a cotton factory in Mississippi and in a Tennessee fertilizer firm that he hoped would relocate in Atlanta. Gordon also acted as a land broker for an English company by overseeing the sale of 500,000 acres of land in Mississippi. His connection with overseas capitalists deepened appreciably when he spent most of the latter half of 1882 in London and Paris, ostensibly to sell Georgia Pacific bonds to European investors. Although initially successful in placing some three million dollars in bonds in London, Gordon ran into considerable difficulty when the value of American railroad stocks, especially those of the R & D, plummeted. Nevertheless, when questioned after his return about what effect the English reluctance to invest would have upon the Georgia Pacific, Gordon reassured his interviewer that the road was in excellent shape and that the bonds could be placed in New York if overseas investors backed out.[15]

14. Atlanta *Constitution*, September 27, 29, 1881; Gordon to Barlow, August 18, 1881, in Barlow Papers; Clement A. Evans, "General Gordon and General Longstreet," *Independent*, LVI (February, 1904), 313.

15. Atlanta *Constitution*, January 17, February 9, March 30, April 5, August 11–13, 25, November 26, December 14, 17, 1882; Felton, *Memoirs*, 304, 542.

In addition to his attempts to obtain foreign backing for the Georgia Pacific bonds, Gordon also undertook several other missions while on his European trip. In the words of one correspondent, the main object of his visit was "to put the material interests and the vast possibilities of the south before the capitalists of Europe . . . presenting a rich field for investment and emigration." In that vein, Gordon must have devoted a great deal of his time to drumming up interest in another of his railroad projects. He had already investigated the possibility of building a railroad in Florida that stretched all the way to Key West. But Gordon hoped to develop this enterprise into something much more than merely a railroad traversing Florida. Gordon's vision included steamship and telegraph lines across the Caribbean, as well as a wide variety of agricultural ventures in Latin America. It would make Florida, in the words of another commentator, "the great commercial center of the Western World" by calling "to her shores the great trade of South America, Mexico and Cuba." Gordon did indeed have grand plans; and upon his return to America in December, 1882, he let it be known that he had "several large interests outside of the Georgia Pacific" that would demand his attention and keep him extremely busy the following year.[16]

By February, 1883, Gordon had convinced the Florida legislature to approve a bill of incorporation granting a charter to the International Railroad and Steamship Company of Florida. Gordon organized the I.R.R. & S.S. Co. "for the purpose of constructing and operating a railroad from a point on the line of the State of Georgia to Key West and Tampa, in the State of Florida." In addition to the authorization to locate, build, equip, and operate a railroad, the charter also empowered the company to lay underwater telegraph lines and establish shipping lines between Florida and overseas ports. In return for the construction of the railroad and the benefits that would accrue to Florida, the charter granted fifteen thousand acres of land to the I.R.R. & S.S. Co. for every mile of completed track. On March 22, 1883, the company formally organized in Jacksonville, Florida, and Gordon, as the leading spirit of the enterprise, was selected president. Gordon subscribed to 991 of the first 1,000 shares ($100 per share) of the I.R.R. & S.S. Co. stock issued at that time. He then established a construc-

16. Atlanta *Constitution*, August 12, December 17, 1882; Felton, *Memoirs*, 538; David L. Willing, "Florida's Overseas Railroad," *Florida Historical Quarterly*, XXXV (April, 1957), 288–89; Carlton J. Corliss, "Building the Overseas Railway to Key West," *Tequesta*, XIII (1953), 4.

tion company and, on June 20, entered into a contract with the I.R.R. & S.S. Co. in which he personally assumed responsibility for the construction of the Florida road. One week later, the New York, Florida, and Havana Construction Company purchased the contract from him for $999,000, with payment to be made in stock in the New York, Florida, and Havana. Clearly, with the exception of the bonds, which he had necessarily to open to outside investors, Gordon organized the entire project so that it would be his.[17]

Gordon commenced work in Florida even before his construction company officially organized. Survey and work teams already dispatched to Tampa began laying out a route northward toward the Georgia line. In several strictly confidential letters to his chief engineers in Florida, Gordon stressed the necessity of concealing the actual location of the road. He had several reasons for his obsessive secrecy. He used the placement of the road as a point of leverage to extract concessions from Florida communities and, in effect, forced them to bid for the railroad to pass through their locales. Gordon was also interested in buying large chunks of land along the route of the railroad, well in advance of public announcement. Once word leaked out as to where the line would run, land values would skyrocket and provide handsome profits to those individuals owning the adjacent properties. Gordon was, as he put it, often "offered such large inducements" that he was willing to relocate his road even though the new route might be more expensive. On one occasion, when he wanted to conceal a change in the path of the road, he encouraged his representative to employ all forms of deception in order to avoid arousing suspicion: "Discretion, caution, secrecy and the blinding of the public to our real designs is absolutely necessary to the accomplishment of my purposes." Orders like this, by no means uncommon, indicate that Gordon was intensely involved in the Florida project. As he soon found time for little else, he decided to resign as president of the Georgia Pacific. In his June 30, 1883, letter of resignation, Gordon explained that his Florida railroad "requires so much of my attention

17. Atlanta *Constitution*, February 28, 1883; Minutebook of the International Railroad and Steamship Company of Florida, March 22, June 20, 1883, in Records of the Public Service Commission, Record Group 17, Bound Transportation Division's Railroad Minute Books, GDAH, hereinafter cited as Minutebook, I.R.R. & S.S. Co.; Minutebook of the New York, Florida and Havana Construction Company, June 14, 27, 1883, in Records of the Public Service Commission, Record Group 17, Bound Transportation Division's Railroad Minute Books, GDAH, hereinafter cited as Minutebook, NY, FLA and Havana Co.

as to make it impossible for me to give my time to the Georgia Pacific."[18]

Gordon's wholehearted involvement in the I.R.R. & S.S. Co. is amply shown in a set of personal letter books he maintained during the 1880s. These seven letter books, spanning a period from May, 1883, to November, 1890, include numerous letters to people on both sides of the Atlantic on a wide variety of subjects. The letters of May through July, 1883, convey a dramatic impression of hectic, almost nonstop activity. In a ten-week period, Gordon wrote over 180 letters, the vast majority of which deal with the I.R.R. & S.S. Co. and clearly show that it was his overriding concern. He discussed the proposed route of the road, the marketing of millions of dollars of stock in Europe, and the sale of smaller blocks of construction-company stock to individuals. He wrote to the governor of Florida to inquire about the possibility of using convicts for his labor force, ordered materials for the construction of his railroad, and lobbied support for his Florida claims. He sought trustworthy legal counsel from luminaries such as L. Q. C. Lamar and Logan E. Bleckley and tried to obtain inside information concerning the complicated legal questions involved in the disputes that developed between the I.R.R. & S.S. Co. and other Florida railroad companies. These letters leave no doubt of Gordon's abiding commitment to his newest enterprise. He brought into the boardroom the same tenacity and sense of purpose that he had so often demonstrated on the battlefield. However, the aggressive, gambling nature that had carried him to such great fame in war did not serve him nearly so well in business. He would have been wise to have relied more on the calculated pragmatism that had ensured his success in politics.[19]

18. All of the following letters are located in John Brown Gordon Records, 1883–1890, AC. 00-118, GDAH, hereinafter cited as Gordon Personal Letterbooks. Gordon to Henry Cooper, May 9, 1883; Gordon to J. B. Baird, May 10, 1883; Gordon to John T. Lesley, May 11, 1883; Gordon to Governor W. D. Bloxham, May 14, 1883; Gordon to Charles Smith, May 17, 1883; Gordon to Hamilton Disston, May 17, 1883; Gordon to W. H. Mabry, May 24, 1883; Gordon to S. Wailes, May 31, 1883. See also Atlanta *Constitution*, June 7, July 5, 8, 1883; and Minutebook, I.R.R. & S.S. Co., February 20, 1884.

19. All of the following letters are located in Gordon Personal Letterbooks. Gordon to Governor W. D. Bloxham, May 11, 14, 1883; Gordon to L. Q. C. Lamar, May 12, 1883; Gordon to A. C. Harmer, May 21, June 11, 20, September 13, 1883; Gordon to George Walker, May 26, 1883; Gordon to James Hastings, July 10, 23, 1883; Gordon to James A. Williamson, July 21, 1883; Gordon to Israel Joseph, August 17, 1883; Gordon to Archer N. Martin, September 20, 1883; Gordon to W. L. Watson, October 30, 1883; Gordon to L. E. Bleckley, April 22, 23, 1884. Virtually every day in November, 1883,

The letters also reveal Gordon's concern with a number of related matters. He purchased substantial property in Florida in the belief that it would become quite valuable when his road was completed. In addition to his attempts to acquire orange groves so that he might establish a produce business for his sons, Gordon planned to build a winter home in Florida for himself. He investigated the possibility of bringing in settlers and establishing colonies along the railroad. Further, Gordon continued to operate as a land broker for English interests; and even after he had severed his connection with the Georgia Pacific, he remained actively concerned with real-estate speculation in Mississippi. Obviously, Gordon was exceedingly active.[20]

Legal problems with other railroads in Florida soon became the Georgian's paramount concern. In its haste to construct railroads in the state as quickly as possible, the Florida legislature had granted too many charters with extraordinarily generous terms. It was claimed, probably accurately, that the state of Florida gave away more public land than there was acreage in the state. Thus, there were many overlapping claims and numerous legal uncertainties concerning them. Moreover, several companies that had earlier secured charters had failed to commence work; others that had begun construction had stopped or were not progressing rapidly enough to comply with the terms of their contracts. The resulting muddle left Gordon unable to proceed freely. With so many legal questions unanswered, he found it increasingly difficult to attract investors. When efforts to place his bonds in Europe failed and similar efforts in New York also collapsed, the I.R.R. & S.S. Co. stagnated. Even as early as the end of 1883, legal entanglements and the problems they generated had dampened Gordon's prospects for success in Florida.[21]

---

Gordon wrote one or more letters about the financing for his railroad. See also Gordon to Barlow, April 14, May 25, June 29, 1883, all in Barlow Papers.

20. All of the following letters are located in Gordon Personal Letterbooks. Gordon to Nathaniel Greene, May 9, 1883; Gordon to S. J. Wailes, May 10, 31, 1883; Gordon to J. W. Johnston, May 10, 1883; Gordon to Governor W. D. Bloxham, May 11, 1883; Gordon to Reynolds and Eckford, June 11, 20, 1883; Gordon to Charles Smith, June 14, 1883; Gordon to J. T. Lesley, June 18, July 14, 1883; Gordon to C. G. Megrue, June 20, 1883; Gordon to Israel Joseph, June 20, 1883; Gordon to Jonathan A. Fitten, July 14, 1883; Gordon to J. S. Thrasher, July 14, 1883; Gordon to Son, July 18, 1883; Gordon to J. H. Lyman, February 29, 1884.

21. All of the following letters are located in Gordon Personal Letterbooks. Gordon to L. Q. C. Lamar, May 12, 1883; Gordon to Charles Smith, May 21, 1883; Gordon to N. H. Barnum, June 9, 1883; Gordon to R. A. Lancaster, June 21, 1883; Gordon to Board of Trustees of International Improvement Fund of Florida, June 29, 1883, February 14, 20, 1884; Gordon to H. B. Plant, June 29, 1883; Gordon to A. B. Mason, July 1, 11, 13, 21, 24,

Added to Gordon's legal problems with the International Railroad and Steamship Company were troubles of a different nature, reaching back to his days in the Senate. In December, 1883, several national newspapers printed hundreds of the private letters between Collis P. Huntington, a California railroad mogul, and one of his partners on the West Coast, David D. Colton. Huntington, vice-president and general manager of the Central Pacific, was also vitally involved in the building of the Southern Pacific Railroad. In the 1870s, he spent much of his time in the nation's capital, where he lobbied fiercely on behalf of his roads. The correspondence between Huntington and Colton revealed the shocking nature and enormous influence of the various railroad lobbying machines active in Washington. During the period covered by the letters, October, 1874, to October, 1878, Huntington and his Southern Pacific were frequently locked in battle with Tom Scott and his Texas and Pacific Railroad. While Scott sought political and financial favors to aid in the construction of his road to the Pacific, Huntington worked to block Scott's efforts in Congress. In their struggle to best one another, both men employed virtually every means at their disposal, regardless of legal or ethical considerations. The so-called Colton Letters exposed a startling web of fraud, deception, bribery, and corruption that had ensnared numerous legislators and cabinet officers. Publication of the Huntington-Colton correspondence, wrote one historian, was "second only to the Crédit Mobilier scandal as a soiler of Congressional names."[22]

---

August 24, 1883; Gordon to John W. Candler, July 13, 1883; Gordon to D. C. Forney, August 3, 1883; Gordon to A. C. Harmer, September 13, 17, 1883; Gordon to P. A. Wellford, November 23, 1883; Gordon to W. D. Bloxham, November 24, 1883; Gordon to Charles Harris, November 30, 1883. See also Minutebook, I.R.R. & S. S. Co., June 27, 29, 1883, March 4, 1884; Minutebook, NY, FLA and Havana Co., February 21, June 11, 1884; Gordon to Barlow, May 25, June 29, 1883, both in Barlow Papers; Atlanta *Constitution*, July 12, 1883, February 2, 1884, February 3, 1885; and J. E. Dovell, "The Railroads and the Public Lands of Florida, 1879–1905," *Florida Historical Quarterly*, XXXIV (January, 1956), 236–58.

22. C. Vann Woodward, *Reunion and Reaction: The Compromise of 1877 and the End of Reconstruction* (Rev. ed.; Boston, 1966), 69–142, *passim*; Woodward, *Watson*, 3; Woodward, *Origins of the New South*, 37. A copy of the short pamphlet, *The Colton Letters: The Inside Story of an Infamous Procedure* (N.p., n.d.), containing extracts of some thirty-eight letters, can be found in the Bancroft Library, University of California, Berkeley. The December 23, 1883, issue of the San Francisco *Chronicle* reproduced verbatim most of Huntington's letters to Colton. The New York *World* and the Chicago *Tribune* also published extensive portions of the Huntington-Colton correspondence in late December, 1883. See also Cerinda W. Evans, *Collis Potter Huntington* (2 vols.; Newport News, Va., 1954), I, 340–58; and David Lavender, *The Great Persuader* [C. P. Huntington] (Garden City, N.Y., 1970), 307–17, 325–29.

Although there are no direct indications of payoffs to Gordon or of willful wrongdoing on his part, six letters mention him by name and leave no doubt that Gordon and Huntington were frequently in contact with one another. It is unclear what effect their relationship had upon Gordon's senatorial actions, and particularly on railroad matters such as Gordon's opposition to the Texas and Pacific Railroad Bill. With this bill, Scott solicited government endorsement of approximately $50 million in bonds (with an aggregate interest over a fifty-year period amounting to almost one-quarter of a billion dollars) in order to assure the building of his railroad. As early as December, 1874, Scott was using his contacts in Congress to gain Gordon's support. The following month, Gordon expressed in a letter his reluctance to authorize subsidies even though the Texas and Pacific appeared to offer significant benefits for the South. Scott, in his effort to drum up southern support for his bill, continued to court Gordon. In September, he prevailed upon P. G. T. Beauregard to contact the Georgian and stress the necessity for united southern action. As active as Scott's wooing of Gordon may have been, it paled in comparison to that of Huntington.[23]

Despite uncertainty as to when Gordon and Huntington first met, it is clear that the two had established contact by mid-1876. In a July, 1876, letter, Huntington informed Colton that he had told Gordon that "if he [Gordon] could get up a party of the best men of the South" to visit California and observe how work on the Southern Pacific was progressing, "we [the railroad lobby] would pay all their expenses." The cost might exceed ten thousand dollars, but the railroad baron thought "it would be money well-expended." Gordon evidently had no qualms about traveling at the railroad's expense, but he advised Huntington "that some of his friends do not like to go on an invitation from a railroad company." Accordingly, Huntington instructed Colton to have "some of the prominent men in San Francisco" invite Gordon and other leading southerners to visit California. These invitations were issued almost immediately, whereupon Gordon assured the railroad man that he could gather perhaps as many as thirty southerners for a trip that September. Huntington, however, expressed doubts in mid-August that a substantial party of southerners

23. Atlanta, *Constitution*, January 17, 1884; Woodward, *Reunion and Reaction*, 80, 128–29; Felton, *Memoirs*, 541–44; Tom A. Scott to M. W. Ransom, December 15, 1874, in Matt W. Ransom Papers, SHC; Gordon to Barlow, January 23, 1875, in Barlow Papers; Huntington to Colton, September 18, 1875, in San Francisco *Chronicle*, December 23, 1883.

254 · JOHN BROWN GORDON

could be induced to travel to California that fall, especially since elections were nearing. Apparently his fears were well founded because it does not appear Gordon ever made the trip. In any event, the general continued to oppose the Texas and Pacific Railroad Bill.[24]

Gordon's introduction of a sinking-fund bill on January 12, 1877, presents a more serious dilemma in determining the rectitude of his actions. "The most urgent legislative problem the Union Pacific and the Central Pacific had in common," wrote a historian of the complicated economic maneuverings underlying the Compromise of 1877, "was the large debt they owed to the Federal government and their combined effort to forestall impending steps to collect that debt." These roads, along with lesser railroads, owed the national government approximately $55 million for the subsidies that permitted completion of a transcontinental railroad. Gordon's proposal would create a sinking fund to help retire that debt, but at a much slower rate than that provided by a second bill sponsored by Senator Allen G. Thurman. Unquestionably, the Pacific railroads preferred Gordon's bill to the more rigorous repayment provisions of Thurman's so-called Judiciary Bill. In spite of immense pressure by Huntington and other lobbyists, Gordon's sinking-fund measure never had much chance of passage. Although Huntington admitted as much in February and March, 1877, he optimistically reported that the Gordon bill, or "our Sinking Fund bill," as he styled it, "is in a much better shape to pass than it has ever been before." He probably based his optimism on his ability "to fix up the Railroad Committee in the Senate . . . just as we want it." Huntington miscalculated his capacity to influence the composition of that key Senate committee. One week later, after appointments were made for the special session that began in March, he lamented Scott's success in replacing "one of our men" with one of his own. "Gordon of Georgia was taken off and [Lewis V.] Bogy of Missouri put on." Huntington undoubtedly considered Gordon a man whom he could count on for support in the Senate.[25]

24. Huntington to Colton, July 26, August 7, 14, 25, 1876, all in San Francisco *Chronicle*, December 23, 1883.

25. *Congressional Record*, 44th Cong., 2nd Sess., 589, 736, 1308; App., 107–10; 45th Cong., 1st Sess., 39; Woodward, *Reunion and Reaction*, 122–25; Huntington to Colton, February 12, March 7, 14, 1877, all in San Francisco *Chronicle*, December 23, 1883. Mrs. Felton, in her obsessive effort to portray Gordon in the worst possible light in her *Memoirs*, repeatedly used a January 17, 1876, letter but cited it as January 17, 1877. In the letter, Huntington informed Colton, "I believe with $200,000 I can pass our bill." By incorrectly citing this letter, Mrs. Felton constructed a false scenario in which five days after Gordon introduced his bill, Huntington bragged he could pass it. Felton, *Memoirs*, 83, 89, 102–103, 507, 514, 520, 541–44, 630.

Gordon's opposition to both the Texas and Pacific bill and the Thurman bill, as well as his sponsorship of a sinking-fund proposal of his own, are not in and of themselves sufficient reasons for indictment. However, in light of his relationship with Huntington, these actions certainly do raise some questions. Following publication of the Colton Letters, when accusations were made that Gordon bore a large share of the responsibility for the defeat of the Scott bill, he apologized in no way whatsoever for his opposition. He saw no reason, he said, for the government to endorse $50 million in bonds to build a railroad, when along the same general line, Huntington was already actively constructing a road without any assistance from the government. In addition to his belief that the government should not guarantee loans made to private corporations, Gordon maintained that the Southern Pacific offered greater penetration of the South than did the Texas and Pacific and thus would be more beneficial to the region. Two years later, when political opponents charged that his votes against Scott's bill stemmed from bribes, he contemptuously dismissed such accusations with the claim that "my silence could have won for me a colossal fortune." Gordon asserted that he could have secured both money and immunity from criticism had he but feigned an illness and been silent; instead, he openly opposed the measure because, as he maintained, it was not in the best interests of the people or the nation. Similarly, when he introduced his sinking-fund measure, Gordon contended that it would "exact from these railroads the last dollar due to the Government, and exact it by the shortest and safest process" compatible with the previous contracts and governmental good faith. He opposed the Thurman bill because he feared the railroad companies would reject its more stringent restructuring of earlier contracts and that would lead to a costly lawsuit, further complicating and delaying the repayment process. Even after his proposal had died, Gordon persistently opposed the Judiciary Bill and was one of a handful of congressmen to vote against it when it finally passed and became law.[26]

Strangely, few Georgians ever demanded a fuller explanation by Gordon of his actions or his relationship with Huntington. Indeed, public reaction ranged from mild surprise to total lack of concern. An eyebrow may occasionally have been raised in 1877 because of Gor-

26. *Congressional Record*, 44th Cong., 2nd Sess., App., 107–10; 45th Cong., 1st Sess., 2384, 2790; Atlanta *Constitution*, January 17, 1884, May 27, 1886; Atlanta *Evening Capitol*, June 18, 1886, quoted in James Gaston Towery, "The Georgia Gubernatorial Campaign of 1886" (M.A. thesis, Emory University, 1945), 53.

don's backing of a measure obviously beneficial to the huge railroad interests, but most Georgians simply paid no attention to the matter. Following publication of the Huntington-Colton correspondence, some Georgia newspapers expressed a desire to learn more about the affair; but with the exception of the Feltons' Cartersville *Free Press*, most papers refused to follow up on the "revelations." A frustrated, almost incredulous Mrs. Felton wrote, "[N]othing can account for this remarkable silence save the power of money and triumvirate patronage." National newspapers were more willing to question Gordon's actions; yet, in the main, their responses generally reflected more sadness and disappointment than anger or indignation. The San Francisco *Chronicle*, which first published the story, found it difficult to reconcile Gordon's image "as the representative of everything that was highly respectable in the South" with the correspondence's allusions to him as a "more than eager friend of the monopoly." Echoing these sentiments, the New York *World* concluded that Gordon had become "a servant of the corporation." Mrs. Felton may have derived some satisfaction from these mild indictments, but in spite of her steadfast condemnation of Gordon and her relentless search for materials damaging to him, she never uncovered conclusive proof that he had either sold his vote or betrayed the public trust. By and large, Georgians ignored the implications of the letters both at the time of their publication and later, when opponents of the general attempted to use them to defeat him in a political contest.[27]

Nevertheless, the Colton Letters do furnish grounds for suspicion that Gordon did receive money from the Huntington interests. Reference to Gordon as "one of our men," or to his proposal as "our Sinking Fund bill," plus the smug sense of confidence with which Huntington banked on Gordon's support, raise questions concerning the senator's actions. Also, the more optimistic tone of Gordon's letters to Barlow in 1877 indicates that his desperate financial plight of the previous year had substantially improved. Rather than bemoaning his economic distress or pleading with Barlow to assist him in securing urgently needed loans, Gordon discussed almost exclusively matters of investment and speculation. He was definitely more active financially after he introduced the Huntington-backed, sinking-fund proposal than he had been during any previous period of his senatorship.

27. Felton, *Memoirs*, 114–18, 488, 508–12, 514, 541–43, 630; San Francisco *Chronicle*, December 23, 1883; Arnett, *The Populist Movement in Georgia*, 30; Woodward, *Watson*, 63; Towery, "Georgia Gubernatorial Campaign," 50–53.

His increased ability to engage in all sorts of speculative ventures tends to lend credence to charges that Gordon sold his votes or became a paid servant of Huntington.[28]

Yet, even in the depths of his economic misery, Gordon wrote a letter to Barlow that would seem to contravene such conduct. In July, 1876, Gordon informed the New York attorney that he had received two offers of loans but had rejected them because they were "from sources which will not permit acceptance by me . . . as long as I am in the senate." This persistence in trying to borrow the money, plus his apparent ability to discriminate between acceptable creditors and those who would place him in a compromising position, is perhaps indicative of a moral resolve not easily seduced. Gordon's decision to refuse questionable loan offers at a time when he wrote "I don't know what I am to do" demonstrates his unwillingness—at least at that point in time—to compromise his office. Certainly the people he represented were confident that he possessed such strength. In the following months, he may have secured his long-sought loan, or he may have found other legitimate means of obtaining money; or, of course, it is possible that the financial pressures became so acute that he finally succumbed to the dollars Huntington undoubtedly dangled before him. The limited evidence available strongly suggests that Gordon did receive a substantial amount of money in late 1876 or early 1877, but it is simply impossible to ascertain the source.[29]

C. Vann Woodward, a keen student of leading southerners of the last third of the nineteenth century, refrained from attributing Gordon's actions to "conscious duplicity" and asserted that those who did so were "likely to credit him [Gordon] with a complexity of mind of which he was innocent, for it must be remembered that the General was an authentic hero, and heroes have never been notorious for complex mentalities." Although possibly correct, this assessment of Gordon's involvement in the Huntington affair is perhaps too summary a judgment of the man. Granted that Gordon did not possess first-rate business acumen—a fact borne out by his long list of financial failures—but the inability to distinguish oneself in business does not consign one to the ranks of the mentally infirm. Moreover, Gordon's reputation as a genuine military hero, a reputation he earned on

28. Huntington to Colton, February 12, March 14, 1877, in San Francisco *Chronicle*, December 23, 1883. See Gordon to Barlow, [undated, 1876], May 19, 31, June 7, July 10, 1876, May 5, 17, June 13, 1877, all in Barlow Papers.

29. Gordon to Barlow, July 10, 1876, in Barlow Papers.

the battlefield, does not preclude his possessing a sharp mind or a well-developed sense of integrity. Indeed, for those men who had accomplished as much as he had militarily, the opposite would often seem to be true. Gordon was certainly an intelligent man, entirely capable of differentiating between bribery and subtle pressure.[30]

If Gordon did receive money from Huntington, he assuredly knew what he was doing. His willingness to accept railroad passes and to allow Huntington to pay his expenses is readily apparent, but that is not to say that he would have permitted himself to be bought and controlled by the railroad magnate. Still, in view of the unexplained improvement in Gordon's financial situation, the subsequent prearrangements that resulted in his resignation from the Senate in 1880, and the generally low level of morality pervading American politics at the time, it is likely that Gordon did receive illicit payments. Perhaps at some point during the last half of 1876, his financial burdens finally became too overwhelming. But no conclusive proof of any illegality or betrayal of public trust has ever surfaced. Gordon may have appeared eager to ally himself with the railroad mogul— and in fact he may have done so—but the people chose to believe otherwise. Gordon's popularity, both in Georgia and in the South as a whole, suffered little, if at all, from the Huntington revelations.

Scarcely fazed by publication of the Huntington-Colton correspondence, Gordon continued his efforts to develop the I.R.R. & S.S. Co., and since 1884 was a presidential election year, he also renewed his involvement in national politics. Spending most of his time at his business office in New York, Gordon was able to maintain close contact with many of the power brokers within the Democratic party. Whenever interviewed, Gordon refrained from publicly endorsing a specific candidate and instead stressed the necessity of selecting a man who would run well in New York and other crucial states. Although he appears to have preferred Grover Cleveland early in the year, at the July national convention he labored extensively on behalf of Thomas F. Bayard. Yet, when Cleveland emerged as the party's standard-bearer, Gordon readily supported the New Yorker.[31]

Shortly after the convention, Gordon made several suggestions to

30. Woodward, *Watson*, 63.
31. New York *Tribune*, April 3, 1884; Atlanta *Constitution*, April 6, June 17, 1884; Henry L. Bryan to T. F. Bayard, July 8, 15, 1884, both in Bayard Collection; Gordon to A. H. Colquitt, April 5, 1884, Gordon to Harry, May 17, 1884, both in Gordon Personal Letterbooks.

the Democratic nominee. He urged Cleveland to refrain from any "reference whatsoever to the war or to the sections of our common country or to the existence of any passion or prejudice engendered by the war." Gordon thought such a course would be best for the country and for "your reputation as a reformer and the nonpartisan character of your administration." He also encouraged Cleveland to make favorable overtures toward those "influential Republicans belonging to a class known as 'business men' "—those men with whom Gordon had been heavily involved since leaving the Senate. In light of the current rift within the Republican party caused by James G. Blaine's nomination, Gordon believed that several of these prominent Republicans could be induced to support Cleveland. Volunteering his services in the upcoming campaign, the Georgian asserted, "I sincerely believe that your election will inaugurate an era of sectional concord, of higher peace, better administration of the government and a satisfaction which will be so nearly universal as to extend to all parties, classes, creeds and colors of the American people."[32]

Cleveland's victory in the fall elections surely gratified Gordon, as did the Democrats regaining control of the national government for the first time since the war. When he learned of the Democratic triumph, he wired Senator L. Q. C. Lamar, "Thank God! Cleveland is elected. Turn the rascals out!" However, the party's success was not foremost in the general's mind during the final months of 1884. In September, his youngest son died unexpectedly of typhoid fever. John Brown Gordon, Jr.'s death robbed his father of the jubilation he would normally have felt after the Democratic victory in the national election. Moreover, the loss of the nineteen-year-old, who had been "a source of pride to himself and gratification to his parents and friends," devastated the entire Gordon family. This shock came only three years after Caroline Williams Gordon, wife of Gordon's eldest son, Hugh, had died at the age of twenty-seven. Tragedy would again strike the Gordon family less than two years later, when Walter S. Gordon, John's brother and frequent partner in business, died in October, 1886; and two weeks before Christmas, the Reverend Zachariah H. Gordon also died. So much sorrow in such a short period of time had to leave its mark on Gordon. But his greatest loss, the one that pained him most, was the death of his namesake.[33]

32. Gordon to Cleveland, July 24, 1884, in Gordon Personal Letterbooks.
33. Edward Mayes, *Lucius Q. C. Lamar. His Life, Times, and Speeches. 1825–1893* (Nashville, 1896), 460; Atlanta *Constitution*, August 16, 1881, September 13, 14, 1884,

The burden of personal grief and business frustration lightened in the early days of 1885 when the prospect of a return to an active role in national politics beckoned. The Democrats' November triumph meant a significant turnover in government, especially in the executive branch. Following a celebratory banquet of some two hundred of New York's Democratic elite, at which Gordon sat at the table of honor, word began to circulate that the president would tap the Georgian for some cabinet post. There seemed to be sufficient basis for such speculation, because Cleveland had recently alluded to Gordon as "one of the southern men to whom he would look for advice." Indeed, Gordon did have substantial backing among prominent Democrats. Alfred H. Colquitt, then United States senator from Georgia, wrote an enthusiastic letter of recommendation to the president-elect less than two weeks after the November election. Similarly, Senator L. Q. C. Lamar, in a February 6, 1885, letter to Cleveland, strongly endorsed Gordon as a man "full of ardor *vim* & energy; & his abilities are fully equal to the responsibilities of a Cabinet position." Acknowledging that Gordon "had not escaped criticism & detraction in his public career," Lamar asserted that in his opinion, "the imputations have not the slightest foundation in truth . . . [and] I have not a shadow of doubt about his purity of character in every respect."[34]

Gordon may not have publicly professed a desire for a cabinet position, but he certainly did so in private. In a "strictly confidential" letter to Barlow on February 3, 1885, he related his discussion that morning with Lamar about the selection of Cleveland's cabinet. The Mississippian told Gordon that he was not interested in a cabinet post, but that he intended to do all that he could on Gordon's behalf. Lamar's strong letter several days later evinced his desire to secure a position for the Georgian. Although he did not openly request Barlow's assistance, Gordon did write, "If you see your way clear you could not do me a greater service than to get Governor Cleveland to ask the leading Southern Senators . . . what they think of Gor-

October 20, December 11, 13, 1886; Gordon to Barlow, August 18, 1881, in Barlow Papers; Hugh H. Gordon to John Hancock, September 12, 1884, in Gordon Personal Letterbooks; Cemetery Records, Block 341–2, Oakland Cemetery, Atlanta, Ga.; Hugh H. Gordon, Jr., *A Letter to My Sons about their Forebears* (Privately printed, 1954); Fanny to her daughter, September 14, 1892, in Gordon Family Collection, UGA.

34. New York *Times*, December 13, 1884; Atlanta *Constitution*, December 14, 1884, January 14, 1885; A. H. Colquitt to Grover Cleveland, November 18, 1884, L. Q. C. Lamar to Grover Cleveland, February 6, 1885, both in Grover Cleveland Papers, LC.

don. These men . . . the real representatives of the best people of the South . . . w'd indicate how my appointment w'd be rec'vd at the South." Gordon closed his private letter by adding, "You & others could tell him [Cleveland] how it [Gordon's appointment] w'd be rec'vd at the North." Gordon must have been disappointed when Cleveland passed him over, but he could take heart that his friend Lamar had received the much-discussed cabinet appointment.[35]

Once his flurry of political activity had spent itself, Gordon resumed his quest for crowning success in business. Both of his sons, especially Hugh, took on greater responsibilities as they became more involved in their father's businesses. The wide range of enterprises included dredging for gold in the rivers of Georgia, speculating in real estate both for himself and for overseas investors, cultivating Latin American contacts, investing in and promoting inventions, and raising huge herds of cattle. But above all else, Gordon persisted in his efforts to sell I.R.R. & S.S. Co. bonds that would permit work on the road to continue. Gordon's struggle to place the railroad's bonds had peaked in 1884. Of the over five hundred letters he wrote during that year, well over half of them dealt specifically with the increasingly difficult task of securing outside financing. In his numerous letters to agents, brokers, and potential investors on both sides of the Atlantic, Gordon continually insisted that large issues of bonds for his railroad would soon be taken and that full-scale construction would commence at any moment. He attempted to attract interest in his project by offering land bonuses to investors. He also circulated thousands of pamphlets that purported to provide the "real facts" about the Florida situation and thereby attempted to inspire confidence. Similarly, in a February, 1885, article in the Atlanta *Constitution*, Gordon went to great lengths to reassure the public that his company was a going concern and that the laying of track would begin as soon as rails arrived by boat in Florida. Despite such assurances, by 1885, it had become apparent to most observers that the railway-steamship project was fizzling.[36]

35. Gordon to Barlow, February 3, 1885, in Barlow Papers.

36. January–December, 1884, *passim*, in Gordon Personal Letterbooks (see especially Gordon to James A. Williamson, April 14, 1884, and Gordon to New, April 14, 1884); Gordon to W. D. Simpson, June 2, 1884, in Simpson, Young, Dean, and Coleman Families Papers, SCL; Felton, *Memoirs*, 538–40; Atlanta *Constitution*, February 3, 1885; Minutebook, I.R.R. & S.S. Co., February 20, March 4, 1884; Minutebook, NY, FLA and Havana Co.; February 21, 1884, June 12, September 29, 1885; see also Hugh H. Gordon Letterbook, 1887–1891, AC. 00-013, GDAH.

Even though Gordon devoted himself to a variety of nonagricul-
tural pursuits, he never lost touch with the agrarian roots of his
native South. Throughout the last three decades of the 1800s, he
engaged in all sorts of agricultural experimentation both at Sutherland and at his Beechwood plantation on the Flint River in Taylor
County. Located near Reynolds, Georgia, about eighty miles south of
Atlanta, and almost equidistant from Macon and Columbus, Beechwood provided an ideal refuge to which Gordon escaped whenever
possible. There his agronomic dabblings included the planting of
many different types of grass, the cultivation of exotic fruits, and the
growing of apples, peaches, and pecans, as well as staple crops. But
Gordon derived his greatest pleasure from the stock he raised at Beechwood. Goats, shepherd dogs, sheep, thoroughbred horses, "Texas
ponies," hogs, and several varieties of cattle roamed the fields between his plantation home and the levees along the Flint River. On
one occasion, when the levee ruptured and flooded the "cane-breaks"
of the overgrown bottomland, Gordon lost most of his herd of 250
Brahman cattle. The loss of these prized animals and the grisly task of
disposing of the drowned creatures broke not only Gordon's heart but
that of one of his daughters, who never forgot "the ghastly and pathetic sight." Despite this disaster and similar occurrences, Gordon
loved this pastoral retreat, a place where he could truly feel close to
the land.[37]

Overall, however, Gordon enjoyed little more success as a farmer
than he did as a businessman. Engrossed in either public service or
private enterprise, Gordon found it impossible to manage the plantation himself. Consequently, he often rented his lands to neighboring
farmers and was forced to employ overseers to manage Beechwood.
The shortcomings of these managers, generally former Confederate
soldiers, combined with Gordon's willingness to experiment, rendered Beechwood, in his daughter's words, "a white elephant." Even
in her partisan evaluation of her father, she acknowledged that his
business sense left something to be desired: "My father was a military
genius, a man of imagination and creative ability, and a great states-

37. Caroline Lewis Gordon, "De Gin'ral an' Miss Fanny"; Richard Frotscher to
Gordon, October 24, 1893, S. M. Tracy to S. D. Lee, October 31, 1893, S. M. Waymon to
Gordon, November 8, 1893, N. Dietzen to Gordon, November 9, 1893, all in Gordon
Family Collection, UGA; Gordon to Barlow, June 8, July 5, 1878, February 28, March
29, April 2, 22, 24, 1879, August 30, 187[8 or 9?], April 16, 1880, all in Barlow Papers;
Atlanta Constitution, January 14, 1883; Atlanta Journal, January 27, 1929.

man, but he was not a practical business man." Apparently Fanny possessed a much shrewder business sense than did her husband. And though he generally looked to her for advice and trusted her counsel, she was frequently unable to dissuade him from making unfortunate decisions and disastrous appointments of men to manage the plantation. Years later, Gordon's daughter recalled how her mother used to joke when a wagonload of goods from the plantation arrived at Sutherland. Fanny would invite their neighbors "to come and enjoy some of her $1,000 turkey and her $100 a pound butter." Regardless of Beechwood's unprofitability, Gordon never tired of his country retreat. In addition to enjoying long horseback rides over his property, Gordon, in his later years, wrote large portions of both his lectures and his reminiscences at Beechwood.[38]

Convicts leased from the state supplied much of the labor employed on Gordon's Beechwood plantation. The practice of leasing out the state's prisoners dated back to the early days of Reconstruction. When he first began using convicts is uncertain, but under the act of February 25, 1876, Gordon became one of the four original lessees of Penitentiary Company No. 2. This company was composed of B. G. Lockett, L. A. Jordan, W. B. Lowe, and Gordon, and it leased convicts for twenty years to labor in camps in Taylor and Dougherty counties. In December, 1876, however, Gordon, for whatever reasons, tried to divest himself of his interest in the convict lease system. The governor refused his request because the legislature had not made any provisions for the release of the original lessees. Although Gordon persisted in his efforts to free himself from direct responsibility for convicts that he could not personally supervise, he retained his share of the penitentiary company and legal accountability for the prisoners leased to him.[39]

In August, 1878, Gordon sublet the sixty convicts at work on

38. Atlanta *Journal*, January 27, 1929; Gordon, "De Gin'ral an' Miss Fanny"; Fanny to her husband, May 10, 1873, Fanny to daughter, September 14, 1893, both in Gordon Family Collection, UGA.

39. A. Elizabeth Taylor, "The Origin and Development of the Convict Lease System in Georgia," *Georgia Historical Quarterly*, XXVI (June, 1942), 113–20; *Georgia House Journal*, 1886, pp. 412–16; Derrell Roberts, "Joseph E. Brown and the Convict Lease System," *Georgia Historical Quarterly*, XLIV (December, 1960), 399–401; Atlanta *Constitution*, May 21, June 6, 1886; Scrapbook No. 16, p. 71, in Rebecca Latimer Felton Collection, UGA. The uncertainty surrounding how or when Gordon managed to rid himself of his legal obligations under the terms of the 1876 contract led to charges during Gordon's governorship that he was, in effect, suing himself when he officially brought suit against the penitentiary companies.

Beechwood to Edward Cox. At some point prior to this, Gordon and Cox had entered into an agricultural partnership in Taylor County. Evidently, Cox managed and operated Gordon's plantation, in addition to working his own holdings in central Georgia. It is possible that Gordon had earlier leased his convicts to Cox or that Cox merely oversaw their labor while they remained Gordon's responsibility; nonetheless, under the terms of their 1878 contract, Cox agreed to pay Gordon fifty bales of cotton annually in return for use of the prisoners and all products raised on Gordon's land. Details are lacking, but whether as a result of Cox's mismanagement of Beechwood, his mistreatment of the convicts, or the several law suits for nonpayment brought against the firm of Gordon & Cox, relations between the two partners deteriorated almost immediately. Less than seven months after subletting his convicts to Cox, Gordon again sought to sever his connection with the convict labor system. On April 1, 1879, Gordon sold his share in Penitentiary Company No. 2 to C. B. Howard for four thousand dollars in cash, an annual payment of fifty bales of cotton for eight years, and Howard's assumption of most of the debts of Gordon & Cox. In addition to turning over sixty convicts, Gordon rented Beechwood to Howard for eight years, by signing away "his right to enter and take possession of his plantation in Taylor County." Technically, however, Gordon remained a convict lessee as prescribed by the 1876 contract.[40]

In a tragic footnote to Gordon's attempt to sell his interest in the convict lease company, an incident of violence occurred on March 11, 1879. Forced to remain in Washington during the early months of 1879 because of congressional duties, Gordon authorized a friend, Robert A. Alston, to find a suitable buyer for his share of the company. Alston proceeded to negotiate with a number of interested parties, including Howard. Trouble arose when Alston concluded the arrangement with Howard, who refused to sublet convicts to Cox as Gordon had. An irate Cox confronted Alston and demanded that he rescind the Howard deal and accept another from Jessie Walters, a close friend of Cox. Tempers flared immediately and threats were

40. Felton, *Memoirs*, 488, 498–501, 515; Scrapbook No. 16, p. 71, No. 28, pp. 15–16, both in R. L. Felton Collection; *George P. Swift and Son v. John B. Gordon and Ed Cox*, March, 1880, *John D. Mitchell v. John B. Gordon and Ed Cox*, March, 1881, *Swift and Son v. Gordon & Cox* and Cox as an individual, March, 1881, all in De Kalb County Superior Court Minutes, Decatur, Ga.; Real Estate Deeds and Mortgages, April 11, 1878, in De Kalb County, Superior Court, Decatur, Ga.

exchanged. Later that day, the two engaged in a spectacular shoot-out in the Georgia State Capitol, in which Cox mortally wounded Alston, who in turn gravely wounded his assailant. Cox recovered from his wounds and received a sentence of life imprisonment. His assignment to light duty at Joe Brown's Dade County convict camp and his subsequent pardon after serving less than three years gave rise to new rumors concerning Brown and Gordon. Some Georgians, most notably Mrs. Felton, suspected that Brown gave preferential treatment to Cox, Gordon's former business partner, in order to gain damaging information that he might later use against the general. Although Gordon's resignation from the Senate and Brown's appointment one year after the shoot-out might seem to lend credence to these rumors, it is doubtful that the Cox-Alston tragedy had any impact whatsoever on the actions of May, 1880.[41]

Gordon's unhappy association with Cox also reveals a distressing tendency that surfaced frequently throughout the general's life. Gordon & Cox's failure to pay its debts often brought the two men into court. Gordon, both as an individual and as a codefendant, was involved in a large number of additional legal actions in which he was sued for nonpayment of debts, particularly loans. Most of the suits originated during the 1870s, when he served in the Senate; but he continued his irresponsible fiscal course well after leaving political office. On several instances, though the sums rarely exceeded two thousand dollars, Gordon refused to make the necessary arrangements to repay his loans until steps to seize his property were actually begun. It is ironic that a man so acutely sensitive to all affronts to his personal honor could display such a remarkable lack of concern for his financial trustworthiness. Gordon evidently saw nothing dishonorable or dishonest in his reluctance to meet his financial obligations. Whether Gordon even recognized this inconsistency is impossible to determine. However, it is certain that his lax approach to his own indebtedness frequently created problems for him. But these personal troubles were of little consequence when compared to the legal and financial difficulties associated with Gordon's Florida railroad.[42]

41. Atlanta *Constitution*, March 12, May 12, 1879, December 12, 1882; Felton, *Memoirs*, 372–73, 490–91; 496–97; Scrapbook No. 16, p. 71, in R. L. Felton Collection; Derrell Roberts, "Duel in the Georgia State Capitol," *Georgia Historical Quarterly*, XLVII (December, 1963), 420–24; Roberts, "Brown and the Convict Lease," 406–407.
42. *John R. Dos Passos* v. *John B. Gordon and Hugh H. Gordon*, March, 1887,

In spite of persistent legal complications concerning land grants and rights-of-way for the I.R.R. & S.S. Co., Gordon appears to have been close to undertaking actual construction of a portion of the road in January, 1886. With surveying and heavy grading along a forty-mile stretch near Tampa completed, Gordon prepared to lay crossties and rails. As always, the most serious problem facing him was a lack of funds. Having already spent $200,000 of his own money and having been repeatedly frustrated in his efforts to place his bonds, Gordon concentrated upon securing a loan. He believed he had found his backer when John R. Dos Passos of New York apparently agreed to loan him $250,000 by January 20, 1886. That amount, Gordon believed, would allow him to complete the forty-mile portion of the railroad, and the profits gained from the completion of that line would permit construction to begin along other sections of the proposed five-hundred-mile railroad. In return for the loan, Gordon agreed to divide equally with Dos Passos all the profits he realized from the completion of the road and from speculation along the line. Gordon's creditor would receive a $50,000 bonus, as well. These generous terms evince the extent of Gordon's desperation to see his Florida railroad built. Dos Passos, however, dashed the general's hopes as quickly as he had raised them when, for unknown reasons, he backed away from the enterprise. Gordon's inability to secure the funds necessary for construction brought work on the railroad to a halt and sounded the death knell of the I.R.R. & S.S. Co.[43]

Gordon would continue to try and revive his railway-steamship project, but for all intents and purposes, it was dead. With it died Gordon's dreams of a financial empire in Florida and the Caribbean. Fresh from his stunning accomplishments in the early 1880s, Gordon had wholeheartedly committed himself to this immense enterprise

---

*Campbell Brown* v. *John B. Gordon and E. C. Gordon*, March, 1877, *J. W. Smart and B. W. Smart* v. *Alfred H. Colquitt and John B. Gordon*, March, 1887, *Atlanta National Bank* v. *John B. Gordon*, September, 1880, all in Circuit Court of the United States for Northern District of Georgia, Federal Archives and Records Center, East Point, Ga.; *William P. Phillips* v. *John B. Gordon and Thomas C. Howard*, September, 1874, *Wood, Tabor and Moore* v. *John B. Gordon*, March, 1881, *Julius L. and Joseph M. Brown as Executors* v. *John B. Gordon*, February, 1900, all in De Kalb County Superior Court, GDAH.

43. Hoke Smith and Burton Smith to Gordon, October 20, 1888, in Letterbooks, Hoke Smith Collection, Richard B. Russell Memorial Library, UGA; Gordon to J. R. Dos Passos, September 15, December 2, 1886, March 7, 1888, all in Gordon Personal Letterbooks. The last entries in the I.R.R. & S.S. Co. Minutebook and the NY, FLA and Havana Co. Minutebook are August 4, 1886, and June 9, 1887, respectively.

that he believed would open up Florida and aid the economy of the entire Southeast. Certainly the successful development of the I.R.R. & S.S. Co. would have made him a fabulously wealthy man. But more important than the potential for riches was the impact it would have had on his reputation. Heavily laden steamships and railroad cars steaming northward as part of a Gordon transportation system would have completely removed the stigma of failure that marked his earlier business career. Gordon the businessman could then have finally assumed the lofty, respected position attained by Gordon as soldier and politician. But by 1886, Gordon's grand vision had been all but destroyed. Instead of winning new glories and new accolades, he found his financial future seriously clouded.

Even though he lost most of his money in his Florida enterprises and was, in the words of a contemporary, "somewhat out at the elbow," Gordon retained his willingness to speculate and to engage in any number of "sure-fire" schemes. His active participation in a variety of business ventures during the next two decades demonstrates that he was neither financially nor spiritually broken. Nonetheless, by 1886, Gordon must have been tired, and surely frustrated. Six years of almost obsessive involvement in railroading and numerous other facets of the burgeoning New South economy had exacted a heavy toll on the general. The steady erosion of both his fortune and his newly established reputation as a railroad developer forced him to step back and assess both his past and his future. His uneven course in the years after leaving the Senate had, in a very real sense, led him right back to the point where he began. Spectacular success had given way to dismal failure.[44]

As he turned away from his frustrating business career, he must have longed for a respite, a peaceful interlude in which he could recoup his strength and regain his equilibrium. He yearned for a comfortable milieu wherein he might again bask in the glory and respect that he had grown accustomed to in the decades after the war. New military laurels were impossible; however, a revival of his political career seemed within reach. Thus, weary from his years of battle in the boardrooms of New York and the courts of Florida, Gordon limped home to Georgia. Bowed but not beaten, he prepared to enter the familiar waters of Georgia politics once again. Perhaps they would provide him with the stability he desperately needed and now sought.

44. Raymond B. Nixon, *Henry W. Grady: Spokesman of the New South* (New York, 1943), 226.

# XIII · Governor of Georgia

Prospects for Gordon's immediate reentry into Georgia politics did not appear particularly promising. Although he received occasional mention as a possible successor to Governor Henry D. McDaniel, few Georgians considered him a serious candidate. T. J. Simmons and Augustus O. Bacon, who lived in Macon, were the two names most frequently bantered about, with the latter, the former speaker of the Georgia House, having a decided advantage. Since his unsuccessful bid for governor in 1883, Bacon had established an extensive machine with some fifteen hundred former members of the Georgia legislature actively working on his behalf throughout the state. Given his strength among county political leaders, Bacon appeared to have the nomination secured. But once again, as he had in 1880, Gordon was about to shatter Georgia's political calm. With the able assistance and brilliant guidance of Henry W. Grady, Gordon set out to capture the governorship of Georgia.[1]

In the 1880s, Grady had devoted his immense talent and energy to centralizing the economic and political power of the state in Atlanta. He had steadfastly resisted all challenges to the capital city's dominance from other Georgia cities, but now, in 1886, he faced a serious threat from Macon with the imminent election of Bacon. Although most observers considered Gordon's nomination "a forlorn hope," Grady thought he had a "sure-fire plan" to elect the general and keep

1. Atlanta *Constitution*, March 14, 28, April 6, 9, 19, 1886; James Gaston Towery, "The Georgia Gubernatorial Campaign of 1886" (M.A. thesis, Emory University, 1945), 1–5; Raymond B. Nixon, *Henry W. Grady: Spokesman of the New South* (New York, 1943), 225–26; Judson Clements Ward, Jr., "Georgia Under the Bourbon Democrats, 1872–1890" (Ph.D. dissertation, University of North Carolina, 1947), 177–78.

the city of Macon from claiming the governorship. Even so, numerous problems faced the young managing editor of the *Constitution*. He had to place his candidate in the limelight immediately and find a means to keep Bacon from winning the nomination before a Gordon organization and the general's natural strengths could be developed. In order to have any chance whatsoever in the upcoming campaign, it was absolutely imperative that Gordon recapture the political prominence he had willingly foresaken almost six years earlier. Gordon needed a vehicle to reawaken the tender, bittersweet memories of the Confederacy; he needed an event or action that would allow him to capitalize again on the reputation he had gained as a soldier. Gordon and Grady found such a vehicle ready-made for their purposes in the upcoming tour of the former president of the Confederacy.[2]

The scheme centered around the May 1 unveiling and dedication of a statue of Benjamin H. Hill in Atlanta. Gordon had already accepted an invitation to deliver, in late April, the major address at the laying of the cornerstone of a Montgomery monument to honor the Confederate war dead of Alabama. Jefferson Davis would also attend the ceremonies and speak briefly. Upon learning of Davis' journey to Montgomery, Grady persuaded the B. H. Hill Monument Commission to invite the Mississippian to continue his trip on to Atlanta and participate in the Hill festivities as an honored guest. Davis' acceptance of this invitation undoubtedly thrilled Gordon and Grady. Fully cognizant of the depth of Georgians' emotional attachment to the "dear old Confederacy," Grady envisioned the former president acting as a magnet, drawing countless Confederate veterans to Atlanta to see and hear their former leader. He would not play a prominent role in the Atlanta dedication, but Davis would naturally serve as the center of attention. Gordon's mere presence at the side of his now enfeebled chieftain would warm the hearts of most Georgians, and certainly rekindle old fires in those of the veterans. As Grady's biographer noted, "[T]hose veterans could determine the outcome of any political battle in Georgia."[3]

2. Harold E. Davis, "Henry W. Grady, Master of the Atlanta Ring—1880–1886," *Georgia Historical Quarterly*, LXIX (Spring, 1985), 1–38; Walter G. Cooper, *Official History of Fulton County* (1934; rpr. Spartanburg, S.C., 1978), 833; Nixon, *Grady*, 226.

3. Cooper, *History of Fulton County*, 833; Nixon, *Grady*, 226; Dunbar Rowland (ed.), *Jefferson Davis, Constitutionalist: His Letters, Papers and Speeches* (10 vols.; Jackson, Miss., 1923), IX, 409, 412–13; Atlanta *Constitution*, March 28, 1886; address of Major R. J. Guinn, in *Editor's Forum*, VIII (July, 1936), 7–8.

The ceremonies in Montgomery unquestionably bolstered the newspaperman's confidence. In order to guarantee full and colorful coverage, he had sent one of his best reporters to the Alabama capital, and Grady himself supplemented these accounts with personal reports. The receptions for both Gordon and Davis were overwhelming, as thousands of southerners descended upon the first capital of the Confederacy to recapture a piece of their past. Gordon's dedicatory speech focused upon the valor, courage, and devotion of the southern soldiery. After briefly recounting the North's innumerable advantages in the war, he asked how southerners—those of the same race and common ancestry as their foes—could have resisted so doggedly in the face of such odds. He concluded that "the great, distinctive, primal thought that moved, dominated and inspired the southern people . . . [was] the law of self defense." For Gordon, it was this "one controlling, all pervading thought" that served as "the tower of her amazing strength." As he usually did in similar laudatory addresses, Gordon closed on a nationalistic note, by appealing to his listeners to "let your fidelity to the whole country be as conspicuous in peace as was your devotion to the south during devastating war." That evening, after the ceremonies, Gordon renewed friendships with his former comrades of the 6th Alabama, many of whom he had not seen in years. It was a touching occasion, one that certainly provided a hint of what was to come in Atlanta.[4]

The following day, Gordon, along with members of the monument committee, rode with Davis on the train to the Georgia capital. At numerous stops along the way, both in Alabama and Georgia, adoring crowds turned out to catch a glimpse of their heroes and coax them to speak. Davis, impaired by old age and physical infirmities and exhausted by the excitement in Montgomery, was physically unable to honor the repeated requests. At Opelika, Davis finally heeded Gordon's warnings against overexerting himself. He placed his hand upon the Georgian's shoulder and declared, "This is my Aaron; let him speak for me." From that point on, Gordon spoke in place of the man he reverently styled "this dear old chief of ours." He explained that the former president's "heart, as well as his tongue, is full of eloquence, but his years are almost gone, and it is enough for us to look upon his face." Even after their arrival in Atlanta that evening,

4. Atlanta *Constitution*, April 28–30, 1886; Nixon, *Grady*, 227; Ward, "Georgia Under the Bourbons," 180.

Gordon continued to speak on behalf of Davis, excusing the latter's fatigue and expressing his gratitude for the overwhelming welcome.[5]

Nearly 100,000 spectators gathered in Atlanta for the May 1 dedication ceremonies. Grady had the *Constitution* publish a special "Davis Issue" on April 25, recalling "The Days of '61," and he took every other opportunity to whip up enthusiasm. Throughout the morning and afternoon, Gordon maintained a relatively low profile, since he had no direct role in the unveiling exercises. Grady, who presided as master of ceremonies, Davis, and J. C. C. Black shared the day's spotlight. Grady had made sure that the dedication retained "an appropriate non-political atmosphere" by selecting Black, a leading supporter of Bacon, as the principal orator. Despite frequent calls from the overflowing crowd for him to speak, Gordon "could not be found" because he was "lost" among his former comrades, with whom he had chosen to march. In truth, the proper moment to usher Gordon onto center stage had not yet arrived.[6]

But later in the day, with veterans milling about the Kimball House, a hotel long recognized as "the political center and beehive of Georgia," Gordon's time was at hand. Colonel Melville Dwinell of Rome, a friend and former employer of Grady, climbed on a chair on the balcony overlooking the main lobby. He gained the attention of the crowd below and proposed that Gordon deliver an address that night. Immediately, a wild cry arose from the lobby, "Gordon! Gordon for Governor!" Almost "magically," Gordon appeared on the balcony. Although he declined to speak that evening, he tenderly informed the enthusiastic throng, "This is the happiest day of my life. My heart is full and it is all yours." Gordon had barely retreated from the frenzied crowd at the hotel when angry Bacon supporters vocally protested what they perceived as the politicalization of the dedication ceremony. However, the tumult reigning after Gordon's brief appearance drowned out their protests. Excitement quickly spread from the hotel into the streets of Atlanta, leaving little doubt that Gordon would soon enter the gubernatorial race. Indeed, Grady's skillful strategic use of the veterans had been so successful that the newspaperman boasted to a friend, "Confederate money will be good before midnight!" The fire set by Grady had begun to blaze.[7]

5. Atlanta *Constitution*, May 1, 1886; Nixon, *Grady*, 227–28.
6. Nixon, *Grady*, 227–29; Atlanta *Constitution*, May 2, 1886.
7. Nixon, *Grady*, 229–30; Cooper, *History of Fulton County*, 833–34; Atlanta *Constitution*, May 2, 1886, May 23, 1921.

His editorial the next morning in the *Constitution* called for Gordon's nomination for governor. Speculation about when he would officially enter the race abounded, but Gordon did not formally announce his candidacy until nearly a week later. After the Hill dedication ceremonies, Davis, again in the company of the Georgian, traveled to Savannah to review the troops of the Chatham Artillery. There Gordon told a reporter that he would become a candidate because the "pressure from all parts of the state urging me to run is so great that I do not see how I can resist it." Finally, in a May 8 letter to the people of Georgia, Gordon announced his candidacy for the office of governor. He related that "somber thought and full consideration" and the increasing evidence of widespread support among the people "profoundly stirred my heart and satisfied me of my duty." As if to anticipate the bitter assault upon his character and integrity that would mark the ensuing campaign, he declared, "[I]f the life I have led for more than half a century . . . is not a sufficient answer to my enemies, who are enemies without cause or excuse, no reply from me would satisfy them." He was in the race and would make every effort to speak in as many counties as possible.[8]

Even before Gordon officially announced his candidacy, charges were circulating that Davis' tour "was but a means of furthering General Gordon's political claims." The Atlanta *Constitution* emphatically denied such assertions, maintaining that Gordon had been selected to speak in Alabama by men unassociated with Georgia politics. Grady minimized his manipulation of May 1 affairs by contending that Gordon had refrained from participating in the official Hill Monument ceremonies for fear that he might detract from "the declared purpose of the day." In fact, claimed the *Constitution*, if there was any blame to be attached to Gordon's advancement, it had to rest upon the people themselves, for calling him to the fore. If it was "the revival of memories" that elevated Gordon to political prominence, then the real cause went back much further than just the Montgomery or Atlanta ceremonies. "If the popular heart kindled into applause whenever his scarred face was shown or his name mentioned, the cause is to be found in the popular heart. The people speak when they feel like speaking, and they are responsible to themselves for what they do." Thus, according to the *Constitution*, Gordon merely exercised "the indisputable right" of any citizen to answer the summons of the people.[9]

8. Cooper, *History of Fulton County*, 834; Atlanta *Constitution*, May 3, 7–9, 1886.
9. Atlanta *Constitution*, May 7, 9, 1886.

The *Constitution*'s protests that neither Grady nor anyone else had schemed to use the Davis tour for Gordon's political benefit have a hollow ring to them. The skillful manner in which Gordon emerged as a candidate suggests the guidance of the same master manipulator who carefully orchestrated Gordon's resignation in 1880. Accurately perceiving the political capital to be gained by a rekindling of the passions stirred by Davis' journey from the Mississippi coast, Grady constantly kept his man in the right place at the right time. Gordon's intimate association with Davis on the train ride through Alabama and Georgia, as well as their appearance together in Atlanta and Savannah, allowed him to reap benefits from remembrances of the Confederacy. Yet, by keeping Gordon at a distance from the actual Atlanta ceremonies and having an active Bacon supporter as the primary orator, Grady softened later charges that the tour and dedication were used for political purposes. The veterans' demand for Gordon at the Kimball House, though carefully contrived, took on the appearance of a spontaneous call from the people. The deft handling of Gordon's dramatic move back into Georgia politics in late April and early May evinces the brilliant manipulation present in so many of Grady's dealings.

Gordon's participation in the Davis tour was a calculated means of reawakening old memories and of tapping the wellspring of Confederate patriotism still running deep in the South. It can be viewed as the first phase of the plan to elect the general; the second phase followed quickly on its heels. The May 9 edition of the Atlanta *Constitution*, which printed Gordon's letter announcing his candidacy, also carried a letter from Gordon to Bacon and all other candidates. In it, Gordon asked his opponents to join with him in requesting that the Democratic State Executive Committee recommend primary elections in every county "in order that the will of the people may be surely ascertained." This appeal for direct primaries was a crucial tactic in Gordon's quest for the gubernatorial nomination. Although the idea of holding primaries instead of traditional courthouse meetings was, as one student of the contest noted, "entirely nonexistent before Gordon entered the campaign, it was now a vital issue that was to play an important part in the final results of the campaign."[10]

The call for primary elections in the counties served a multitude of

10. *Ibid.*, May 9, 1886; Ward, "Georgia Under the Bourbons," 182; Nixon, *Grady*, 230–31; Towery, "Georgia Gubernatorial Campaign," 26. See Towery, "Georgia Gubernatorial Campaign," Ch. II, "Primaries versus Courthouse Meetings," for a thorough discussion of this issue.

purposes. First and foremost, it helped forestall the delegate selection process. Since some counties, employing courthouse meetings, had already chosen delegates pledged to Bacon, Gordon's people had to work quickly. By interjecting popular primaries into the campaign, the Gordon forces sought to buy the time necessary to organize and combat Bacon's already established organization. Moreover, if the contest were moved out onto the hustings, Gordon's oratorical ability and his personal magnetism could be fully employed. Although "deeply pious, hard working, highly respected, and successful," Bacon lacked the warmth and the heroic stature that Gordon so effectively exuded whenever he faced an audience. On the stump, Gordon's fiery, enthusiastic appeals to the jury would invariably overshadow Bacon's cold, logical statements to the court. The general's voice, remembered one chronicler, "rang like a clarion; and, when he raised it to the highest pitch, it seemed to wake up all the echoes of the forest." Similarly, Gordon's scarred face vividly reminded his listeners that he had fought and bled for Georgia and the South. The deep, noticeable scar on his left cheek from his wound at the Bloody Lane served as a mark of distinction that he bore proudly. Robert Toombs, a combative Georgia political leader who often clashed with Gordon, cynically proclaimed "that if Gordon's scar was somewhere else than on his face he would be a failure as a politician." Referred to by contemporaries as "the dimple of Antietam," "the signet-stamp of gallantry," "the most ornate jewel" and "the handsomest feature of his manly face," Gordon's scar obviously stirred emotions in his audiences. If Gordon was afforded the opportunity to showcase his eloquence and capitalize on his superb war record, Bacon would be in trouble.[11]

As a result, Bacon, already stung by Gordon's sudden entry into what heretofore had not been considered much of a race, refused to accede to Gordon's call for primaries. In his public letter of refusal, Bacon explained that he believed Georgia voters themselves "can

11. Nixon, *Grady*, 231; Ward, "Georgia Under the Bourbons," 178, 182–83; Towery, "Georgia Gubernatorial Campaign," 24, 27–28, 79–81; Isaac W. Avery, *History of the State of Georgia From 1850 to 1881* (New York, 1881), 391; Lucian Lamar Knight, *Reminiscences of Famous Georgians* (2 vols.; Atlanta, 1907–1908), II, 418–19; Morris Schaff, *The Sunset of the Confederacy* (Boston, 1912), 57; *Minutes of the Annual Meetings and Reunions of the United Confederate Veterans*, 1892, p. 108; Atlanta *Constitution*, February 26, 1869; John S. Wise, "Two Great Confederates. General John B. Gordon and General James Longstreet: Characterizations By a Friend of Both," *American Monthly Review of Reviews*, XXIX (February, 1904), 207.

determine better than the Executive Committee, or perhaps better than you or myself, the mode best suited to the situation of their several communities." Courthouse meetings that had been good enough in the past were still eminently satisfactory for Bacon. Although he may have been genuinely concerned with each county's right to select its delegates by whatever method it chose, Bacon unquestionably saw through the opposition's strategy—a strategy that banked on the primaries as the best way to offset Bacon's established relationship with county political leaders. The dilemma facing him, however, was how to oppose the primary elections without lending credence to the Gordon camp's charges that he was resisting the will of the people. It proved a difficult task; for once popular primaries emerged as a major issue, Bacon's carefully cultivated strength began to dissipate. Thus, the campaign evolved into a race in which Bacon worked to speed up the selection of delegates while Gordon struggled to delay the voting until he could visit with and speak to the people in the various counties.[12]

Gordon and his supporters were quick to exploit Bacon's dilemma. He and the *Constitution* stressed, almost *ad nauseam*, that the request for primaries asked for nothing more than that "the democratic voters of the state be allowed to express their opinions through the ballot box." While a paper supporting Bacon likened primary elections to the opening of Pandora's box, the *Constitution* confidently asserted that Gordon had nothing to fear in an open, fair fight. Rarely a day passed in May, 1886, that the *Constitution* did not editorialize upon the issue of primaries and the wisdom of giving the people a voice in the selection of their officials. Grady relentlessly hammered away, reminding his readers that only "conspirators and wire-pullers," who based their hopes "on little courthouse meetings and back room caucuses," sought to avoid the ballot box. When opponents renewed old charges accusing Gordon of being a candidate of the "Atlanta ring," Gordon supporters enjoyed a field day. They dismissed the accusations and declared there was "but one 'ring' in Georgia politics, and that is the little 'ring' at Macon"—the same one that had been laboring to elect Bacon for six years and was now desperately "muzzling the voices of the people with the hands of politicians." Despite the rhetoric of the campaign, most Georgians

---

12. Atlanta *Constitution*, May 11, 1886; Towery, "Georgia Gubernatorial Campaign," 32–36, 101–102.

probably concurred with the Fort Gaines *Tribune's* assessment that "politics is nothing but a game of 'rings' anyway." For in Georgia at this time, two strong machines were indeed locked in combat. Nevertheless, Gordon profited from Bacon's apparent reluctance to allow the people to express themselves directly through primary elections.[13]

In addition to calling for primaries, Gordon and his lieutenants employed virtually every means at their disposal to erect a statewide organization as quickly as possible. After Gordon officially entered the race, Grady assumed personal command of the campaign and established campaign headquarters in a large storeroom near the offices of the *Constitution*. Although he professed in his editorials "to furnish the news fully, fairly and promptly," Grady unmistakably placed the *Constitution* squarely behind the general. The editor's tactics were varied and often innovative. Early on, he mailed lithographed letters to all identifiable Georgia voters; these facsimile letters bore Gordon's signature, and since few Georgians were acquainted with the lithographic process, many believed they had actually received a personal message from Gordon himself.[14]

The general and Grady also sent personal letters to influential Georgians soliciting support and urging prompt action. "The campaign before us is so short," wrote Gordon, "that I am compelled to rely largely on the organization of my friends in the counties which I am unable to reach. . . . My competitor has a compact and trained following in every section. This must be met immediately by similar organization of my friends." Grady, in a letter to Colonel W. H. Harrison, wrote, "I know that you can do him [Gordon] a great deal of good if you will, and you may rest assured it will not hurt you to do it. . . . Help him out . . . and the reward of the just will be yours." In addition to these mailings, Grady dispatched trusted assistants to critical counties prior to the selection of delegates. On one occasion, an aide carried two notes with him, one for each of the county's leading politicians. Grady's instructions were both succinct and pointed: "If you find that No. 1 is for Gordon, give him the note. Otherwise, see No. 2. He's bound to be against No. 1."[15]

13. Atlanta *Constitution*, May 18, 9, 12, 14, 30, 1886; Fort Gaines *Tribune*, quoted *ibid.*, May 18, 1886.

14. Nixon, *Grady*, 231, 234; Atlanta *Constitution*, May 9, 1886; Towery, "Georgia Gubernatorial Campaign," 28–29, 72–73.

15. Cooper, *History of Fulton County*, 834; Nixon, *Grady*, 231–32; H. W. Grady to Colonel W. H. Harrison, May 11, 1886, in Henry Woodfin Grady Papers, Records of the

These devices were skillfully employed, but the cornerstone of the Gordon-Grady strategy lay in the appeal of Gordon's glorious war record. Unquestionably, Grady succeeded in igniting old passions with the Montgomery ceremonies and Jefferson Davis' visit to Georgia. Now that these memories had been reawakened, it was time to use them on behalf of the Hero of Appomattox. And it would be the old soldiers, the veterans who had followed Gordon into battle so often, that would serve the general again. They would act as Gordon's vanguard to victory. Grady sent word to Gordon supporters in the individual counties "to station *one-armed* or *one-legged* Confederate veterans at all the crossroads to enlist the attendance of other veterans in the county at a caucus one hour before the convention opened." If this informal meeting determined that the county convention would probably select Gordon, the veterans were to proceed with the regular convention. But if, on the other hand, the Gordonites believed Bacon supporters would dominate, the old soldiers were instructed to disrupt the courthouse meeting, demand a primary, and allow Gordon time enough to canvass the county. In Americus, a wagonload of one-legged Confederate veterans appeared at a Gordon rally with a banner, "One Leg only, but Will Get There All the Same." Throughout the campaign, at all political gatherings, whenever Gordon spoke, maimed veterans, war widows, and orphans invariably occupied conspicuous positions. Grady's biographer stated that this tactic "created the impression that the former Confederates were unanimously behind their hero." Although it is impossible to document, it seems certain that the overwhelming majority of veterans were solidly behind Gordon. Emotional appeals to memories of the Confederacy and wartime experiences were extraordinarily powerful devices. As an unhappy Bacon was soon to discover, a reputation gained on the battlefield was rarely lost in politics or business.[16]

Gordon and Bacon discussed few substantive issues during the course of the campaign. Questions concerning Georgia's Railroad Commission, the proposed lease or sale of the state-owned Western and Atlantic Railroad, and the fate of the state's convict lease system were occasionally raised, but these issues did not provide the central

---

Department of Archives and History, Record Group 4, File II, GDAH; John B. Gordon to [unknown], May 15, 1886, in John Brown Gordon Papers, Emory.
16. Nixon, *Grady*, 232; Towery, "Georgia Gubernatorial Campaign," 81–82; Atlanta *Constitution*, May 13, 1886.

278 · JOHN BROWN GORDON

focus of the contest. Beyond the debate over the advisability of primaries, the campaign revolved around the effort of the Bacon camp to "prove that General Gordon had been such a complete failure in both public and private life" that he was unworthy of Georgians' trust as governor. Bacon and his followers inaugurated and sustained a vicious assault upon Gordon's honesty, integrity, and ability, as can be seen in virtually any Georgia newspaper between May and July, 1886. His vilification of his opponent dictated the tone of the campaign and forced Gordon to answer Bacon's charges by retaliating in kind.[17]

Nowhere was this more evident than at the "joint discussions" between the two candidates in late May. Seeking, as he put it, "the opportunity of meeting the people face to face and of giving them the fullest information on all the issues involved in the campaign," Bacon proposed that a speaking tour be arranged. Gordon accepted the proposal and a series of joint appearances began at Eatonton on May 17. Meetings at Sparta, Augusta, Lexington, Greensboro, and Conyers took place successively on the next five days.[18] But Bacon's supporters became so bitterly abusive of Gordon that after these six were held, the state Democratic committee reluctantly recommended a cessation. Nevertheless, Bacon and his followers continued to vilify the general with unrelenting fury. Old charges that Gordon had been a paid lackey of the railroad interests and that he had betrayed Georgians' trust by resigning his Senate post again surfaced. Similarly, Gordon's affiliation with the Atlanta ring and his involvement in the convict lease system served as major points of criticism. Gordon's opponents, as if to provide a capstone for their assaults, also pounded away at his abysmal business record and questioned whether a man of such dubious financial ability could be entrusted with Georgia's fiscal well-being. Whatever validity these charges may have possessed was obscured and all but eviscerated by the malicious tone of this assault upon the most popular man in all of Georgia.[19]

Popular though he was, Gordon certainly did not enjoy the admiration of all Georgians. Until late in the campaign, Grady's *Consti-*

17. Towery, "Georgia Gubernatorial Campaign," 8–11, 42.
18. Although the organized tour included only these six meetings, Gordon and Bacon also met at Leesburg, Cuthbert, and Albany prior to Eatonton. Atlanta *Constitution*, May 15–17, 1886.
19. *Ibid.*, May 11, 19–23, 1886; Ward, "Georgia Under the Bourbons," 184–85; Towery, "Georgia Gubernatorial Campaign," 42, 69–72.

*tution* was the only major daily active in his support. Patrick Walsh and J. F. Hanson, editors of the Augusta *Chronicle* and the Macon *Telegraph*, respectively, violently assailed Gordon. Their opposition to the "Atlanta ringster," however, paled in comparison with that of Gordon's most persistent nemeses, the Feltons. Dr. and Mrs. Felton renewed their war upon "the Artful Dodger" with a vindictiveness that exceeded even Bacon's. Writing under the pen name "Plain Talk," Mrs. Felton sent letters and articles to numerous newspapers and even published these exposés in a pamphlet, *General J. B. Gordon as a Financier and Statesman*. She reveled in referring to her hated foe as "a fourth rate lawyer" and "a political gymnast." And in response to the Gordon camp's evocation of his martial glory, or as she styled it, "military slush joined to political gush," she took great pains to point out to Georgians that they were electing a governor, not a general. Whenever campaigning for Bacon, Dr. Felton matched his wife's undying enmity and flatly declared he would not support Gordon for governor even if he won the Democratic nomination. Dr. and Mrs. Felton's barbs unquestionably irritated their enemies and delighted their allies, but, as her biographer concluded, "they won few votes for Bacon among the Veterans, or among their sons reared in the Confederate tradition." In relying upon charater assasination, Bacon and his supporters were sowing an evil seed that would soon bear a bitter fruit.[20]

On the stump and in print, Gordon and Grady met the opposition's savage thrusts and repelled them with the skill of master duelists.[21] Gordon dismissed charges that he had used the Senate to enrich himself as ludicrous and maintained that he left Washington poorer than

20. Towery, "Georgia Gubernatorial Campaign," 82–88; John E. Talmadge, *Rebecca Latimer Felton: Nine Stormy Decades* (Athens, Ga., 1966), 82–85; Atlanta *Constitution*, June 4, 1886; Mrs. William H. Felton, *My Memoirs of Georgia Politics* (Atlanta, 1911), 625, chapter "The Gordon-Bacon Campaign," *passim*. Both the Doctor William Harrell Felton and Mrs. Rebecca A. Latimer Felton Collection and the Rebecca Latimer Felton Collection, UGA, contain numerous anti-Gordon letters written in May and June, 1886, that concern the gubernatorial campaign. See particularly T. J. Simmons to W. H. Felton, June 28, 1886, A. O. Bacon to W. H. Felton, May 15, 1886, M. R. Tunno to W. H. Felton, July 26, 1886, all in Dr. and Mrs. Felton Collection; D. B. Harrell to W. H. Felton, May 24, 1886, in R. L. Felton Collection; Felton, *Memoirs*, 631–33; and Mrs. William H. Felton [Plain Talk], *Gen. J. B. Gordon as Financier and Statesman* (Macon, 1886), a pamphlet found in her collection.

21. Gordon and Grady were ably assisted by a number of fine speakers. Former governor James M. Smith, Dupont Guerry, Colonel Albert Cox, and Colonel W. C. Glenn all spoke effectively and convincingly in the general's behalf. Towery, "Georgia Gubernatorial Campaign," 88–89.

he was when he had arrived. He reiterated that he resigned his office when he was satisfied that his mission there had been accomplished and then continued his service to the state after entering the railroad business. Whenever his departure from the Senate came up, Gordon masterfully turned the resignation controversy back upon his opponent. He slyly inquired about Bacon's resignation from active duty in the Confederate army in 1862, owing to illness, and effectively contrasted their war records, when he asked, "[W]here was this gentleman who argues that I laid down office for personal gain? Where was he from '62 to '65?" The answer was obvious: while Gordon had braved the fire of battle, Bacon had remained safe and secure behind the lines, serving in the commissary. In the same manner, the general rebuffed "ring" charges by relying on his support of and Bacon's opposition to primaries as sufficient evidence of who was truly a ring candidate. Thus, the resort to abusive character assassination— though many of Bacon's charges had some basis in fact—boomeranged on him.[22]

Gordon responded with similar effect to questions about his record as a convict lessee and as a remarkably unsuccessful businessman. He freely admitted his previous involvement with the system of convict labor. He explained that the state's impoverishment at the war's end made the leasing of prisoners for labor "a valuable temporary expedient to care for these men until the white voters of Georgia" could regain control of their own affairs. Gordon did not apologize for leasing convicts because he "believed it to be the best system to use at the time." However, "when the usefulness of the system had passed I sought to end my connections with the lessee interests, and was finally able to do so" legally by 1883. Gordon contended that the system had served a vital purpose; but now that its "baneful effects" outweighed any positive benefits, he promised to work toward its abolition if elected. Gordon discussed his well-chronicled failure as a businessman with a forthrightness that silenced many of his critics. In one speech, he frankly declared, "It is true that nearly all of the business enterprises with which I was connected failed for one reason or another, but I assure you I was not the monetary beneficiary of any

22. Ibid., 44–48, 60–64; Atlanta Constitution, May 13, 14, 20, 31, 1886. Although these specific dates have been cited, almost every issue of the Constitution in May and early June boldly presented the general's arguments in coverage of Gordon's speaking engagements, in Grady's pointed editorials, and particularly in the reporting of the "joint discussions." Atlanta Constitution, May 19–23, 1886.

of these failures." Gordon never squarely addressed the most important consideration—whether he was capable of managing the state's finances prudently—but few seemed to notice. Gordon evidently managed to arrest fears concerning his financial responsibility; by the end of the campaign, most Georgia Democrats found his answers and explanations satisfactory.[23]

In an effort to present his case to the people, Gordon spoke in almost every county in Georgia during the campaign. Except in hotbeds of Bacon support, the general successfully blunted his opponent's criticisms, thereby overcoming Bacon's early lead and organizational advantages. Following the first major round of delegate selections in early June, Gordon had drawn almost even. Later in the month, after another large number of counties voted, he took the lead and began pulling away, so that by early July, the campaign, for all intents and purposes, was over. When the state convention assembled on July 28 in Atlanta, Gordon secured the necessary majority on the first ballot, garnering 252 votes to Bacon's 70. A move to make his nomination unanimous proved unsuccessful, but Gordon, nonetheless, amassed 322 of the 332 votes cast and thus became the Democratic nominee. In a state where "nomination had become tantamount to election," there was no doubt Gordon would be Georgia's next governor. Gordon ran unopposed in the October general election.[24]

Gordon's remarkable triumph in 1886 was the result of the combined efforts of Gordon and Grady. Together they charted a bold course, and together they steered the campaign to victory. Several years later, the Atlanta *Constitution* admitted as much when assessing Gordon's gubernatorial triumph: "[T]he *Constitution*, with the mighty arm of Henry Grady, was put under his [Gordon's] shoulder and stood by him, at the sacrifice of all else in the way, until his election. No such contest was ever seen in Georgia, and no such master hand as that of Grady ever piloted a canvass as he conducted that." The spectacular emergence of Gordon as a candidate, the skillful use of the primary-election issue, and the effective utilization of

23. Towery, "Georgia Gubernatorial Campaign," 53–57, 64–67; Atlanta *Constitution*, May 12, 21, June 6, 24, 1886; Marietta *Journal*, July 18, 1886, quoted in Towery, "Georgia Gubernatorial Campaign," 66. See also Atlanta *Constitution*, May–July, 1886, *passim*.

24. Towery, "Georgia Gubernatorial Campaign," 36, 76–79, 90–97; Atlanta *Constitution*, July 7, 29, October 6, 7, 1886; Ward, "Georgia Under the Bourbons," 188; *Georgia House Journal*, 1886, p. 46; *Georgia Senate Journal*, 1886, p. 49.

Gordon's greatest strengths all provide evidence of careful planning on the part of the general and the journalist. Gordon's personal magnetism and his natural speaking ability allowed him to harness the powerful emotional commitment to the Confederacy. Gordon became the "Very Embodiment of the Lost Cause" for many Georgians, and especially for veterans. As a result, Bacon's campaign of slander, as a student of the contest concluded, "proved an utter failure and served only to arouse in the supporters of Gordon a determination to swing the tide of victory for their candidate." Bacon's failure to destroy Georgians' faith in the integrity and honesty of Gordon actually gained the general even greater support. The Atlanta *Evening Capitol* echoed this sentiment when it declared that Gordon's "whole life gives the denial to such a charge, and the accusation will continue to rally, as it has drawn to him, the masses of people in its indignant repudiation." A particularly succinct and astute analysis of the campaign came from the Savannah *Morning News*: "[T]he skill of his managers, the abuse heaped upon him by his opponents and, more than all, his record as a soldier have given General Gordon the victory." Gordon was and would remain the most popular man in Georgia. His banner, once darkened by the smoke of battle, could not be tarnished by political rhetoric.[25]

Gordon's inauguration took place on November 9, 1886, in a light rain at the State Capitol in Atlanta. In his brief inaugural address, Gordon concentrated on what he considered at that time the greatest danger facing Georgia and all other states. He feared the states' steady loss of "constitutional vigor or power of self-preservation . . . by gradual accretions to federal power and imperceptible absorption of state functions." This distressing trend toward centralization had to be reversed because, he believed, the "freest government is that which is not controlled by homogeneous communities; and the strongest government for a country like ours is that which devolves upon the states the largest responsibilities." In addition to this re-echoing of Jeffersonianism, Gordon urged his fellow Georgians to develop their industrial concerns, to promote agriculture, and to make broad and practical education "an object of universal concern." The gala festivities surrounding Gordon's induction into office re-

---

25. Towery, "Georgia Gubernatorial Campaign," 98–99, 101–102; Nixon, *Grady*, 234–35; Savannah *Morning News*, July 8, 1886, quoted in Ward, "Georgia Under the Bourbons," 187; Atlanta *Evening Capitol*, June 29, 1886; Atlanta *Constitution*, May 23, June 12, November 10, 1886, November 16, 1890.

sumed after his speech and culminated with a banquet and military ball that evening. Former president Rutherford B. Hayes, attending the inauguration of the southerner who had so often aided his administration, recorded the prevailing excitement: *"Balls, parties, processions. A wide-awake time indeed."*[26]

Gordon's elevation to chief executive of Georgia represented the height of the Bourbon Triumvirate's rule of Georgia. With Colquitt and Joe Brown in the United States Senate and Gordon in the governor's mansion, the three most powerful positions in Georgia politics were securely in the hands of the leading Conservative Democrats. Independentism, which had been in decline in Georgia since the early 1880s, was for all intents and purposes dead as a significant political force. The political calm that had existed in Georgia prior to Gordon's dramatic reentry in May, 1886, once again settled over the state. To be sure, protests against single-party control and opposition to the policies of the triumvirate were not completely silenced. Disputes over local issues persisted and the developing Farmers' Alliance movement continually gained strength in the second half of the 1880s; but, as a historian of this period concluded, none of these "local skirmishes" or "family quarrels . . . was sufficient to ruffle the placidity of the Bourbon control." Relative peace prevailed in Georgia during Gordon's tenure.[27]

The new governor's first official act—his authorization of a one hundred dollar warrant for a Confederate soldier who had lost a leg—seemed particularly appropriate as a symbolic gesture because the veterans had played such a prominent role in his gubernatorial victory. The general declared that "he was glad his entry into office had been signalized by an act in the interest of one of them." On December 1, 1886, Gordon sent a special message to the General Assembly in which he considered the state's penitentiary system and agricultural interests. He briefly discussed the major criticisms of the convict lease system—probably the most troublesome being its placing "pecuniary interests in conflict with humanity"—but averred that they were not grave enough to demand wholesale change. Rather

26. Atlanta *Constitution*, November 10, 1886; Hugh H. Gordon to Charles Herbst, November 15, 1886, in John B. Gordon Collection, Kentucky Historical Society, Frankfort; Charles Richard Williams (ed.), *Diary and Letters of Rutherford B. Hayes* (5 vols.; Columbus, Ohio 1922–26), IV, 292.

27. Kenneth Coleman (ed.), *A History of Georgia* (Athens, 1977), 222; Ward, "Georgia Under the Bourbons," 189; Lewis N. Wynne, "The Bourbon Triumvirate: A Reconsideration," *Atlanta Historical Journal*, XXIV (Summer, 1980), 39–40, 53.

than return to the costly old scheme of incarceration or use convicts
to improve state roads, Gordon proposed a plan which he thought
would both improve the penal system and possibly benefit Georgia's
agriculture. He called for the establishment of a state-controlled ex-
perimental farm that would be worked by thirty or forty convicts.
This minimal investment, he contended, would provide an excellent
laboratory for scientific experiments that individual farmers had neither the time nor the money to undertake. Moreover, his farm proposal would eliminate walled incarceration; confine convicts, yet
employ them where they would not compete with free labor; restore
control of prisoners to the state; and make the system self-sustaining
if not, in fact, profitable. Despite the apparent merits of Gordon's
plan, the General Assembly did not enact such a program.[28]

Within two weeks, however, Gordon delivered additional messages concerning the convict lease system: one to the House detailing
the history of the system; and another to the Senate providing requested information, as well as recommending "careful investiga-
tions" of convict camps and "sworn reports" by impartial observers.
This emphasis upon penal concerns early in his administration set
the tone for much of Gordon's first year in office. It was ironic that
Gordon, one of the original lessees of Penitentiary Company No. 2,
would devote so much attention to convict lease matters. Several
plans for reforming the system were presented and debated in the
legislature, but none attracted so much attention or interest as that
resulting from a special investigation conducted by Gordon in the fall
of 1887. After receiving two anonymous letters in late August that
charged Camp Bingham officers with dispensing cruel and inhumane
punishment, the governor sent the Principal Keeper of the Penitentiary, Colonel John R. Towers, and the Principal Physician, Dr. Willis
F. Westmoreland, to the Spalding County convict camp.[29]

During the preceding month, Gordon, acting on the recommenda-

28. Atlanta *Constitution*, November 11, 25, December 2, 1886; Minutes, December
1, 1886, in Records of the Executive Department, Record Group 1, November 1886–
November 1890, GDAH, hereinafter cited as Executive Minutes. See also *Georgia
Senate Journal*, 1886, pp. 215–21; and *Georgia House Journal*, 1886, pp. 296–302.

29. *Georgia House Journal*, 1886, pp. 412–16; *Georgia Senate Journal*, 1886, pp.
332–33; Executive Minutes, December 10, 15, 1886; Order Books, November 10, 1886,
in Records of the Executive Department, Record Group 1, November 1886–November
1890, in GDAH, hereinafter cited as Executive Order Books; Incoming Correspondence, December 15, 1886, in Records of the Executive Department, Record Group 1,
November 1886–November 1890, in GDAH; Atlanta *Constitution*, August 26, 1886.

tions of Towers and Westmoreland, had ordered that a camp in Richmond County be broken up unless certain evils were remedied. When one of the lessees complained, Gordon wrote a letter exonerating him of any personal culpability. More important, though, this letter clearly explained Gordon's perception of his responsibilities as chief executive. "So long as the present system of leasing out prisoners to individuals and corporations shall exist," he wrote, "all the protective agencies furnished by our laws must be supported and all the restraining regulations must be enforced by the Executive." In other words, he felt compelled not only to enforce court-determined penalties but to protect the convicts, as best he could, from excessive punishment or labor. Questions testing the strength of Gordon's dedication to this duty came to the fore even as he penned these words.[30]

In August, after receiving preliminary reports from Towers and Westmoreland that confirmed the existence of the filthy conditions of the camp and the brutal beating of four black convicts, Gordon removed Camp Bingham's whipping boss, C. C. Bingham. He issued a second executive order, instructing that legal prosecution of Bingham be initiated, that suits to recover damages for cruelty to the prisoners be brought against Company No. 2 and Company No. 3, and that both companies appear before him on September 1 "to show cause why their contracts with the state for the lease of convicts should not be annulled and cancelled." In addition, Gordon immediately sent a special observer to Spalding County to serve as a watchdog on his behalf. Having taken these actions, he informed a reporter that "I shall hold the strong arm of the state between the convicts and such treatment at any cost and at any hazard."[31]

Public hearings into the convict lease system began on September 1. Defense attorneys and skeptical opponents of the governor, particularly those associated with the Feltons, argued that Gordon's original connection with Company No. 2 disqualified him as the presiding officer. They contended that if the terms of his 1876 contract with the state still legally bound him in some manner, then Gordon as governor was in effect suing himself as an original leaseholder. These ob-

30. Executive Minutes, July 27, 1887; Governor's Letterbooks, August 13, 23, 1887, in Records of the Executive Department, Record Group 1, November 1886–November 1890, GDAH, hereinafter cited as Governor Gordon Letterbooks.
31. Incoming Correspondence, August 26, 1887; Executive Minutes, August 25, 31, 1887; Governor Gordon Letterbooks, August 25, 1887; Atlanta *Constitution*, August 26, 28, 1887.

286 · JOHN BROWN GORDON

jections were considered but dismissed by the attorney general, who, as chief law-enforcement officer of the state, attended all sessions and served as the governor's legal adviser. Thus, Gordon chaired this inquiry, which broadened far beyond the incidents at the two camps in the summer of 1887; it developed into the most thorough examination of Georgia's penal system ever conducted. With the state's reputation at stake and with the pecuniary interests of the lessees in jeopardy, Gordon devoted most of September to these questions of "utmost importance." Following final arguments by both sides in early October, Gordon adjourned the investigation, thanking all the participants and promising to deliver his verdict as soon as possible.[32]

Gordon did not render his judgment until November 8, 1887. A particularly difficult problem for him was what the state would do if he voided the leases and the prisoners were returned to its care. Funds necessary to provide for the convicts had not been appropriated, nor had provisions been made for entering into new contracts. And though closely counseled by the state attorney general, Gordon could not be absolutely certain that he even had the right to cancel the convict contracts. So despite evidence of periodic mistreatment and frequent overworking of prisoners, there simply did not seem to be a practicable way to nullify the leases. These considerations obviously influenced Gordon, because when he announced his decision, he attempted to steer a prudent course between appearing to condone the brutal actions of some camps and revoking outright the leases on state convicts. Gordon forcefully asserted that the governor did have the right to cancel the leases for any number of abuses, including unreasonable or oppressive labor, unauthorized subletting, and excessive brutality. Although he determined that the lessees of the penitentiary companies were not personally responsible for any misdeeds, they, nevertheless, were strictly accountable for the actions of their subordinates. Violations of the terms of their contracts and occasionally cruel and inhumane treatment of the prisoners had taken place, but Gordon concluded that such abuses were not of sufficient number or seriousness to justify rescinding the leases at present. Consequently, his only punishment of Company No. 2 and

32. Atlanta *Constitution*, September 2–October 6, 1887, *passim*. See also October 9, 1887; Ward, "Georgia Under the Bourbons," 428–29; Incoming Correspondence, undated, unsigned five-page letter stating Gordon must disqualify himself, [1886–1887?]; and Charles L. Bartlett to Mrs. Felton, December 4, 1886, in Dr. and Mrs. Felton Collection, UGA.

Company No. 3 was to fine each company $2,500 for cruelty. Despite his rather light sentence, Gordon threatened that future violations would result in much more stringent penalties, and perhaps even cancellation of their contracts.[33]

Gordon's decision unquestionably frustrated opponents of the convict lease system, but he did face a difficult dilemma. "The problem of disposing of convicts," observed a student of penology, "in such a way as to render them least troublesome and expensive to the government and, at the same time, insure them humane and proper treatment has always been a perplexing one." Abolition or wholesale reform of Georgia's established program was legally and practically almost impossible during Gordon's administration. The state had committed its convicts in binding leases until 1896 and, more important, had neither the plans nor the means for more conventional forms of incarceration. Nor was there any significant ground swell of public support for reformation of a system that had successfully and inexpensively kept undesirable elements away from society at large. Despite cries for more humane treatment of prisoners, few Georgians exhibited any concern whatsoever. In that sense, wrote one Georgia historian, Gordon's gubernatorial record, as it concerned the convict lease system, "was better than might have been expected from one who personally was a lessee of convicts and who so closely associated with the powerful group of men who dominated the penitentiary system."[34]

His decisions following this public investigation and his handling of convict matters throughout his four years as governor generally met with the approval of the public. He called for tighter state regulation of the system and more frequent visitation of the camps, and he repeatedly pleaded for the establishment of a pardon board. Even though a new commission specifically designed to handle pardons and commutations would both lighten the work load of the governor and ensure that each case would have a proper hearing, the General Assembly did not act upon Gordon's proposal. In fact, no major reforms were implemented during his governorship. Nevertheless, Gordon, in November, 1888, praised the operation of the penal sys-

33. Atlanta *Constitution*, November 9, 1887; Executive Minutes, November 8, 1887; Ward, "Georgia Under the Bourbons," 429–31.

34. A. Elizabeth Taylor, "The Origin and Development of the Convict Lease System in Georgia," *Georgia Historical Quarterly*, XXVI (June, 1942), 113; Ward, "Georgia Under the Bourbons," 431–32.

tem, particularly its decreased rates of crime, violence, and mortality. And when he left office two years later, Gordon described the Georgia Penitentiary as "superior in the care of the health, and morals and comfort of its inmates to any county chain-gang in the State of Georgia." Gordon may have been correct, and he probably did take pride in the manner in which he handled the state's convicts; but he could have done much more than he did. He failed to lead the state toward a new policy, and as a result, the convict lease system continued. It was, as one historian has styled it, "the blackest chapter in the record of the Bourbon regime in Georgia." The end of this brutal and inhumane practice lay twenty years in the future.[35]

The investigation into the convict lease system was one of the most spectacular official happenings of his governorship, yet Gordon's involvement with national politics had forced him to delay the announcement of his decision for over a month. In mid-October, President Grover Cleveland traveled to Atlanta, in part to visit the city's ambitious Piedmont Exposition. Because he was the "first democratic president that ever set foot on Georgia soil," his visit attracted as much attention as any event in recent years. Throughout the president's two-day stay, which included a seemingly endless series of receptions, parades, and dinners, Gordon rarely strayed far from Cleveland's side. The president had barely departed for Washington when Gordon himself ventured northward. Prominent Democrats in Ohio had long been beseeching Gordon to come to their state and speak to their citizens, but owing to his responsibilities, he had been forced to decline. However, the ending of the penal inquiry and the Ohioans' continued insistence finally persuaded him to answer the call of the Democracy.[36]

During the last week of October and the first week in November, Gordon spoke frequently to large audiences in the Buckeye State, especially in Cincinnati, Columbus, and Cleveland. Even before his arrival, Ohio Republicans, particularly Governor J. B. Foraker, assailed the southerner as a "kukluxer" who perpetuated the oppression of the black man in the South. Gordon was forced to devote much of his efforts to refuting charges of mistreatment of blacks and

35. Executive Minutes, July 7, November 8, 1887, November 7, 1888, November 8, 1890; Ward, "Georgia Under the Bourbons," 431–32. See also Incoming Correspondence, May 5, 1888, April 2, August 2, 1889.

36. Atlanta *Constitution*, October 16–20, 22, 1887; Sue Harper Mims Scrapbook, 1876–1887, in AHS; Allen Nevins, *Grover Cleveland: A Study in Courage* (New York, 1953), 319–23.

to repelling what he branded "unwarranted, ungracious and un-gentlemanly attacks upon my character." But primarily, he exhorted his listeners "to forego the passions of the past and unite in a common purpose to promote the prosperity and exalt the greatness of our country." Although enthusiastically received and widely praised, Gordon was unable to boost the Ohio Democracy to victory. The Republicans triumphed in the elections that took place shortly after his tour.[37]

In spite of the flurry of activity during his first year in office, Gordon's tenure as governor proved rather ordinary. Renominated in 1888, he won reelection for another two years, again without any Republican opposition. Although Gordon's biennial reports glow-ingly praised the prosperity of the time and cited impressive figures that seemed to indicate tremendous material and social advance-ment for the state, very little changed in Georgia between 1886 and 1890. Indeed, it is difficult to say much about Gordon's governorship because little of importance occurred during his four-year tenure. The official papers of his administrations, the records of the General Assembly, and contemporary newspapers reveal that Gordon did not do much in his official capacity and in fact spent a great deal of time out of state. He sent a number of special messages to the legislature, but these communications charted no new directions, calling for minor changes but no major reforms. Gordon maintained a relatively low profile and pursued a myriad of personal interests, allowing other Georgians to lead the way.[38]

As a result, Gordon failed to deal with many of the state's prob-lems. Although he frequently praised Georgia's farmers and was even referred to by a leading farm spokesman as "warmly and especially concerned" with Georgia agriculture, Gordon made no real effort to alleviate the agrarian distress that plagued the state. He did recom-mend an increase in state spending and the use of convict labor to improve country roads; however, that recommendation did not come

37. Atlanta *Constitution*, October 28-November 3, November 9, 1887; Huber W. Ellingsworth, "The Ohio Raid of General John B. Gordon," *Southern Speech Journal*, XXI (Winter, 1955), 120–26; Willie D. Halsell (ed.), "Some Correspondence Between Lucius Q. C. Lamar and John B. Gordon," *Georgia Historical Quarterly*, XXVIII (March, 1944), 49–50. A pamphlet incorporating some of Foraker's speeches, entitled *Stand Up, Governor Gordon, Sit Down, Governor Gordon,* can be found in the Georgia Room, UGA.

38. Concerning Gordon's governorship, see especially Executive Minutes, 1886–1890, *passim*; and *Georgia Senate Journal*, 1888, pp. 39–43; 1890, pp. 19–20, 22–26.

until 1890, when he was leaving office. Gordon and other Bourbon leaders largely ignored the pleas of small farmers and the tenant class and concentrated upon the needs of the wealthy landholders. Bourbons like Gordon, one Georgia historian concluded, "were content to leave the burden of taxation on real property, and to employ a legal system to protect the interests of landlords against the tenants, to leave the farmers with muddy roads, to abandon tenants to the exploitation of time prices, and to acquiesce in the *laissez faire* philosophy of government." This unwillingness to address legitimate agricultural concerns set the stage for, even hastened, the agrarian upheaval of the 1890s.[39]

Agriculture, despite the lack of governmental assistance, remained the dominant sector of Georgia's economy; however, commerce and industry steadily gained importance in the post-Reconstruction period—not surprisingly, given the Bourbons' espousal of the capitalistic New South spirit. During the 1880s, Georgia made great advances when several established industries underwent explosive growth and many new industries also began to flourish. Gordon, who frequently extolled the wisdom of diversifying Georgia's economy, naturally supported the development of the state's mineral and industrial resources. Yet, he apparently played only a minor role in attracting out-of-state capital. Indeed, most of his labors along this line involved personal, not official, concerns. As Georgia's chief executive, he continued the policy of reducing the state's debt and holding down taxes; in keeping Georgia on a sound fiscal course, Gordon proved himself a successful administrator of public finances. Still, his emphasis on economy in government had some less than beneficial results.[40]

Gordon often called for the improvement and expansion of Georgia's educational system, but the advances that were made during his two administrations resulted primarily from the efforts of the commissioners of education, not from those of the governor. He generally backed their proposals; however, as was so often the case while he served as the state's chief executive, Gordon did not assume a leading role. Even though school appropriations increased and public

39. Ward, "Georgia Under the Bourbons," 299, 300; *Georgia Senate Journal*, 1890, pp. 49–50. See also Ward, "Georgia Under the Bourbons," 246–300.
40. See Ward, "Georgia Under the Bourbons," 301–78, especially the table on 328. Also, for a fine statement of Gordon's views on economic diversification for Georgia, see Atlanta *Constitution*, March 13, 1888.

education made steady but slow progress during the Bourbon years, Georgia remained shackled with an inferior school system, largely because of reluctance to levy the taxes necessary for marked improvement. Georgia public schools, though free, had few well-trained teachers and were guaranteed to be in session for only three months each year. The record at the college level proved every bit as dismal. Despite the establishment of the Georgia Normal and Industrial School at Milledgeville and the Georgia School of Technology at Atlanta, higher education received a mere pittance of state funds.[41]

The only time during the Gordon years that collegiate concerns received more than passing mention occurred in 1887, when problems with Atlanta University surfaced. Since 1874, this institution had received an annual appropriation of eight thousand dollars for the express purpose of educating only blacks. Yet, in the summer of 1877, the Board of Visitors—a committee appointed to oversee examinations at the University of Georgia as well as Atlanta University— discovered white students attending this black institution. After discussing the situation with university faculty members and learning that they intended to admit all whites who applied, the board reported to the governor, recommending that he take action to prevent this breaking down of racial barriers. The board regarded the university's action as both "intrinsically wrong [and] . . . an improper use of the money appropriated by the State to this institution."[42]

Obviously concerned with this commingling of the races in an educational setting, Gordon sent a special message to the legislature on July 7, 1887. He concurred with the Board's findings and explained that the state constitution required that separate facilities be maintained for blacks and whites. Convinced that Georgians "in every form in which public opinion can be expressed have declared their unalterable opposition to the co-education of the races," Gordon maintained that such a position "must be considered as part of the settled policy of the State in reference to the colored race." He further asserted that biracial education was, in his opinion, detrimental to both blacks and whites because "all races which have achieved anything in this world have been homogenous." The governor thought that the best way for blacks to improve themselves was through the

41. *Georgia Senate Journal*, 1888, pp. 43–44; 1890, pp. 39–41; Ward, "Georgia Under the Bourbons," 435–78.
42. Ward, "Georgia Under the Bourbons," 475–77; *Georgia Senate Journal*, 1887, pp. 11–12; Atlanta *Constitution*, July 3, 8, 1887.

use of "separate and distinct" facilities. Accordingly, he suggested that Atlanta University's annual appropriation be used to maintain "colored institutions, taught by colored teachers, and presided over by colored president and officers." Segregation of the races was to remain the rule. As a consequence of Atlanta University's refusal to turn away white students and the government's unwillingness to break down the color line, the eight thousand dollars earmarked for the black university was withheld in each of the next three years. Finally, in 1890, this yearly appropriation for Atlanta University was revoked, and the money was awarded to a totally black institution.[43]

The desire to curb spending, which dramatically inhibited education at all levels, similarly left social services in Georgia badly underfunded. The three state-supported charitable institutions—the Lunatic Asylum, the Academy for the Blind, and the Institute for the Deaf and Dumb—continued to receive only small allocations, despite frequently severe overcrowding. Gordon did, however, go out of his way to provide one group of Georgians with sorely needed funds and facilities. These were the men he had led into battle more than thirty years ago. He routinely requested funds for numerous causes, but he always "most earnestly recommended" aid for "his boys." He never tired in his efforts to liberalize governmental allowances for veterans and their widows or to remind contemporary Georgians of their obligation to those who had fought for the Confederacy. In 1889, he presented a comprehensive plan, which he had developed, to build a home for disabled Confederate veterans and their families without using government money. Even though his grand plan for a self-sustaining "confederate cooperative industrial home" capitalized at one million dollars was never implemented, Gordon both contributed to and worked for the establishment of a dramatically scaled-down version of his veterans' home, which was eventually built without governmental help. So Confederate veterans did receive some assistance, and some progress was made in meeting the ever-growing needs of the state's population for social services. However, as noted by a Georgia historian, "the question of economy largely outweighed considerations of reform and humanity."[44]

The drive toward economy in government—always the watch-

43. *Georgia Senate Journal*, 1887, pp. 11–14; 1888, pp. 54–57; 1890, pp. 35–39, 55–71.

44. Ward, "Georgia Under the Bourbons," 479–518; *Georgia Senate Journal*, 1888, pp. 53–54; 1890, pp. 33–34; Atlanta *Constitution*, April 9, 1889.

word of southern Conservative Democrats—continued unchecked during Gordon's governorship. In his espousal of the philosophy of limited government, he differed little from other southern leaders of his day. In Georgia, this commitment to keeping governmental expenses down "enabled the state to emerge in a strong financial condition from a period in which most of her people were relatively poor, but at the same time schools, roads, charitable institutions, and other public services languished." Thus Gordon and his counterparts left Georgia with a heritage of one-party control and a weak, limited government, unwilling to support state services adequately.[45]

During his governorship, Gordon engaged in a wide variety of personal activities. He was often—both in and out of the state—dedicating monuments, attending reunions, or looking after his businesses. His attention to the world of business may necessarily have been restricted by his official duties, but he and his sons continued to promote a large number of diverse enterprises and often used his official position in efforts to attract investors to their projects. They sought to develop mining interests in north Georgia; they invested in the invention and manufacturing of a railroad coupler device; they dredged for gold in the rivers of Georgia and Florida; and they formed land and livestock companies for grazing animals. Gordon also helped to establish and served as president of both a company that manufactured sewing-machine motors and a firm that extracted and sold oil from cottonseed. Clearly, his concern with business continued as his quest for financial success went unfulfilled. In addition to these involvements and his responsibilities as governor, Gordon accepted the position of commander-in-chief of the United Confederate Veterans (UCV) when it organized in June, 1889. Although limited during the first few years, Gordon's commitment to the veterans association would later expand, and he would play a central role in the organization's development and success. And as he increased his efforts to promote national reconciliation in the 1890s, he would use the UCV as a vehicle toward that end.[46]

45. Ward, "Georgia Under the Bourbons," 519–25.

46. Hugh H. Gordon Letterbook, 1887–1891, AC. 00–013 *passim*, in GDAH; John Brown Records, 1883–1890, AC. 00–118, 1887–1900, *passim*, in GDAH, hereinafter cited as Gordon Personal Letterbooks; Incoming Correspondence, 1886–1890, *passim*; Atlanta *Constitution*, August 28, September 25, 26, November 13, 1890; Wynne, "Bourbon Triumvirate," 41–42; *Proceedings of the Convention for Organization, and Adoption of the Constitution of the United Confederate Veterans, June 10th, 1889* (New Orleans, 1891), 8.

Yet before hoisting the banner of nationalism to its fullest height, Gordon felt compelled once again to defend the South against an external threat. In June, 1890, Henry Cabot Lodge introduced the so-called force bill to provide for greater federal control of elections. Specifically designed to protect black voters in the South against state measures depriving them of the vote, the Lodge bill, noted a southern historian, "caused more alarm and excitement in the South than any Federal measure since 1877." This effort to alter racial affairs in the South brought forth a swift, vigorous response from white southerners. In fact, three months before the actual introduction of the force bill, Gordon, while addressing fellow Georgians, made clear his belief that northern interference in this strictly southern concern remained the greatest source of sectional discord. He casually dismissed charges of discrimination against blacks by explaining that he as governor would surely know if a race problem existed in Georgia. Not surprisingly, he affirmed that there was no such problem, and even if there was, southerners—and southerners alone—must be permitted to resolve relations between the races.[47]

In July, 1890, after the Lodge bill passed the House, Gordon responded to queries by several northern newspapers. If "the useless and infamous force bill" became law, he promised, "I shall use whatever influence and ability I may possess to arouse the southern people to the necessity of looking only to their own exhaustless resources." In other words, Gordon advocated a southern boycott of northern businesses in reprisal. Defeat of the bill in the Senate in January, 1891, thwarted this attempt at tighter federal control of elections, but the furor generated by the force bill nonetheless demonstrated the concern many white southerners had about a renewed federal commitment to the black man. As a major spokesman for Georgia and the South, Gordon reechoed the traditional southern white response to outside pressure: "[L]eave the south's destiny to those whose every interest is involved in that destiny." Or, to put it more pointedly, leave the race problem in the South to white southerners. So while preparing to step down as Georgia's chief executive, Gordon again positively asserted that where race was concerned, southern prejudices must prevail over national designs.[48]

As the end of his second term neared, plans were announced for

47. C. Vann Woodward, *Origins of the New South, 1877–1913* (Rev. ed.; Baton Rouge, 1971), 254–55; Atlanta *Constitution*, March 29, 1890.

48. Atlanta *Constitution*, July 22, 23, 1890.

Gordon to replace Senator Joe Brown, who was to retire to private life in 1891. The prospect of Gordon returning to the United States Senate was not the least bit unexpected. In fact, only eight months after he first captured the governor's chair, rumors were already circulating that the general would serve two terms and then take Brown's post in Washington. But the man who had assisted Gordon in many of his postwar business and political affairs would not again guide his actions. Henry W. Grady, at only thirty-nine years of age, died in 1889. Although Gordon attended Grady's funeral and later delivered a brief but eloquent eulogy of the brilliant newspaperman, relations between the two had soured since the 1886 gubernatorial campaign. Evidently, Gordon became piqued in the aftermath of his election by reports that Grady had been "the master hand" who piloted him to victory. This estrangement grew more marked in 1888, when a movement to send Grady to the United States Senate gained strength. An "encouraging word" from Gordon might have enabled Grady to displace A. H. Colquitt as senator, but the general withheld his assistance and, as friends of the editor charged, allowed his office to become the opposition's headquarters. The following year, Gordon wrote a blistering letter to Grady accusing him of leaking information to the family of the seriously ill Joe Brown that should he die, the governor desired his Senate seat. The letter has not survived, but it contained language that an associate of the newspaperman thought "would make the friends of Governor Gordon blush." Although Grady refrained from publicly severing relations with the man he had so long admired, Grady's secretary later recalled that "Governor Gordon's conduct hurt him [Grady] more than the outside world ever knew."[49]

This collapse of the friendship of two of Georgia's most prominent public figures reveals a darker side of Gordon's character. His point of view in the controversy has never been adequately aired, but his silence, in and of itself, tends to substantiate the statements of Grady's friends. It seems certain that Gordon chose to cast the young

49. Clipping of Charleston *Sunday News* July 3, 1887, in Scrapbook III, p. 37, in Francis Warrington Dawson I Collection, Duke; Nixon, *Grady*, 255–56, 291–96; Joel Chandler Harris, *Life of Henry W. Grady including his Writings and Speeches* (New York, 1890), 382–84; *Life and Labors of Henry W. Grady* (Atlanta, 1890), 82–83, 96–97; Atlanta *Constitution*, November 18, 1888, December 21, 23–26, 1889, November 16, 18, 1890; Gordon to Grady, June 24, July 5, 1889, both in Gordon Personal Letterbooks. Although the text of the July 5 letter is largely illegible, this is probably the letter in which Gordon violently assailed Grady.

man aside. He did so probably more because of his ego or his pride than for any concrete reasons. Since his splendid military record had elevated him to heights of belovedness and popularity far beyond the reach of all other Georgians, Gordon was unaccustomed to sharing the political limelight with anyone. That same sense of self-importance or ambition that had helped make Gordon such a remarkably successful soldier would not allow him to tolerate a rival for the accolades of Georgians. The general must have considered himself the only actor worthy of occupying the center stage of Georgia politics. Resentful of the gifted newspaperman's immense abilities or perhaps fearful that Grady would eclipse him in the hearts of the Georgia people, Gordon turned on the man who had provided him with such invaluable advice and guidance. Gordon's treatment of his friend, wrote one Grady intimate, "marks a tale of ingratitude which has not its parallel in the history of Georgia." This biting assessment sadly appears to be true. Gordon had abandoned Grady for a new crowd; new men would direct his next campaign.[50]

As Gordon made plans to return to the national forum, he must have pondered the differences between the Congress he had served in the 1870s and the one he hoped to reenter in the 1890s. Unquestionably, much of the passion and enmity engendered by the war and Reconstruction had abated, but as his speaking tour in Ohio had proven, a willingness on the part of some to "wave the bloody-shirt" still existed. When previously in the Senate, Gordon had labored tirelessly to restore home rule to all the southern states while at the same time working to extinguish the fires of sectional animosity. Now that Reconstruction was but a memory and the South was redeemed, Gordon could concentrate more fully on uniting the country. Although he had become involved in a myriad of financial and business dealings—and would continue to exhibit an adventuresome spirit of financial acquisitiveness—Gordon's final years were devoted more than ever to healing the long-festering wounds of the war that had been inflicted over a generation earlier. In doing so, Gordon moved beyond his established reputation as southern spokesman and national statesman. He became the most outspoken and the most widely traveled proponent of national reconciliation during the last years of the nineteenth century.

50. Atlanta *Constitution*, November 16, 1890.

# XIV · Return to the Senate

When Joe Brown let it be known in March, 1890, that he would not seek reelection to the United States Senate that November, a friend asked him who his successor would be. The senator, enfeebled by a long illness, replied, "I have never thought of but one man as likely to fill my place, and Governor Gordon is that man." To be sure, Brown and many other Georgians thought it only natural that the general move on into the national forum after his term as governor expired in October. Gordon immediately announced his candidacy, and throughout most of 1890, he remained the only serious aspirant for Brown's Senate seat. However, the emergence of a vibrant, newly united force in Georgia politics soon threatened Gordon's plans.[1]

Impoverished by more than two decades of agricultural depression and frustratingly ensnared in the pernicious crop-lien system, farmers in Georgia and other states had begun to organize. As their efforts to ameliorate their desperate plight gained momentum, farmers entered the political arena, and the Farmers' Alliance became a potent force that had to be reckoned with. By 1890, only three years after its inception in the state, the Georgia alliance boasted 100,000 members and over 2,000 lodges. The farmers' organization so thoroughly dominated state elections that year that it seemed as if the alliance had swallowed up the Democratic party. With this vocal, assertive element now in the ascendancy, all politicians who wished

---

1. Atlanta *Constitution*, March 11, 1890; Alex Mathews Arnett, *The Populist Movement in Georgia: A View of the "Agrarian Crusade" in Light of Solid-South Politics* (New York, 1922), 110–11.

to succeed in Georgia had to come to terms with the organization. Even the Gallant Gordon would have to stand the test.[2]

A self-professed friend and ally of the farmer, Gordon appeared to have sufficient support among alliance members to assure his election. However, his August 20 address to an audience composed largely of alliance men attending their annual state convention in Atlanta dramatically undercut Gordon's strength. In a speech sprinkled with martial analogies, Gordon referred to the alliance and the Democratic party as "two armies with a single flag; or rather, one great army in a dual capacity, and yet holding the unity of faith." He praised the farmers' organization for "waging its special warfare within the democratic lines; marshalling its forces beneath the democratic flag; and battling as democratic veterans with ancestral democratic faith for cardinal democratic principles." It was these same principles, Gordon maintained, that had guided him throughout his public career in his struggles to provide for the prosperity and well-being of all the people. He averred that despite the numerous obstacles in the path of reform charted by the alliance, success could be attained. But he stressed above all else that the triumph of the principles of both the alliance and the Democracy could only be realized through organization; and the organization had to be firmly rooted in conservative leadership and a broad-based unity embracing all classes and all sections. Clearly, Gordon was attempting to forestall the divisiveness that would eventually lead to the formation of a third party.[3]

Although it may have seemed strange, it was for precisely this reason that Gordon revealed his opposition to a major plank in the alliance platform, the subtreasury plan. This program involved an arrangement whereby farmers could store nonperishable produce in government warehouses and granaries at minimal cost. Then they

2. E. Merton Coulter, A Short History of Georgia (Athens, 1933), 369–71; Kenneth Coleman (ed.), A History of Georgia (Athens, 1977), 295–96; Judson Clements Ward, Jr., "Georgia Under the Bourbon Democrats, 1872–1890," (Ph.D. dissertation, University of North Carolina, 1947), 191–94, 196; James C. Bonner, "The Alliance Legislature of 1890," in James C. Bonner and Lucien E. Roberts (eds.), Studies in Georgia History and Government (Athens, 1940), 159–60, 163; Lewis Nicholas Wynne, "The Alliance Legislature of 1890" (M.A. thesis, University of Georgia, 1970), passim; Arnett, Populist Movement in Georgia, 77–100. See also Steven Hahn, The Roots of Southern Populism: Yeoman Farmers and the Transformation of the Georgia Upcountry, 1850–1890 (New York, 1983), 137–289; and Barton C. Shaw, The Wool-Hat Boys: Georgia's Populist Party (Baton Rouge, 1984), 1–30.

3. Atlanta Constitution, July 23, 25, August 21, 1890.

could obtain low-interest loans from the government based on the value of those crops. This system would allow the farmers to stagger the marketing of their produce, thus preventing a glut of the market and the accompanying decline in prices. Quickly capturing the imagination of many farmers, the subtreasury plan represented in their minds a panacea for the ills besetting the agrarian sector. More important, the plan rapidly became the single standard by which many farm leaders measured all people, alliance members and nonmembers alike. That is why Gordon's announcement had the effect of an exploding bombshell.[4]

Gordon cited the distressing tendency of some farmers to focus solely on the subtreasury plan as his main reason for opposing the proposal. In addition to believing that it would not provide the relief farmers sought, he expressed his fears that reliance upon a single standard for determining party loyalty could be disastrous for the Democratic party and the alliance. He warned farmers, "You cannot afford to pin your destinies to any one programme or cast all your future in any one specific boat, which may be engulfed and lost." Gordon contended that the subtreasury plan was far too controversial, even among Georgians, to serve as the bulwark of party support. Unity of purpose and strength in numbers were, for Gordon, more effective means of improving the farmers' lot. By concentrating on electing alliance members and supporters, Gordon assured farmers, they could dominate the legislative process and enact the laws and measures necessary to effect relief. Unity and organization, more than any specific measure, would open the road to success, or so Gordon asserted.[5]

Although the tone and intended thrust of Gordon's speech was markedly sympathetic and apparently solicitous of the cause of the alliance, few alliance men saw beyond his opposition to the subtreasury plan. A roar of indignation arose immediately from many of the delegates. Gordon's position quickly became the major topic of discussion that evening and also during the following day's session of the convention. The unanimous endorsement of the plan by the

4. *Ibid.*, August 21, 1890; Lawrence Goodwyn, *Democratic Promise: The Populist Movement in America* (New York, 1976), 166–71; John D. Hicks, *The Populist Revolt: A History of the Farmers' Alliance and the People's Party* (1931; rpr. Westport, Conn., 1981), 186–204; Shaw, *Wool-Hat Boys*, 25–26; Bonner, "Alliance Legislature," 160–62.

5. Atlanta *Constitution*, August 21, 1890.

Georgia alliance that day heightened the sense of a developing confrontation. Some believed Gordon's bold stance would ensure his election, but most insisted that the general had sealed his own doom with his declaration against the plan. Nonetheless, as discussion about what effect Gordon's speech would have on his Senate chances increased, one point became abundantly clear. In the words of one alliance man, "It makes certain . . . that he will have a straightout subtreasury opponent for the senate." With his hopes of running unopposed dashed, Gordon faced the prospect of another fight for his political life.[6]

Speculation as to who would oppose the general abounded, but opponents were slow in presenting themselves. Even though he refused to declare himself a candidate, Thomas M. Norwood emerged as the most likely opponent. By mid-September, he and Gordon were engaged in a heated exchange of public letters and verbal barbs, leaving no doubt that the ensuing campaign would be filled with rancor and bitterness. In spite of the extremely harsh words that passed between them, Norwood delayed announcing his candidacy until mid-October. His decision, as well as those of several others who entered the contest soon thereafter, was probably influenced by the stunning victory of the alliance in the state elections on October 1. Winning the governorship and almost 80 percent of the seats in the legislature, the Farmers' Alliance assumed a commanding position. Gordon and the other Senate hopefuls—Judge James K. Hines, N. J. Hammond, Patrick Calhoun, and Norwood—all actively courted the farmers' votes. Even so, during the course of the campaign, Gordon often crossed swords with prominent national and state leaders of the alliance. Irked by the general's opposition to the subtreasury plan, they issued strident calls for his defeat. As a result, Gordon increasingly accused alliance leaders of misquoting and misrepresenting him for their own personal advantage. In doing so, Gordon generated substantial opposition to his election outside of Georgia as well as within the state.[7]

6. *Ibid.*, August 21, 22, 1890.
7. *Ibid.*, August 24, 26, 30, September 7, 13, 14, 16–18, 20, 22, 25, 26, October 5, 9, 11, 1890; Arnett, *Populist Movement in Georgia*, 105, 116–20; C. Vann Woodward, *Tom Watson: Agrarian Rebel* (New York, 1938), 162–63; Shaw, *Wool-Hat Boys*, 30; Bonner, "Alliance Legislature," in Bonner and Roberts (eds.), *Studies in Georgia History and Government*, 163–65; Burton Smith to Frank Gordon, October 31, 1890, in Hoke Smith Collection, Richard B. Russell Memorial Library, UGA. The Samuel Houston Brodnax Collection, Duke, contains numerous farmers' letters of opposition

Even before opposition crystallized and opponents emerged, Gordon had taken the stump to plead his case. He spoke throughout the state in the two and a half months preceding the mid-November election. Whether in front of county suballiances, or in an open circular letter to the people of Georgia, or before the newly elected Georgia legislature that would decide the Senate race, Gordon focused over and over on several main themes. He consistently portrayed himself as an ardent, lifelong friend of the farmer. He said he had joined the Georgia Agricultural Society at twenty and since then had become a member of every farmers' organization to which he could be admitted, including the Grange. Having supported all efforts by the "tillers of the soil" to organize, Gordon contended that he now felt that his long-cherished hope had at last been realized with the establishment of the Farmers' Alliance. Gordon also maintained that he had unwaveringly championed the cause of the agrarian sector from his earliest days in the Senate. Styling himself as just another soldier who had long served in the ranks of the agrarian army, the general reiterated that the farmers' enemies were also his enemies. High tariffs, national banks, restrictions on silver, contraction of currency, and all other measures that imposed unequal burdens on farmers were their common foes. Gordon insisted, "I have been as consistent and persistent in my defense of those principles [of the alliance] . . . as any man living. . . . I have defended those principles for a long series of years, and under circumstances which make it impossible for any fair-minded man to doubt my sincerity or question my motives." Many did, however.[8]

Gordon explained that his refusal to endorse a major plank in the alliance program stemmed not from opposition to the farmers' movement but from the harm he believed would be "caused by making the endorsement of the subtreasury bill a test of democratic fealty." Having detected substantial opposition to the plan within the Georgia Democracy and in other states as well, he again voiced his fear that internal dissension "would not only threaten the integrity of the democratic party, but would assuredly defeat some of the alliance

to Gordon. See especially W. L. Peek to Brodnax, October 2, 1890, J. H. Stewart to Brodnax, October 11, 1890, G. R. Brown to Brodnax, October 11, 1890, N. J. Day to Brodnax, October 12, 1890, N. H. Grumter to Brodnax, October 15, 1890, M. K. Bennett to Brodnax, October 16, 1890, and [author unknown] to Brodnax, October 20, 30, 1890.

8. Atlanta *Constitution*, August 31, September 3, 13, 14, October 11, 19, November 11, 1890.

candidates, and bring serious embarrassment to the alliance cause in Georgia." The possibility that the newly developed strength of the farmers' organization would be dissipated, he declared, made it imperative that he speak out. "I knew full well that silence on my part meant unanimous election to the senate but . . . I could not afford to be silent and see unauthorized tests applied which were separating democrats, and which, if persisted in, must rend the party in twain, and drive from the alliance cause throughout the union millions of votes." Along this line, Gordon's objections to the subtreasury scheme seem to have been sincere, for had he remained silent on the issue, his election, as he asserted, would have been virtually guaranteed.[9]

Gordon constantly reemphasized that his failure to endorse the plan did not make him an enemy of the alliance. To the contrary, he told the farmers, "you are firing at the wrong man. Turn your guns on the enemy!" For Gordon, it was ironic, almost tragic, that an effective farmers' organization—the cause for which, he maintained, he had labored so long and so earnestly—might be the instrument of his defeat. In a speech delivered to the alliance-dominated legislature one week before the election, Gordon protested, "Call me a traitor to the south, to my country, to my church and to society, but don't put your vote against me upon the pretense that I am not a friend of the Farmers' Alliance."[10]

Gordon, as he had done so often before, relied heavily on the support of his former comrades-in-arms. And because many members of the Farmers' Alliance were veterans of the war, the rekindling of memories of the Confederacy proved especially effective. Whenever he spoke, the aging general shamelessly appealed to those fond remembrances of Confederate service that few individuals wished to forget. Although Gordon genuinely sought to bury the violent passions engendered by the war, he was ever ready to capitalize on the sentimentality increasingly associated with it. He repeatedly referred back to the days when he commanded many of his listeners and often couched his arguments in martial terms or employed military analogies to emphasize his points. All of these references were carefully calculated to draw back into the Democratic fold those veterans who were considering political alternatives that more directly addressed their economic distress. Gordon even told his audiences that though

9. *Ibid.*, September 3, 1890.
10. *Ibid.*, September 3, November 11, 1890.

he certainly wanted to win, the loss of political office would not particularly trouble him; however, the "keenest pang would be the consciousness that among those who dealt the blow were my confederate
comrades in the alliance brotherhood acting under leadership of men
who never shared with them the dread fortunes of war." He refused to
believe that those brave veterans, whom he styled "the Old Guard of
the confederate army," would turn against him.[11]

In addition to his appeals as the "farmers' best friend" and as "the
man who led you into battle," Gordon touched another particularly
sensitive nerve. He implored Democrats, both in and out of the alliance, to remember that "the integrity of your party is essential to
the continued supremacy of the white race in Georgia," which, in
turn, was essential "to the security of your property and the safety of
your homes." Bitter memories of Republican-imposed Reconstruction, when Federal troops occupied the South and the specter of black
equality threatened the established social order, still haunted many
white southerners. Fears of renewed Federal intrusion into the affairs
of southern states had been revived only weeks earlier when discussion of the force bill was renewed and occupied headlines throughout
the South. His efforts to capitalize on a resurgence of racial fear demonstrated Gordon's willingness to employ all the weapons at his disposal in his quest for the Senate.[12]

As the campaign drew to a close, the outcome seemed to be in
serious doubt. A major element of the uncertainty stemmed from the
phenomenal success of alliance candidates in the October state elections. Rumors and speculation about how the "Farmers' Legislature"
would handle the old warrior generated intense excitement as both
houses convened on November 18. Earlier in the week, the Atlanta
Constitution—no longer a supporter of Gordon, in part because of his
falling out with Henry Grady—had announced that Patrick Calhoun
had already gained the endorsement of a majority of the legislature
and thus would be elected. In spite of Calhoun's extensive railroad
connections, the Constitution reported, his strong endorsement of
the subtreasury plan would win the nomination for him. Supporters
of Norwood likewise appeared confident. Many Georgians believed

11. *Ibid.*; Bonner, "Alliance Legislature," in Bonner and Roberts (eds.), *Studies in
Georgia History and Government*, 164–65. Gordon's speeches during the campaign
were all loaded with martial references. See Atlanta *Constitution*, September–mid-
November, 1890, *passim*.

12. Atlanta *Constitution*, September 3, 1890.

that "it is doubtful if ever again such an exciting election will be held," but the drama proved short-lived. On the first ballot, Gordon won a clear majority in the Senate and, after some hasty vote-switching, gained a slim majority in the House as well. His consolidated total stood at 122, compared to Norwood's 43, Calhoun's 25, and Hines's 13, with the remaining 10 votes divided between two other candidates. Garnering votes from throughout the state, Gordon won a clear-cut though narrow victory. According to one account, "for a quarter of an hour the din of applause was deafening." His election set off a wild celebration that carried over well into the night. Indeed, it seemed to the *Constitution* that even the supporters of the defeated candidates were happy. The following morning's edition of the paper saluted the senator-elect and pledged him its "hearty support." Assuring its readers that Georgia's interests were truly safe with Gordon, the paper urged all Georgians to forget past differences and to rally around him "in the good old-fashioned democratic way."[13]

To explain Gordon's remarkable success as merely the result of the duping of political novices by a machiavellian political schemer is too simplistic an assessment to be of value. Gordon probably considered himself a genuine friend of farmers, but he was by no means a bona fide spokesman for them. It is true that he appreciated the importance of southern agriculture, and he did sympathize with the plight of farmers; however, he had never truly championed their cause. His postwar career leaves no doubt that his economic philosophy revolved more around the business and industry of the New South than it did around the staple-crop agriculture that dominated the Old South. Why or how, then, did he succeed in the face of marked agrarian opposition? Quite simply, in spite of all the controversy surrounding his postwar career and in spite of his nonagrarian inclinations, Gordon retained the firm hold on the affections of Georgians that he first won while wearing the gray.

The years in which he gained his fame and earned the confidence and respect of his fellow southerners were almost three decades in the past, but most Georgians still adored and trusted him. Just as in 1873, when one veteran characterized Gordon as one of the very few men you could "shut your eyes and go it blind on," an alliance man in 1890

---

13. *Ibid.*, November 14, 16, 18, 19, 1890; Bonner, "Alliance Legislature," in Bonner and Roberts (eds.), *Studies in Georgia History and Government*, 164–65; *Georgia House Journal*, 1890, pp. 203–206, 217; *Georgia Senate Journal*, 1890, pp. 113–14, 121–22; Arnett, *Populist Movement in Georgia*, 116–18.

claimed, "We have all sorts of plans, and we can change 'em, and fix 'em up any way we please, but we've got only one Gordon." Or as another farmer explained, "I am for Gordon as well as the subtreasury plan, [but] I am for Gordon first." These sentiments were not isolated; many of the alliance men were "for Gordon on any sort of a platform." Whether donning the soiled, sweat-soaked overalls of a tenant farmer, stuffing himself into the faded, blood-stained gray uniform he had worn during the war, or even figuratively pulling on the vestments of the Klan, Gordon remained Georgia's most beloved figure.[14]

The Senate that he joined in December, 1891, differed significantly from the one he had served in during the 1870s. Most of the heated passions that had forced Gordon to defend his native South against Radical onslaughts had passed. Even though questions concerning the reconstruction of the nation had been resolved, new and equally troublesome problems were arising. In the 1890s, agrarian discontent flourished, labor unrest abounded, the battle of monetary standards raged, and social tensions assumed frightening proportions. Amid this growing anxiety and the raging Populist conflagration, Gordon remained remarkably inactive. He frequently campaigned for Democratic candidates in Georgia who faced the growing Populist challenge; but with the exception of the period between August, 1893, and July, 1894, his involvement in Senate affairs was negligible, almost nonexistent. Although he presented numerous petitions and resolutions on behalf of his constituents, Gordon did not play as important a role as he had during his earlier tenure. He introduced very few bills, rarely entered into debates, made only a handful of speeches, and was often absent from Congress. Indeed, on well over half the votes during his tenure, he paired with opponents so as to permit his absence. In sum, Gordon did very little.

A number of factors contributed to the minor role he played in the

14. Atlanta *Constitution*, January 14, 1873, August 31, 1890; Arnett, *Populist Movement in Georgia*, 120; Woodward, *Watson*, 163; Gordon to C. C. Jones, November 28, 1890, in John Brown Gordon Papers, Emory. Amid substantial speculation as to his intentions, Gordon finally joined the Farmers' Alliance in January, 1891. When he announced his decision to join, he reiterated that he had wanted to join the order for a long time; however, because of his candidacy for the Senate, he deferred such action, fearing his motives might be misrepresented. Once elected in his own right, Gordon no longer worried about his actions being misconstrued. New York *Times*, January 19, 1891; Atlanta *Constitution*, November 11, 19, December 7, 1890; Hoke Smith to Gordon, December 30, 1890, in Smith Collection.

Senate in the 1890s. His advanced age, frequent bouts of ill health, new business ventures, involvement with veterans organizations, and extensive lecture tours all explain in part Gordon's lackluster performance. But, most important, he found little of interest in Senate affairs in the 1890s. For him, the sense of excitement and urgency that animated him in battle and during Reconstruction no longer existed. And with political leadership increasingly passing into the hands of younger men, men not of Gordon's generation, only the most serious of national crises could bring him out of the shadows of the Senate chamber.

His first action of any note came on January 13, 1892. He had missed the initial meeting of the Committee on Coast Defenses due to a misunderstanding but felt compelled to voice his opposition to a bill that the committee had reported upon favorably. Although he had no objections to voting appropriations for national defense whenever necessary, Gordon believed that "the present condition of the country and of the people" and the absence of "war clouds" made the expenditures in question unwise and inappropriate. "The burdens of taxation from which the people are suffering," he contended, posed a far greater threat than "any invasion from a foreign foe." Accordingly, he urged Congress to economize by curtailing expenditures and cutting taxes. "Let us first relieve our people, as far as we may, from the present exactions of taxation and then, when the occasion arises, look to the remote and contingent danger from outside." This rather insignificant speech basically represented the extent of Gordon's participation in the Senate until late summer, 1893.[15]

Victories in the 1892 fall elections swept the Democrats back into control of the national government, but with the onset of the panic of 1893, cause for celebration evaporated almost immediately. Agricultural prices plummeted, unemployment skyrocketed, and currency contracted as the economy of the nation spiraled downward, leaving the Democracy "the party of depression." With economic dislocations working ever greater hardships upon the American people, Gordon stirred from his lethargy and assumed a more active role in the Senate. It was as if he had received his call to arms. On August 14, 1893, he submitted a series of resolutions dealing expressly with the financial policies he believed should be pursued by the Fifty-third Congress. In essence, Gordon called upon his fellow Democrats (and

15. *Congressional Record,* 52nd Cong., 1st Sess., 283.

Republicans so inclined) to honor the pledges they had made during the previous campaign: to repeal the Sherman Silver Purchase Act of 1890; to develop a sounder, more flexible currency system based on bimetallism; and to repeal the federal tax on the issue of state bank notes. Although not specifically enumerated in his program of reform, Gordon also considered a stricter sense of economy in government essential to recovery.[16]

The following day, he introduced a bill to suspend for six months the 10 percent tax on state bank issues. Realizing that repeal of the tax was impractical on such short notice, Gordon nevertheless understood the urgent need to increase the amount of money in circulation, particularly at this critical juncture when the current cotton crop was about to reach market. A temporary suspension, he asserted, would allow state banks to inject into the economy hundreds of thousands of dollars, which would permit the marketing of the crop. Gordon announced that the increase in circulating medium "would be equivalent to a ship of gold emptied into our markets" and would relieve "all the cotton States within a few days from the embargo now imposed by want of currency." He dismissed several criticisms of his bill and claimed that even though "it is not a panacea for all our ills," its enactment "would end the panic in the South, at least, within fifteen days." Despite his plea for early action on the measure by the Finance Committee, it remained buried beneath the avalanche of proposals presented to alleviate the nation's economic woes. When Gordon introduced a bill calling for the outright repeal of the tax during the following session, it met a similar fate.[17]

Gordon delivered his major address on the money question on August 29, 1893. He focused mainly on the silver issue, but began by admonishing his fellow Democrats to fulfill the promises of financial reform that had paved the way to victory. The time had come to redeem their pledges to lower the tariff, to repeal the Sherman law, to repeal the state bank tax, and to put gold and silver on the same footing. Gordon cautioned the Senate to heed the people's demand for "the inauguration of a sound and stable but more liberal policy of finance." As he maintained, the loudest cries of the public centered around the repeal of the Sherman Silver Purchase Act of 1890. Even though he admitted his uncertainty as to the effect the silver-purchase provision had upon the panic, Gordon observed that the "Sher-

16. *Ibid.*, 53rd Cong., 1st Sess., 288. See also *ibid.*, 52nd Cong., 1st Sess., 283.
17. *Ibid.*, 53rd Cong., 1st Sess., 329–30; 2nd Sess., 3882–83.

man law, rightfully or wrongfully, justly or injustly, in the public estimation is the alarming agency which has brought the chill, frozen the currents, and stifled the heart-throbs of trade." Recognizing that "belief in such case is as hurtful as reality," Gordon called for the immediate repeal of the act. Even "if we can not at once rescue the country bodily from the dead sea of distrust in which it is drowning, let us at least lift its head above the waves . . . [so] it may gather breath and strength for the next struggle." Repeal would serve as a first step in the right direction toward restoring public faith and confidence. When the Senate voted in late October, Gordon was one of only a few southerners favoring the repeal.[18]

Yet, even while heartily endorsing President Grover Cleveland's call for repeal of the silver-purchase act, Gordon went to great lengths to ensure that no one would misinterpret his position on bimetallism. Disavowal of the Sherman act by no means signaled a reversal of his long-held conviction that the soundest monetary system had its basis in the use of both gold and silver. He proclaimed that the Senate contained no "more consistent, ardent, and sincere" friend of bimetallism than himself. Indeed, bimetallism had been, in his opinion, "the most popular, if not the most potential, factor in the last campaign"; all parties had "bowed before its altar and worshipped at the common shrine." Gordon renewed his appeal to his fellow Senators to place gold and silver on an equal footing. As he saw it, once the repeal of the silver-purchase provision had broken "a rift in the clouds," the Congress could go forward "then with more light and more time for deliberation . . . in the effort to arm the country with the double strength of its two great metals, and start it once more on a broader road to increased and permanent prosperity."[19]

But as economic conditions worsened and social disorder grew more pronounced, Gordon turned his attention away from specific financial reforms and toward apparent threats to the system. The arrival of "Coxey's army" in Washington in May, 1894, aroused concern among many legislators. Jacob S. Coxey, an Ohio Populist, had called for a march on the nation's capital to dramatize his plans for government-sponsored work-relief projects for the country's unemployed. Although only about five hundred of his followers actually

18. *Ibid.*, 53rd Cong., 1st Sess., 862, 1013–16, 2958; Arnett, *Populist Movement in Georgia*, 172, 179–80.

19. *Congressional Record*, 53rd Cong., 1st Sess., 1013–16. See also Gordon to Grover Cleveland, September 23, 1892, March 15, 1894, both in Grover Cleveland Papers, LC; Arnett, *Populist Movement in Georgia*, 167–72.

reached Washington, police prevented them from entering the Capitol and arrested Coxey and several others on concocted charges. When a resolution was introduced in the Senate to establish a committee to investigate the incident, Gordon took the opportunity to look at Coxeyism "from a Southern standpoint." He smugly asserted that the nation could learn a valuable lesson by closely examining that movement. Appeals for relief like those of Coxey and his supporters were coming, he erroneously contended, from every section of the country save one, the South. What explained "the remarkable freedom of the South from these ill-omened agitations?" Clearly, the South had not been spared poverty or unemployment and it, too, suffered from the same lack of currency that harassed the entire country. Also, the South had not gained any special benefits from the tariff, nor had southerners received bountiful subsidies from the federal government. Why then, inquired the Georgian, had the South—if no better off materially than the rest of the country—been exempted from such agitations?[20]

For Gordon, "the towering, the overshadowing reason" was the South's special sense of self-reliance, a strength southerners developed as a result of the Civil War. "Shut out from all hope of governmental relief, they learned to lean not upon the legislative arm, but upon their own right arm." Southerners, Gordon explained, did not "look upon the Government as a fostering mother from which they were to draw sustenance or obtain relief in their periods of depression." Necessity, "that most relentless of taskmasters," had taught southerners to rely on no one but themselves and their own state governments. Gordon maintained that all states could learn an important lesson from the example of the South: "[D]ecentralize, as far as may be consistent with safety, this General Government, and devolve upon the States, as far as practicable, the responsibility of dealing with these ill-advised movements which agitate and disturb communities." In his opinion, the individual states, and not the federal government, must be empowered to deal fully with their own problems. Having reiterated his conviction that state governments were the safest repositories of their citizens' interests, he closed by renewing his call for repeal of the state bank tax. States and state banks could better address the problems facing them than Congress could.[21]

20. *Congressional Record*, 53rd Cong., 2nd Sess., 4564–65.
21. *Ibid.*, 4565; Atlanta *Constitution*, May 11, 1894; See also *Congressional Record*, 53rd Cong., 2nd Sess., 3882–83.

Less than two months later, however, Gordon found it remarkably easy to temper his life-long views on states' rights. As the strike of the American Railway Union against the Pullman Company widened during the summer of 1894, and despite strenuous objections from Illinois governor John P. Altgeld, President Grover Cleveland ordered federal troops into the Chicago area to ensure delivery of the mail. In a July 9 conference at the White House, Gordon assured the president "that his course was eminently proper and that it would be endorsed by the entire country." The Georgian also tendered his services should volunteers be necessary to suppress the disturbance. Later that day, in an interview, he insisted—unjustifiably, though—that his sympathies had always lain with the laboring classes, but he simply would not countenance lawlessness on their part. Mob violence, wherever it appeared, "must be put down at any cost or the government cannot last." When asked what the result of the current crisis would be, he replied that "but one thing is certain, the law will be enforced and the public peace preserved." Clearly, Gordon supported the employment of federal forces to break the strike even though Governor Altgeld resisted such intervention.[22]

An opportunity to enunciate his views more fully presented itself on July 10, 1894. Following Populist senator William A. Peffer's blistering attack upon the Republican and Democratic parties for their responsibility for the current disorders, Gordon rose to address both Peffer's comments and the issue of escalating social tensions. He began by expressing his disdain for the Kansas senator's attempt to enlist support for the Populist party by placing the blame for the "present unhappy conditions" at the doorstep of the two major parties. At a time "when our very civilization, not to say the form of government under which we live, is heaving under the mighty ground-swell of a great agitation," Gordon indignantly proclaimed, partisan political concerns were of little consequence. If anarchy was to be averted, "we must stand now shoulder to shoulder for the enforcement of its [the nation's] laws, for the preservation of its peace, the support of its dignity, and the perpetuity of its freedom." Gordon therefore disclaimed political or sectional affiliation and instead spoke as a "lover of his country and of his whole country" because the present situation involved "not only labor and law and personal liberty, but the life of the Republic itself." Fearful that the disorder in

22. Atlanta *Constitution*, July 10, 1894.

Chicago might ignite further outbreaks of violence, he stressed the imperativeness of meeting lawlessness firmly and immediately. A warning had to be issued to those who would defy the laws. And to remove any doubt as to how the South stood on the matter, Gordon dramatically proclaimed, "[T]he men who wore the gray from 1861 to 1865, under strong convictions, will be found side by side with the men who wore the blue, following the same flag, in upholding the dignity of the Republic over which it floats, and in enforcing every law upon its statute books." He closed his brief address with a sincere wish that further bloodshed could be avoided, but felt "impelled to add that the blood which has been shed or may yet be shed is nothing as compared to the value of this Republic, and that the sons of the men who established it will save it, whatever may be the cost."[23]

Gordon's eloquent statement lasted barely fifteen minutes; even as he spoke, excitement and applause rippled through the galleries and about the floor. When he had finished, prolonged and wildly enthusiastic applause swept through the Senate chamber. Senators from both sides of the aisle converged on the Georgian with warm congratulations. Former Union generals Daniel Sickles and Newton M. Curtis remarked that Gordon's speech would "do more to quell disorder and revolution than a regiment of soldiers, sent by federal or state authorities." Editorial comments from around the nation lavishly praised Gordon for his patriotic expressions at a time when many feared that the security of the country hung in the balance. Gordon also received a large number of letters from private citizens throughout the country—particularly from the North and the West— lauding his "patriotic and soul-inspiring" remarks. Some considered this speech his greatest. Certainly he uttered few, if any, more positive endorsements of the federal government's enforcement powers.[24]

Shortly after his nationalistic speech and prior to the adjournment of Congress, Gordon returned to Georgia, where he lent his efforts to heading off Populist inroads in his home state. At Barnesville on August 25, 1894, he delivered a lengthy speech in which he discussed the current national situation. Feeling that the worst had passed,

23. *Congressional Record*, 53rd Cong., 2nd Sess., 7231–35, 7240–41.

24. *Ibid.*, 7240–41; Atlanta *Constitution*, July 11, 12, 1894; New York *Times*, July 11, 1894; John F. Rudisill to Gordon, July 21, 1894, N. S. Dickson to Gordon, July 17, 1894, both in Gordon Family Collection, UGA. A large number of resolutions, letters, and editorial clippings congratulating and praising Gordon for his July 10, 1894, speech can be found in Gordon Family Collection, UGA.

Gordon proclaimed that only "an over-ruling providence and the democratic party" had enabled the country to weather "the most gigantic and alarming industrial upheaval of the century." He again painted the remarkable spectacle of a serene South reposing amid the anarchy that threatened from all sides. Even though the South and Georgia were similarly racked by the convulsions of Populism, Gordon refused to acknowledge this turmoil. Instead, he asserted, "[H]ow comforting, sustaining, and inspiring is the reflection that while these industrial and social storms have been raging around us, we of the South have been resting in peace, in safety, and comparative comfort." In addition to that splendid, well-developed sense of self-reliance that he had referred to in the Senate, Gordon also supplied another reason for the supposed absence of disturbances in the South: the South's strength lay in the sound conservative policies of the Democratic party. With the Populists now posing a genuine third-party threat to Democratic domination, Gordon renewed his call for loyalty to the party. Just as he had done in his 1890 senatorial campaign and again during the 1892 campaigns, he decried the decision of many farmers to resort to a third political party. After discussing several Populist proposals, showing to his satisfaction the impracticality of radicalism, and stressing the potentially disastrous consequences of abandoning the conservatism of the Democracy, he hopefully concluded that Georgians "will stand in solid line against all hazardous experiments in government, and, above all, against the socialistic tendencies of the populists." As long as southerners eschewed radicalism, Gordon predicted, the country would continue "on the ascending highway now open before us to unprecedented prosperity, security and peace."[25]

Gordon's three 1894 speeches again illustrate the dual allegiances under which he had labored since entering public service in 1873: he continued to defend and promote southern interests while at the same time struggling to foster a nationalism that encompassed all sections of the country as equal partners. Yet, with all their emotional rhetoric and high-sounding platitudes, they have a superficial ring to them. The apparent simplicity of the speeches—particularly those portions in which he asserted that the South was devoid of social unrest—evinces a certain naïveté or sense of unreality on Gordon's part. It is true that the South experienced fewer outbreaks of

25. Atlanta *Constitution*, August 26, 1894; New York *Times*, August 7, 1892; Woodward, *Watson*, 226–29.

industrial violence and labor disorder, but that was attributable more to demographics and agricultural domination of the southern economy than to self-reliance or party loyalty. And despite the less frequent incidence of violence, the South certainly had its share of unrest in the 1890s. Indeed, the South and Georgia were inflamed with Populist unrest. Gordon, however, was either unaware of these disorders or—as is more probable—chose to ignore them.[26]

Both possibilities raise questions about his capacity as a senator, especially in light of his almost total lack of involvement in national affairs during his final two and one-half years of service. His speeches in the summer of 1894 seem to display more concern with style and appearance than with content and results. In the 1870s, he had played an active, important role in national politics until the South had been redeemed. After 1877, however, his involvement rapidly waned. Similarly, in the 1890s, when he sensed imminent danger to the nation, he was excited by the prospect of meaningful service. Once the most serious threat had passed, he again lost interest and ceased to be active. Gordon was a man made for turbulent times. Probably the best explanation of his poor record in the Senate is that the aging general had become not only an elder statesman but an elderly statesman, as well. Thirty years of public life after four years of military service had taken their toll. Physically, he had grown increasingly infirm. Gordon was now an old man, and politics no longer held much attraction for him. It was almost as if his final burst of activity during the summer of 1894 burned up the last of his enthusiasm for politics. When he announced, in June, 1895, that he would not seek reelection, Gordon informed his fellow Georgians that he had reached that decision more than a year earlier. In 1896, when talk of running him for vice-president surfaced, as it had often during his career, Gordon squelched the possibility by proclaiming he would not accept any nomination to any political office. As he turned his attention away from the Senate and toward other concerns of more interest, Gordon seems to have lost touch with the realities of national politics, as well as those of his section.[27]

26. C. Vann Woodward, *Origins of the New South, 1877–1913* (Rev. ed.; Baton Rouge, 1971), 265–69.

27. New York *Times*, June 16, 1895, January 10, 1904; Atlanta *Constitution*, August 4, 1896; Gordon to George Moorman, November 21, December 11, 1891, March 1, 15, June 2, 1892, Gordon to John C. Underwood, March 1, 1892, all in United Confederate Veterans Collection, LSU; clipping from St. Paul *Pioneer Press*, July 21, 1896, in Gordon Family Collection, UGA; Tomlinson Fort to Joseph Wheeler, December 23, 1893, in Joseph Wheeler Papers, ADAH.

Even so, Gordon retained his abiding commitment to nationalism or, more specifically, to national reconciliation. The steady erosion of sectional animosity that each passing year brought most assuredly gratified the man who had buried his own wartime passions at Appomattox. Much of his postwar career had been devoted to helping other Americans—northerners and southerners alike—to cleanse themselves of their hatreds for one another. Gordon's Pullman-strike speech, more than merely reflecting his concern for law and order, also served as another example of his continuing pacification efforts; and the timing and the circumstances under which it was delivered made it extremely important. The reactions of national newspapers reflect the reconciliatory benefits it afforded. The New York *Telegram* concluded that his effort "must go far toward convincing the country and the world that the old time lines of difference between Southern thinking and Northern thinking are at length obliterated." Speaking not as a southerner but as an American, Gordon convincingly demonstrated to the Youngstown, Ohio, *Telegram* "that the American people are a nation and that patriotism and love for the flag now knows no North or South." Realizing that most of the war-generated bitterness had dissipated and sensing in the uneasy mood of the country a desire for stability and a reaffirmation of old values, he redoubled his efforts to heal completely those wounds still festering. Indeed, during the final years of his life, Gordon's commitment to national pacification overshadowed all his other activities.[28]

28. Clippings from New York *Telegram*, July 12, 1894, and Youngstown (Ohio) *Telegram*, July 11, 1894, both in Gordon Family Collection, UGA.

# XV · The Southerner as American

During the last decade of his life, Gordon remained extremely active in his efforts to vindicate the South and at the same time to establish a new spirit of nationalism. He did not, however, avail himself of the forum that his Senate post afforded him. Instead, he chose a less official yet more effective means of reaching the American people. He embarked on a career as a lecturer. Although precisely when he decided to develop a public lecture is not known, by mid-1893, Gordon had begun to work on such a project. He chose "Last Days of the Confederacy" as his title. Rather than analyze the causes of the Confederate defeat or describe the battles themselves, Gordon proposed "to speak of those less grave but scarcely less important phases or incidents of the war which illustrate the spirit and character of the American soldier and people." He would tell his story from a southern point of view but show that neither side enjoyed a monopoly on virtue. His use of this broader nationalistic perspective helped establish a common vantage point from which northerners and southerners alike could view the war and derive pride and honor from their participation.[1]

Although concentrating heavily upon the final days of the war, Gordon included several anecdotes that effectively humanized his lecture. He related the story of the staunchly Unionist woman at Wrightsville who provided breakfast for the Confederates, the humorous account of the gregarious Yankee who crossed the Rapidan to visit with Gordon's troops, the remarkable Barlow saga that began on

1. New York *Times*, June 11, 1893; Gordon to Moorman, July 18, 1893, in United Confederate Veterans Collection, LSU, hereinafter cited as UCV Collection, LSU; John Brown Gordon, "Last Days of the Confederacy," in Thomas B. Reed (ed.), *Modern Eloquence* (15 vols.; Philadelphia, 1900–1903), V, 471–72.

the battlefield of Gettysburg, and other touching tales that stirred the emotions of his listeners. Yet, it was his deft description of the closing scenes of the Civil War—the bone-tired fatigue of the seemingly ceaseless retreat from Petersburg, the anxiety of leaving his wife and newborn baby in Yankee hands, the magnanimous treatment of the Confederates by their humble victors, and the high drama of the surrender procession—that elicited the most tender responses. "Heroic bravery of Union soldiers, the undaunted courage of the Southern men, the self-sacrifice of noble Southern women, the patriotism of Northern womanhood, interspersed with lively anecdotes and abundant incidents illustrating the grim humor of the camp and the deep pathos and the suffering in the field and in the home"—containing all these elements, Gordon's lecture warmed the heart of even the coldest of listeners.[2]

Gordon first delivered "Last Days of the Confederacy" at the Tabernacle of Brooklyn in New York City on November 17, 1893. The audience and the reviewers in the northern city favorably received the southerner and his message. For two and one-half hours, his "magnetic eloquence" enthralled the five thousand listeners, many of whom had fought against him during the war. In "low but earnest tones," with a powerful and resonant voice, Gordon spoke with "a Southern warmth, dash, brilliancy and force" one reviewer rarely found among northern orators. "Aroused to the highest pitch of enthusiasm," the hugh throng frequently interrupted the general with "long continued applause." Although a reporter praised the sprightliness of the written speech, he found Gordon's departures from the text particularly effective and moving: "The lecturer literally ran away from his manuscript so often to tell a story or relate an incident full of pathos, or patriotism, or both," that the audience did not even notice the exceptional length of the lecture. Gordon received a rousing three cheers upon concluding, and spent a long time thereafter shaking hands with his appreciative listeners. Gordon's efforts proved so effective that New Yorkers immediately prevailed upon him to deliver the lecture again the following week at Carnegie Music Hall.[3]

2. Gordon, "Last Days of the Confederacy," in Reed (ed.), *Modern Eloquence*, V, 471–94; St. Louis *Republic* quoted in Southern Lyceum Bureau program for Gordon lecture, 1897–98 season, in John B. Gordon Biographical File, AHS, hereinafter cited as Southern Lyceum program.

3. New York *Tribune*, November 18, 1893; quote from "Special Announcement," in Southern Lyceum program; clipping from Brooklyn *Citizen*, November 18, 1893, in

During the next ten years, Gordon would deliver his lecture hundreds of times as he traversed the country on extensive tours. He enlisted the services of several lyceums and booking agencies to organize his speaking engagements. Even while serving as senator, Gordon conducted a series of tours when Congress was not in session. Soon after adjournment in March, 1895, he set out on a ten-state tour through the Midwest and trans-Mississippi South in which he fulfilled twenty-two engagements in six weeks. When freed of his political duties in 1897, Gordon devoted most of his time to lecturing. Indeed, it may have seemed to the general that he lived on a train, for his engagements kept him constantly on the move. So many of his letters closed with "hurriedly" or "on the run" that it is obvious he was "constantly on the wing."[4]

Gordon's brutal speaking schedule frequently kept him away from his wife and family for extended periods. Fanny occasionally accompanied him on tour, but generally she remained behind and attended to business and family matters as she had done throughout much of the postwar period. While he was in the Senate, she screened newspapers for him, negotiated with his creditors, handled much of his correspondence, managed the family budget, and performed countless other important tasks. Even after he left political office, Fanny continued her efforts to lighten his always-heavy burden by freeing him of many of the more mundane, day-to-day responsibilities. But, giving more than financial or clerical assistance, Fanny provided John with a sense of stability and serenity missing in his public career. Ever on the go and harried by indebtedness, Gordon derived strength from the affection and devotion of his wife. He was not the type of man to express publicly the depth of his feeling for Fanny, but on her birthday in 1891—their thirty-seventh wedding anniversary—he

Gordon Family Collection, UGA; Slaton Lyceum Bureau program for Gordon lecture, n.d., in Gordon Family Collection, UGA, hereinafter cited as Slayton Lyceum program; New York *Times*, November 25, 26, 1893.

4. Southern Lyceum program; Slayton Lyceum program; J. B. Gordon to Moorman, October 24, 1894, March 13, April 13, 1895, March 15, 27, November 26, 1897, January 30, October 23, 27, 1899, J. B. Gordon to Robert C. Woods, July 16, 1895, Frank Gordon to Moorman, April 30, 1897, February 7, March 5, 26, 1902, all in UCV Collection, LSU; J. B. Gordon to Miss Marry Carrington, November 20, 1899, in Isaac Howell Carrington Papers, Duke; J. B. Gordon to B. T. Johnson, November 26, 1897, in Bradley T. Johnson Papers, Duke; J. B. Gordon to W. E. Mickle, April 30, 1903, in United Confederate Veterans Collection, UGA, hereinafter cited as UCV Collection, UGA; Gordon to Scribner, October 24, 1902, in Charles Scribner's Sons Papers, Princeton.

penned a touching poem which reveals that his love for her had scarcely diminished over the years:

> Of all the days I now remember,
> The sweetest far was in September
> When woods and fields and star-lit skies,
> And mellow suns and Autumn sighs,
>
> Made earth so fair and life so sweet,
> As Heaven bowed this world to greet,
> And threw it's sheen o'er Nature's face
> And clasped all things in love's embrace.
>
> 'Twas natal day to fair young bride,
> 'Twas natal day to new born pride,
> In him whose life and hope and care,
> This fair young bride henceforth must share.
>
> So young she was, so winsome, coy,
> So lithe her form, so pure her joy,
> So rare her grace, so e'er discreet,
> So trusting, true, so fair and sweet,
>
> That happy man ne'er won for wife,
> To lift his aims and brighten life,
> More helpful hand or mind I ween,
> Than this sweet girl of seventeen.
>
> Though birthdays come and years pass by,
> Though clouds may dim September's sky,
> Though threads of gray may streak thy hair,
> And roses fade from cheeks so fair,
>
> Still beauty's seal is on thy brow,
> No brighter, nobler, then than now,
> And love's still warm, as 'twas when you
> Were seventeen, I twenty-two.[5]

Despite a longing to spend more time with his beloved Fanny, Gordon felt compelled to continue his long tours, for debt remained an ever-present companion. As his fame as a lecturer swept the country, he took precautions to guarantee himself a steady income as long as the lecture remained popular by copyrighting his speech. His fre-

5. Fanny Gordon to her daughter, Tuesday night [undated], and September 14, 1893, both in Gordon Family Collection, UGA; Gordon to Moorman, December 26, 1896, April 25, 1900, both in UCV Collection, LSU; Gordon to Scribner, September 11, 1903, in Scribner's Sons Papers, Princeton; Caroline Lewis Gordon, "De Gin'ral an' Miss Fanny," and untitled poem, both in Gordon Family Collection, UGA.

quent admonitions to reporters not to record his address demonstrated Gordon's concern for continued drawing power and the concomitant continued income. Nevertheless, he rarely gave exactly the same lecture twice. His constant polishing and reworking, his tailoring of the lecture to particular locales, his proclivity to ad-lib, and his stentorian delivery made his lecture an attraction of the first order. Even though he later developed a second companion lecture, "First Days of the Confederacy," it was his treatment of the last days of the Confederacy that captivated audiences throughout America.[6]

Reviews of Gordon's lectures seldom varied, except perhaps in reporters' efforts to outdo one another in their praise of the general. His stage presence rarely escaped mention. Described as "every inch a soldier, both in bearing and sentiment," and as "attractive, romantic, and courtly," Gordon was the archetypal southern general. He brought with him to the lectern the "same spirit of dash and vivacity" that had distinguished him on the battlefield and in the Senate. His clear, ringing voice filled auditoriums, and his oratorical talents allowed him to move his audiences alternately from laughter to tears to outbursts of wild enthusiasm. His skillful mingling of humor, pathos, and patriotism made the lecture a masterpiece. Observers marveled at his "mastery over the human heart" and his ability to cast "a spell which enchanted and enhanced them through every word of his resounding eloquence." Whenever Gordon apologized for the length of his speech and offered to close quickly, audiences throughout the country pleaded with him not to stop but to go on. Perhaps the Minneapolis *Sunday Times* best assessed Gordon's powers and presence when its reviewer wrote, "There was something so much deeper in the man than even in what he uttered that his very presence lent a solemn and sacred grandeur to the occasion."[7]

But as inspiring and captivating as Gordon's abilities and image were, it was his message that moved the American people so deeply.

6. Howard Dorgan, "A Case Study in Reconciliation: General John B. Gordon and 'The Last Days of the Confederacy,'" *Quarterly Journal of Speech*, LX (February, 1974), 83–91; Southern Lyceum program; Slayton Lyceum program.

7. New Haven *Morning News* and Minneapolis *Sunday Times*, quoted in Southern Lyceum program; Atlanta *Constitution*, January 8, 1904; Clement A. Evans, "General Gordon and General Longstreet," *Independent*, LVI (February, 1904), 314; New Orleans *Times-Democrat*, and New Orleans *Daily Picayune*, quoted in Slayton Lyceum program; Extracts from Press Comments on Gen. Gordon's Lecture (September 1894 tour), in John Brown Gordon Papers, Emory; Southern Lyceum program, *passim*; Slayton Lyceum program, *passim*.

More than "a gem of oratory," Gordon's lecture became a timeless and "superb outburst of patriotism." Newspapers called it a "matchless sermon from the gospel of peace," in which every sentence "was wreathed in an olive branch" and every thought "sweetly tempered with magnanimity." Certainly, Gordon's purpose was nationalistic, to present the war and wartime experiences in a manner removing the heated passions and transforming the struggle into a trial by fire wherein the American character had been tempered and strengthened. Thus the war and participation in it could be glorified. A Kansas editor wrote, "He is keeping green the memories of the war and its heroes on both sides, but he is obliterating the asperities of that strife." And a Georgian asserted that Gordon instilled "into the hearts of thousands of people, North and South, a higher appreciation of the gallant men who fought under Grant and Lee; a deeper veneration for American valor and unswerving fidelity, and a warmer love and a loftier pride in this great and reunited country."[8]

Gordon's effort to break down the barriers of hate and sectional animosity frequently brought about touching scenes, none more dramatic than an episode in Vermont. At the conclusion of Gordon's lecture before what had been a particularly icy crowd at the outset, an old man, with tears trickling down his cheeks, confronted the general and boldly proclaimed, "General Gordon, I have hated you for more than thirty years; I have hated everything South. I had cause for hating. You killed the noblest boy of my home, and he lies buried now in an unknown grave. We have mourned his loss all these years." But, the elderly gentleman then added, "when I had listened to you and heard you tell the history of your hardships, how the soldier marched barefooted, how he lived without a bite some days, how he suffered, I can see that he was fighting for the cause which he esteemed more dear than life." As he extended his hand to the former Confederate, the bereaved but now unburdened father pronounced, "I will never hate you any more. . . . My hatred for the South is gone forever."[9]

Although few of Gordon's experiences were as dramatic, his efforts to draw the people of the North and the South closer together through

8. Louisville *Courier-Journal*, St. Louis *Republic*, and Kansas City *Times*, quoted in Southern Lyceum program; Augusta *Chronicle*, quoted in Extracts from Press Comments; Southern Lyceum program, *passim*; Slayton Lyceum program, *passim*; Extracts from Press Comments, *passim*. See also Judge Selwyn N. Owen to Calvin Brice, July 6, 1894, W. H. Anderson to Gordon, November 10, 1903, both in Gordon Family Collection, UGA; Robert H. Cartmell Diary, October 13, 1894, in TSLA.

9. Atlanta *Journal*, January 9, 1904.

his lecture met with considerable success. Gordon nurtured his image as a peacemaker and made sure that nothing would detract from his mission of reconciliation. When on tour, he refused to enter into political discussions. Instead, he concentrated exclusively on the nonpartisan, nationalistic message of his lecture, which served as "a healing balm for sectional ill-will." Gordon explicitly stated his intent at the opening of his lecture: "[A]lthough you are to listen tonight to a Southern man, a Southern soldier, yet I beg you to believe that he is as true as any man to this Republic's flag and to all that it truly represents." Still, in his native South, Gordon's ability to make these old memories of heroism, comradery, and commitment to the Confederate cause come alive proved just as appealing and effective. In 1894, when Gordon's friend and fellow senator from North Carolina, Matt Ransom, appeared headed for defeat in an upcoming election, another Tar-Heel politician recommended that Ransom enlist Gordon's support. "Getting Genl Gordon to deliver his lecture on 'the last days of the Confederacy,' . . . and getting him to make an allusion to you" might be the trick needed to turn defeat into victory. Clearly, Gordon's lecture was immensely popular in both the North and the South. The gradual lessening of the bitterness engendered by the war and the changing times account in part for the tremendous popularity of the "Last Days of the Confederacy"; however, it was the old general's adeptness at stirring southern emotions without offending northern sentiments that primarily explains the success of the lecture. Carefully treading along the narrow path of common ground that he had helped to establish, Gordon contributed significantly to cementing national bonds between the former warring sections.[10]

In addition to his commitment to national reconciliation, Gordon also played an important role in helping southerners finally come to grips with their defeat in the Civil War. In doing so, he contributed mightily to the development of both the myth of the Old South and the cult of the Lost Cause. Southerners, in the wake of physical and psychological devastation wrought by the war, were a troubled people and slow to emerge from their disorientation in the years after Appomattox. The trauma of having to deal with defeat—an atypical American experience—largely explains the creation of an idealized

10. Dorgan, "Case Study in Reconciliation," 85–86; Gordon, "Last Days of the Confederacy," in Reed (ed.), *Modern Eloquence,* V, 471; R. J. Brevard to M. W. Ransom, July 3, 1894, in Matt W. Ransom Papers, SHC; Waldo W. Braden, *The Oral Tradition in the South* (Baton Rouge, 1983), 77–78.

heritage by postbellum southerners. They seized upon two powerful symbols to ease the burdens of their defeat. They painted a picture of the antebellum era as one of boundless prosperity, societal harmony, honorable and chivalrous whites, contented slaves, and, in every sense, a peaceful, pastoral South—something certainly worth preserving. The Old South that they envisioned, however, was a myth, an invention designed to help justify southern actions and erase the haunting sense of inferiority. Similarly, the celebration of the Confederacy and of the war, which grew during the final decades of the nineteenth century, also aided southerners in their effort to come to terms with defeat. This Confederate celebration, writes a historian of the movement, "incorporated an historical interpretation that maintained that the South had acted rightly in 1861–1865, reassured southerners that their honor and manhood had survived, and praised the common soldier as well as the leaders of the Confederacy." By the 1880s, southerners had begun to look back upon their past with more of a sense of nostalgia and pride than uneasiness and uncertainty. Curiously, the same men who fostered and embellished the vision of the old order and conjured up the ghosts of the Confederacy with the greatest gusto were generally the architects of the new order. And among the most important of these New South figures glorifying the past was John B. Gordon.[11]

Gordon's postwar career offers numerous examples of his determination to ensure that southerners not be stripped of their heritage because of their participation in the Civil War. His address before the Confederate Survivors' Association of Augusta, Georgia, on April 26, 1887, most vividly revealed his stylized vision of the past. Gordon discussed how portrayals of the South and its association with slavery that he felt were inaccurate endangered not only the present generation but succeeding ones as well. If these misrepresentations went unchallenged, the future would be fraught with peril: first would come "a decrease of our appreciation of this section and of its people"; then, "a diminution of our own self-respect" followed by a "gradual but certain retrogression and impairment of our manhood; and, finally, the loss of those distinctive characteristics which are the traditional, recognized, and chief sources of this people's greatness." Southerners must cherish their heritage, for, he claimed, "no age or

---

11. C. Vann Woodward, *Origins of the New South, 1877–1913* (Rev. ed.; Baton Rouge, 1971), 154–58; Gaines Milligan Foster, "Ghosts of the Confederacy: Defeat, History, and the Culture of the New South, 1865–1913" (Ph.D. dissertation, University of North Carolina, 1982), 4.

country has ever produced a civilization of a nobler type than that which was born in the southern plantation home." Even though he admitted that the gentility of that "old plantation life of the South" was gone forever, Gordon implored southerners not to forget their past and the immense contributions their forebears had made to republicanism in America. "The great problem of our future," he asserted, "is how to hold to the characteristics of our old civilization, when that civilization itself is gone; how to send the current which so enriched and purified the old, coursing forever through the new life before us; how to relight the old fires upon the new altars."[12]

Here, within the bounds of a single speech to Confederate survivors, lies a fascinating irony. Gordon, one of the most vocal proponents of and active participants in the new industrial order, was at the same time one of the greatest cultivators of the myth of the Old South. Although the incongruity appears obvious today, neither Gordon nor his contemporaries saw the apparent contradiction. The reason lies less in the duplicity of men like Gordon and more in the South's desperate need for a past of which its residents could be proud. Defeat deeply scarred many southerners. Rather than face the possibility that the sufferings and exertions of war might have had been in vain, southerners created an idealized Old South worth defending and dying for. In this manner, they also enabled former Confederates, as well as their descendants, to derive an intense, ardent pride from participation in the war. Their motives were ennobled, and their cause sanctified. Few, if any, propositions afforded Gordon greater pleasure than the opportunity to glorify the Confederate soldier and the Confederate cause.

Gordon dreaded the possibility that children of former Confederates might turn on their parents for their part in the war. He always

12. John B. Gordon, The Old South. Addresses Delivered Before the Confederate Survivors' Association in Augusta, Georgia, on the Occasion of Its Ninth Annual Reunion, on Memorial Day, April 16th 1887 by His Excellency, Governor John B. Gordon, and by Col. Charles C. Jones, Jr. (Augusta, Ga., 1887), 6–14. For a keener appreciation of the irony of ardent New South proponents embracing and developing a mythical vision of the Old South, see Michael M. Cass, "Charles C. Jones, Jr. and the 'Lost Cause,'" Georgia Historical Quarterly, IV (Summer, 1971), 222–33; Gordon to C. C. Jones, Jr., June 6, 1889, in John Brown Gordon Papers, Duke; A. H. Colquitt to C. C. Jones, Jr., July 27, 1889, in Alfred Holt Colquitt Papers, Duke. See also Waldo W. Braden, "Repining over an Irrevocable Past: The Ceremonial Orator in a Defeated Society, 1865–1900," in Waldo W. Braden (ed.), Oratory in the New South (Baton Rouge, 1979), 8–37; Howard Dorgan, "Rhetoric of the United Confederate Veterans: A Lost Cause Mythology in the Making," in Braden (ed.), Oratory in the New South, 143–73; Braden, Oral Tradition in the South, Ch. 4.

asserted that vigilance was especially necessary because "victory it-self vindicates, while defeat dooms to disparagement and misrepresentation the cause of the vanquished." He had long labored to see that the motives and actions of southern whites were fully explained. In order to provide impartial textbooks for southern school children, he became involved with the University Publishing Company. Gordon gave freely of his time and money to southern movements devoted to preserving the record of service of his beloved veterans. When veterans in Virginia organized the Association of the Army of Northern Virginia, Gordon joined his former comrades and also participated in several efforts to honor his former chieftain, Robert E. Lee. As statues and memorials to Confederate officials and soldiers began to appear in the 1870s and proliferated in the 1880s, Gordon knew no peer as a dedicator of monuments. He also lent his support to movements to provide assistance for Confederate widows, orphans, and disabled veterans. Fearful that the valiant conduct and honorable service of the Confederate soldiery might be forgotten or disparaged, he warned his fellow southerners that "a people without the memories of heroic suffering and sacrifice are A PEOPLE WITHOUT A HIS-TORY." It was for these same purposes, on behalf of which Gordon had toiled so long—accurately preserving and presenting the history of the Confederacy, keeping alive the fraternal spirit born in the trials of war, and aiding survivors and dependents—that Confederate veterans organized in New Orleans in June, 1889. His election and annual reelection as commander-in-chief of the United Confederate Veterans (UCV) provided Gordon with a source of great pride. He considered the privilege of leading the old soldiers once again·to be among his highest honors, and certainly the most gratifying.[13]

13. William E. Mickle (ed.), *Orders, U.C.V., General and Special* (2 vols.; New Orleans, 1911–12), I, General Orders No. 1, hereinafter cited as *UCV Orders; Minutes of the Annual Meetings and Reunions of the United Confederate Veterans*, 1898, p. 26, hereinafter cited as *UCV Minutes*; J. William Jones (comp.), *Army of Northern Virginia Memorial Volume* (Richmond, 1880), 13, 22–27, 37, 41–43, 48; "Appeal of the Lee Monument Association," *SHSP*, V (January–June, 1879), 141–42; "Annual Reunion of the Virginia Division, A.N.V.," *SHSP*, VI (July–December, 1879), 289; "Sketch of the Lee Memorial Association," *SHSP*, XI (July, 1883), 388–90; "Annual Reunion of the Association of the Army of Northern Virginia," *SHSP*, XVII (1889), 112; "The Monument to General Robert E. Lee," *SHSP*, XVII (1889), 190, 193; "Soldiers Monument," *SHSP*, XVII (1889), 391; "General Jubal A. Early," *SHSP*, XXII (1894), 284; "Unveiling of the Soldiers and Sailors Monument," *SHSP*, XXII (1894), 342; Atlanta *Constitution*, October 18, 25, 1870, November 12, 1874, June 2, 1875, May 23, 1878, June 16, 1883, April 10, May 3, 1884, April 9, May 10, 1889; Gordon to Fish, April 7, 1884, in Hamilton Fish Collection, LC; Alberta Malone, *History of the Atlanta Ladies Memo-*

The organizers of the UCV gave scant consideration to anyone other than Gordon for the post of commander-in-chief. There were other Confederate officers of higher rank, but none was more popular than the Georgian. Although it is difficult to determine the extent of Gordon's involvement in the early development of the UCV, he kept well abreast of its affairs. Even with his other interests and responsibilities, Gordon was in almost constant communication with the man most responsible for the success of organization, George Moorman. Prior to Gordon's appointment of Moorman as adjutant general in mid–1891, the UCV had grown very slowly; but once Moorman assumed responsibility for the management of the fledgling association, membership skyrocketed. Clearly, Moorman was the driving force behind the UCV. However, the heavy volume of correspondence between him and the commander-in-chief demonstrates that Gordon was vitally concerned with the organization. During the year and a half after Moorman took control of the UCV office, Gordon continually prodded the adjutant to wage an active campaign to bring more and more Confederate veterans into the fold. Particularly interested in having Georgia camps join, Gordon wrote that he felt "it is a reflection on me to have Georgia lagging behind." In addition to pressing the effort to pull in all existing groups in the South, he encouraged the organization of camps in New York and Chicago. Gordon did not manage the UCV—that was left to Moorman—but he did oversee its operations.[14]

rial Association, 1866–1946 (Atlanta, 1946), 4, 31–32 (copy in AHS); Gordon to T. K. Oglesby, September 7, 1903, in Thaddeus K. Oglesby Collection, Duke; J. B. Gordon to Editor of the Richmond Dispatch, May 19, 1894, in Munford-Ellis Family Papers, Duke; William W. White, The Confederate Veteran (Tuscaloosa, Ala., 1962), 20–21; C. Vann Woodward, Tom Watson: Agrarian Rebel (New York, 1938), 63.

14. Proceedings of the Convention for Organization, and Adoption of the Constitution of the United Confederate Veterans, June 10th, 1889 (New Orleans, 1891); Confederate Veteran, III (1895), 145, and XII (1904), 425; New Orleans Times-Picayune, June 10, 11, 1889; W. W. White, Confederate Veteran, 26–35; Gaines M. Foster, Ghosts of the Confederacy (New York, 1987), 105–106, 110–12; Herman Hattaway, "Clio's Southern Soldiers: The United Confederate Veterans and History," Louisiana History, XII (Summer, 1971), 214; Herman Hattaway, "The United Confederate Veterans in Louisiana," Louisiana History, XVI (Winter, 1975), 15; Clement A. Evans (ed.), Confederate Military History (12 vols.; Atlanta, 1899), XII, 512a–512h; Gordon to Moorman, June 9, September 17, October 29, November 12, 16, 21, December 26, 1891, March 1, 15, June 2, July 7, October 26, 27, 1892, Gordon to J. C. Underwood, March 1, 1892, all in UCV Collection, LSU; Gordon to W. E. Mickle, February 27, 1892, S. D. Lee to W. E. Mickle, April 4, 1897, February 4, 1904, in UCV Collection, UGA. For a brief history of the UCV, see clippings of William E. Beard, "The UCV Marches in Review," from the Nashville Banner, 1941, in Gordon Family Collection, UGA.

Even in later years, when his extensive speaking commitments and his deteriorating physical health restricted his involvement, Gordon directed the course of the UCV quite effectively. He took his position as the symbolic head of all Confederate veterans quite seriously and displayed an acute concern for guarding the image of the organization. Wary of offending other Confederates, Gordon saw to it that the UCV generally refrained from endorsing specific magazines or books as officially sanctioned works. The UCV, under Gordon's supervision, however, did lend support to organizations like the Sons of the Confederate Veterans and United Daughters of the Confederacy. When questions concerning the conduct of officials in local camps were raised, Gordon expressed his concern about possible disgrace such individuals might bring to the UCV. Gordon similarly maintained a firm control on what went before the public. Following Moorman's death in 1903, Gordon instructed his successor not to send out any public orders involving the association until he had personally reviewed them. Later he added, "[I]n all matters of any moment that go to the public press with my name, I naturally w'd like to see them before publication." More than mere personal considerations prompted Gordon's discretion; he was determined to protect the UCV's image. His vigilance, along with Moorman's skillful management, prevented the minor controversies that surfaced frequently within the membership from erupting into serious threats to the organization.[15]

As the UCV grew in size, the annual reunion became the central focus of the organization. Each year, thousands of aging veterans, often accompanied by their families, descended upon a designated southern city. These meetings grew to be magnificent spectacles. Transportation and lodging discounts were often provided as each city struggled to outdo the efforts of previous hosts with even more elaborate preparations. Indeed, for most veterans, attendance at the UCV reunions became the major social event of the year; there they attempted to recapture those magic moments of their youth. And just as the annual reunion served as the "central ritual of the Confederate celebration," Gordon served as the celebration's "primary ceremo-

15. Gordon to Moorman, December 13, 1895, February 19, 1900, March 25, 1902, S. A. Cunningham to Moorman, February 11, 1898, all in UCV Collection, LSU; Gordon to W. E. Mickle, February 5, 15, 1903, in UCV Collection, UGA. Evidence of numerous minor controversies which sprang up among UCV members can be found throughout the voluminous correspondence of the organization, in UCV Collection, LSU.

nial figure." As it was recorded in the minutes of one UCV meeting, the "name of Gordon is the electric spark that always makes the Veterans wild with joy." His arrival in the assembly hall frequently set off spontaneous demonstrations of tremendous enthusiasm, and when he appeared on stage and spoke to the men he fondly referred to as "my boys," all the memories came flooding back. "His eloquence and spirited delivery never fail[ed] to have a marked effect on the veterans." The bond of love between the commander-in-chief and his "boys" was as mutual as it was genuine.[16]

The wildest, most unrestrained outbursts of affection occurred when Gordon attempted to step down as head of the UCV. He first expressed his desire that another veteran should be allowed to share the honor of heading the organization at the second reunion, but the rank and file would have none of it. They refused his request and unanimously reelected him. Obviously moved, Gordon responded, "I cannot speak to you my brethren. My heart full, is at your feet; my life and all I have is at your service." This same scene was repeated time and time again, for on every occasion that Gordon broached the subject of his retirement, his "boys" shouted him down and unanimously reelected him amidst the wildest of scenes. Hats and umbrellas were thrown into the air, handkerchiefs fluttered, flags waved with the vigor of old, enthusiastic cheers mingled with strains of "Dixie," and the old "Rebel yell" reverberated off the walls as the "old warriors shouted themselves hoarse." Although these "love feasts" took place annually, perhaps the most touching of these always emotional scenes came during the seventh annual reunion in Nashville. Two weeks before the veterans assembled, Gordon issued a letter declining his sure-to-come nomination. At the reunion, he reiterated his desire to pass the mantle of command on to another and to take his place "by the side of those untitled heroes who bore the battle's brunt in the bloody work of war." But despite his protestations and a farewell speech, the veterans ignored his wishes, and instead, nominated and elected him by acclamation. A tearful, grateful Gordon, "humbled to dust," replied, "My comrades there is nothing left me as a soldier, but to bow to your will, and God being my helper I shall serve you to the best of my ability." There would be no further discus-

16. W. W. White, *Confederate Veteran*, 35–41; Hattaway, "Clio's Southern Soldiers," 215; Foster, *Ghosts of the Confederacy*, 133–39, 112; *UCV Minutes*, 1898, p. 59; 1899, p. 10; 1901, p. 72; New Orleans *Times-Picayune*, June 14, 24, 1897.

328 · JOHN BROWN GORDON

sion of the matter; the old general would remain at the head of his men until death intervened.[17]

It would be difficult to exaggerate the central role Gordon played in the southern quest for vindication. As the living symbol of the Confederacy, he became the principal ceremonial figure in the Confederate celebration, the embodiment of the Lost Cause. In his scarred face, veterans could catch a glimpse of their own past. The smell of powder, the smoke of battle, the roll of artillery, and din of musketry, as well as the fatigue of the march and the comradery in camp—all came alive as the proud, erect figure of the Georgian strolled about the stage. The Hero of Appomattox stood as a representation of chivalry, honor, and bravery, all that was worthy of preserving in the Old South and in the Confederate war effort. Revered by the South and respected by the North, Gordon became even more important as a symbol than he was as a man.

As commander of the UCV and as a private citizen, Gordon resolutely strove to open channels of communication between northern and southern veterans. In the Senate and in his business dealings, he had developed associations with northerners, many of whom had fought against him. In the 1880s, as chairman of a committee to provide a home for disabled Confederate soldiers, Gordon solicited contributions from numerous former foes. In addition to attending the funerals of several Union generals, Gordon poignantly eulogized his friend President Grant in the southern press upon the general's death in 1885. And when the movement to establish national military parks began to grow, he frequently joined with northern veterans at the dedications of the battlefields. Many of the barriers that once stood between the soldiers of the North and the South had been removed by the late 1880s, when steps to organize joint reunions were undertaken. Gordon not only supported these blue-gray reunions, but also participated in many of them as well. In his commitment to bring veterans on both sides closer together, Gordon attempted to use the UCV as something more than just a celebration of

17. *UCV Minutes*, 1891, pp. 13–14; 1897, pp. 52–60; 1898, p. 59; 1899, p. 10. See also *ibid.*, 1892, pp. 107–109; 1894, pp. 13–14; 1895, p. 62; 1896, p. 115; 1897, pp. 54–60; 1898, pp. 58–59; 1899, p. 175; 1900, p. 68; 1901, p. 72; 1902, pp. 82–83; 1903, p. 87. Although the wildest reactions came when Gordon attempted to step down, the *UCV Minutes* are full of examples of similar enthusiastic outbursts. A reunion was held each year except 1893, when national economic conditions forced its cancellation. Gordon to Moorman, July 3, 1893, in UCV Collection, LSU; *UCV Orders*, I, General Orders No. 99; I, General Orders No. 103; I, General Orders No. 108.

the Confederacy and the mythical southern past. For him, the UCV served as another section of the bridge spanning "the bloody chasm" that still yawned between the North and the South.[18]

In 1898, the Spanish-American War added impetus to Gordon's reconciliatory efforts. Eleven years prior to the outbreak of war with Spain, he had told an Ohio audience, "I have sometimes thought that I would be willing to see one more war, that we might march under the stars and stripes, shoulder to shoulder, against a common foe." Gordon seized upon the opportunity the war presented to expound on the vindicatory benefits southern participation offered. At the eighth UCV reunion in July, 1898, in Atlanta, Gordon declared that the war would lead "to the complete and permanent obliteration of all sectional distrusts, and to the establishment of the too long delayed brotherhood and unity of the American people, which shall neither be broken nor called into question no more forever." Later in the meeting, at Gordon's prompting, the convention rose as one to approve a patriotic memorial pledging the full support of the UCV for President William McKinley. The president's reply to the Confederates' resolution echoed Gordon's sentiments: "The present war has certainly served one very useful purpose in completely obliterating the sectional lines drawn in the last one. The response to the Union's call to arms has been equally spontaneous and patriotic in all parts of the country. Veterans of the gray, as well as of the blue, are now fighting side by side, winning equal honor and renown." It seemed as if the final obstacles on the road to reunion were being removed.[19]

Despite the satisfaction Gordon unquestionably derived from the increased evidence of reconciliation at the turn of the century, events

18. Atlanta *Constitution*, June 4, 1876, March 22, April 10, May 3, 1884, April 10, July 31, August 13, 1885, July 3, 9, 1888, April 9, May 10, 1889, July 5, August 22, 1890; New York *Times*, August 17, 1891, September 20, 1895; Gilbert E. Govan and James W. Livingood, *The Chattanooga Country, 1540–1976: From Tomahawks to TVA* (Knoxville, 1977), 367–68; Gordon to Hamilton Fish, April 7, 1884, in Fish Collection; Gordon to J. Madison Drake, May 27, 1889, Gordon to Thomas J. Kennan, Jr., May 23, 1894, both in Gordon Papers, Duke; William O. McDowell to Gordon, November 1, 1891, in UCV Collection, LSU; [Gordon?] to C. A. Williams, April 19, 1884, Gordon to A. W. Rand, April 23, 1884, Gordon to J. Z. Westervelt, May 2, 1884, O'Beirne to Gordon, May 3, 1884, all in John Brown Gordon Records, 1883–1890, AC. 00-118, GDAH; U. S. Grant to Gordon, April 21, 1884, in Gordon Family Collection, UGA; "Editorial Paragraphs," *SHSP*, XII (May, 1884), 238–39.

19. Gordon, quoted in Huber W. Ellingsworth, "Southern Reconciliation Orators in the North, 1868–1899" (Ph.D. dissertation, Florida State University, 1955), 77; *UCV Minutes*, 1898, pp. 22–27, 55–57; New York *Times*, July 24, 1898; Atlanta *Constitution*, July 24, 1898.

in the middle of 1900 revealed that sectional antagonisms were still alive. A minority within the organization continued to generate an undercurrent hostile to all moves toward fraternization with the UCV's northern counterpart, the Grand Army of the Republic (GAR). At the tenth annual UCV meeting in Louisville in June, the introduction of a resolution "calling for expressions of fraternal feeling between the North and South threw the convention into an uproar." Amid a wildly chaotic scene, Gordon rose to head off the minority challenge by speaking in favor of the proposal. "I trust the day shall never come," he told the veterans, "when I shall refuse to send a message of cordial greeting to an enemy gallant enough to greet a foe of thirty-five years ago." Following his forceful endorsement, the resolution passed; nevertheless, the hostile opposition it inspired showed that not all Confederates accepted increasing fraternization with their former enemies.[20]

A brief but potentially explosive incident at a large blue-gray reunion in Atlanta six weeks later could have provided substantial ammunition for these irreconcilables. Both Gordon and Albert Shaw, commander of the Grand Army of the Republic, attended and spoke at the ceremonies. Relations between the old foes were cordial until Shaw interjected an objectionable request into his otherwise warmly reconciliatory address. The Union commander urged southerners to refrain from teaching their children that the Confederate cause had been just and correct. Such teachings, he maintained, were "all out of order, unwise, unjust" and fanned the flames of sectionalism. Shaw meant no disrespect whatsoever to the Confederate veterans themselves in his call for a common history for all sections of the country. But Gordon, sensing personal and sectional impugnment, leaped to his feet immediately upon the conclusion of Shaw's speech. Having labored so earnestly since the war's end to ensure that southerners' motives would not be misconstrued and that the exertions of the southern soldiery would not be denigrated, Gordon could not allow what he perceived as an affront to the South to pass unchallenged. He protested against the insinuation "that teaching our children that the cause for what we fought and our comrades died is all wrong." Rather than assail his Union counterpart, however, Gordon again presented his nationalistic interpretation of the war, "namely, that both sides were right because both were fighting for the constitution of the

20. *UCV Minutes*, 1900, pp. 111–13.

fathers as they had been taught to interpret it, and both were right." Shaw, realizing how his remarks lent themselves to misinterpretation, endorsed Gordon's comments and stated that though confusion had resulted, he and the Georgian were of the same sentiment. Prudence on the part of the two commanders, particularly Shaw, avoided what could have developed into a fiery and damaging confrontation.[21]

Continued criticism from a few disgruntled Confederate veterans for his participation in blue-gray activities quickly brought forth a public letter of explanation from the general. He did not apologize in the least for his actions; on the contrary, he insisted, "I shall continue the efforts which I have made for nearly thirty years in the interest of sectional harmony and unity." Gordon reiterated his commitment to do whatever he could "for the truth of history, for justice to the South, and to all sections for fostering our cherished memories . . . and for the settlement of all sectional controversies on a basis consistent with the honor and the manhood and the self-respect of all." In essence, Gordon summarized the major influences on his postwar career. While steadily working to eradicate sectional differences, he remained on guard to see that the interests of the South were protected and that its inhabitants were not portrayed in an uncomplimentary light. His efforts continued to widen that narrow path leading toward national unity that he had helped to establish with his lecture and other, earlier actions.[22]

Still, Gordon's most enduring contribution to nationalism came with the publication of *Reminiscences of the Civil War*. Friends had long urged him to write a book about his war experiences, but Gordon found it difficult to devote time to the project. In addition to his Senate responsibilities, his lecture tours, his commitments to the UCV, his various business ventures, and his private interests, Gordon's health noticeably began to fail. Beset by the infirmities normally associated with old age, Gordon frequently fell victim to overexertion. In his later years, broken bones, dislocated and sprained joints, and a variety of other incapacitating injuries and illnesses increasingly plagued the general. Nevertheless, in December, 1896,

21. Atlanta *Constitution*, July 20, 21, 1900; New York *Times*, July 20, 21, 1900; Mary R. Dearing, *Veterans in Politics: The Story of the G.A.R.* (Baton Rouge, 1952), 495; *Confederate Veteran*, VIII (1900), 297; Gordon to Moorman, July 25, 26, August 14, 1900, all in UCV Collection, LSU.
22. New York *Times*, August 21, 1900.

he first approached Charles S. Scribner's Sons about a book on the Civil War that he had been preparing for some time. Modeling his work on the informal style he used in his lecture, Gordon proposed to develop "another side of that war, as yet unwritten, the story which should not be lost." He wanted to preserve the story of the soldiers who had fought on both sides. His purpose was "first to intensify, if I can, the National patriotic and fraternal spirit and second, to make money for myself. The one I trust is a high and laudable purpose; the other is with me a stern necessity." Once again, Gordon tied his own fortunes to a higher goal.[23]

Gordon and the publishing firm finally reached an agreement in 1902. The terms of his contract with Scribner's Sons provided him with a 15 percent royalty on the first ten thousand copies sold and 20 percent on all books sold thereafter. Gordon would receive a three thousand dollar advance and agreed to allow Scribner's Sons to publish articles from his manuscript in *Scribner's Magazine*. For each of the three articles published prior to the release of his book, he received four hundred dollars. The general also gained the right to purchase copies of the book at half price, so that he could sell them on his own. And in addition to the 50 percent discount, Gordon arranged for a personal commission on all books that he helped sell for the publisher. Although he would not permit the UCV itself to become directly involved in the marketing of the book, Gordon clearly sought to capitalize on his contacts with the veterans and on his lecture engagements.[24]

23. John B. Gordon, *Reminiscences of the Civil War* (New York, 1903), xi; Gordon to Gentlemen, December 22, 1896, in Scribner's Sons Papers, Princeton; New York *Times*, May 1, 1897; Frank Gordon to Moorman, May 3, 5, December 11, 1897, February 25, 1898, June 13, 1899, J. B. Gordon to Moorman, December 23, 1897, September 7, November 26, 1898, January 2, 10, July 24, September 13, September [n.d.], October 31, 1899, February 16, August 26, 1900, January 8, 1901, March 27, 1902, Caroline Lewis Gordon to Moorman, October 7, 1898, March 25, May 31, 1899, Hugh H. Gordon, Jr., to Moorman, July 15, 1901, J. B. Gordon to W. E. Mickle, February 9, July 13, 1903, all in UCV Collection, LSU; J. B. Gordon to W. E. Mickle, February 5, 15, March 10, 21, August 21, 1903, all in UCV Collection, UGA; J. B. Gordon to W. E. Mickle, December 29, 1903, in John Brown Gordon Papers, Emory; J. B. Gordon to Mrs. Bryan, March 16, 1900, in Mary Norcott Bryan Scrapbook, SHC; J. B. Gordon to James Callaway, July 4, 1898, in John Brown Gordon Paper, Collection No. 317, GHS; J. B. Gordon to S. D. Smedes, September 7, 1899, in Papers of the Dabney Family, Box 1, (No. 7690-p), Manuscripts Department, University of Virginia Library, Charlottesville; Atlanta *Journal*, January 8, 1904.

24. Gordon to Scribner, January 17, 1901, May 24, June 11, July 2, September 29, October 24, November 1, 1902, September 7, 11, 1903, and Memorandum of Agreement between Gordon and Charles Scribner's Sons, June 2, 1902, all in Scribner's Sons Papers, Princeton. See also "Points of Advantage on Gordon Book," (Typescript in

Gordon made numerous suggestions concerning the printing, illustrating, and marketing of the book, but he was unable to press his proposals because he needed money badly. Even as he and his sons moved toward establishing another southern life insurance company, he bemoaned his indebtedness: "[D]ebt, debt—what a horrible master it is & how I long to get from under its dominion so I can rest & take it easy." Obviously, the financial pressures under which he had labored much of his life continued to weigh upon him in his later years. In June, 1899, his Sutherland estate was destroyed by fire. Even though Gordon saved most of the furniture and carried insurance, the destruction of his magnificent estate and the cost of rebuilding it "block for block" in the style of the original worked a significant hardship on the general. Perhaps even worse than the financial burdens it imposed was the keen sense of loss he felt at the destruction of most of his private correspondence and personal mementos. Almost as quickly as word of the sad fate that had befallen their commander reached prominent members of the UCV, movements were undertaken to ease his distress. Gordon graciously thanked his fellow veterans, but he declined to accept any assistance and disavowed all such efforts. It seems almost ironic that the man who had so often organized and contributed to similar efforts to aid other Confederates would adamantly prohibit his "boys" from assisting him.[25]

*ibid.*), and Gordon to W. E. Mickle, August 21, 27, September 11, 1903, all in UCV Collection, UGA. Gordon's three articles in *Scribner's Magazine* are "My First Command and the Outbreak of War," XXXIII (May, 1903), 514–28; "Antietam and Chancellorsville," XXXIII (June, 1903), 685–99; and "Gettysburg," XXXIV (July, 1903), 2–24.

25. Gordon to Scribner, May 6, August 26, September 3, 5, 7, 11, 1903, Clark Howell to Gordon, September 4, 1903, in Scribner's Sons Papers, Princeton; Atlanta *Constitution*, June 22, 1899; Atlanta *Journal*, January 8, 1904; C. L. Gordon, "De Gin'ral an' Miss Fanny"; J. B. Gordon to my dear General, October 26, 1899, in Gordon Family Papers, Collection No. 318, GHS; E. G. Gordon to Moorman, July 8, 1899, G. W. Gordon to Moorman, July 25, 1899, J. B. Gordon to Moorman, December 26, 1896, September 13, September [n.d.], 1899, April 25, 1900, all in UCV Collection, LSU; Gordon to W. E. Mickle, December 29, 1903, in John Brown Gordon Papers, Emory. For details concerning Gordon's Sutherland home and its eventual razing, see Atlanta *Journal*, March 16, 1924, January 16, 1927, February 21, 1937, October 11, 1942; C. L. Gordon, "De Gin'ral an' Miss Fanny"; and Paul W. Miller (ed.), *Atlanta: Capital of the South* (New York, 1949), 218–20. Also, for a brief sketch of Gordon's new life insurance company, the American Annuity and Mutual Life Company, see J. B. Gordon to Moorman, February 27, 1900, January 8, October 19, 1901, Hugh H. Gordon to Moorman, November 10, 1900, Frank Gordon to Moorman, December 4, 1900, all in UCV Collection, LSU; Gordon to B. N. Duke, September 7, 1900, Confidential Circular Letter from General J. B. Gordon, September 1, 1900, both in Benjamin N. Duke Collection, Duke; Gordon to E. P. McKissick, September 19, 1900, in Edward Perrin McKissick Papers, SCL.

Nevertheless, many aided him in a less direct manner by buying his book. *Reminiscences of the Civil War* became an immediate success and went through several printings within the first year. Reviewers lavished praise upon both the author and his work. Written with "charming simplicity" in a "style unaffected, luminous and often eloquent," *Reminiscences* was heralded as "genial, magnanimous and tolerant," a "model of modesty and clarity." Many readers marveled at Gordon's ability to bring to life the humorous, tragic, and pathetic scenes of the Civil War while avoiding "the peculiar egotism" that often marred works of the kind. The absence of personal and sectional prejudice made it appealing to all parts of the country. Northerners found no bitterness or animosity toward themselves and southerners praised the book's lesson "that it is un-American and untruthful to contend that all the honorable motives rested with one side and all the ignoble motives in the other." One journal, the *Outlook*, called *Reminiscences* "not only one of the most important contributions yet made to the literature of a great period, but one of the most fascinating and charming books that has come from the hand of an American man of action."[26]

Gordon's uplifting, nationalistic message contributed significantly to the success of the book. Gordon did not discuss the causes of the war at length; instead, as he put it in his introduction, he endeavored "to make a brief but dispassionate and judicially fair analysis of the divergent opinions and ceaseless controversies" that precipitated the war. Although he admitted that "slavery was undoubtedly the immediate fomenting cause of the woful [sic] American conflict," he contended that it was not the sole cause. For Gordon, the fundamental issue originated in "the clashing theories and bristling arguments of 1787," those matters so earnestly debated by the Founding

26. Advertisements in *Dial*, XXXV (July-December, 1903), 241, 329, 377, 445; "Reminiscences of a Confederate General," *Dial*, XXXV (November, 1903), 302–305; John S. Wise, "Two Great Confederates. General John B. Gordon and General James Longstreet: Characterizations by a Friend of Both," *American Monthly Review of Reviews*, XXIX (February, 1904), 204; New York *Evening Sun*, quoted in *Dial*, XXXV (November, 1903), 329; New York *Times*, November 21, 1903; Thomas G. Jones to Gordon, November 10, 1903, in Gordon Family Collection, UGA; "Soldier and Gentleman," *Outlook*, LXXVI (January, 1904), 152. See also George F. Hoar to Gordon, November 2, 1903, Grover Cleveland to Gordon, January 7, 1904, clipping from New York *Sun*, November 1, 1903, all in Gordon Family Collection, UGA; "A Volunteer General," *Spectator*, XCII (April, 1904), 667–68; "Gen. Gordon's Reminiscences," *Nation*, LXXVIII (May, 1904), 373–75; "General Gordon's Reminiscences," *Independent*, LV (December, 1903), 3127–28.

Fathers. As he had maintained since the war's end, differing constitutional interpretations with regard to the powers of the states and the national government provided the genesis of conflict. Over time these opposing constitutional concepts took on sectional dimensions and eventually led to war. Gordon explained that southerners, believing that efforts to restrict the expansion of slavery infringed upon their constitutionally prescribed rights, merely exercised another constitutional right when they seceded. Southerners, therefore, were as justified in their effort to dissolve the Union as northerners were in theirs to preserve it. Yet, Gordon did not dwell upon constitutional differences because, for him, the northern victory in the war finally and forever settled all questions concerning the nature of the Union. Continued controversy over who was right or wrong was pointless because, as he asserted, "[t]ruth, justice and patriotism unite in proclaiming that both sides fought for liberty as bequeathed by the Fathers, one for liberty in the Union of the States, the other for liberty in the Independence of the States."[27]

The dominating spirit of *Reminiscences*, however, emanates from Gordon's desire to preserve a record of both the soldiers who wore the blue and those who wore the gray. Gordon's glorification of the honor, bravery, and patriotism of the American soldier and of American manhood spills over onto every page of this charming, completely inoffensive account of his wartime experiences. Gordon paid equally high tributes to the leaders and men of both armies. His praise of "Yank" and "Reb" alike is so overflowing that it impossible to ascertain any point of distinction between the character of the two. A portrait of a chivalrous, humble, spiritual, gallant American soldier emerges from Gordon's vivid descriptions of battle and camp scenes. In his veneration of the character of the American soldier, Gordon hoped to accomplish "a still higher aim." He wanted to establish a "common ground on which all may stand; where justification of one section does not require or imply condemnation of the other." It was Gordon's fervent wish that all Americans recognize the strength of character exhibited by soldiers in both armies. Recognition that each side had fought equally hard for what it believed was right would open the door to complete reconciliation. Once again, Gordon propounded a nationalist interpretation of the war that was acceptable to northerners and southerners alike.[28]

27. Gordon, *Reminiscences*, xi–xiii, 13–25.
28. *Ibid.*, xii-xiii, 25, *passim*; "Reminiscences of a Confederate General," 303.

*Reminiscences of the Civil War* preached virtually the same sermon that Gordon had delivered so often during the last third of the nineteenth century. In the "Last Days of the Confederacy," at joint functions between the UCV and the GAR, and on so many other occasions, he worked to reunite the North and the South more completely. Gordon probably reached more people with his lecture than he did with *Reminiscences*, and his public role as a conciliator for nearly forty years was his most far-reaching contribution to national reconciliation; but *Reminiscences* is the most complete statement of his feelings. Gordon summarized his message best in the final pages of the book.

> The unseemly things which occurred in the great conflict between the States should be forgotten, or at least forgiven, and no longer permitted to disturb complete harmony between North and South. American youth in all sections should be taught to hold in perpetual remembrance all that was great and good on both sides; to comprehend the inherited convictions for which saintly women suffered and patriotic men died; to recognize the unparalleled carnage as proof of unrivalled courage; to appreciate the singular absence of personal animosity and the frequent manifestation between those brave antagonists of a good-fellowship such as had never before been witnessed between hostile armies. It will be a glorious day for our country when all the children within its borders shall learn that the four years of fratricidal war between the North and the South was waged by neither with criminal or unworthy intent, but by both to protect what they conceived to be threatened rights and imperilled liberty; that the issues which divided the sections were born when the Republic was born, and were forever buried in an ocean of fraternal blood. We shall then see that, under God's providence, every sheet of flame from the blazing rifles of the contending armies, every whizzing shell that tore through the forests at Shiloh and Chancellorsville, every cannon-shot that shook Chickamauga's hills or thundered around the heights of Gettysburg, and all the blood and the tears that were shed are yet to become contributions of the upbuilding American manhood and for the future defence of American freedom. The Christian Church received its baptism of pentecostal power as it emerged from the shadows of Calvary, and went forth to its world-wide work with greater unity and a diviner purpose. So the Republic, rising from its baptism of blood with a national life more robust, a national union more complete, and a national influence ever widening, shall go forever forward in its benign mission to humanity.

For Gordon, the Civil War served as the crucible of the American nation. This testing, purifying, and strengthening of the character of its citizens in both the North and the South convinced him that the future of America was indeed bright.[29]

In *Reminiscences*, Gordon brought together all his earlier efforts. Published less than three months before his death, *Reminiscences* represented the capstone of a nearly forty-year career devoted in large part to reconciling the formerly warring sections. One contemporary regarded the book as "a monument to his memory more beautiful than any that will be built by those who loved and honored him, a tribute more eloquent than any that can ever be paid by those who knew him best." With the publication of his book in October, 1903, Gordon's labors were at an end. He said as much just before Christmas. Stopping briefly in Atlanta on his way to his winter home near Miami, Gordon confided to a friend, "I feel in my heart there is not much left for me to do" now that "the bitterness of civil strife [is] forgotten" and replaced with "a promise of universal brotherhood under a reunited flag." Looking forward to a period of rest and recuperation, he continued on to Florida where the Gordon family would spend the holidays. There, in the state where Gordon had envisioned an empire and yet had experienced his greatest business failure, the vital spirit that had driven him so fiercely on the battlefield, in the Senate, and in business would finally be stilled.[30]

29. Gordon, *Reminiscences*, 464–65.

30. Advertisement in *Dial*, XXXV (October, 1903), 241; "Soldier and Gentleman," 152; Frances Gordon Smith, "Memorial Sketch of the Last Hours, Death, and Funeral of General John B. Gordon," in John B. Gordon, *Reminiscences of the Civil War* (New York, 1904), xxi.

# Epilogue

Shortly before Christmas, 1903, Gordon headed south to Biscayne Bay, seeking to escape the wintry blasts of Georgia in favor of the tropical breezes of Florida. Having just finished a lecture tour through New England, Gordon seemed tired, but no more so than usual; speaking tours always wore heavily on the nearly seventy-two-year-old General. As two weeks in the warm sun and ocean air again appeared to work their recuperative magic, Gordon revived and "was feeling unusually well." On Tuesday, January 5, he and his grandson tramped through the fields and orchards surrounding his home. That evening Gordon talked with members of his family and speculated about further developing his farming interests on the Florida property. All seemed fine and the general appeared healthy.[1]

Early the next morning, however, almost immediately upon arising, Gordon took a chill. Although he returned to bed at once, the chill persisted and then grew more violent. Alarmed, his family summoned a physician from Miami; but before the doctor arrived, the chill became a fever that quickly rose to 105 degrees. The general worsened, suffering severely from an attack of nausea. Soon he was delirious and fighting for his life. Almost from the outset, his physicians doubted Gordon would recover, citing his "advanced age and general depleted strength from previous impaired health." Through-

1. Frances Gordon Smith, "Memorial Sketch of the Last Hours, Death, and Funeral of General John B. Gordon," in John B. Gordon, *Reminiscences of the Civil War* (New York, 1904), xxi-xxii; Atlanta *Constitution*, January 8–10, 1904; Atlanta *Journal*, January 7–9, 1904. For additional information on Gordon's agricultural plans in Florida, see Henry F. Emery-J. B. Gordon letters, in Gordon Family Collection, UGA.

out Wednesday, Thursday, and Friday, he showed no real signs of improving; his kidneys began to fail and his heart became weak and beat intermittently. Briefly regaining consciousness on Saturday morning, he gazed upon a sun-drenched Biscayne Bay and in "low and broken tones" spoke to those gathered at his bedside. " 'It seems,' he sighed, 'a poor use of God's beautiful gifts to us to be ill on a day like this!' " For the remainder of the day, Gordon alternated between unconsciousness and semiconsciousness. Although apparently aware of those around him at times, he was simply too weak to speak. By early evening, all hope was lost: his kidneys ceased to function and uremic poisoning set in. Finally, at 10:05 P.M., January 9, 1904, "as peacefully as a little child falls asleep," John B. Gordon died.[2]

As word of Gordon's death flashed across the country, Georgians prepared to honor their most beloved native son. Plans for a massive state funeral were undertaken immediately, and proposals to erect a statue in his memory were widely discussed. Before the Gordon family returned to Atlanta, they acceded to the request of Miamians and permitted them to pay their final respects to the general. Gordon's body lay in state in the Presbyterian Church of Miami until a special railroad car, provided by the transportation magnate Henry M. Flagler, arrived on Monday. Early on the morning of Tuesday, January 12, the black-draped funeral car began the long journey to the Georgia capital. All along the train's route, Floridians and then Georgians turned out to pay their last respects. Nearly twenty-four hours later, about seven o'clock on the chilly, gray morning of January 13, the funeral train pulled into the Atlanta terminal, where a large crowd had gathered. As the pallbearers, veterans all, sadly bore the casket of their fallen chieftain to the hearse, one old veteran surged forward. Removing his worn and faded gray jacket, he meekly inquired, "May I lay it on his coffin just one minute?" Receiving permission, he accomplished his purpose. As the aged Confederate stepped back from the coffin and slipped the jacket over his shoulders, he sobbed, "Now thousands couldn't buy it from me!"[3]

2. Gordon Smith, "Memorial Sketch," xxii; Atlanta *Journal*, January 8–10, 12, 1904; Atlanta *Constitution*, January 8–10, 1904.

3. Atlanta *Journal*, January 10–13, 1904; Atlanta *Constitution*, January 11–14, 1904; Gordon Smith, "Memorial Sketch," xxiii–xxiv. An imposing equestrian statue of Gordon was sculpted by Solon H. Borglum and erected on the State Capitol grounds in Atlanta, where it still stands. In addition to voluntary contributions that poured in from all over the country, the state of Georgia appropriated $10,000 for the monument. The dedication and unveiling ceremonies took place on May 25, 1907. Report of the

Drawn by four magnificent white horses, the hearse proceeded to the State Capitol, where Gordon's simple black casket was placed in the center of the rotunda. There, beneath Confederate battleflags drooping at half-mast and surrounded by oceans of flowers, Gordon lay in state. The doors of the capitol opened shortly after nine and the mourners slowly, silently began moving past the funeral bier in single file. Thousands of southerners, availing themselves of special discounts offered by all railroad lines south of the Potomac and east of the Mississippi, flocked to the capital city to pay their respects to the Hero of Appomattox. The crowd soon grew so large that one line was insufficient, and two lines were arranged. For the numerous veterans who passed in final review of the general, the experience must have been particularly moving. More than the grief they felt, many were overwhelmed by visions of the past. Gordon's death dramatically compelled the aging veterans to confront their own mortality. His passing, only one week after that of General James Longstreet, another of Lee's lieutenants, drove home the somber reality that their days, too, were drawing to a close. In a very real sense, they were paying tribute to their own past, as well as to the Gallant Gordon. These old veterans composed a large portion of the upwards of fifty thousand mourners who steadily filed past Gordon's coffin well into the night.[4]

The following day, January 14, was an official day of mourning in Georgia. Memorial services were held throughout the state. In Atlanta, flags hung at half-mast, a seventeen-gun salute was fired every half hour, and state offices, courts, schools, businesses, and shops were closed in honor of Gordon's funeral. At 10:00 A.M., a two-hour memorial service commenced at the state house, during which many of his friends delivered eloquent eulogies, each limited to ten minutes. Then pallbearers carried Gordon's casket across the street into the Central Presbyterian Church for religious services. Although the church was small, Mrs. Gordon specifically requested that veterans "be given every opportunity of witnessing these services." Shortly after 1:00 P.M., Gordon's final march began. Moving to muffled drumbeats and escorted by military units from all sections of the state, as

Gordon Monument Commission, in GDAH; Gordon, *Reminiscences*, 101–102; Atlanta *Constitution*, May 26, 1907; New York *Times*, May 26, 1907.

4. Gordon Smith, "Memorial Sketch," xxiv–xxv; Atlanta *Constitution*, January 10, 14–15, 1904; Atlanta *Journal*, January 10, 13–14, 1904.

well as United States regulars and a contingent from the Grand Army of the Republic, the solemn funeral procession made its way to Oakland Cemetery through streets lined with mourners. The Gordon family already owned a large plot at the cemetery, but the Ladies Memorial Association of Atlanta donated "the most beautiful site in the confederate burying ground" for the general. Gordon would rest among his fallen comrades near the Confederate Memorial Monument. The day was raw, but thousands attended the simple ceremony at Oakland, which one reporter styled "the most touching spectacle ever seen in Georgia." Immediately following the brief, poignant graveside service, Gordon's body was lowered into the ground as taps sounded and muffled drums beat "the soldier's last tattoo." As a band played "Nearer My God to Thee," the family and then the assembled mourners filed past the grave in final tribute to the man who had devoted so much of himself to his state, his section, and his country. The "last and knightliest of the Paladins of Lee" would not be forgotten. As another eulogist proclaimed, "[H]is name becomes the heritage of his people, and his fame the glory of a nation."[5]

John Brown Gordon died one month before his seventy-second birthday, leaving behind more than forty years of prominent public service and a life of intriguing contradictions. He was a brilliantly successful soldier and a dismally unsuccessful businessman, a devout Christian and an equally devout Klansman, a chivalric moralist and a greedy opportunist, the living embodiment of the Lost Cause and an early proponent of postwar nationalism, a romantic symbol of the Old South and a paradigm of the hustling entrepreneurial spirit of the New South. To explain these fascinating contradictions is partly to explain the man and partly to explain his times. Gordon loved the spotlight and he had the energy and enthusiasm to withstand its glare for decades. Southerners trusted him to defend their section, and though he often lost interest after a crisis had passed, Gordon, when called upon, always responded with vigor. The more intense the need, the greater the conflict, the more active he became.

It was not, however, his business activities or his political sagacity that marked him as one of the most visible and important southerners; rather, it was his reputation as a soldier. In a sense, Gordon's

5. Atlanta *Constitution*, January 11–15, 1904; Gordon Smith, "Memorial Sketch," xxv–xxvii; Atlanta *Journal*, January 12–15, 1904; *Confederate Veteran*, XII (1904), 56, 332–33.

success during the Civil War created the rest of his life. An amateur soldier in an army overwhelmingly commanded by professionals, he rose quickly from captain to corps commander. His courage, instincts, moral resolve, and predilection for the offensive made him a superb combat officer. With his speeches before battle, his martial bearing, and his coolness under fire, Gordon inspired men as few others could and thus drew greatness from them. No Confederate emerged from the war with a record more stunning. This record proved to be his glory and his curse, for he would spend his remaining years attempting to achieve as a businessman and a politician the success he had enjoyed as a soldier.

The reputation Gordon earned on the battlefield thrust him into a prominence from which he would not retreat until he died. The general was beloved, respected, and trusted by most white southerners. His association with the Ku Klux Klan demonstrated his commitment to preserving white domination, a commitment for which, at the time, he was honored. Although generally a financial failure, he sought to advance both his own and his region's economic interests, and was respected for it. As a United States senator, he fought tirelessly to remove Federal troops from the South and to restore home rule. Time after time, he ably and eloquently defended the honor and integrity of southern whites. These things firmly established him in southerners' minds and, after Robert E. Lee's death, made Gordon the South's most popular man. And still, his war record loomed over all.

His popularity in the South was matched by his stature as a national statesman. Some disparage his postwar career as empty of contributions and make of Gordon little more than a figurehead orator, but he was demonstrably a central actor in the slow and painful process of national reconciliation. He accepted the South's defeat from the moment of surrender at Appomattox and set out to reunite quickly the former enemies, albeit on terms favorable to white southerners. Often angered by Radical assaults in the 1870s, Gordon usually refrained from joining the bitter sectional polemic so zealously employed by many critics of the South. This restraint and the security of his position in the South made Gordon a favorite of northern politicians and businessmen. They could deal with him confidently. In his efforts to replace sectional antagonisms with a common commitment to building a stronger nation, he contributed mightily to the eventual reconciliation that allowed northerners and southerners to embrace again.

Gordon was guided by the twin stars of regionalism and nationalism. His southern star compelled him to safeguard and foster the South's interests, as well as to preserve and defend its past. His national star led him to propound a new nationalism in his lectures, his book, and even in his position as leader of the UCV. He explained the Civil War primarily as the result of differing interpretations of the Constitution, and he portrayed the soldiers and citizens on both sides as chivalrous, honorable, and patriotic. He helped establish a common vantage point from which northerners and southerners could view the war and take pride not only in their own conduct but in that of their former opponents, as well. It is perhaps the greatest irony of Gordon's life that he achieved a position from which he could help reunite the nation because of the fame he gained while trying to destroy it.

Gordon left his mark on the times, but he was also a symbol of them. The contradiction in him between honor and necessity reflected the same contradiction in America during the Gilded Age. He bristled when his word was questioned and undoubtedly thought of himself as honorable; but he unabashedly solicited inside information, ignored financial obligations, and used political office for personal gain. And yet, he apparently saw no inconsistency in this conduct because such behavior was common in both the North and the South. Gordon typified the laissez faire, devil-take-the-hindmost attitude of the country between the war and the end of the century. It is not coincidental that his political and financial standards mirrored those of the North's leading hero, U. S. Grant.

Although Gordon obviously glorified a new order, he remained true to the old order, as well. He reflected southerners' desire to come to grips with the devastating psychological dislocation of defeat, and he spearheaded their quest for vindication. Similarly, his popularization of the mythical Old South helped satisfy southerners' nostalgia for a more sentimental, chivalrous past, one worth defending. Just as Gordon's war record influenced his postbellum career, so, too, it molded the way southerners—and even some northerners—perceived him. His scarred face and booming voice evoked in those who had worn the gray glorious images of the battles of their youth. To southerners, he was the beau ideal, the gallant cavalier. Northerners regarded him as a model of southern gentility, the Confederate Brigadier. Decades after the war, most Americans remained blinded by Gordon's dazzling military performance. Even many of those who recognized his postwar flaws and failures conveniently ignored them. Gordon's political enemies were frustrated at every turn when they tried to tarnish him. Most Americans saw in Gordon what they wanted to see. He remained for them the Hero of Appomattox.

# Bibliographical Essay

*Manuscripts*

The major problem in writing this biography has been the dearth of manuscript material. The bulk of Gordon's personal correspondence and private papers were destroyed when his home burned in June, 1899. As a result, the search for Gordon material—especially letters to, from, and about him—has not been especially productive. At the outset of my research, no one repository stood above the others as the most important archival source; however, the subsequent acquisition of the Gordon Family Collection by the University of Georgia has made it the single most valuable source. This collection, which the late Hugh H. Gordon III and I assembled and cataloged, contains letters, personal papers, and mementos that survived the fire. Letters between Gordon and his wife—during and after the war—and between Fanny and other members of the family provide an insight into Gordon's personal and family life unavailable anywhere else, making the Gordon Family Collection invaluable. In addition to family correspondence, the collection also includes postwar letters between Gordon and prominent individuals such as R. E. Lee, Jefferson Davis, and U. S. Grant, numerous letters of praise for speeches made or actions taken by Gordon, *A Letter to My Sons about their Forebears* (Privately printed, 1954) by the general's grandson, and a variety of miscellaneous papers. Caroline Lewis Gordon's "De Gin'ral an' Miss Fanny," an unpublished manuscript within the collection, is a wholly uncritical yet valuable source of information on Gordon's home life.

345

Other collections in the University of Georgia's Hargrett Rare Book and Manuscript Library were also helpful. The Doctor William Harrell Felton and Rebecca A. Latimer Felton Collection and the much larger Rebecca Latimer Felton Collection are great storehouses of anti-Gordon material. As the general's most relentless and vocal critic, Mrs. Felton spent decades accumulating information that she deemed damaging to Gordon. In addition to the large body of her correspondence, an impressive collection of scrapbooks contains criticisms of Gordon as a politician and a businessman, as well as clippings of her frequent newspaper attacks upon him. The Joseph E. Brown Papers in the Felix Hargrett Collection shed light on the secret maneuverings that underlay Gordon's resignation and Brown's appointment in May, 1880. (Typescript copies of the originals and the deciphered messages can also be found in the Joseph E. Brown Papers at the Atlanta Historical Society.) Other collections that contain useful material are the Henry P. Farrow Papers, the Alfred H. Colquitt Scrapbooks, the United Confederate Veterans Papers, and the Keith Morton Read Collection, as well as the Hoke Smith Collection, in the Richard B. Russell Memorial Library. The Minutes of the Faculty and the Records of the Demosthenian Literary Society, found in the University of Georgia, Department of Archives, present a sketchy though valuable picture of Gordon's days as a college student.

The official records of Gordon's governorship are located in the Georgia Department of Archives and History. Records of the Executive Department (Record Group 1, November, 1886–November, 1890) contain the Executive Minutes, Executive Orders, Incoming Correspondence, and the Governor's Letterbooks, but in general they are disappointing. The seven volumes of personal letter books that Gordon and his sons maintained between 1883 and 1890 (John Brown Gordon Records, AC. 00-118) are much more valuable. These largely illegible letter books are the richest source of information on the International Railroad and Steamship Company of Florida. The Minute Books of the I.R.R. & S.S. Co. and those of the New York, Florida and Havana Construction Company, both in Records of the Public Service Commission (Record Group 17), are helpful in developing the history of his Florida railroad activities. The John Brown Gordon Letterbooks, along with the Hugh H. Gordon Letterbook, 1887–1891 (AC. 00-013), document the wide variety of other interests in which he and his sons were involved. The Henry Woodfin Grady Papers, (Record Group 4, File II) contain an important letter dealing with

Gordon's gubernatorial campaign in 1886. Alfred H. Colquitt's Governor's Letterbooks, January, 1877–April, 1881, in the Records of the Executive Department (Record Group 1), are useful, as are two poignant letters of 1864 from Fanny to John, in Fanny Haralson (Mrs. John B.) Gordon Letters (AC. 68-432).

In the Southern Historical Collection in the Wilson Library at the University of North Carolina at Chapel Hill, I found a number of collections with helpful letters. The Matt W. Ransom Papers contain correspondence between Gordon and his former comrade-in-arms while they served in the Senate, plus a letter illustrating the political usefulness of Gordon's famous lecture, "Last Days of the Confederacy." The papers of Alexander Robert Lawton are informative concerning Georgia politics. Gordon's involvements with the Southern Life Insurance Company and the Plantation Publishing Company are illuminated in the papers of Benjamin C. Yancey. Letters in the Edward Porter Alexander Papers touch upon the final battle of the war and Gordon's plans in the immediate postwar period. An 1886 letter in the William Gaston Lewis Collection provides additional details on Gordon's attack on Fort Stedman in March, 1865. In the Marcus Joseph Wright Papers, Gordon explains why he remained a major general, even though he exercised the command responsibilities of a lieutenant general. Gordon's letter to the ladies of Columbia, South Carolina, thanking them for the silver service presented to him in honor of his labors on behalf of the Palmetto State, can be found in the Franklin Harper Elmore Papers. Other useful holdings are the Stephen Dodson Ramseur Papers, Stephen Dill Lee Papers, and Samuel Chiles Mitchell Papers.

The Manuscript Department in the Duke University Library also holds several collections that include a small number of Gordon letters. Correspondence between Thomas G. Jones, an officer on Gordon's staff, and John W. Daniel, one of Early's staff members, in the John Warwick Daniel Papers elaborates upon and clarifies many points of controversy between Jubal Early and Gordon. Jones's two long July 3, 1904, letters to Daniel—one in which he answered a number of questions concerning the battles of the Wilderness and Cedar Creek and the other, a *private* letter," in which Jones wrote frankly and freely about points of conflict between Gordon and Early—are invaluable. The Munford-Ellis Family Papers also discuss certain aspects of Gordon's Civil War career and contain important letters from Thomas H. Carter. A large body of letters in the Samuel

Houston Brodnax Collection demonstrate that there was substantial opposition from the agrarian sector to Gordon's 1890 Senate bid. The Herschel Vespasian Johnson Papers provide information on postwar Georgia politics. Other useful collections are the John Brown Gordon Papers, Thaddeus K. Oglesby Collection, Paul Hamilton Hayne Collection, Bradley T. Johnson Papers, Charles Edgeworth Jones Collection, John McIntosh Kell Papers, Richard Launcelot Maury Papers, Frederick W. M. Holliday Papers, Confederate Veteran Papers, and the Francis Warrington Dawson I Collection.

The Special Collections Department in the Woodruff Library at Emory University contains a number of helpful collections. The John Brown Gordon Papers are few in number, but they provide information on a variety of subjects. Letters in the James Pinckney Hambleton Collection and in the L. N. Trammell Letters are useful in the discussion of Georgia politics and Gordon's role therein. A single letter in the John Hill Hewitt Papers deals with Gordon's race for the Senate in 1872. The most valuable material in the Alexander Hamilton Stephens I Collection is an 1871 letter in which Gordon discusses his unsuccessful lumber business at Brunswick and his efforts to resolve his resulting debts.

Collections in the Virginia Historical Society supply additional details on Gordon's military career. Several unpublished reports, especially his April 11, 1865 Report, and postwar correspondence between Gordon and Lee in the Robert Edward Lee Headquarters Papers shed substantial light on his Civil War actions. The Charles Scott Venable Papers and Samuel J. C. Moore Papers help detail Gordon's role in battles during 1864. Two letters in the Robert Edward Lee Letterbooks deal with Gordon's postwar business activities.

The search for Gordon manuscript materials in the holdings of the Manuscript Division of the Library of Congress was somewhat disappointing; nevertheless, I found valuable information in several collections. The Thomas Francis Bayard, Manton Marble, and Alexander H. Stephens Collections, as well as the presidential papers of Grover Cleveland, Benjamin Harrison, and William McKinley, all supply information on Gordon's role in national politics. The papers of both Jedediah Hotchkiss and Jubal A. Early add tremendously to the discussion of Civil War actions that resulted in full-blown controversies during the last third of the nineteenth century.

Other repositories, though they have fewer collections that contain Gordon material, are also of value. The Huntington Library in

San Marino, California, has only one important collection pertinent to my study, but the Samuel Latham Mitchill Barlow Papers are an excellent source of behind-the-scenes information on Gordon. These letters, approximately eighty in number, demonstrate both the activity and diversity of Gordon's business and political involvements in the postwar period. The Thomas Goode Jones Collection in the Alabama Department of Archives and History contains personal correspondence, as well as additional letters between Jones and Daniel not found in the Daniel Papers at Duke. Gordon's Service File in the National Archives and his military records, plus those of the 6th Alabama Regiment in the Alabama Department of Archives and History, supply valuable information on his war record. In the South Caroliniana Library at the University of South Carolina, the papers of Edward Perrin McKissick, the Bratton Family Papers, and the Simpson, Young, Dean, and Coleman Families Papers all contain letters concerning Gordon's life insurance and railroad ventures. The United Confederate Veterans Collection in the Louisiana and Lower Mississippi Valley Collections at Louisiana State University is the best source of manuscript materials on Gordon's involvement with the veterans' organization. John Sutlive's "The Lady and the General" in the John Laffiteau Sutlive Collection, Georgia Historical Society, is an interesting account of the conflict between Mrs. Felton and Gordon. Details concerning the negotiations and publication of Gordon's *Reminiscences* are found in the Charles Scribner's Sons Collection at Princeton University. Other collections that provided helpful information are the William Leroy Broun Papers in the Department of Archives at Auburn University, the Bryan Grimes Papers at the North Carolina Division of Archives and History, the Fairbanks Collection of the Jessie Ball duPont Library at the University of the South, the Papers of the Dabney Family at the University of Virginia Library, and the John B. Gordon Biographical File at the Atlanta Historical Society.

*Newspapers*

The single most important source cited in my biography is the Atlanta *Constitution*. From 1868 to 1904, the Atlanta daily thoroughly covered Gordon's postwar career. Although generally quite favorable to him, the *Constitution* provides a tremendous amount of material on his varied business enterprises and on his political activities that is unavailable from other sources. It not only presents a Georgia perspective on Gordon and his actions but also supplies valuable sectional and national points of view with its reprinting of southern and national editorials. For a broader national perspective, I relied on the New York *Times* and the New York *Tribune*. Their ample coverage of Gordon demonstrates his importance as a national statesman. The late December, 1883, issues of the San Francisco *Chronicle* carried many of the letters between D. D. Colton and C. P. Huntington. Among other newspapers consulted were the Athens *Herald*, the Athens *Southern Banner*, the Athens *Southern Watchman*, the Atlanta *Intelligencer*, the Atlanta *Daily Herald*, the Atlanta *Daily New Era*, the Atlanta *Journal*, the Augusta *Daily Constitutionalist*, the Columbus *Weekly Enquirer*, the Macon *Telegraph*, the Milledgeville *Southern Recorder*, the Milledgeville *Federal Union*, and the Savannah *Daily News and Herald*.

## Official Government Publications, Reports, and Records

The starting point for any study of the military aspects of the Civil War is *The War of the Rebellion: A Compilation of the Official Records of the Union and Confederate Armies* (130 vols.; Washington, D.C., 1880–1901). The *Official Records* is the single most valuable source in determining Gordon's role in the Confederate army. Publications of the United States Bureau of the Census provide useful data on Gordon's financial status over the years. Those most helpful were the 1840 Georgia Slave Schedule, the 1850 Georgia Free and Slave Schedules, the 1860 Alabama Free and Slave Schedules, and the 1870 and 1880 Georgia Schedules. His testimony before the so-called Ku Klux Committee, contained in Volume 6 of *Testimony Taken by the Joint Select Committee to Inquire into the Condition of Affairs in the Late Insurrectionary States* (13 vols.; Washington, D.C.,1872), is an extremely useful source of information not only on the Klan in Georgia but on a myriad of related subjects as well. The *Congressional Record* is invaluable in assessing his activities as a United States senator. Also, federal court documents at the Federal Records Center in East Point, Georgia, reveal Gordon's history of legal problems. The *Georgia House Journal* and the *Georgia Senate Journal* are important publications that provide roll call votes in Gordon's elections, plus legislative details during his governorship. Real estate and court records for the Georgia counties of De Kalb and Taylor contain legal documents involving Gordon and his family.

*Contemporary Observers*

Among the most valuable works by a Gordon contemporary is Isaac W. Avery's *The History of the State of Georgia From 1850 to 1881* (New York, 1881). Although exceedingly favorable to Gordon and other conservative Democrats, Avery provides a particularly informative account of Georgia political history during these three turbulent decades. E. A. Pollard's *The Early Life, Campaigns and Public Services of Robert E. Lee, with a Record of the Campaigns and Heroic Deeds of his Companions in Arms* (New York, 1871) contains a fine early biographical sketch of Gordon. Edward Mayes's *Lucius Q. C. Lamar: His Life, Times, and Speeches, 1825–1893* (Nashville, 1896) points out the close ties between the Mississippian and the Georgian. The pamphlet *The Colton Letters: The Inside Story of an Infamous Procedure* (N.p., n.d.), in the University of California Library at Berkeley, reprints a few of the over four hundred letters between David D. Colton and Collis P. Huntington, some of which seem to implicate Gordon in questionable senatorial activities. And in her testament of hatred, *My Memoirs of Georgia Politics* (Atlanta, 1911), Mrs. William H. Felton catalogs her long list of charges against the general.

Useful works touching on Gordon as a soldier are Robert Underwood Johnson and Clarence Clough Buel (eds.), *Battles and Leaders of the Civil War* (4 vols.; 1887–88; rpr. New York, 1956); John H. Worsham, *One of Jackson's Foot Cavalry* (New York, 1912); Henry Kyd Douglas, *I Rode with Stonewall* (Chapel Hill, 1940); and Jubal Anderson Early, *Autobiographical Sketch and Narrative of the War Between the States* (Philadelphia, 1912). The *Southern Historical Society Papers* (52 vols.; Richmond, 1876–1959) is second only to the *Official Records* as the finest source of printed material on the Confederacy. Also, the *Confederate Veteran* (40 vols.; Nashville, 1893–1932), Clement A. Evans (ed.), *Confederate Military History* (12 vols.; Atlanta, 1899), Dunbar Rowland (ed.), *Jefferson Davis, Constitutionalist: His Letters, Papers, and Speeches* (10 vols.; Jackson, Miss., 1923), and William E. Mickle (ed.), *Minutes of the Annual Meetings and Reunions of the United Confederate Veterans* (3 vols.; New Orleans, 1891–1904) help trace Gordon's military and postwar career. Lucian Lamar Knight's *Reminiscences of Famous Georgians* (2 vols.; Atlanta, 1907–1908) and William J. Northen's *Men of Mark in Georgia* (7 vols.; Atlanta, 1907–12) supply valuable sketches of Gordon and of other prominent Georgians.

*Published Works of John Brown Gordon*

Gordon's *A Boyhood Sketch* (N.p., n.d.) is a brief personal account of his youth in Georgia and, as such, is one of the only sources on his earliest years. The only extant copy of this sketch is in the Atlanta Public Library. A portion of this sketch can be found in "Boyhood in the South," *Youth's Companion: An Illustrated Weekly Paper for Young People and Families*, LXXIV (January, 1900), 15–16. His address before the literary societies of Oglethorpe University in July, 1860, is reproduced in *Progress of Civil Liberty. An Address Delivered Before the Thalian and Phi Delta Societies, of Oglethorpe University, Georgia, at the Last Annual Commencement* (Macon, 1861), a copy of which is located in the Georgia State Library, Atlanta. Gordon's 1887 speech to the Augusta Confederate Survivors' Association is published under the title *The Old South. Addresses Delivered Before the Confederate Survivors' Association in Augusta, Georgia, on the Occasion of Its Ninth Annual Reunion, on Memorial Day, April 16th 1887 by His Excellency, Governor John B. Gordon, and by Col. Charles C. Jones, Jr.* (Augusta, 1887). "Last Days of the Confederacy," his famous lecture, can be found in Thomas B. Reed (ed.), *Modern Eloquence* (15 vols.; Philadelphia, 1900–1903), V, 471–94. An article under the same title dealing with the final winter of the war is published in Rossiter Johnson (ed.), *Campfire and Battlefield* (New York, 1978), 485–94. Gordon dictated this article to Henry W. Grady, who prepared it and originally published it in the Philadelphia *Times* in 1875. A portion of this account was also reprinted in the Atlanta *Constitution* on April 10, 1885.

Gordon's *Reminiscences of the Civil War* (New York, 1903) is preceded only by the *Official Records* as a source for developing the history of his activities during the war; nevertheless, it must be read with care because it was written almost forty years after the war. Gordon wished to present a factual account of the battles in which he fought, but above all else, he wanted to venerate the character of the American soldier and treat the war in a positive way, so that northerners and southerners could take pride in their participation. In doing so, Gordon tended to embellish his wartime experiences. Even so, *Reminiscences* provides additional information and adds a valuable human touch missing in official reports and service records. Several editions of *Reminiscences* were printed in 1903 and 1904, with the 1904 Memorial Edition including an introduction by Stephen Dill Lee, Gordon's successor as commander-in-chief of the

United Confederate Veterans, and a sketch of Gordon's final hours and his funeral by his daughter, Frances Gordon Smith.

## SECONDARY WORKS

A number of books are extremely useful in providing a background of Georgia and southern history. E. Merton Coulter's *A Short History of Georgia* (Chapel Hill, 1933) and the more balanced work edited by Kenneth Coleman, *A History of Georgia* (Athens, 1977), supply brief but informative accounts of Georgia history during the second half of the nineteenth century. C. Mildred Thompson's *Reconstruction in Georgia, Economic, Social, Political, 1865–1872* (New York, 1915), Edwin C. Woolley's *The Reconstruction of Georgia* (New York, 1901), Alan Conway's *The Reconstruction of Georgia* (Minneapolis, 1966), and Elizabeth S. Nathans' *Losing the Peace: Georgia Republicans and Reconstruction, 1865–1871* (Baton Rouge, 1968) aid in understanding Reconstruction in Georgia, but a well-balanced comprehensive interpretation of the period has yet to be written. The final three decades of the 1800s in Georgia are treated by Judson Clements Ward, Jr., in "Georgia Under the Bourbon Democrats, 1872–1890" (Ph.D. dissertation, University of North Carolina, 1947) and by Alex Mathews Arnett in *The Populist Movement in Georgia: A View of the "Agrarian Crusade" in Light of Solid-South Politics* (New York, 1922). Ward's dissertation, "Georgia Under the Bourbons," is the only comprehensive work dealing with the Conservative Democratic regime in Georgia between 1872 and 1890. He details not only the politics of the era, but also investigates the convict lease system, agriculture, railroad policies, education, and social welfare, as well as the commercial, industrial, and financial policies of the Bourbons. E. Merton Coulter's *The South During Reconstruction, 1865–1877* (Baton Rouge, 1947), vol. VIII of Wendell Holmes Stephenson and E. Merton Coulter (eds.), *A History of the South*, though often dismissed as a racist tract, nevertheless provides substantial material on Reconstruction in the South. Volume IX of *A History of the South*, C. Vann Woodward's *The Origins of the New South, 1877–1913* (Rev. ed.; Baton Rouge, 1971), remains the standard study of the South during that period.

Other helpful works include Paul M. Gaston, *The New South Creed: A Study in Southern Mythmaking* (Baton Rouge, 1970); Paul

H. Buck, *The Road to Reunion, 1865–1900* (Boston, 1937); C. Vann Woodward, *Reunion and Reaction: The Compromise of 1877 and the End of Reconstruction* (Boston, 1951); Maury Klein, *History of the Louisville & Nashville Railroad* (New York, 1972); John F. Stover, *The Railroads of the South 1865–1900: A Study in Finance and Control* (Chapel Hill, 1955); Walter G. Cooper, *Official History of Fulton County* (1934; rpr. Spartanburg, S.C., 1978); Franklin M. Garrett, *Atlanta and Its Environs: A Chronicle of Its People and Events* (3 vols.; New York, 1954); Steven Hahn, *The Roots of Southern Populism: Yeoman Farmers and the Transformation of the Georgia Upcountry, 1850–1890* (New York, 1983); and Barton C. Shaw, *The Wool-Hat Boys: Georgia's Populist Party* (Baton Rouge, 1984).

Unfortunately, the two previous major studies of Gordon—Allen P. Tankersley's *John B. Gordon: A Study in Gallantry* (Atlanta, 1955) and Grady Sylvester Culpepper's "The Political Career of John Brown Gordon, 1868 to 1897" (Ph.D. dissertation, Emory University, 1981)—are both limited in scope, methodology, and treatment. Tankersley's biography constitutes a pioneering effort but fails to make adequate use of manuscript sources and is uncritical in its approach. Culpepper's study suffers from similar deficiencies and fails to place Gordon in a national context.

Biographical studies of other prominent southerners were very useful. Among them were C. Vann Woodward, *Tom Watson: Agrarian Rebel* (New York, 1938); Raymond B. Nixon, *Henry W. Grady: Spokesman of the New South* (New York, 1943); John E. Talmadge, *Rebecca Latimer Felton: Nine Stormy Decades* (Athens, Ga., 1966); and Joseph H. Parks, *Joseph E. Brown of Georgia* (Baton Rouge, 1977). And any reference to the Army of Northern Virginia without mention of Douglas Southall Freeman's *R. E. Lee: A Biography* (4 vols.; New York, 1934–35) and *Lee's Lieutenants: A Study in Command* (3 vols.; New York, 1942–44) would be an unforgivable oversight. Possessing a better understanding of the men of Lee's army than does any other twentieth-century writer, Freeman recognized Gordon as one of the finest of Lee's lieutenants. These two classics contributed significantly to the study of Gordon's military career.

# Index

10–11; practices law, 10, 11, 128;
works as newspaper reporter, 11;
owns coal mines, 11, 128, 133;
economic status, 12, 126, 128–29,
132–33, 134, 137, 175, 214, 220, 233–
34, 241, 246–47, 256–57, 266–67,
318–19, 333; becomes a Democrat,
12; defends slavery, 12–13, 14;
supports Breckinridge and secession,
13–14; joins Confederacy, 15–17;
commissioned as major of 6th
Alabama, 17; in Battle of First
Manassas, 19–20; promoted to
lieutenant colonel, 21; promoted to
colonel, 22; in Peninsula Campaign,
21–22; in Battle of Seven Pines, 23–
27; speaks to soldiers, 23, 26, 29, 30,
32, 33, 63, 77, 84, 110–11, 122, 123;
appearance in battle, 26, 52, 78, 84,
122, 123; in Seven Days' Battles, 28–
30; at South Mountain, 31–32; in
Battle of Sharpsburg, 33–36;
wounded, 35–36, 36n, 87n, 112;
recuperates from wounds, 37, 38, 38n;
promoted to brigadier general, 39; in
Chancellorsville Campaign, 40–41;
longs for Fanny, 42, 45–46, 53, 58, 90,
122, 317–18; in Lee's second invasion
of the North, 41–58; in Battle of
Winchester (1863), 44–45; at York,
47–48; at Wrightsville, 48–50; dines
with Mrs. Luther L. Rewalt, 49–50; in
Battle of Gettysburg, 51–57; and
Francis C. Barlow, 53–54, 53n; urges
attack on Cemetery Hill, 54–56;
criticizes Early, 56–57, 65, 92, 98–99,
101–03, 103n; and religious
revivalism, 59–60; in Battle of
Wilderness, 61–72; narrowly escapes
capture, 71–72, 101; elevated to
divisional command, 72; in Battle of
Spotsylvania Court House, 72–80;
and "Lee to rear" incident, 77, 77n;
promoted to major general, 79; moves
to stop Hunter, 81, 82; in Battle of
Monocacy, 83–85; threatens
Washington, 85–86; maneuvers in the

valley, 86–87; in Battle of Winchester
(1864), 87–90; fears for Fanny's safety,
90–91, 115, 122, 316; at Fisher's Hill,
91; reconnoiters prior to Cedar Creek,
92–94; in Battle of Cedar Creek, 94–
101; criticized by Early, 101–103;
returns to Lee, 104, 105; fails to
receive promotion to lieutenant
general, 105, 105n, 123; commands II
Corps, 105–22 passim; serves as Lee's
confidant, 106–107; in Battle of Fort
Stedman, 108–14; evacuates
Petersburg, 115; spares spies' lives,
115n; in Battle of Sayler's Creek, 115–
17; at last council of war, 117–18; in
Battle of Appomattox Court House,
118–21; arranges truce, 119–21;
works on surrender agreement, 121;
leads surrender procession, 121–22;
evaluation of military career, 123–24;
returns to family in Petersburg, 125–
26; journeys to Georgia, 126; fears
indictment and persecution, 126–27,
127n; applies for amnesty, 127;
involved in lumber business on the
coast, 128–29, 129n, 132; dabbles in
agriculture, 129, 140, 262–63, 293,
338; and race relations, 129–32, 131n,
144–45, 146–47, 149, 291–92, 294,
303; and debt, 132–33, 167, 175, 233,
256, 257, 265, 318, 333; uses military
fame, 133, 154, 155–56, 194, 197, 269,
270, 271, 273, 277, 280, 282, 302–303;
moves to Atlanta, 133; as president of
Southern Life Insurance Company
(Atlanta branch), 133–35, 170, 174–
75; courts Robert E. Lee, 135;
association with *Plantation*, 135–36;
as vice-president of University
Publishing Company, 136–39;
promotes non-partisan school books,
136–39, 324; defends southern
participation in Civil War, 137, 139,
150, 320, 322–24, 330–31, 334–35,
336; builds Sutherland, 139–40, 333,
333n; runs for governor (1868), 141,
143–45; criticizes Radical

93; chosen commander-in-chief of
UCV, 293, 324, 325; opposes force
bill, 294; ends friendship with Grady,
295–96; campaigns for Senate, 297–
303; alienates Farmers' Alliance, 298–
300, 301–302; portrays self as
farmers' friend, 298, 299, 301–303,
304–305, 305n; elected senator, 304;
complacency as senator, 305–306,
312–13; suggests financial reforms,
306–308; 309; speaks on Coxeyism,
308–309; forcefully supports national
authority, 310–11, 314; opposes
Populism, 311–12; decides to leave
politics, 313; as national pacificator,
314–37; "Last Days of the
Confederacy" (lecture), 315–17, 318–
21; relies on Fanny, 317–18; idealizes
Old South and promotes cult of Lost
Cause, 321–24; as commander-in-
chief of UCV, 325–31; promotes a
new nationalism, 328–31, 334–35,
336, 337; writes *Reminiscences of the
Civil War*, 331–37; final illness, 338–
39; funeral, 340–41; evaluation of
life, 341–44
—the man: appearance, 2, 26, 52, 78, 84,
122, 123, 194, 221, 274, 319, 327, 328,
343; speaking ability, 2, 8–9, 10, 12,
13, 14, 17, 23, 26, 29, 30, 32, 33, 48,
63, 77, 84, 110–11, 121, 122, 123,
131–32, 142, 159–60, 160–62, 164–
66, 169–70, 171–73, 191–92, 195–96,
221–24, 236–37, 270–71, 274, 280,
281, 298–99, 306, 307, 307–308, 309,
310–11, 312–13, 316, 319–20, 322–
23, 327, 342, 343; pride and honor, 3–
4, 167, 189–91, 198, 200, 233–34,
235, 237, 241–42, 249, 253–58, 265,
295–96, 324, 335, 343
—the soldier: 16–124 *passim*; military
performance praised, 2, 26, 27, 29–30,
32, 37–38, 39, 44, 54, 58, 60, 72–73,
79–80, 85, 105, 123–24, 341–42;
military performance questioned, 40–
41, 92, 98, 99, 101–103, 113–14
—the businessman: owns coal mines,

11, 12, 133; in lumber business, 128–
29, 129n, 132; in life insurance, 133–
35, 170, 174–75; owns magazine,
135–36; publishes school books, 136–
39, 324; as adventuresome investor,
222–23, 241, 244–45, 246–47, 248,
249, 250, 251, 256–57, 261, 262–63,
267, 293; organizes and builds
railroads, 242–45, 246, 247, 248–51,
266–67
—the politician: gubernatorial
candidate (1868), 141, 143–45; as
senator (1873–80), 154–201 *passim*;
as governor, 268–95 *passim*; as
senator (1891–97), 296, 297, 298–314
*passim*
—defender and promoter of the South:
2, 134, 136, 137–38, 139, 143, 149–50,
157, 158, 159, 163–68, 169–70, 173,
180–84, 186, 190–92, 234–35, 248,
294, 308, 321–24, 328, 330–31, 334–
335, 342
—national reconciliator: 3, 143, 156–
57, 158–59, 160, 166–67, 168, 191–
92, 199, 310–11, 314, 315–16, 319–
21, 328–29, 330–31, 334–37, 342–43
Gordon, John Brown, Jr. (son of JBG),
12n, 115, 125–26, 259
Gordon, John George (great-great-
grandfather of JBG), 6
Gordon, Malinda Cox (mother of JBG),
7, 15, 126
Gordon, Sarah (chambermaid to Fanny),
38n, 131n
Gordon, Walter S. (brother of JBG), 242,
245, 259
Gordon, Reverend Zachariah Herndon
(father of JGB), 7, 8, 9, 126, 221, 259
Gordon and Cox, 264, 265
Gordon, Shorter and Company, 128–29,
129n, 132
Gordon Springs, Ga., 7, 10n
Grady, Henry W., 21, 235, 239, 240, 243,
303; on JBG, 9, 12, 215, 217; involved
in secret negotiations, 224–25, 226–
29, 230, 231, 232; and Georgia
Western, 226, 229, 230–31, 243, 245;